JOURNAL FOR THE STUDY OF THE NEW TESTAMENT
SUPPLEMENT SERIES
57

Executive Editor, Supplement Series

David Hill

Publishing Editor

David E. Orton

JSOT Press
Sheffield

ESCHATOLOGY
AND THE
COVENANT

A Comparison of 4 Ezra
and Romans 1–11

Bruce W. Longenecker

Journal for the Study of the New Testament
Supplement Series 57

Copyright © 1991 Sheffield Academic Press

Published by JSOT Press
JSOT Press is an imprint of
Sheffield Academic Press Ltd
The University of Sheffield
343 Fulwood Road
Sheffield S10 3BP
England

Typeset by Sheffield Academic Press
and
Printed on acid-free paper in Great Britain
by Billing & Sons Ltd
Worcester

British Library Cataloguing in Publication Data

Longenecker, Bruce W.
   Eschatology and the Covenant: a comparison of 4 Ezra
   and Romans 1–11.
   1. Christianity. Scriptures. Special subjects,
   Eschatology
   I. Title   II. Series
   236

ISSN 0143-5108
ISBN 1-85075-305-9

CONTENTS

Eschatology and the Covenant

PREFACE

Between May 1988 and March 1990, I set myself the task of researching this project as a PhD dissertation at Durham University, England. After one and a half years of testing the feasibility of other research proposals, I sat down and read through *4 Ezra* with E.P. Sanders's *Paul and Palestinian Judaism* in mind. It was then that I knew I had found a topic which both interested me and needed to be addressed: a comparison of Paul and the author of *4 Ezra* against the background of Sanders's portrayal of Early Judaism. The results of that investigation are included within the covers of this book, largely unaltered in form and content, although I have pruned the footnotes somewhat in the interests of making this a more 'user friendly' book than it otherwise would have been.

My thanks are due to many, only some of whom I can mention here. I am indebted to Professor J.D.G. Dunn, who supervised this project and whose work on the origins of Christianity has shaped my thinking substantially. Several others have taken valuable time to review sections of this thesis, including Dr Robert Hayward, Professor C.E.B. Cranfield, Dr Walter Moberly, Mr David Kupp and Mr Dennis Stamps. I have found especially valuable the comments and criticism of my examiners, Dr Christopher Rowland and Dr A.J.M. Wedderburn; their helpful advice has been greatly appreciated. I am grateful to Tyndale House Council (Cambridge) and to the Committee of Vice-Chancellors and Principals of the Universities of the United Kingdom for providing generous research grants for the undertaking of this effort. A special mention is due also to Sara Kindon, who has been a support throughout the whole project and who by now must know as much as I can claim to know about *4 Ezra* and Romans 1–11. My deep appreciation goes to the editorial staff at Sheffield Academic Press and especially to Professor David J.A. Clines for his efforts beyond the call of duty.

This book is dedicated to my parents, Richard and Frances, who have taught me much and loved me more.

ABBREVIATIONS

AASFDHL	Annales Academiae Scientiarum Fennicae Dissertationes Humanarum Litterarum
AnalBibl	Analecta Biblica
AT	Arbeiten zur Theologie
AUSS	Andrews University Seminary Series
BEvTh	Beiträge zur evangelischen Theologie
Bib	*Biblica*
BJRL	*Bulletin of the John Rylands University Library of Manchester*
BJS	Brown Judaic Studies
BLS	Bible and Literature Series
BR	*Biblical Research*
BZ	*Biblische Zeitschrift*
CBC	Cambridge Bible Commentary
CBQ	*Catholic Biblical Quarterly*
CRINT	Compendia Rerum Iudaicarum ad Novum Testamentum
DUJ	Durham University Journal
EKK	Evangelisch-katholischer Kommentar zum Neuen Testament
FOTL	Forms of Old Testament Literature
FRLANT	Forschungen zur Religion und Literatur des Alten und Neuen Testaments
HSS	Harvard Semitic Studies
HTR	*Harvard Theological Review*
ICC	The International Critical Commentary
Int	*Interpretation*
IOS	Israel Oriental Studies
JBL	*Journal of Biblical Literature*
JETS	*Journal of the Evangelical Theological Society*
JJS	*Journal of Jewish Studies*
JR	*Journal of Religion*

JSJ	*Journal for the Study of Judaism*
JSNT	*Journal for the Study of the New Testament*
JSNTS	Journal for the Study of the New Testament Supplement Series
JSOTS	Journal for the Study of the Old Testament Supplement Series
JSP	*Journal for the Study of the Pseudepigrapha*
JSPS	Journal for the Study of the Pseudepigrapha Supplement Series
JSZ	Jüdische Schriften aus hellenistisch-römischer Zeit
JTS	*Journal of Theological Studies*
LEC	Library of Early Christianity
LumVit	*Lumière et Vie*
NA	Neutestamentliche Abhandlungen
NCB	New Century Bible
Neot	*Neotestamentica*
NovT	*Novum Testamentum*
NovTS	Novum Testamentum Supplement Series
NTD	Das Neue Testament Deutsch
NTS	*New Testament Studies*
PFES	Publications of the Finnish Exegetical Society
RB	*Revue Biblique*
SBLDS	Society of Biblical Literature Dissertation Series
SBLSBS	Society of Biblical Literature Sources for Bible Study
SBT	Studies in Biblical Theology
SC	Sources chrétiennes
SEA	Svensk exegetisk årsbok
SJT	*Scottish Journal of Theology*
SNTSMS	Society of New Testament Studies Monograph Series
SPCK	Society for Promoting Christian Knowledge
StNT	Studien zum Neuen Testament
SR	*Studies in Religions/Sciences religieuses*
ST	*Studia Theologica*
SUNT	Studien zur Umwelt des Neuen Testaments
TLZ	*Theologische Literaturzeitung*
TrinJ	*Trinity Journal*
TynBul	*Tyndale Bulletin*
TZ	*Theologische Zeitschrift*
TPINTC	Trinity Press International New Testament Commentary

TUGAL	Texte und Untersuchungen zur Geschichte der altchristlichen Literatur
UPATS	University of Pennsylvania Armenian Texts and Studies
WBC	Word Biblical Commentary
WMANT	Wissenschaftliche Monographien zum Alten und Neuen Testament
WUNT	Wissenschaftliche Untersuchungen zum Neuen Testament
WTJ	*Westminster Theological Journal*
ZAW	*Zeitschrift für die alttestamentliche Wissenschaft*

Part I

Introduction

Chapter 1

INTRODUCTION

1.1. *New Approaches, New Issues*

It may not be too much to say that New Testament scholarship is currently working in a 'post-Sanders' environment. E.P. Sanders's book *Paul and Palestinian Judaism* is considered by many (particularly in the English-speaking world) to have introduced a new era in New Testament studies; especially in Pauline scholarship, much of the agenda has been set by this one book. So N.T. Wright, in his review of recent scholarship, observes that: 'it is no exaggeration to say that the entire flavour of Pauline studies has been changed, quite probably permanently, as a result' of Sanders's work.[1] Many others have expressed similar appreciation for Sanders's work, citing it as 'a watershed',[2] a study which has '"broken the mould" of Pauline studies'[3] and forced scholarship to enter into 'a new stage of the discussion' concerning Paul's relationship to Judaism.[4]

Acclaim of this sort is not unduly given, for if Sanders's central argument is correct, a new approach is to be undertaken when studying the texts of Early Judaism. Sanders argues (as others have as well[5]) that all too often the texts which were produced within the social and religious matrix of Early Judaism have been analysed from a flawed understanding of the character of Early Judaism. Traditional characterizations of Judaism have portrayed it as an arid wasteland of legalistic works-righteousness with an emphasis on merit and achievement, so that one's good works outweigh the bad works in the final eschatological evaluation of behaviour. In short, Judaism was

---

1. 1988: 424.
2. Moo, 1987: 287.
3. Dunn, 1983: 97.
4. Westerholm, 1988: 3.
5. Cf. e.g. Montefiore, 1914; Moore, 1921; Klein, 1978.

thought to be a religion of scoreboard mathematics. Easy parallels were then drawn between the formalism and bankruptcy of Early Judaism and similar characterizations of sixteenth-century Christianity, against which Luther and other Protestant reformers reacted. In contrast, Sanders contends that such an estimation misses what animates the whole of Jewish thought and practice: an awareness of Israel's election by, and covenant relationship with, God. Sanders's fundamental point concerns the *motivation* for Jewish obedience to the law; rather than seeking to *earn* salvation by merit points and, thereby, putting God under obligation to bestow salvation in the final judgment, pious Jews concerned themselves with obeying God's commandments as the means of *preserving the covenantal relationship already established by God's initiating mercy upon Israel, his people.* Sanders argues that the underlying principles of Early Judaism arrange themselves in a 'pattern of religion' which he names 'covenantal nomism', a term devised to demonstrate that Jewish observance of the law ('nomism') remained firmly rooted within a covenantal context.[1] Thus, Sanders contends that, for too long, the theological agenda of Christian scholars has caused Jewish texts to be evaluated in an environment foreign to their historical context, without regard for the covenantal undergirding which permeated Early Judaism.

Perhaps the clearest indication of the 'watershed' in contemporary studies of Early Judaism facilitated by Sanders's work comes when judging scholarly appraisals of the place of *4 Ezra* within its historical context. In the traditional characterization of Early Judaism, *4 Ezra* is often cited as paradigmatic of the kind of legalistic piety which pervaded contemporary Judaism. For instance, W. Bousset, whose work *Die Religion des Judentums im späthellenistischen Zeitalter* has long been a basic textbook for the study of Early Judaism, describes Early Judaism as 'eine Religion der Observanz und des absoluten Beharrens'[2] in which external formalism ('äussere Betätigung') suffocated true religious sentiment, thereby facilitating the deterioration of Jewish religion. Bankruptcy of this kind, which was founded upon 'eine Frömmigkeit ödester Observanz',[3] promoted a rigid individualism, in

---

1. See his eight-point definition in 1977: 422; revised in 1982: 394-95. For defences of his position, see Sanders, 1976; *idem,* 1977: 33-428; *idem,* 1982: 394-402.

2. 1926: 85; cf. 409.

3. 1926: 101.

which salvation was merited 'durch angespannte Anstrengung'.[1] Since individuals relied upon their own efforts, their salvation was never assured.[2] Nonetheless, hypocrisy took root in Judaism, as is evidenced by the Pharisees who became haughty in their self-achievement.[3] Their arrogant self-sufficiency is indicative of the deterioration of the Jewish religion and is instructive of the dangers of legalism in Christian history: 'Die Parallele mit dem katholischen Klerus der Renaissancezeit drängt sich auf'.[4] For Bousset, *4 Ezra* is most illustrative of the self-reliance and personal piety of Early Judaism; although the author is doubtful about one's abilities to earn salvation,[5] nonetheless he holds fast to the view 'dass der Einzelne verantwortlich ist für sein Tun'[6] in order to earn salvation by those deeds.

R. Bultmann, Bousset's student, maintains his teacher's position concerning the legalistic character of Early Judaism. In his presentations, Early Judaism is represented as the paradigm of the human tendency to grasp at salvation apart from any dependency upon God, concerning itself instead with detailed and trivial regulations which were 'pettifogging'[7] and went 'to the point of absurdity'.[8] Bultmann cites in this regard *4 Ezra* 8.47b-49, thinking it to demonstrate how in Early Judaism 'self-praise can be combined with a sense of sin'.[9] Moreover, for Bultmann, this passage depicts the manner in which 'repentance itself became a good work which secured merit'[10] before God. From this passage in *4 Ezra*, Bultmann concludes that, in Early Judaism, 'the whole range of man's relation with God came to be thought of in terms of merit'.[11]

Similar estimates can be reproduced at some length. Representative is the pronouncement of J. Köberle:

[T]he author of IV Ezra without doubt gives us a correct presentation of the repercussion of the belief in the future judgment on the religious expressions

1. 1926: 115.
2. 1926: 92.
3. 1926: 184, 189.
4. 1926: 101.
5. Bousset cites 7.46; 8.35; 3.35; 7.68.
6. 1926: 405.
7. 1956: 67.
8. 1956: 65.
9. 1956: 71.
10. 1956: 71.
11. 1956: 71.

of individual Jewish piety. *All the many expressions of belief in God's grace and mercy appear to be denied.*[1]

It would be wrong to suggest that estimates of this kind belong to a past day in scholarship. A decade ago M. Knibb commented on the matter of *4 Ezra*'s place within Early Judaism, stating that the author of *4 Ezra*

> in common with other Jews of his day believed that by the strict observance of the law it was possible for an individual to acquire, as it were, a credit balance of good works to earn thereby the reward in the world to come of life.[2]

Estimates of this sort often result in strains of polemic, such as those found in the claims of H.M. Hughes:

> There could be no better illustration of the need for the Christian revelation than ps.-Ezra's doctrine of the will. He grasped the truth, not comprehended by many of his Jewish contemporaries, that the law of itself left the will almost powerless for righteousness. The next step was the realization of the moral dynamic in the life of faith. For this his light was insufficient. . . The step [of faith] which ps.-Ezra was unable to take was taken by Paul when he surrendered to Jesus Christ, and this momentous advance represents the gulf between the moral outlook of the two.[3]

For Hughes, while *4 Ezra* is unique in that it alone of the Jewish literature recognizes the inadequacy of traditional Jewish piety, it remains trapped in the problem characteristic of all Judaism (viz. the powerlessness of legalism)—a problem which is surmounted only by Christian faith.

While not all interpreters of *4 Ezra* have found its author to be a legalist, it is no exaggeration to say that *4 Ezra* has often been found to bolster the traditional understanding of Early Judaism as a legalistic religion. The experience of the 'typical' Jew is clearly represented by the author of *4 Ezra* who is caught in the dilemma of legalism: salvation will come to those who have to their credit works of merit, but few are capable of achieving that end since their works are flawed and sinful.

In Sanders's case, however, *4 Ezra* is not representative of Early Judaism but is something of an oddity within the broader scope of

1. 1905: 657, cited by Sanders, 1977: 41, 427.
2. 1979: 182, emphasis added.
3. N.d.: 240-41.

Judaism: *4 Ezra* is to be distinguished 'from the rest of Judaism as it is revealed in the surviving literature'.[1] In his review of Palestinian Judaism from 200 BCE to 200 CE, Sanders repeatedly speaks of 'the distinctiveness of IV Ezra', 'the unique position of IV Ezra among the literature which remains', qualifying his general depictions of Judaism with notes such as 'except IV Ezra', 'IV Ezra differs', and 'absent in IV Ezra'. Sanders's estimate of *4 Ezra*'s place within Early Judaism, then, is in sharp contrast to those given in the above paragraphs. Sanders argues that a legalistic attitude 'has often been held to be Jewish "soteriology", but we have seen this nowhere to be the case, except in IV Ezra'.[2] In contrast to those who maintain the traditional view of Judaism, Sanders locates *4 Ezra* 'outside' the common pattern of thought and practice of Early Judaism.

This survey demonstrates something of the shift which has been facilitated by Sanders's work concerning the covenantal character of Early Judaism. Although Sanders's view has not been accepted by all,[3] and although it has drawn criticism on several scores,[4] it is expertly argued from a selection of Jewish texts and has been well received by a large number of exegetes and historians. Moreover, it has received added support from the work of other scholars who have gone beyond the texts he himself analysed and who have obtained similar results.[5] Thus, it is not unusual these days to hear scholars speak of the covenant as 'the key to any understanding of Judaism'.[6] Perhaps the

1. 1977: 418.
2. 1977: 543. It should be pointed out, however, that in one sense *4 Ezra* is, in fact, representative of Early Judaism. Neusner, for instance, claims it to be such (1981: 23), but he does so in connection with the eschatological expectancy prevalent in Early Judaism.
3. Cf. e.g. Käsemann, 1980; Hübner, 1984a.
4. These criticisms tend to fall into three categories: (1) Sanders asks his own questions of the texts; (2) Sanders's 'covenantal nomism' is a scholarly, ahistorical abstraction which does not do justice to the diversity within Early Judaism; and (3) some texts refute 'covenantal nomism' itself. Sanders responds to criticisms especially in his 1980 article. The third criticism needs to be noted, for there is a corpus of Jewish literature which Sanders does not cite and which falls outside the pattern of 'covenantal nomism'. He himself notes this in his translation of the *Testament of Abraham* (1983b). The genre of Jewish 'propaganda literature' tends to play down the distinctiveness theme which is inherent in 'covenantal nomism' (cf. Collins, 1985: 164-70), as do some authors who have a more cosmopolitan perspective, such as Philo of Alexandria.
5. Cf. Garlington, 1990a; Dunn, 1988a: lxvii-lxxi; earlier, Limbeck, 1971.
6. Vermes, 1981: 163.

trend of modern scholarship in this matter is best demonstrated by the fact that the most recent university 'textbook' to concern itself with the origins of Christianity begins its introduction to 'Jewish Life and Thought at the Beginning of the Christian Era' by pointing to the covenant as a 'dominant theme in the Jewish religion'.[1]

Fundamental to this project is the conviction that the best starting point for the study of Early Judaism is the recognition of the importance of the covenant for Jewish reflection and practice. Sanders's case is found to be compellingly substantiated by the Jewish texts of the period (see §1.2 below). It may well be, of course, that this approach will need to be subjected to various degrees of nuancing and revision when individual texts are examined in its light (see §1.2.3 below). It is arguable, nonetheless, that inroads can be made into the majority of Early Jewish texts when approached from this angle. It will frequently repay the student of Early Judaism to ask of Jewish texts questions such as: Does the author of this text interact with a covenantal perception of God's ways? If so, what is his 'posture' towards the covenant? Has the situation which gave rise to this text helped to determine the manner in which the covenant is understood by its author(s)? To what extent is a covenantal perspective maintained/abandoned in this text? Questions such as these will, more often than not, help to illumine the purpose behind the writing of those texts. It provides, we believe, a historically sensitive working hypothesis for the study of Jewish texts within the context of Early Judaism.

Of course, the study of Judaism was only part of Sanders's overall project, as the title of his work clearly indicates. Sanders's book is almost two books in one, the first establishing a covenantal pattern of thought and practice pervading Early Judaism (Part I), and the second analysing the contours and content of Paul's thought and its relationship to Judaism (Part II and Conclusions). With regard to this second issue, Sanders makes the following claim:

> Paul's 'pattern of religion' cannot be described as 'covenantal nomism', and therefore Paul presents an *essentially different type of religiousness from any found in Palestinian Jewish literature . . . Paul in fact explicitly denies that the Jewish covenant can be effective for salvation, thus consciously denying the basis of Judaism.*[2]

1. Rowland, 1985: 27.
2. 1977: 543, 551, emphasis his.

An obvious point needs to be mentioned here. That is to say that the accuracy of this provocative statement and others like it (cf. his talk of Paul's radical 'change of "entire systems"'[1]) depends upon the accuracy of Sanders's reconstruction of Paul's thought and of its relationship to Judaism; accepting Sanders's point concerning the covenantal nature of Judaism (Part I) does not necessarily entail the acceptance of his portrayal of Paul (Part II) and Paul's place within or 'without' Judaism (Conclusions). Sanders has been joined by others who share his concern to reapproach the matter of Paul and Judaism with a backdrop of covenantal nomism in view, but, despite their common understanding of Judaism, these scholars have registered different analyses of Paul, his thought and his relationship to Judaism.[2] If it can be said that Sanders has set the agenda for much of Pauline study by his compelling characterization of Judaism, it is not clear that he has offered the definitive presentation of Paul or answered the issue of Paul and Judaism beyond doubt. This remains a matter for investigation and discussion.

The traditional understanding of 'Paul and Judaism' was based upon a legalistic portrayal of Judaism. Paul was seen as the great challenger of religious legalism and institutionalism, attacking the Judaism of his day for this very reason and converting to Christianity with its double emphasis on human inadequacy and divine grace. Obviously, then, renewed study of this issue (Paul and Judaism) is required as a result of Sanders's analysis of Judaism. If the legalistic portrayal of Judaism is to be done away with, how then are we to understand Paul?

At least two possibilities arise. The first is that the traditional understanding of Paul as the challenger of legalism is left intact, despite a revised understanding of Early Judaism as a covenantal 'religion'. If it were shown to be the case that Paul actually did make the charge of legalism against his Jewish contemporaries, it may then be argued that Paul's critique of Judaism has little substance. One would then have to consider whether the Judaism known by Paul was a peripheral and perverse phenomenon within Judaism which is not given voice to by the extant texts of Early Judaism, or whether Paul failed to understand the covenantal context of Jewish obedience to the

---

1.　1977: 550.
2.　Cf. e.g. Räisänen, 1983; Dunn, 1983; *idem*, 1988a; Wright, 1978; *idem*, 1980; Ziesler, 1989; Westerholm, 1988; Barclay, 1988. Donaldson notes 'the increasing recognition within Pauline scholarship that the legalistic depiction of pharisaism is simply false' (1989: 669).

law, or whether he simply misrepresented Judaism to his readership in order to score points for his own controversial programme. In any case, if Paul did charge his Jewish contemporaries with legalistic motives, no doubt they would have found these charges to miss the mark. A second possibility, however, would be that Paul's critiques had nothing to do with legalism but were directed against something altogether different. Those who would advocate this view suggest that the misguided understanding of Judaism as legalistic has, in turn, misguided our perceptions of Paul, that the 'result of the traditional, and false, picture of Judaism has been. . . the manufacture of an imaginary apostle'.[1] All this is still very much a matter of debate; accordingly, it is, as Wright estimates, 'an exciting time to be a Pauline scholar'.[2]

It is the purpose of this project to join in the examination of Paul and Early Judaism by means of a route as yet unexplored. In Sanders's survey of Jewish literature, Paul does not stand alone outside the common pattern of Early Judaism; as we have seen, Sanders cites one other first-century Jew whose work can be shown to fall beyond the bounds of covenantal nomism: the author of *4 Ezra*. Since the issue of Paul and Judaism remains problematic, it would seem quite appropriate, if not imperative, to consider whether any light can be shed on this matter by comparing with Paul another Jew who, like Paul, is something of an enigma within the reconstruction of Judaism offered by Sanders. Sanders himself was not concerned with a comprehensive analysis of *4 Ezra*, as he was with Paul; he does not ask in any detail about how the author of *4 Ezra* constructs his distinctive case against the background of the prevailing covenantalism of his day, or whether, and to what extent, the author interacts with covenantal nomism itself. Sanders's primary point in this regard was simply to show *that* (not how or why) *4 Ezra* falls outside the typical Jewish 'pattern of religion'. These matters of relationship are, of course, applied to the issue of Paul and Judaism, but not to the question of *4 Ezra* and Judaism. While many have joined Sanders in reapproaching Paul against the background of Jewish covenantal nomism, little consideration has been given to whether *4 Ezra* holds any clues to aid in this reinvestigation of Paul and Judaism. Since the publication of

1. Wright, 1978: 80. See especially Räisänen, 1983: 166-77; Sanders, 1983a: 154-60; Dunn, 1983.
2. 1988: 430.

Sanders's work, no detailed study has appeared which sets out to discover what can be learned from a comparison of these two 'exceptional' Jews against the background of Jewish covenantalism. However different they may be, if Sanders is right, *4 Ezra* and Paul have one significant point in common: their common displacement from the covenantal 'pattern of religion' which was so prevalent in Early Judaism. Certainly a comparison of the two is called for, and it is this task which I seek to undertake here.

Such a comparison would appear to have some potential on several scores. The two authors were near contemporaries: not more than half a century separates the time of their writing. Moreover, both authors underwent a profound 'crisis experience' which motivated their respective works—events which necessitated the re-examination of their traditional perspectives: for Paul, the encounter with the risen Christ; for the author of *4 Ezra*, the destruction of Jerusalem in 70 CE. For this reason scholars have often spoken of each author as having had a 'conversion' experience (whether the word is correct or not),[1] thereby indicating that both authors have arrived at their position in distinction from an earlier-held view—a significant point for this project. Furthermore, two or three decades separate those crisis events from the writing of the authors' texts. As such, those texts embody not the initial 'knee-jerk' reflexes but the calculated reflections upon those events and their implications for the situations in which these authors found themselves. Further still, one prominent scholar has claimed that both authors struggled with a common dilemma, and that their solutions are 'structurally very similar'.[2] The structural similarities are especially evident when *4 Ezra* is compared with Paul's letter to the Roman Christian communities, chs. 1–11 in particular. For this reason, the texts of comparison chosen for this study are *4 Ezra* and Romans 1–11.

Before undertaking a comparison of this sort, it is necessary to ground our understanding of Early Judaism in the texts of that period, while highlighting aspects which will prove to be of importance for this project. First, it will become evident early on that the authors of *4 Ezra* and Romans 1–11 develop their respective cases with two common convictions in their sights: (1) the pervasiveness of sin through-

---

1. For *4 Ezra*, see Stone, 1981; Collins 1984a: 165. For Paul, see Donaldson, 1989; Gager, 1981; Wilckens, 1974; Räisänen, 1987b.
2. Stone, 1973: 84.

out humanity, and (2) the effectiveness of God's grace within the covenant. That these are commonplace within Early Judaism will be documented in §1.2.1. Second, many Jewish texts demonstrate how easily a covenantal self-identity could result in a sense of national distinctiveness, thereby promoting an attitude of Jewish ethnocentrism, as §1.2.2 will illustrate. This aspect of Early Judaism is of fundamental importance to the cases of the authors of this study, which Parts II and III below will demonstrate. In §1.2.3, the social diversity of Early Judaism will be called to mind since, if we hope to analyse correctly the position of these authors to or within Early Judaism, the 'variations' upon the covenant 'theme' must first be recognized. With these considerations in mind, the issue of particular interest for this project will be established in §1.2.4. Then in §1.3, several terms will be defined and the perspective and approach of this study will be set out.

1.2. *Aspects of Early Jewish Covenantalism*

1.2.1. *Human sinfulness and the covenant of divine grace.* Much of Jewish literature demonstrates a common conviction concerning the wickedness of all humanity. Throughout 1QH, for instance, there are repeated statements to this effect. It is said that a human has no defence before God (1.25-27), for to 'man' belongs 'the work of iniquity and deeds of deceit' (1.27). No one, 'when he is judged, shall be righteous before thee. . . nor can any withstand thy wrath' (7.28-29; cf. 9.14-17; 12.24-31). There is 'no fleshly refuge' (7.17); a creature of clay and dust—itself 'a source of pollution, a melting pot of wickedness and an edifice of sin' (1.22; cf. 12.25)—stands 'in the realm of wickedness' (3.24) and therefore has no hope of standing upright before a just God (cf. 10.3-12; 12.19). Such a one's beginning is in sinful iniquity (13.15) and he remains 'in iniquity from the womb and in guilty unfaithfulness until his old age' (4.29-30). Righteousness 'is not of man nor is perfection of way of the son of man' (4.30; cf. 15.12), for he inclines all his days towards sin and guilt (11.20-21).

From this, it is clear that, despite a strong sense of separateness and distinctiveness from the rest of society, those who recited these hymns and psalms affirmed their position in sin right alongside the rest of humanity. This condition of sinfulness includes all humanity; social distinctions were considered to be inappropriate when one's position before God was in view. There are none who are righteous before God since sin is pervasive throughout the human race. This conviction is evident in much of the literature of Early Judaism,[1] and expands upon the pronounced confessions of sinfulness and personal inadequacy as recorded in the psalms, the Jewish prayerbook. One needs only to glance briefly at Pss. 25, 51, 79, 90, or 105 to see that such convictions concerning sin were hardly unique; it was a Jewish commonplace to recognize the indiscriminate stamp of sin upon all humanity: 'No one living is righteous before you' (Ps. 143.2; cf. 1 Kgs 8.46 = 2 Chron. 6.36; Eccl. 7.20; Ps. 14.1-3; 53.1-3; 11QPs 155.8; *Pss. Sol.* 3.5 with 3.9; 9.7; *Ps.-Philo* 12; 13.9; 26.14; 19.9-10, 44; 1QS 11.9-11; Philo, *Vit. Mos.* 2.147).

Nonetheless, such all-embracing declarations are outnumbered in Jewish literature by statements concerning the efficacy of the grace of God (cf. *Pss. Sol.* 10.4; 11QPs 155.20-21; Pr. Man. 13–14; *Jos. Asen.* 10–13), grace which is bestowed upon those in covenant relationship with God. This is perhaps nowhere clearer than in *Pseudo-Philo* (cf. 11.1, 6; 13.10; 14.2; 18.10; 19.8-11; 21.4, 9; 22.5-7; 23.4-14; 28.4-5; 30.7; 32.1-13; 35.3-4; 39.4-6; 47.3; 49.3). Repeatedly we hear pronouncements therein such as this one, spoken by God: 'For even if my people have sinned, nevertheless I will have mercy upon them' (31.2; cf. 19.11; 39.6; 49.3). Divine grace is granted to the people of Israel 'because of his covenant that he established with your fathers and the oath that he has sworn not to abandon you' (30.7). Divine grace is effective through the channel of covenant relationship. Although God may punish his people when they sin, this is the natural result of a prior relationship, a relationship compared to that of a father and a son (16.5; cf. Exod. 4.22-23; Hos. 11.1; Wis. 18.13; *Pss. Sol.* 18.4; *Jub.* 19.29). This relationship is assured through God's faithfulness to his people:

> It is easier to take away the foundations and the topmost part of the earth and to extinguish the light of the sun and to darken the light of the moon than for anyone to uproot the planting of the Most Powerful or to destroy his vine (18.10).

Throughout, *Pseudo-Philo* is animated by this notion of the unique covenant relationship between God and Israel. One can turn to almost any page of the text and find the fundamental concern of its author(s) to be the preservation of the covenant. At every point, the various episodes of Israel's history are explained according to covenantal

1. Cf. Sanders, 1977: 279; Charlesworth, 1988: 49.

dynamics; the people's faithfulness or unfaithfulness provokes God to act in various ways, thereby shaping the course of Israel's history. This in itself is not very original, and the work may well be typical of 'mainstream' Jewish piety:[1] God is merciful to his people as they walk in the ways which are pleasing to him, living by the law (10.4-6; 19.9; 23.10) which he gave them in order to establish an 'eternal covenant with the sons of Israel' (11.5; cf. *Pss. Sol.* 10.4; *Jub.* 1.4-5; 1 Macc. 1.57). Offences of the law threaten the covenant relationship but can be set right (especially 'unintentional' sin; cf. *Ps.-Philo* 6; 22; 30; *Pss. Sol.* 3.7-8; Lev. 4.2, 13, 22, 27; 5.15, 18; 22.14; Num. 15.22-31) by means of repentance and atonement (contrast the unrepentant sons of Eli in *Ps.-Philo* 53 with the repentant Israelites in *Ps.-Philo* 39).

Although the Qumran sectarians revalued the covenant between God and Israel in a manner distinct from that found in *Pseudo-Philo*, the pattern is nonetheless much the same. In their literature, the members of the Qumran community emphasized the necessity of divine grace as the means of salvation. While recognizing that all are sinful before God, the speaker of 1QH nonetheless considered himself to walk in righteousness (7.14), but only through the goodness of God: '*By thy goodness alone* is man righteous' (13.16-17); 'Thou wilt pardon iniquity and *through thy righteousness* (thou wilt purify man) of his sin' (4.37; cf. 7.18-19; 16.11; 1QS 10.11; 11.2-3, 12-15). This cleansing from sin by God's goodness was thought to occur only as one participated in the membership of the 'children of thy grace' (12.20) who were 'purified' and 'made holy' and who had 'no abominable uncleanness' or 'guilty wickedness' (11.10-11). So the confessor blessed God: 'Thou hast (caused the perverse heart to enter) into a Covenant with thee' (16.24; cf. 3.21-22; 16.26-29). Despite recognizing the pervasiveness of sin throughout all humanity, the author of 1QH urged his fellow covenanters in the following manner: 'O just men, put away iniquity! Hold fast (to the Covenant), O all you perfect of way' (1.36).[2] It is, then, in the community of the covenant (albeit redefined here in narrow sectarian terms) that one is rescued from the condition of sin which pervades the whole of humanity. In various hymns, the recognition of the unworthiness of all humanity and the belief that as a

---

1. Cf. Perrot, 1976: 23, 28-39; Murphy, 1988: 275; but see Alexander, 1988: 111.
2. For 'you perfect of way' as a community signifier, cf. 1QS 4.22a and 1QSa 1.28.

member of the covenant community one is righteous stand together without apparent contradiction.[1] These two convictions—of standing among the righteous and of personal unworthiness before God—are labelled by G.W.E. Nickelsburg 'the public and private sides of the speaker',[2] a distinction which is possible only on the basis of divine grace.

Since they considered themselves to be the exclusive members of the covenant people, the members of the Qumran community claimed for themselves such titles as 'the just', 'the elect of righteousness', 'the Holy Ones', 'the upright of way' and 'the council of Holiness', and distinguished themselves from 'the wicked', 'the seekers of falsehood', 'the horde of Satan' who 'wallow in sin'. These titular distinctions illustrate a (perceived) fundamental social difference between those in the covenant and those outside it, a difference which is evident in the behaviour of the two groups; the status of an individual is demonstrated by his manner of life. The sectarian, believing himself to be enlightened concerning the ways of God (cf. 11.16-28), loathes 'all the ways of iniquity' (14.26) so as not to turn aside from God's commands or to be separated from his laws (15.11-12). He walks in the ways of God's holiness (15.15; cf. 6.20), keeps his hands free from iniquity (16.10), and loves God by keeping his commandments (16.13; cf. 12.24). For this reason, the sectarian claims to have the law of God 'engraved on my heart' (4.10) or hidden within (5.11). Conversely, those outside the covenant 'walk in the way which is not good' because they have 'loathed thy (truth)', taking 'no delight in all thy commandments' (15.18). Teachers of lies with stubborn hearts (4.10, 15) lead astray 'thy people' (viz. ethnic Israel; 4.11, 16) by worshipping idols and setting them before the people (4.15, 19). Their idolatry and 'the multitude of their sins' (4.14) proves them to be 'the wicked' who have no share in the community of God's grace. The law is the strict possession of the covenant people (viz. the Qumran community); those

---

1. Cf. especially (following Vermes's structure of twenty-five hymns) Hymn 1 (cf. 1.22 and 1.25-27 with 1.36), Hymn 5 (cf. 3.23-25 with 3.19-23), Hymn 7 (cf. 4.29-30 with 4.31-33 and 4.35-37), Hymn 11 (cf. 7.16-17 with 7.17-25), Hymn 12 (cf. 7.28-29 with 7.29-31), Hymn 14 (cf. 9.14b-16 with 9.12-14a), Hymn 17 (cf. 11.3 with 11.9-12), Hymn 18 (cf. 11.20 with 11.17-18 and 11.29-32), Hymn 19 (cf. 12.19 and 12.24-31 with 12.20-23 and 12.32), Hymn 20 (cf. 13.13-16 with 13.16-19), Hymn 25 (cf. the interspersing of the two emphases throughout 17.26–18.30).
2. 1981: 139.

who fail to live up to the standards of the law demonstrate their unworthiness of community membership, and are thereby deserving of God's wrath.

Noticeable in all this is the dual character of adjectives such as 'righteous' and 'sinful' in Early Jewish literature. As one scholar states on evidence from the *Psalms of Solomon*, the godly 'are not free from sin, but are sinfully pious, unrighteously righteous. Their opponents are the sinners.'[1] The antithetical status of these two groups (viz. the righteous and the sinners) is wholly determined by whether or not one is, and intends to remain,[2] a member of the covenant community, for common to both groups is sin, but restricted to the covenant community is the grace of God which is efficacious for the repentant members of that community who seek his forgiveness. So W.D. Davies writes: 'To be righteous was to be within the Covenant despite one's failures'.[3] The law plays a role in this, itself serving to testify to the fact that God has promised to be merciful to Israel, his servants. Thus, *Pss. Sol.* 10.4 reads: 'And the Lord will remember his servants in mercy, for the testimony of it (is) in the Law of the eternal covenant'.

1.2.2. Jewish distinctiveness, separation and ethnocentrism. It is significant for this project to note the manner in which Israel's covenant relationship with God and possession of God's law facilitated a sense of nationalistic distinctiveness for many Jews. Israel, having been selected as God's unique people, were to live in a manner worthy of their calling; since YHWH is holy (קָדוֹשׁ) so too are they to be holy (קְדֹשִׁים, Lev. 11.44), a holy nation (גּוֹי קָדוֹשׁ, Exod. 19.6). It is this characteristic, shared by covenant God and covenant people, which distinguishes Israel from the nations who do not enjoy a covenant relationship with God. So, for instance, Deut. 4.6-8 praises the people of Israel over all the other nations because of their possession of the law and their observance of God's commandments: '[The gentile nations] will say, "Surely this great nation is a wise and understanding people. . . What other nation is so great as to have such righteous decrees and laws?"' Similar pronouncements concerning the privilege and distinctiveness of Israel are made on the basis of this same

---

1. Franklyn, 1987: 8.
2. Schoeps: 'intention is man's affirmation of the covenant' (1961: 196). Cf. Sanders, 1977: 135.
3. 1984b: 18.

connection between wisdom and the law given to Israel. So Ben Sira, contending that a life of wisdom is lived in devotion 'to the study of the Law of the Most High' (Sir. 39.1), personifies wisdom as a divine figure who wanders throughout the world looking for a place to take up residence (24.3-7) until she is commanded: 'Make your dwelling in Jacob, and in Israel receive your inheritance' (24.8; cf. 24.23; Bar. 3.36–4.4). This intricate connection between the law and the people of Israel is presupposed by the author of *Pseudo-Philo*, who describes the law as containing the 'rules for *our race*' (*Ps.-Philo* 12.2). The law, then, served not only as a symbol or 'testimony' (*Ps.-Philo* 11.2; cf. *Pss. Sol.* 10.4) of the covenant relationship between God and Israel ('the book of the covenant of the Most High God', Sir. 24.23) but as a guide book for moral living which gives to the people of Israel the 'ethical edge' over the gentile nations.

While it was the case that a good many Jews sought to highlight the universal character of the Mosaic legislation in order to encourage gentiles to respect (at least, and perhaps to adopt) Jewish practices and beliefs (e.g. Philo), for many Jews just the opposite was the case. Israel's election by God, their possession of the law, and their concern for holiness frequently promoted a Jewish concern to keep separate from others by adhering to practices which distinguished them from their gentile contemporaries. Various ritualistic observances became recognized throughout the Graeco-Roman world as distinctively *Jewish* practices, since they were for the Jews symbols of covenant membership. These practices were to be maintained upon penalty of forfeiting one's covenantal standing. Of them, circumcision was normative, being considered the mark of the covenant *par excellence*[1]—'the covenant of the flesh' (*Ps.-Philo* 9.13, 15). Genesis 17 records the divine command in this regard:

> This is my covenant with you and your descendants after you, the covenant you are to keep: Every male among you shall be circumcised. . . My covenant in your flesh is to be an everlasting covenant. Any uncircumcised male. . . will be cut off from his people; he has broken my covenant (17.10, 14; cf. Exod. 4.24-26).

While some Jews in Alexandria considered this command to have symbolic rather than literal significance (cf. Philo, *Migr. Abr.* 89–94), their view was certainly somewhat idiosyncratic; if P. Borgen is right,

---

1. Cf. Nolland, 1981; Collins, 1985.

such Jews were persecuted by their contemporaries in view of the scriptural injunction.[1] For the vast majority of Jews, circumcision seems to have been essential for covenant membership (cf. *Jub.*. 15.11-15; 15.23-34; 16.14). So, for instance, when speaking of the physical attribute which identified Moses as a Jew, the author of *Pseudo-Philo* spoke not of Moses' circumcision but, instead, of his 'covenant' (9.15), thereby signalling how the two terms could be used virtually interchangeably. Other practices which were regarded as necessary for the preservation of the covenant included especially the observance of the Sabbath rest (*Ps.-Philo* 44.7; *Jub.* 2.17-33; 50.1-13) and Jewish dietary regulations (*Jub.* 6.4-16).[2] Thus, when these practices were threatened by pagan influences and overlords (1 Macc. 1.41-50; 2 Macc. 5.27–6.11), some pious Jews passively 'welcomed death rather than defile themselves and profane the holy covenant' (1 Macc. 1.63; cf. 1.54-62; 2.50; 2 Macc. 6.10-11; 6.18–7.42; so also the passive character of Daniel 7–12 and, if dated to this time, *Ass. Mos.* 9), while others actively took up arms against their rulers in order to preserve the covenant, even if that entailed their death (1 Macc. 2.15-28; 2 Macc. 8.1-36; *Jub.* 23.20; *1 En.* 90.13-19). Such measures were said to be motivated by Jewish 'zeal' (1 Macc. 2.54; *4 Macc.* 18.12), a 'zeal for the law' (1 Macc. 2.26-27, 54, 58). The 'renegade Jews' (1 Macc. 1.11) who adhered to the Hellenizing programme of this period argued that Jewish separation from the gentiles resulted in 'disaster' for the Jews (1 Macc. 1.11). Accordingly, they 'removed their marks of circumcision. . . intermarried with the Gentiles, and abandoned themselves to evil ways' (1 Macc. 1.15). Those who maintained the distinctively Jewish practices denounced these 'renegades' as having 'broken the covenant with the Lord our God' (*Jub.* 15.26; cf. 15.28-34; Dan. 11.30; 1 Macc. 1.15) and having entered 'into a covenant with the Gentiles' (1 Macc. 1.11).[3]

As a consequence of their distinctiveness as God's people who live in accordance with the law, the people of Israel could be acclaimed as 'a race of most righteous men' (*Sib. Or.* 3.219). This attitude has a

---

1. 1983: 38.

2. Further textual support is given by Stern, 1974: §§195, 258, 281, 301.

3. Bickermann proposed that the 'renegade' Jews legitimized this on the basis that distinctively Jewish practices were later additions to the original Mosaic law, having been incorporated into the Mosaic code through the efforts of 'superstitious priests' (1979: 86). Cf. Hengel, 1974: 1.258-60; Blenkinsopp, 1981: 16-17; Cohen, 1987: 42.

converse side to it, of course: the denigration of other nations. Since
the gentiles did not possess the law (they are 'unlawful', *Pss. Sol.*
17.24) and 'have not learned my [God's] Law' (*Ps.-Philo* 10.2), so
they were perceived by many Jews as being 'sinners' (*Pss. Sol.* 2.1;
17.23 [1.1?]; *Jub.* 23.24; Gal. 2.15) and 'rabble' (*Pss. Sol.* 17.15).
They are likened to 'spittle' before God, being as significant to him as
a drop of water (*Ps.-Philo* 7.3, 12.4; *2 Bar.* 82.5; *4 Ezra* 6.56). All
this follows from the fundamental point of Israel's unique election:
God chose Israel alone to be his 'portion and inheritance' (*Pss. Sol.*
14.5), blessed 'above all the nations' (*Pss. Sol.* 11.9; cf. 11.8-11; *Ps.-
Philo* 11.1; 19.8; 30.4; 35.2). Consequently, just as distinctively *Jewish*
practices (circumcision, Sabbath and dietary observance) were to be
maintained, so also practices which were distinctive of the *gentile*
nations were to be avoided, for gentiles were a polluted people. Denigration of this sort is obvious, for instance, in *Jub.* 22.16:

> Separate yourself from the gentiles, and do not eat with them, and do not per-
> form deeds like theirs. And do not become associates of theirs. Because their
> deeds are defiled, and all of their ways are contaminated, despicable, and
> abominable.

The concern to maintain Jewish distinctiveness (with the denigration
of the gentile nations as its corollary) is especially apparent in *Pseudo-
Philo*. Throughout that work, idolatry is cited as characteristic of the
practice of the gentiles; it is the sin which provokes all other sins (*Ps.-
Philo* 27; 44).[1] Accordingly, idolatry heads the list of practices which
compromise the covenant relationship between God and Israel and
which, naturally, should be avoided lest other gentile practices be
adopted (cf. 12.2-10; 19.7; 25.7-13; 27.2 with 27.15; 34.1-4; 41.3;
44.1-10). The author repeatedly makes the point that if one is truly to
shun this fundamental evil (idolatry), one must refrain from mingling
or associating with the pagan nations in any way (9.1; 18.13-14; 21.1;
25.10; 30.1; 34.1-5; 43.5; 44.7; 45.3).[2] A most dramatic portrayal of
this is evident in *Ps.-Philo* 9.5, where Tamar is depicted as devising a
plan to have sexual intercourse with her father-in-law in order to keep
herself from having to have intercourse with gentiles; the former
would be pardonable since it prevented her from 'mixing' with gentiles, an unpardonable sin. Here is clear indication of the Jewish concern to keep themselves separate and distinct from the gentile nations

---

1. Cf. Murphy, 1988: 279-80.
2. Cf. Murphy, 1988: 276, 284.

who fall outside the boundaries of the covenant of God's grace. Necessarily, then, ethical distinctions demarcate the covenant boundaries (those 'within' are ethically superior to those 'without') and ethical behaviour situates a person accordingly.

As a result of their election by the merciful covenant God, the people of Israel awaited their final vindication in the ultimate eschatological conflict through which God will establish his reign on behalf of his people. Although expectations concerning the fate of the gentiles in the eschatological age vary greatly,[1] one common expectation is clearly given voice in the messianic section of the *Psalms of Solomon*. Therein, God's grace and protection upon Israel is contrasted with the condemnation and destruction of the 'unlawful' nations (8.23; 17.22-28; *Ps.-Philo* 10.4-6) who are deserving of God's wrath because of their rampant sinfulness. God will be compassionate to the people of Israel, being faithful in mercy towards them forever (cf. *Pss. Sol.* 7.6-10; 8.23-34; 10.5-8; 11.1-9; 12.6; 17.1-46).

1.2.3. *The covenant and its diversity in Early Judaism.* As we have seen from §§1.2.1 and 1.2.2, the covenant of God in relationship with Israel should be regarded as a fundamental building block of Jewish thought and practice in the first century CE. Nonetheless, it is important to add here that the covenant, while being commonplace throughout much of Early Judaism, proved to be a point of contention among the various segments of Jewish society—a society which has been described as 'a swirling dynamo full of life'.[2] The concept of the covenant did not function in the same way or mean the same thing 'across the board'. In fact, although the covenant is fundamental to much of the literature of Early Judaism, those texts themselves suggest that two central components of covenantalism—the law and the people of Israel—are subject to (re)definition. If we extract these two components from particular texts in order to notice common themes and the like, we must also recognize that what we are left with is something quite bare-boned which tends to be an ahistorical abstraction. As soon as flesh is given to this 'skeleton', what becomes visible is not so much that which was common to the various groups which comprised Early

---

1. Cf. e.g. Sanders, 1985b: 213-28.
2. Charlesworth, 1987: 227.

Judaism but, instead, their idiosyncratic definitions of that common-place.[1]

For this reason, it is in one sense preferable to speak not of the 'Judaism' of the first century of our era but of the then-current 'Judaisms'.[2] If it is true that, as a rule, Jewish texts of that period give evidence of a vibrant sense of Jewish election and covenantal self-definition, it is also true that the understanding of the covenant varies from text to text, from situation to situation, thereby contributing to a significant degree of tension among the variety of Jewish groups of that time (for instance the way in which the covenant is understood in *Pseudo-Philo* with the sectarian definitions of the covenant in the Thanksgiving Hymn scroll from Qumran or in the *Psalms of Solomon* [which we read as sectarian][3]). That God had called for himself a people was not in doubt, but what that people was meant to be and how they were to act was subject to interpretation. It is one thing for the historian to recognize the covenant as a common 'given' of Jewish self-awareness, the foundation upon which much Jewish reflection rested. It is another thing to consider the shape which the covenant took in any given situation. When the former is emphasized, one can speak of covenantal theology, rather than legalism, as the warp and woof of Jewish identity. When the latter is emphasized, however, one is reminded of the variance within Early Judaism itself—that is, of the Judaisms which were jostling each other in their bids for recognition and dominance. They may have shared a basic recipe, but various seasonings produced a *pot pourri* of flavours.[4] Evidently, it is not too much to say that what characterized the Judaisms of this time was not uniformity, but diversity. Variation and controversy arose when

---

1. So Sigal, after laying out in *two* pages 'A Basic Portrait of Judaism' (along the lines of Sanders's covenantal nomism), proceeds in *forty-eight* pages to discuss 'The Varieties of Judaic Religious Experience' of Early Judaism (1988: 36-86).

2. So Neusner, Green and Frerichs, editing a recent collection of articles, entitle their book, *Judaisms and Their Messiahs* (1987b). Moreover, Simon notes that each form of Judaism 'could claim with some justification to represent the most authentic form of Judaism' (1967: 7).

3. Cf. Hann, 1988.

4. This consideration has led Sanders, in reflection upon his work of 1977, to admit that his study is prone to highlight a commonality in Early Judaism at the expense of its diversity (1980: 66). In a more recent article, Sanders discusses the character of Early Judaism without once making mention of 'covenantal nomism'. Instead, he speaks less rigidly of the relationship between God's mercy and human obedience (1985a; see e.g. 1985a: 369, 371).

determining what obedience to YHWH involved and what being his covenant people meant in practice. Accordingly, whereas the modern historian sees the various groups of first-century Jews as indicating the diversity and spread of Early Judaism, those particular parties themselves often thought that they alone embodied true Judaism while the others were in grave error or had fallen away altogether.[1] If the covenant proved to be commonplace throughout much of Early Judaism, it also proved to be vulnerable to definition so that, in practice, the commonplace itself became a medium towards diversity.

1.2.4. *Establishing the issues of this study.* This scenario of Early Judaism, as set out in above, provides the context for formulating the primary issues of the present study, taking into account three characteristics of Early Judaism which we find to be fundamental: (1) its covenantal nature, (2) its ethnocentric focus, and (3) its social diversity. In this regard, Sanders recognizes 'two pillars to all forms of Judaism: the election of Israel and faithfulness to the Mosaic law'.[2] Covenantal perspectives, no matter their form, included these as two central components: Israel and the Torah. So also S. Sandmel comments: 'Israel and the Torah constitute a blended entity; without Israel the Torah had no significance, and without the Torah Israel had no uniqueness'.[3] These two components are so intertwined in the covenantal undergirding of Early Judaism that the one intersects directly with the other, however the covenant is defined. Accordingly, our primary interest in this project will lie in discerning how the law and the covenant people are presented by the authors of *4 Ezra* and Romans 1–11, against the background of Jewish covenantalism. If these two Jews do, in fact, fall outside a common 'pattern of religion', their distinctiveness will no doubt be most evident in their handling of Israel and the significance of the law. These matters, then, will provide the focus for the study of these two texts.

---

1. Neusner believes that in reconstructions of E rly Judaism, 'an essentially philosophical construct, "Judaism", is imposed upon wildly diverse evidence deriving from many kinds of social groups and testifying to the state of mind and way of life of many sorts of Jews, who in their own day would scarcely have understood one another' (1981: 21).

2. 1983a: 208.

3. 1978: 182.

1.3. *Definitions and Perspective*

Before proceeding, a few terms which are frequently used in this project need to be cited and explained. First, although I accept as a starting point Sanders's description of Early Judaism as marked out by what he calls 'covenantal nomism', it will be more helpful for this project to rename this 'pattern of religion' as 'ethnocentric covenantalism'. We have seen how a covenantal awareness undergirds a wide selection of Jewish literature. Accordingly, it is arguable that, when formulating a descriptive phrase to characterize Early Judaism, the covenant is to take central position in that formulation and is deserving, therefore, of the position of the noun ('covenantalism') rather than the adjective ('covenantal').[1] The adjective, then, can serve to describe the kind of covenantalism which is found in particular texts. Instead of 'nomistic covenantalism' (reversing Sanders's order), it is necessary for this project to highlight the ethnocentric character (cf. §1.2.2) of Jewish covenantalism. No matter how the covenant was (re)defined, its ethnocentric character was retained throughout most Jewish texts of the time.[2] Even in sectarian definitions of the covenant this is true, since the members of the sect considered themselves to constitute the exclusive participants in the covenant established by God with Israel;[3] although the requirements for membership in the covenant proved to be open to definition, the ethnocentric character of the covenant was not called into question. As we will see, 'ethnocentric covenantalism' provides the best backdrop against which *4 Ezra* and Romans 1–11 should be read, since their authors argue independently of each other that an ethnic exclusivism of this kind involves an inherently flawed understanding of the covenant, which they then seek to repattern along different lines. These facts demonstrate something of the motivation for coining this phrase, 'ethnocentric covenantalism'.

Second, references will be made on occasion to the 'anthropological condition of sin' and 'the covenantal corrective'. Whereas the concept of 'sin' can contain various connotations in Jewish literature, it has as

---

1. Cf. the appropriate remarks by Davies, 1984b: 17-18.
2. This is not to imply, however, that Jewish ethnocentrism is incompatible with a more universalistic concern, since such is not necessarily the case. The issue is too large to enter into here since it is only a related issue, but we note in this regard Urbach's article of 1981, which demonstrates how particularistic and universalistic concerns often reinforced one another in Early Jewish perspectives.
3. Exemplified in Qumran; cf. Vermes, 1981: 163-88; Sanders, 1977: 240-57.

its 'coherent centre' the fundamental notion of a breach of relationship with God.[1] The adjective 'anthropological' is employed in order to highlight the commonplace (noted above) that this condition of 'sin' is not restricted to particular peoples or groups but is shared by all indiscriminately before God. As Sanders explains: 'During this life, man never ceases to be "nothing" vis-à-vis God'.[2] Social distinctions are improper when this position of sin before God is in view. The corrective, of course, comes through God's grace, which re-establishes relationship through the channels of the covenant; those who are within the covenant may be vulnerable to falling out of favour with God through transgression,[3] but by God's grace they have been rescued from the anthropological condition in which the sinners remain. Whereas the anthropological condition of sin is anterior to the covenantal relationship, God's gracious initiative is the salvific antidote which legitimates a distinction between the righteous and the sinners. These dynamics, which were noted in §1.2.1, are explained by Sanders in this way:

> On the one hand, there is the sense of human inadequacy before God. . . no one can be righteous or perfect before God. . . On the other hand, there is the consciousness of being elect; thus some are righteous (*tsaddiq, yitsdaq*), but only by the grace of God.[4]

Accordingly, the sinful condition of all humanity is offset within the social unit of God's people (however that group be defined by various Jewish factions), established as such by his grace (cf. the structure of Gen. 1–11 [the anthropological condition of sin] and Gen. 12ff. [the covenantal corrective]).[5]

1. Cf. Stählin: 'It is almost always a matter of "offense in relation to God"' (in Grundmann, 1964: 295). Cf. in the same article, Quell, 274, 276; Bertram, 289; Stählin–Grundmann, 289.
2. 1977: 279. He finds this in rabbinic and tannaitic literature, in the Dead Sea Scrolls, Sirach, *1 Enoch*, *Psalms of Solomon*, and *4 Ezra*. See his index entry 'Sin' on p. 626 for references.
3. Cf. the interesting comment by Green: 'The boastful proposition "we are men and they are crocodiles" implies that "we were, or could have been, or might yet be crocodiles too"' (1985: 50).
4. 1977: 311-12.
5. Accordingly, the blessing of God to Adam in Gen. 1.26-30 to 'be fruitful and multiply' is reissued after the sin of Adam and transposed onto the covenant people of Abraham's offspring. Cf. (with Gen. 1.26-27) Gen. 17.2, 6, 16; 22.17; 26.4; 28.3; 35.11; 47.27; 48.3-4; Exod. 1.7; 32.13; Lev. 26.9; Deut. 1.10; 7.13-14; 8.1; 10.22; 28.11, 63; 30.5, 16.

With these terms defined, several remarks need also be registered here concerning the perspective and approach of this study. First, I formed the opinion early on that the historical roots of Christianity lie within Judaism and, for the most part, remained fundamentally 'Jewish' at least until the destruction of Jerusalem in 70 CE. With hindsight, of course, it can be argued that a religion quite distinctive from Judaism was born with the life, death and resurrection of Jesus Christ, and that only time was needed to reveal the incompatibility of the old and the new, Judaism and Christianity. It is suspected, however, that the divorce of Christianity from Judaism may not have been inevitable from the start, as is commonly thought. In any case, we locate the beginnings of Christianity under the umbrella of Early Judaism. As a result, in order to avoid dichotomizing Judaism and Christianity, I have chosen to speak not of 'Christianity' but of the 'early christian movement' within Judaism. For the same reason, I have attempted in what follows to employ the word 'christian' only as an adjective (instead of 'Christian(s)' or 'Christianity'). And, moreover, it is cited throughout with a lower-case 'c'. It is hoped that the reader can humour me regarding these little idiosyncrasies, all of which spring from the same conviction: The christian movement of Paul's day remained (from the historian's point of view) a sect within the broad scope of Early Judaism. The extent to which this perspective has shaped the results of this project or its nuancing, the reader may judge.

Second, the title of this project should not give the impression that what follows herein is a detailed study of the *whole* of *4 Ezra* and of Romans 1–11, for such is not the case. I have concerned myself only with those passages which are most relevant to the question of how each author interacts with ethnocentric covenantalism on matters of the law and the people of God. Different approaches are taken to accomplish this in the two texts. Although *4 Ezra* is examined section by section (since it is constructed as a piece of narrative theology), whatever is not relevant to our concern is quickly passed over. The analysis of Romans 1–11 is structured thematically rather than sequentially, and no attempt has been made to undertake a comprehensive analysis of the whole of the eleven chapters.

With these considerations in mind, we set out now to examine these two texts in comparison against the background of ethnocentric covenantalism. Each author has proven to be something of a 'Pandora's Box' for those who attempt to look inside. Accordingly, the hope is to highlight issues, submit proposals, and perhaps generate discussion of these exhilarating religious figures from the Judaism of the first century CE. The remainder of this project will follow a simple three-part structure. In Parts II and III, *4 Ezra* and Romans 1–11 (respectively) will be analysed in relation to ethnocentric covenantalism. Each text will be approached independently of the other in order to avoid (as much as possible) allowing the interests of one text to determine the investigation of the other. Only in Part IV will a large-scale comparison of the two authors be attempted—a comparison with the aim of shedding light on Paul's situation and argument by way of another whose situation will be seen as somewhat analogous. Therein we will also include reflections concerning these two Jews in relation to Early Judaism and the emerging christian and rabbinic movements of their day.

PART II

4 EZRA

Chapter 2

INTRODUCTION TO 4 EZRA

2.1. *Introduction to 4 Ezra*

The book of *4 Ezra* (2 Esd. 3–14) is identified by J.J. Collins as 'one of the greatest of the apocalypses', written by 'a sensitive and perceptive Jew'[1] engaged in a profound reflection upon the ways of God. It is the product of one Jew's reflections after the destruction of Jerusalem in 70 CE—an event which left the Jewish 'religion' never the same again. The author of *4 Ezra* is one of the first to grapple with the implications of this event for Jewish thought and practice, in the light of traditional beliefs concerning the faithfulness and justice of Israel's God. Throughout Part II the interest will be to examine the author's concerns, techniques and solutions, with a view towards fixing his case in relation to the ethnocentric covenantalism of his day.

Most scholars are agreed on three textual and structural matters. First, the original text appears to have been written in Hebrew, although no Hebrew document survives. (The place of writing is most probably Palestine,[2] although Rome is a possibility.) The Latin and Syriac translations are thought to be the most reliable extant versions, themselves produced in dependence upon a Greek translation of the Hebrew.[3] Second, any interpretation must take into account the dialogical format of the narrative, for different perspectives are given voice to by different characters of the story. Third, in the extant texts of *4 Ezra*, the narrative progresses according to a seven-episode structure, the first three Episodes (I–III) being given over to lengthy and sometimes frustrating dialogues between Ezra (the questioner) and

1. 1984a: 156, 168.
2. Cf. e.g. Harnisch, 1969: 15; Gunkel, 1930: 352; Box, 1912: 552-53.
3. See Stone, 1989: 33-43; Klijn, 1981; Thompson, 1977: 83-85. The Latin text used herein is Klijn, 1983; the Syriac text is Bidawid, 1973. The English translation used herein is Metzger's, 1983, unless otherwise stated.

the angel Uriel (the respondent). These dialogues then give way to three visions (IV–VI) and an 'epilogue' (VII).

Despite these points of general agreement, various assessments have been proposed of the purposes of the text. Especially important in this regard are the dialogues of I–III. Although the two characters are actively engaged in dialogical exchange throughout, there is no proposition which both characters formally agree upon in the end. No conclusion appears in the dialogues; they simply come to an end. The dialogue weaves in and out of issues, often without any obvious gains being made along the way. Questions are left unanswered, concerns are often ignored, and neither Ezra nor Uriel can claim to have proven his case by the end of III. The author sets up a curious tension between these characters without an explicit indication of where he himself stands. One cannot arrive at 'the theology of the author of *4 Ezra*' simply by blending Ezra's and Uriel's positions together. Instead his position must be pieced together after consideration of various matters: Is there any indication that one character, Ezra or Uriel, speaks on behalf of the author? Or might it not be better to ask, instead, how Ezra and Uriel together play a role in the crafting of the author's case? What, then, is the point of these extended debates in I–III?

Similar questions may be asked concerning Episodes IV–VII. What is the purpose of the visions, especially in relation to the dialogues of I–III? Is the author addressing here a second matter of concern, leaving behind his interests voiced in I–III? Is the integrity of the text to be accepted in IV–VII or has textual transmission corrupted an originally coherent work and introduced foreign material which should be disqualified from consideration?

Before setting out to answer questions of this sort, it will be helpful to note briefly the solutions of some others. The review which follows in §2.2 is not meant to be exhaustive of *4 Ezra* scholarship. Instead, it is meant to be representative of the kinds of solutions given to the issues cited here.[1]

2.2. *A Selective Survey of 4 Ezra Scholarship*

In his still-valuable commentary of 1912, G.H. Box contributed to *4 Ezra* scholarship by applying to the text the source-critical interests

---

1. For more extensive reviews, see Thompson, 1977: 85-120; Brandenburger, 1981: 22-57.

which were especially popular then.[1] Box isolated five separate sources which were collected, edited and fused together by a single redactor. The main text of Episodes I–III attracted the attention of the redactor because of its 'pure legalism' and 'lofty individualism'. Nonetheless, the redactor appended apocalyptic visions (IV–VI) to this source, allowing their 'eschatology of the nation' to provide a corrective to the 'eschatology of the individual' of I–III. Finally, VII was included to attract the attention of the rabbinic school, which was supposedly hostile to the apocalyptic mindset, in order to solicit rabbinic approval for apocalyptic literature. For Box, therefore, the redactor has (at least) two concerns, which are inconsistent with each other but which are fused together to form a somewhat disjointed piece.

In reaction to this source-critical approach, H. Gunkel insisted that the author was an independent thinker whose ideas need not be attributable simply to underlying sources.[2] Despite the presence of source material, the book is a unity, produced by an author who wrestled with disturbing reflections concerning the problem of evil and the fate of sinners. Gunkel identified what he thought to be two independent issues which the author addressed at different points of the book: (1) religious problems and speculations, and (2) apocalyptic and eschatological mysteries.[3] The former is addressed in I–III. There, the dialogues between Ezra and Uriel objectify the author's own inner struggle. Each character gives voice to one aspect of the author's penetrating enquiry—Ezra embodying his scepticism, and Uriel his faith.[4] The author, Gunkel claims, speaks through *both* characters simultaneously as he grapples with his own existential dilemma. Gunkel notes, however, that there is a noticeable transition between the end of III and the beginning of IV, which facilitates Ezra's consolation in IV–VII.[5] There, the author's religious problems are left behind and the eschatological mysteries are explored. In the process, the author became assured that God is in control of history, an assurance which lifted him out of his despair. The author came to expect that only in the future age will the religious problems that plagued his faith be resolved. Finally, in Gunkel's estimation, VII is a supplement

1. Cf. also Kabisch, 1889; Charles, 1896.
2. 1900: 350-52.
3. 1900: 335.
4. 1900: 340.
5. 1900: 347-48.

to *4 Ezra* which gives to the whole work 'einen ästhetisch gefälligen Abschluss'.[1]

A completely different picture is given by R.H. Pfeiffer. Analysing the author's concern to be the reconciliation of the existence of evil with the existence of a righteous God, Pfeiffer thinks that the author failed to solve the matter rationally. The author came to believe that God's ways are inscrutable, and that the human intellect is unable to find an answer to doubt, a theme met with already in the book of Job. But the author of *4 Ezra* differs from the author of Job in his deliberate search for comfort 'in the world of make-believe'.[2] Once intellectual enquiry failed, the author resorted to a 'mirage of a future golden age'.[3] But, according to Pfeiffer, even this failed to comfort him, since his intellect was plagued by doubts which Uriel's answers could not satisfy. Pfeiffer characterizes *4 Ezra* as 'a work of a truly great writer and thinker, an utterly sincere and candid spirit, who strove honestly and earnestly to solve ultimate problems but finally admitted sadly his failure to explain the tragic lot of his nation—and of all human beings'.[4] In Pfeiffer's scheme, Ezra represents the author in his search for the truth which ultimately evaded him. The author was left without a rational solution of any kind.

W. Harnisch understands Ezra and Uriel to represent not the inner wrestling of the author himself, as Gunkel had suggested, but two sides of a live dispute between the author and his opponents—Ezra mouthing the position of the author's opponents and Uriel representing the author's own view.[5] Harnisch considers Ezra to advocate an extremely sceptical view which sprang from a gnosticizing heresy. Ezra portrays God as distanced from his creation, and humanity as being above reproach for sin since one has no control of one's actions; each person is under the unbending control of fate. This estimation is vetoed at every point by Uriel, the author's mouthpiece. As a solution to Ezra's concerns, Uriel sets forward a doctrine of the two ages of history. Because of the corruption of the present age, things are not as they should be, but the present age will give way to another age. In that age, God will grant salvation to those who obey the law in the present age. Harnisch thinks that, in the course of the dialogues, Ezra

1. 1900: 348.
2. 1949: 85.
3. 1949: 86.
4. 1949: 86.
5. 1969: 64-65, 86-87.

is progressively won over to the angel's view.[1] In the beginning of IV, in fact, Ezra seems to have conceded the angel's position and addresses the people as the angel had addressed him previously.[2] Three visions are then recorded by the author in order to depict the events leading up to the age-to-come. These enabled the author to end on a note of assurance concerning salvation.[3]

Another approach is taken by E. Breech, who argues that the hermeneutical key to *4 Ezra* lies not so much in the specifics of the dialogical debates but in the *form* of the work as a whole. He argues that 'the structure and meaning of *4 Ezra* are mutually determinative',[4] the whole of *4 Ezra* being animated by a 'pattern of consolation'. While Ezra is the representative of the people and expresses the various concerns of the community, neither he nor Uriel voices the author's position *per se*. Instead, each contributes to the author's progressive journey from distress to consolation, which takes place in the movement from dialogues to visions, from Ezra's room (I–III) to the open field (IV–VI). The visions of IV–VII are themselves 'firmly rooted in the pattern of consolation',[5] giving assurance to the community despite their despair. VII is the necessary conclusion to this pattern since the prophet must return to the community and console them. That the author was concerned more with form than content[6] is obvious to Breech from the fact that Ezra's questions are never answered to his satisfaction throughout the whole work. Neither the dialogues nor the visions provide a propositional solution to his religious dilemma. Ezra finds his solution not through an intellectual process of problem-solving but, in the final sections of the book, through the consoling reassurance that their God is 'the true source of life and death for the community'.[7]

Admitting Gunkel's influence, A.P. Hayman suggests that the author was trying to solve two distinct problems:[8] (1) sin, its origin and the means by which one can escape its power to gain salvation, and (2) the

1. 1983: 477-78.
2. 1969: 173.
3. 1969: 248-57.
4. 1973: 269.
5. 1973: 272.
6. Breech remarks that one should focus 'on the motif of consolation, instead of on the contents of the several sections' (1973: 270).
7. 1973: 274.
8. 1975: 54-55.

sovereignty of God and his faithfulness to the promises to Israel. To answer these two issues, the author made use of two different eschatological traditions. In answer to (1), he utilized (in I–III) the doctrine of the Two Ages in which sin has so permeated this world that God has left it to itself, and only the future age and those who dwell in it are of concern to him. But the usefulness of this eschatological perspective runs aground after III, evidently because the author found from it no satisfactory answer to the issue of who is worthy of membership in the future age. Ezra himself is never convinced by the argument and no conclusion is reached. In this way, we have a window into the author's view of the inadequacy of the way Judaism traditionally dealt with the problem of sin and justification. On the other hand, in answer to (2), the author made greater gains in IV–VI, where a more traditional eschatological expectation was well suited to explain the desperate situation in which the Jewish people found themselves. Although the people are at present being punished for their sin, the future hope of a messianic era of vindication for Israel is maintained. In this way, two issues were answered by two different means. Hayman distinguishes himself from Gunkel when he characterizes the author's two distinct concerns as common elements in Hebrew literature whereby faith is stimulated by intellectual examination, and doubt is overcome by religious experience.[1]

In 1977, A.L. Thompson highlighted the function of *4 Ezra* as a theodicy. He considered the Ezra of I–III to be the defender of humanity's case who appeals to God for mercy in the light of the desperate situation of Adam's race. Ezra, then, has a tendency towards individualism. Uriel, on the other hand, has a tendency towards Jewish nationalism and, thereby, simply mouths orthodox assurances that salvation is bestowed upon those who are obedient to the law.[2] Thompson thinks the author to have sympathized with Ezra's struggle to comprehend the problem of evil which plagues the whole of humanity; it is Ezra's voice which the author really wanted to be heard.[3] On the other hand, both the book itself and the dialogues within it begin and end with a nationalistic interest. In fact, Ezra himself abandons his universalistic concerns of III in the transition episode of IV, not because his questions have been answered but because he takes refuge

1. 1975: 55-56.
2. 1977: 209-18, 267.
3. 1977: 296.

from his troubled heart in the knowledge that God is righteous.[1] Although Uriel's 'doctrinal' nationalism wins in the end, in the dialogues between Uriel and Ezra the author has looked beyond the easy answers of traditional Judaism and examined a more fundamental condition which permeates human existence: the problem of evil. The author found no valid solution to this issue in the arsenal of Jewish theodicy but, in the process of his work, explored the outer fringes of traditional Judaism and beyond, while simultaneously retaining his place in Judaism and affirming faith in God. The author did not stray; instead, he tried to correct Jewish theology from within by forcing it to accept a more universalistic outlook.[2] In the end, however, he resorted to a traditional Jewish understanding whereby salvation is gained through legalistic works and merit points. For this reason, he wrote under the name of Ezra in order to keep one foot within Judaism while stepping out with the other foot from Judaism's traditional stance.[3] He speaks neither through Uriel nor Ezra exclusively, but together, in order to reveal the tension of his inner struggle.[4]

Quite differently, E.P. Sanders believes that the position of the author has nothing whatsoever to do with Ezra. In the dialogues, says Sanders, Ezra's case fluctuates greatly, while Uriel's is consistent throughout. Ezra's arguments on behalf of Israel almost always meet with negative replies from Uriel and cannot be said to represent the author's voice. Through the figures of Ezra and Uriel, the author allowed various propositions (voiced by Ezra) to be confirmed or denied (by Uriel).[5] What emerges from Uriel's comments is a pattern of 'legalistic perfectionism' in which salvation is granted to the individuals whose obedience to the law is without fault. In the beginning of IV, in fact, Ezra drops his questioning and resigns himself to Uriel's view.[6] In Sanders's opinion, V and VI do not follow from the pen of the author of I–IV, but are instead the addition of a later redactor. This conclusion is based on the fact that in V and VI Sanders finds a nationalistic hope to be revived which was lacking in Uriel's position of I–III. As such, it is not inherent to the work of the original author but was tacked on later 'to make it palatable and to bring it into

1. 1977: 239, 340-42.
2. 1977: 187, 269.
3. 1977: 269.
4. 1977: 157, 215.
5. 1977: 412.
6. 1977: 416.

conformity with the prevailing Jewish hope'.[1] A later redactor has overruled the original author. Similarly, Sanders does not think VII to be integral to the book. It too is an appendix which was added to the rest in order to make the book more acceptable to the Jewish community. Nothing in IV–VII, therefore, should be allowed to overshadow the legalism of the original author which is given voice to by Uriel in I–III.[2]

In his review of Jewish apocalypticism, J.J. Collins finds *4 Ezra* to represent the spiritual journey of a pious Jew after the cataclysmic events of 70 CE. In the dialogues, the author struggles with various questions concerning the covenant and the problem of human sinfulness. Although none of Uriel's arguments consoles Ezra, Ezra's despair is gradually eroded by repeated assurances from Uriel concerning the eschatological cure to the disease of sin.[3] Ezra learns in IV (10.20ff.) that if 'problems cannot be solved we must look away from them and contemplate what is positive'.[4] Instead of reviving a nationalistic hope (cf. Sanders, Box, Gunkel, Hayman, Thompson), the visions of V and VI confirm Uriel's insistence that eschatological salvation is based on merit apart from divine grace.[5] In VII the Mosaic law is supplemented by the eschatological wisdom which Ezra has received.[6] On the whole, the author maintains a traditional understanding of the covenant, but only by revaluing it along new lines throughout the seven episodes.[7]

It was not until 1989 that M.E. Stone published his 1965 Harvard PhD dissertation, entitled 'Features of the Eschatology of IV Ezra'. Stone sets for himself the project of examining the 'two eschatology' approach to *4 Ezra*. As we have seen, despite differences in approach, many students of *4 Ezra* share the conviction that the author of *4 Ezra* constructed a case which included two 'solutions' to two different 'issues' which disturbed him. Traditional formulations of the 'two-

---

1. 1977: 417. Cf. Räisänen: 'the concluding chapters of IV Ezra itself are designed to mitigate the rigorism displayed in the bulk of the book' (1983: 123). Syreeni, Räisänen's pupil, argues the same (1987: 223 n. 16).

2. 1977: 417-18. In a later article, Sanders maintains his belief that *4 Ezra* is a composite work, 'against the advice of most of my colleagues' (1983c: 454).

3. 1984a: 162.

4. 1984a: 168.

5. 1984a: 167, 169.

6. 1984a: 168.

7. 1984a: 168.

Eschatology and the Covenant

eschatology' approach (especially prior to 1965) tended to cite inconsistencies in the eschatological portrayals of *4 Ezra* as evidence of two distinct eschatological traditions (the national and the universal) which have been fused together by the author/redactor. Stone argues, however, that it is inappropriate to expect complete logical consistency within the author's descriptions of eschatological events; the apocalyptic mode of thought is 'non-logical in that it employs other organizing principles than logical consistency between the meanings of its statements'.[1] Stone demonstrates that the author's presentation at any given point is not explained by the 'two-eschatology' approach and that various inconsistencies within the text are the result of variations in 'the context, the subject under discussion and the association of themes and ideas'.[2] These three considerations alone ('context, purpose and association') explain any inconsistencies in the author's eschatological portrayals, without the need to revert to some version of the 'two-eschatology' theory. Throughout the book, Stone demonstrates that the author used various eschatological ideas simply to support different points of argument at different places in his presentation.

This review of a handful of scholars highlights the various issues which will need to be addressed in the following chapters. Perhaps a few preliminary observations may be in order here concerning what we have seen from this survey. First, it needs to be noted that interpreters usually include in their estimations a differentiation of some sort in order to arrive at a consistent explanation of the text. For instance, some scholars work with a 'two-issue' approach, differentiating between the issue addressed in I–III and that addressed in IV–VII (Gunkel, Hayman, Thompson, Box). Others find it necessary to differentiate between original and interpolated material within the text (Sanders), or deny that the voice of one character (Ezra) has any significance in recovering the author's position (Harnisch, Sanders). Still another differentiates between the form and content of the book, and tends to sit loose to the content altogether (Breech).

Secondly, it is important to note that all too often investigations of the text have been carried out with an inaccurate perception of the character of Early Judaism, thereby postulating inaccurate characterizations of the book within its historical context (especially Thompson). In my opinion, these two tendencies represent errors in the study of

1. 1989: 23.
2. 1989: 31.

the text. For these reasons, Collins's analysis, which achieves a historically sensitive and consistent reading of the text without postulating the presence of different issues or interpolated sources, is greatly appreciated. Collins in particular reads IV–VII with the dialogues of I–III in view. As the remaining chapters of Part II will demonstrate, the general results of this project will come closest to Collins's, despite the inevitable differences. This analysis, however, will be far more in-depth than that of Collins, who is not able in fourteen pages to defend his interpretation with a detailed investigation of the text, a task which is necessary in view of Collins's somewhat distinctive stance in *4 Ezra* scholarship. It is this task which is accomplished in the remainder of this part of the present study.

Because development is inherent in the sevenfold structure of the book, the best means of interpretation is to follow the progression of the author's case sequentially throughout the course of the book. This approach simulates an environment closer to the one in which the author intended his work to be heard and lessens the degree to which scholastic agendas determine the approach and results. In the following chapters of Part II, each episode will be analysed individually and a concluding chapter will set out some initial reflections concerning *4 Ezra* and *4 Ezra* scholarship. Further reflections are postponed until Part IV, where a comparison of *4 Ezra* and Romans 1–11 is set out in some detail with the interests of this project in view.

Chapter 3

EPISODE I

The first dialogue (I) will be analysed according to the following outline:

1. The occasion of Ezra's reflections (3.1-3)
2. God's judgment upon sinful humanity (3.4-12)
3. God's grace upon Israel (3.13-19)
4. The evil heart remains in Israel (3.20-27)
5. Why is God's grace upon Israel ineffective? (3.28-36)
6. A debate about human understanding (4.1-25)
7. The doctrine of the two ages (4.26-32)
8. The ages are determined (4.33-43)
9. How much time remains? (4.44-52)
10. The signs of the end of the age (5.1-13)
11. Ezra encounters Phaltiel, a chief of Israel (5.14-20)

3.1. *Analysis of Episode I*

3.1.1. *The occasion of Ezra's reflection (3.1-3)*. Ezra begins by identifying himself as 'Salathiel, who am also called Ezra', living in Babylon thirty years after the destruction of Jerusalem. Whereas the author wants his readers to think that he is referring to the first destruction of Jerusalem in 587 BCE, the modern critic considers this to be a pseudepigraphic device which signals the actual date of writing as being thirty years after the second destruction of Jerusalem and the temple in 70 CE, thereby putting the date of composition at 100 CE, or thereabouts.[1]

The identification of the speaker as both Ezra and Salathiel has given impetus to source-critical analyses of *4 Ezra*, the assumption

1. The contents of the eagle vision in VI would suggest a similar date. See Stone, 1989: 1-11; Schürer, 1973: 3.298-300.

being that the author has utilized an original source (an apocalypse
attributed to Salathiel) in which the name of the main character is subsequently changed from Salathiel (which appears only in 3.1) to Ezra,
the scribe of the Jewish scriptures.[1] Others postulate that, rather than
intending his pseudonym to indicate this historical figure of Israel's
past, the author has invented another Ezra to be the protagonist of the
story.[2] But instead of a fictitious hero or a traditional source, it is
better to understand the importance of the name Salathiel according to
its Hebrew meaning. If, as most scholars now accept, *4 Ezra* was
originally composed in Hebrew, the name 'Shealthiel' (שְׁאַלְתִּיאֵל),
which means 'I have asked of God', would capture well the the character of Ezra throughout the dialogues.[3] The occasion of his asking of
God is described in this introduction. While lying on his bed, Ezra
(alias Shealthiel) reflects upon the desolation of Jerusalem and the
prosperity of Israel's captor, Babylon. Because of these disturbing
reflections, he is 'troubled' and 'greatly agitated'. It is this concern for
Israel's well-being which gives him cause to state his complaint (that
is, to ask of God). What follows are his 'anxious words to the Most
High'.

3.1.2. *God's judgment upon sinful humanity (3.4-12).* Ezra prefaces
his complaint (which begins in 3.20) by retelling the ways of God
from creation to the giving of the law to Israel (3.4-19). His retelling
forms two parts (3.4-12, 13-19), the first of which calls to mind God's
creation of Adam, Adam's transgression, the sinfulness of humanity,
the destruction of the inhabitants of the world by the flood and the
rescue of the one righteous man, Noah, and his household. In all this,
Ezra is following the general structure of Genesis 1–11: (1) God acts
and all is good, (2) humanity acts and all turns bad, (3) God destroys
and begins again. Ezra, in this first section, has done nothing other
than voice traditional beliefs concerning God and his relationship with
creation.

3.1.3. *God's grace upon Israel (3.13-19).* Just as the portrayal in Genesis 1–11 of the creator God and his creation gives way to the por-

---

1. Cf. Burkitt, 1914: 41; Brockington, 1961: 28-29.
2. Cf. James, 1917. This suggestion has not been well received, but see Collins's
revamped version of it, 1984a: 157.
3. Cf. Oesterley, 1933: xiv; J. Schreiner, 1981: 311; Lacocque, 1981: 245.

trayal of the covenant God and his covenant people in Genesis 12ff.,
so Ezra follows the same outline. He notes that the nations of the
world were exceedingly sinful (cf. Gen. 11), but God chose from
among them one man, Abraham, whom he loved and with whom he
made 'an everlasting covenant', promising never to forsake his
descendants (3.15). This covenant was demonstrated especially in two
events: the exodus of the people from Egypt by means of God's intervention on their behalf (3.17), and God's giving of the law to the
people on Mt Sinai, the latter being vividly described in 3.18-19. Here
too, Ezra has followed the scriptural account of God's dealings in
history, highlighting two of the most significant events in Jewish history: the exodus and the giving of the law. (His emphasis is upon the
latter since it will become the point around which his argument in
3.20-36 will revolve.) This scenario contrasts with that of the sinful
nations; while sin increased throughout the nations, God chose Abraham and established for the people of Israel deliverance by means of
the covenant which he initiated with them.

3.1.4. The problem: The evil heart remains in Israel (3.20-27). At this
point, the optimism of the Pentateuchal review of the events surrounding Israel's election drops out of sight. Instead, Ezra, preoccupied
with Israel's present situation, moves from confidence in God's election to despair concerning the ineffectiveness of the law and the
covenant. He focuses directly on the problem: 'You did not take away
from them [Israel] the evil heart, so that your law might bring forth
fruit in them' (3.20). Here Ezra cites the complication which arose in
God's plan for Israel: the nation has not escaped the sinful condition of
humanity which provokes God's judgment. Adam's evil heart has
become permanent, even in the hearts of God's people. The law did
not root it out (3.21-22). Returning to his review of Israel's history,
Ezra notes how God took the initiative once again and raised up for
himself a servant, David, who built a city 'for your name'—a city
wherein oblations were offered up to God in the temple (3.23-25). But
rather than solidifying Israel's special relationship with God, even this
epoch of Israel's history serves merely to prove the people's helpless-
ness; despite their possession of the holy city and the sacrifices of the
temple, Israel's Adamic condition did not change (3.26). Consequently, God delivered the city into the hands of his enemies (3.27).

It is important to recognize the technique of Ezra's polemic. He has
already painted the anthropological condition of sin in 3.4-12, and

then juxtaposed that picture with God's initiative in establishing the covenant with Israel as the corrective to that condition (3.13-19). Already, then, the two categories laid out in Chapter 1 have been employed by Ezra (namely the anthropological condition of sin, the covenantal corrective). But Ezra works his case quite differently in 3.20-27, for there the covenantal corrective is said to be no corrective at all because the anthropological condition prevails. Israel's privileged position before God is enveloped by their Adamic condition, illustrated by the fact that in everything they did 'as Adam and all his descendants had done' (3.26). Because the anthropological condition includes no ethnic differentiation, Ezra has abandoned confidence in the salvific effectiveness of the covenant for the nation of Israel.

3.1.5. *Why is God's grace upon Israel ineffective? (3.28-36).* After setting in tension God's election of Israel (3.13-19) and the desperate condition of Israel (3.20-27), Ezra completes his initial speech with a complaint: 'Are the deeds of those who inhabit Babylon any better? Is that why she has gained dominion over Zion?' (3.28; cf. 3.31b). This bitter tone continues throughout the complaint, wherein Ezra defends Israel on two grounds: (1) in comparison with all the other nations, and (2) in view of their responsiveness to God. The first leads him to note that although Babylon's iniquities are immense, yet it prospers. The nation of Israel, on the other hand, whose sin is much less, has been crushed by Babylon, with God's consent. Here, Ezra does all he can to fault God himself, and accentuates this with his second judgment against God; whereas Israel has 'believed your covenants' (3.32)[1] and expected not to be forsaken by him, the other nations who 'are unmindful of your commandments' (3.33) abound in wealth. While God endures the sins of other nations and allows them to prosper, all he sees of Israel ('your people') is their sin. The people of Israel have not received a reward for their confidence in God but have, instead, been punished for their sin (3.33-34), despite the fact that no other nation 'has kept your commandments so well' (3.35).

3.36 has, it seems, proven to be a red herring for the interpretation of *4 Ezra*. There, Ezra concludes this most nationalistic speech with the words, 'You may indeed find individual men[2] who have kept your

---

1. Here, 'to believe' has the sense of 'to have confidence in'. Cf. Thompson, 1977: 248 n. 47.
2. Latin: *homines per nomina*.

commandments, but nations you will not find'. This verse has been used as evidence of Ezra's transition from national to universal concerns.[1] So J.J. Collins writes of 3.36: 'If only "exceptional individuals" can keep the commandments, then membership of a covenant people becomes irrelevant'.[2] This, however, is not Ezra's concern at this point, nor does covenantal membership become insignificant. In fact, Ezra has not shifted his attention from his national interest at all. The main thrust of Ezra's comments in 3.36 lies in the second half of the verse, where he claims that God will not find a nation which has kept his commandments. Although Ezra does admit elsewhere that even Israel has not kept the commandments of God, here his statement that no nation has kept them (the commandments) is not a chastisement of Israel, but a chastisement of the other nations. Ezra is calling on God to examine Israel and compare it with other nations. When God looks around with this in mind, Ezra is convinced that Israel has nothing to fear. He will find no other nation which has kept the law. Ezra's remarks in 3.36, therefore, are meant to favour Israel. Ezra is still fighting for his people. He has not abandoned Israel for the sake of the concerns of humanity. As Box states, 'the point of the passage is that Israel as a people have kept the divine precepts',[3] at least in comparison with the pagan nations.[4] Israel is distinct from all other nations.

Support for this reading is also gained from the first half of the verse. There, it must be determined to whom the phrase 'individual men' is referring. In this regard, J.H. Charlesworth has argued that 'your commandments' in 3.36 should not be viewed as signalling the Mosaic law but, instead, the Adamic or Noachic commandments which, in Jewish thought, were applicable to the whole of the gentile world.[5] As such, 'individual men' refers only to those gentiles who live by the standards God has established for the gentiles themselves, since the mention of 'commandments' here is not a reference to the Mosaic law. This is a significant suggestion. Unfortunately, Charlesworth does not defend his suggestion, so one can only guess as to what led him to this conclusion. Herein, his suggestion will be evaluated on the basis of word usage and contextual indicators.

1. Cf. Thompson, 1977: 71-76, 211-12, 299, 302, 311-12.
2. 1984a: 160.
3. 1912: 20.
4. Cf. de Villiers, 1981: 361.
5. Read Charlesworth, 1979b: 466 with Thompson, 1977: 171.

One can suppose that Charlesworth's suggestion is based upon a vocabularic peculiarity in the Latin of 3.19-22, wherein the Mosaic law given by God to Israel is spoken of as *lex* ('the law', 3.19, 20, 22) and *diligentia* (usually translated as 'the commandment', 3.19). In the Latin text of 3.36, however, the word for commandment is *mandata* (cf. *mandasti* in 3.7 in reference to God's command to Adam), which is used in 3.33 of God's commandments which the nations have broken, and in 3.35 in the comparison of the nations who have not kept God's commandments with Israel who has kept them better. Perhaps Charlesworth thinks that the different terminology signals different concepts—that is, the distinction between *lex/diligentia* and *mandata* indicates an intentional distinction between Mosaic and Noachic laws, a distinction which will need to be evaluated on contextual grounds. Initially, however, it needs to be recognized that a distinction between the Mosaic and Noachic laws cannot be maintained in the Syriac text. Therein, the Mosaic 'law' of 3.19, 20 and 22 (*nmws'*) equals the Mosaic 'commandments' of 3.19 (*pwqdn'*), the same word which is used in 3.33, 35 and 36 to speak of the 'commandments' which the nation of Israel has tried to observe and of which the other nations have been unmindful. In this way, the 'commandments' are to be identified with the Mosaic law of 3.19, 20 and 22.

The question remains, however, whether a distinction between Adamic and Noachic laws can be maintained even in the Latin text. No evidence can be found in support of such a distinction. In the verses which precede 3.36, *mandata* is used twice (3.33, 35), and neither reference necessitates the idea of *Noachic* commandments. This is especially true of 3.35, where Ezra can only be speaking of the Mosaic commandments, since it is this point on which Israel can be compared favourably with the other nations. Ezra states: 'What nation has kept your commandments so well?' What the nation of Israel has kept better than any other nation is not the Noachic but the Mosaic law which was given specifically to it. What Israel holds dear, other nations have despised. This identification of the 'commandments' with the Mosaic law in 3.35 should govern the reading of 3.36 if Ezra's case is to have its force.

Also in this regard, the parallelism of 7.72 is significant. There, Uriel declares: 'though they received the commandments (Lat. *mandata*; Syr. *pwqdn'*) they did not keep them, and though they obtained the Law (Lat. *legem*; Syr. *nmws'*) they dealt unfaithfully with what they received'. Here too, as W. Harnisch writes, 'zwischen "mandata" und "lex" wird bemerkenswerterweise sachlich nicht differenziert!'[1]

In the light of this, when Ezra speaks of those 'individual men' from among the nations who have kept the commandments, he means those gentiles who have obeyed the Mosaic law[2]—that is, he seems to be thinking of gentile proselytes to Judaism.[3] His reference to 'individual men', therefore, does not indicate a change in Ezra's concern from Israel to humanity, whose rule is the Noachic law. Rather, this passage underlines the fact that Ezra is concerned precisely with those whose self-awareness is defined by the Mosaic law. He has Israel's welfare wholly in mind. Except for the few gentiles who have converted to the religion and ways of Israel, the nations *en masse* have disregarded God's commandments, the law that God gave to Israel as a sign of the covenant. The point of Ezra's argument, then, is this: If the gentile nations have wholly disregarded God's law (except for a few gentile proselytes) and if the people of Israel by comparison have kept the law, why is God not honouring the covenant with them? As such, the whole of 3.28-36 is permeated with ethnocentric concerns, with 3.35-36 serving as the conclusion to the nationalism of the whole prayer.[4]

Ezra's opening speech concludes here. In it, he has traced out God's works in relation to his creation, with Israel especially in mind. It is important to be aware of the complexities of Ezra's thoroughly ethnocentric speech. First, it should be recognized that Ezra's characterization of Israel is contingent upon the stage to which his argument has developed. That is, with regard to Israel's status vis-à-vis the gentile

1. 1969: 162. One can compare also 7.11, where Adam is said to have transgressed God's statutes.

2. Of course, Ezra has just argued that the descendants of Adam are unable to keep the law, but his point here is made in the context of a contrast between Israel and the other nations. He asks, What other nation has kept the commandments as well as Israel (3.35)? He answers, Except for a few converts, none (3.36).

3. See Box, 1912: lvii; Watson, 1986: 215 n. 44. Contrast Myers, who understands the 'individuals' to be a few pious within Israel who have kept the law (1974: 180).

4. Thompson's attempt to read 3.35-36 as springing from the author's concern for humanity is strained (1977: 171-76). It stands only (1) when the passage is extracted from the nationalistic context, (2) when terminological distinctions are forced (i.e. 'inhabitants of the world' in 3.34 is contrasted with 'inhabitants of the earth', although the same terms appear together in 7.72-74 where no distinction can apply), and (3) by a conjectural emendation to the text which is nothing but speculation. Unfortunately, Thompson makes so much of his incorrect reading of 3.35-36 throughout his book that many of his conclusions suffer accordingly.

nations, Ezra's estimate varies according to the point he is trying to make. In 3.13-19, Israel is portrayed in traditional covenantal terms as the prize of God's eye, in distinction from the nations. In 3.20-27, however, such nationalistic distinctions are removed, Israel's distinctiveness being flattened out by the anthropological condition of sin. In 3.28-36, however, Ezra once again invokes the idea of Israel's distinctiveness. Although this theme has been crippled by Ezra's remarks in 3.20-27, it is again put to use in order to plead on Israel's behalf. Here Ezra argues that despite the universality of the evil heart, the other nations are much worse than the nation of Israel, which has believed and better kept God's commandments.

Alongside these various portrayals of Israel, one finds an even more complex depiction of Israel's God. Initially, God is portrayed as the one who animates life and seeks relationship with his creation, Adam: 'you made him alive in your presence'. With the introduction of sin, however, God became the God who judges and destroys the unrighteous. And yet, Ezra continues, God has acted to remedy Israel's situation. Whenever history has been marked out by rebellion (i.e. between Adam and Noah, between Noah and Abraham, between Abraham and Moses, and between Moses and David), God has initiated corrective measures (the saving of Noah, the covenant with Abraham, the giving of the law, the building of Zion), most of which have Israel specifically in mind. Thus, Ezra has set up a bad news/good news situation. The bad news is the condition of humanity in general; the good news is the works of God which he has initiated on behalf of Israel.

But the good news is not good for long. Despite all that God has done on Israel's behalf, Israel has not escaped the human condition of the evil heart. There can be no doubt that Ezra holds God responsible for this dilemma, as is evident from his words in 3.20. There Ezra says that the law brought forth no fruit, not because the people paid no heed to it but because God did not remove the evil heart from them.[1] True, Israel may not have kept the law as well as they ought to have kept it (3.25), but they cannot be held wholly responsible for that since their transgression results from an underlying situation which

---

1. Harnisch's argument that Ezra advocates a theory of 'den Verhängnischarakter der Sünde' is not convincing (1969: 44-51). Ezra's position is a natural result of Jewish covenantalism minus the covenantal efficacy. This will be demonstrated in §5.2 below.

God has not remedied: the evil heart.[1] Despite all that God has done
for Israel (giving the law, initiating the covenant, establishing the holy
city), he has not done enough. Although the people of Israel have been
favoured by God, their privileges amount to nothing. In this way,
Ezra makes God responsible for Israel's condition.[2]

That Ezra indicts God is all the more clear from his complaint in
3.28-36. There, the God of Israel is not the righteous judge who
destroys sinners and rewards the righteous, as Ezra described him
earlier in 3.4-12 (in his review of Gen. 1–11). Instead, just the opposite is true; God has allowed sinners to prosper, while those who have
'known' him and trusted his word have been destroyed. It would seem
that Ezra intentionally juxtaposes these two characterizations of God
in 3.4-12 and 3.28-36 to highlight their incongruity. In Ezra's opinion, Israel's situation is due to a fundamental inconsistency in *God's*
dealings. Thus, just as in 3.20, Ezra holds God responsible. But Ezra's
rationale is somewhat different here than in 3.20. At this point God is
faulted not for what he *has not* done (that is, his failure to remove the
evil heart, as in 3.20), but for what he *has* done (that is, his allowance
of the evil nations to prevail). Or, to put the emphasis differently, God
is faulted not because of what he has not done *for* his people but
because of what he has done *to* them. His dealings are incomprehensi-
ble. Their present state is incompatible with their favoured (they have
known God) and superior (they have kept his commandments better)
position. Ezra's dilemma is expressed in 3.31a, where he accuses God
of not allowing anyone to understand his 'way'.

Although Ezra blames God for the atrocity of Israel's condition, it
is of utmost importance to recognize what Ezra is *not* blaming him
for, since the intention of these opening paragraphs has occasionally
been misunderstood. Although God did not remove the evil heart
from his people, Ezra nowhere holds God responsible for the presence
of evil itself in the world. In 3.4-7, Ezra relates how God brought life
out of dust. Accompanying the giving of life was the giving of one
commandment which was to be obeyed. With the transgression of the
commandment, death replaced life. Who is to be blamed for this? Ezra

---

1. Nothing in *4 Ezra*, however, approaches the extreme of Sedrach's accusation
against God that 'It was *by your will* that Adam was deceived' (*Apoc. Sedr.* 5.1).
2. So Thompson: 'Ezra virtually accuses God of complicity in the crime' (1977:
271). Cf. Harnisch, 1969: 20-23; Brandenburger, 1981: 166; Stone, 1981: 201;
Willett, 1989: 66. Kirschner's analysis does not do justice to this aspect of Ezra's
case (1985: 35-39).

states it clearly: 'he [Adam] trangressed it [the commandment]' (3.7). The appointing of death by God is not unjust but, in fact, proves God's justice in the face of Adam's sin.[1]

The justice of God is again demonstrated in that Noah, the righteous one, escaped God's destruction of sinners. This portrayal of God in 3.4-12 is important for Ezra since God's temperament towards sinners as related in Genesis 1–11 is wholly at odds with Ezra's estimation of the present situation in which gentile sinners prosper and the 'righteous' nation, Israel, is punished. It is essential to Ezra's case, therefore, to keep God free from blame in 3.4-12. As in Genesis 1–11, the presence of evil in the world is not due to God. He cannot be held accountable for it, or for the destruction of the sinners whose hearts are evil. Evil entered the created realm with Adam's trangression and is not inherent in God's own structuring of creation.[2] Thus, it will not do to interpret Ezra's comments in 3.4 ('you formed the earth—and that without help' [*et hoc solus*]) as problematic for the justice of God, as Gunkel and Schreiner have suggested.[3] Whatever Ezra intends by this, he does not think it to infer God's responsibility for the existence of evil.

It must be clear, therefore, what God is and is not accountable for, in Ezra's speech. The presence of evil in the created order is a responsibility shouldered by Adam, through whom the evil heart was introduced into God's creation. The condition of God's people, on the other hand, is a responsibility attributed to God since (1) despite all he has done for them, he did not remove the evil heart in them (3.20-27), and (2) his justice has soured—that is, he has allowed the unrighteous to prosper and those who have trusted him to be humiliated (3.28-36).

Many other reviews of Jewish history are evident in Jewish literature. These operate usually in one of two ways:[4] (1) in praise of God who has done good things on Israel's behalf (cf. Pss. 105; 135), or (2)

---

1. So de Villiers: 'A stark contrast is depicted between the positive life-giving deeds of God and the disregarding, death deserving act of Adam' (1981: 358). This is made especially clear in the Armenian version of 3.7-8; cf. Stone, 1979: 45.

2. Contra Harnisch, who argues that, in true gnostic fashion, Ezra blames the dust of the earth for the presence of evil (1969: 52). Correctly, Stone, 1989: 183; Levison, 1988: 114-17; Charlesworth, 1979a: 79. There is no evidence in *4 Ezra* that 'Satan planted an "evil seed"', or that 'the ultimate cause of the evil in history could be traced to the satanic will', as Murdoch supposes (1967: 172-73).

3. Gunkel, 1900: 352-53; J. Schreiner, 1981: 312.

4. Cf. Brandenburger, 1981: 170.

in reproach of the Jewish people for their unfaithfulness (cf. Ps. 78; Ezek. 20). 'By contrast', as M. Knibb notes, 'Ezra retells this same history as the basis of his accusation that God has treated his people unfairly.'[1] Ezra's point, then, is that if unfaithfulness is anyone's responsibility, it is God's. In this way, he has neither praise for God nor reproach for his people.

Despite the complexities of Ezra's opening speech, one aspect gives it coherence: his nationalistic concern. He is not interested in harmonizing God's righteousness with the existence of evil. Nor is he attempting to break out of Jewish particularism. Nor is he grappling with a humanitarian concern for the gentile nations. He has set his agenda, and it is restricted to the relationship between the people of Israel and their covenant-initiating God. This is what motivates his speech from beginning to end, just as the setting of 3.1-3 illustrates.

3.1.6. *A debate about human understanding (4.1-25).* Ezra does not get an answer in reply to his enquiry. Instead, the angel Uriel ('God is my light'), who is sent to him, questions Ezra's right even to enquire into the ways of God (4.2). The importance of this section (4.1-25) for the whole of *4 Ezra* can hardly be overemphasized. It is here—immediately after Ezra's lengthy posing of his complaint and before Uriel's response really begins—that the stage is set for what will transpire thoughout dialogues I–III. A fundamental difference between Ezra and Uriel is cited, a difference which promotes their lengthy disputes throughout I–III. Uriel insists that Ezra should be mindful of his place (4.13-21), for the ways of God are beyond the powers of human understanding (4.2, 3-11). But Ezra insists that he has the right to question (4.22), since the ways in which God is acting in the present are inexplicable in relation to the ways in which he acted previously. To enquire into such matters is not to forget one's place, Ezra maintains. God has loved the people of Israel, but now they have been given to godless nations. The law, through which God established a covenant with Israel, has been to no advantage for them, for they have evidently been deemed unworthy of God's mercy. What will God do about this?[2] How will he redeem his name by which Israel is called?

---

1. 1979: 114. He notes that Ps. 89 is the closest parallel to this. See also Knibb, 1982: 68.

2. Cf. Harnisch: 'Leitend ist die Frage nach der Gültigkeit der im Gesetz garantierten Heilszusage Gottes' (1969: 40).

These matters, Ezra holds, *are* susceptible to human investigation (4.23-25).

These two positions are wholly at loggerheads, and they motivate the discussions that will develop in I–III. This section captures, in miniature, the dynamics of the following dialogues, and isolates the fundamental problem which will plague the entire debate: the characters of the debate maintain two incompatible understandings of the ways of God.[1] They have such fundamentally different perspectives on this issue that even the validity of Ezra's complaint is in doubt. What is an obvious and reasonable request for explanation to Ezra is completely out of place to Uriel, since it is based on a misunderstanding of God's ways. As J.J. Collins puts it, Uriel's point 'is that Ezra cannot hope to make sense of the world by ordinary human wisdom, *even on the premise of the Deuteronomic covenant*'.[2] Much more of this will be seen before the dialogues conclude.

Moreover, it is important to note Ezra's words in 4.12, which reveal his attitude that suffering is bearable only when one correctly *understands* one's situation. This conviction underlies the whole of his words in I–III, and it helps to explain the peculiar events later in IV.

3.1.7. *The doctrine of the two ages (4.26-32)*. If Uriel ever gives Ezra an answer in explanation of the ways of God it is imbedded in the two-age scheme which he propagates for the first time (*in nuce*) at this point. Uriel simply bids Ezra wait and see what God will do (4.26-27). The evil of this age must be allowed to run its course before the good things of the next world will come (4.28-32). This age is not all there is. It is passing away, so that marvellous things will happen and evil will be rooted out. As T.W. Willett says: 'Implicit with this appeal to the eschaton, though not explicitly stated, is the idea that Ezra's complaints about the present inequities will be redressed in the eschaton'.[3]

3.1.8. *The ages are determined (4.33-43)*. From this point on, the dialogue proceeds not out of Ezra's nationalistic concerns but on the basis of Uriel's two-age doctrine. And so, Ezra asks, 'How long and when will these things be?' (4.33). Uriel's answer is quite simple: The new

1. Koch, 1978: 59.
2. 1984a: 160, emphasis mine.
3. 1989: 67.

age cannot be rushed (4.34-37), nor can it be delayed (4.38-43). It will come when the full number of the righteous has been registered (4.36).

3.1.9. *How much time remains? (4.44-52).* Here again, the dialogue remains rooted in Uriel's doctrine of the two ages. Ezra's concerns have been disqualified by the recognition that the two ages, which remain fixed, are determinative for the manner in which God works now and will work in the future. Accordingly, appeals to God's mercy are worthless, since it is not mercy which defines his actions but, rather, an established time scale into which all things are fitted. Ezra's question, therefore, is a simple one: How much time remains? (4.44-46). It will be soon, Uriel assures him (4.47-50), but more than that he cannot say, and he does not know whether Ezra will be alive at the inauguration of the new age (4.51-52).

3.1.10. *The signs of the end of the age (5.1-13).* Here, Uriel predicts a series of events which, when they occur, will indicate that the end of this age is near.[1] It will be a wholly atrocious time:

> The way of truth shall be hidden, and the land shall be barren of faith [or better, 'faithfulness'[2]]. And unrighteousness shall be increased. . . And one country shall ask its neighbor, 'Has righteousness, or anyone who does right, passed through you?' And it will answer, 'No' (5.1-2, 11).

While most of the signs have to do with natural catastrophes, there is also a political note of prediction concerning the overthrow of the Roman empire (5.3-4)—perhaps a belated reply to Ezra's political concern for Israel. After relating all the signs which he was permitted to reveal, Uriel commands Ezra to weep, pray and fast for seven days so that more may be revealed to him. Here the dialogue proper comes to an end.

3.1.11. *Ezra encounters Phaltiel, a chief of Israel (5.14-20).* Before the second dialogue begins, the author describes a meeting of Ezra with a leader of Israel, Phaltiel ('God is my deliverer'). Recognizing that Ezra's face is sad, Phaltiel reminds him that Israel has been

---

1. Harnisch thinks that the author has borrowed an older apocalyptic source (1969: 151). Cf. J. Schreiner, 1981: 132.
2. Cf. Schreiner: 'Der Sinn unserer Stelle dürfte sein: Das Land (die Erde) wird keine *Treue* kennen' (1981: 324, emphasis added).

entrusted to his (Ezra's) keeping (5.17). He urges Ezra to rise up and eat bread in order to have strength to defend Israel's cause. Without strength for the task, Ezra is like 'a shepherd who leaves his flock in the power of savage wolves' (5.18). This is a curious account for several reasons. First, it reinforces the fact that Israel is in Ezra's charge and his assignment is to defend the interests of his people. His occupation is to be the ambassador of Israel before God.[1] Second, it creates an obvious tension between Uriel's command to fast in order to learn more and Phaltiel's command to eat in order to defend Israel properly. It would perhaps be premature to draw conclusions of any sort about the author's purpose in constructing this tension. It is worth noting, however, that Ezra directs Phaltiel to leave him alone and proceeds to obey Uriel's request to fast. Ezra points out that he did 'as Uriel the angel had commanded me' (5.20).

3.2. *Summary of Episode I*

Throughout Episode I, Ezra's complaints have run along three lines: (1) Israel's failure to keep the law is due to the evil heart which resides in every descendant of Adam, a condition which God has not remedied, no matter what else he may have done for Israel (3.20-27); (2) Israel may not have kept the commandments as well as they should have done, but they are a far better nation than any other and should be protected by God (3.28-36); and (3) God has made a covenant with Israel and Israel has trusted him. Has he now gone back on his word and withheld his mercy to Israel (4.23-25), which he has shown them in the past (3.13-19)?

Each of these three issues is concerned wholly with the interests of Israel. The first digs deeper to examine the human condition, but Ezra's concern is not to speculate about the desperate state of humanity. Scholars continue to insist that Ezra's questions 'revolve round the impossibility for a man to obtain eschatological salvation on this earth',[2] or that Ezra 'raises numerous penetrating questions centered on humanity's plight. The individual is uppermost in his mind.'[3] But Ezra is not interested in philosophical anthropology. He is the repre-

1. Cf. Koch, 1978: 58.
2. Lebram, 1983: 200. Likewise, he depicts Ezra as 'grieving about the hopelessness of existence in the present age' (p. 201). Cf. Collins, 1984a: 160; Thompson, 1977: 187; Charlesworth, 1979b: 466.
3. Charlesworth, 1985b: 295. Cf. Brandenburger, 1962: 27.

sentative of *Israel's* case, and his bleak survey of the human condition serves this role since it removes Israel from blame and places the responsibility of the nation's condition on God himself. Despite their repeated offences, God has done great things for Israel. In the end, however, he has not done anything for his people if he has not rectified the condition of their heart. Thus, Ezra is not jostling universalistic and particularistic issues at random. Instead, the universalistic issues serve his particularistic interest.

In view of this, there seems little reason to agree with Thompson's claim that here Ezra's position tends towards individualism.[1] Such a label has no validity when tagged on Ezra's wholly nationalistic concerns. Better, perhaps, is A. Jaubert's conclusion that the opening paragraphs of *4 Ezra* comprise 'le plus beau poème sur l'élection d'Israël'.[2] Certainly, the national interest displayed in Ezra's words springs from his awareness of the unique covenant relationship which God established with Israel, his people.

Uriel's response to Ezra is commonly written off as, in Stone's words, 'trite', 'pat', and 'evasive'.[3] In the same vein, Charlesworth judges that Ezra's 'questions are without doubt superior here in the first vision to the vapid answers'.[4] This is sometimes construed to mean that the author cannot possibly be using Uriel as his spokesman since Uriel's answers fail to get to the heart of the issues raised by Ezra. Any estimation of this issue, however, must be judged according to the dynamics of 4.1-25. The whole point of this passage is to illustrate that, in Uriel's opinion, the manner of Ezra's probing into the ways of God is completely misguided; one's vantage point must be proper before proper understanding can be gained. Uriel is not so much evasive as he is convinced that Ezra's complaint is fundamentally ill-founded and that Ezra's understanding is in need of radical revision concerning the ways of God. Accordingly, rather than responding to Ezra's complaint, Uriel merely introduces his own vantage point. Uriel refuses to interact with Ezra's point of view and simply imposes his own understanding upon the discussion which Ezra is expected to accept.

1. 1977: 212, although he admits earlier that 'no categorization is tidy' (p. 211).
2. 1963: 287.
3. See e.g. Stone, 1981: 199; *idem*, 1984: 413 n. 166.
4. 1985b: 295.

What Uriel puts forward is a scheme of the relation of the two ages. As soon as it is introduced, this scheme sets the agenda for the dialogue. Since the ages are determined and determinative for the way in which God acts, Ezra's conviction that God's covenant mercy should be effective before the dawning of the eschatological age is completely out of place. In other words, Ezra is asked to judge the present not in terms derived from his understanding of past history but in terms of the timetable of future events; the 'particular events of the ongoing historical process are no longer the arena in which the struggle for understanding is conducted'.[1] In this regard, what W. Schmithals says concerning apocalyptic literature in general is especially true of Uriel's position:

> History is made thoroughly secular, profane. *What* happened in history has no significance theologically. There is no salvation in this eon; how then is God supposed to perform saving acts in it?[2]

With the conclusion of the dialogue, however, Phaltiel's appearance serves as a reminder that the people of Israel are taking their cues not from future revealed events but from their covenantal history and from God's promise never to forsake them.[3] Although Uriel's two-age scheme vindicates God's righteousness by introducing a temporal distinction between the ages, this would explain very little to the people of Israel whose perspective is shaped by a historical understanding of God's covenant mercy upon them within history.

In many ways, then, the debate about human understanding stands at the heart of the whole of Episode I. In 4.1-25, two perspectives on the ways of God collide: Ezra's ethnocentric covenantalism and Uriel's two-age doctrine. What preceded 4.1-25 is Ezra's case, and what follows is Uriel's case. Like water and oil in the same flask, two positions appear in this episode but never mix. Although Uriel gets the last word, the author reminds the reader (through the appearance of Phaltiel) that the people's concerns persist. And so, the drama is sure to continue in II.

---

1. Stone, 1981: 198. Cf. Collins, 1974: 20.
2. 1975a: 81.
3. Ponthot speaks of a Jewish 'believing mentality' 'which experiences and understands the historical condition as the place of encounter with the divine action' (1985: 161).

Chapter 4

Episode II

This short dialogue, as M.A. Knibb notes, has 'a similar structure to the first and goes over a good deal of the same ground'.[1] The outline of the second dialogue (II) illustrates that well:

1. The occasion of Ezra's reflections (5.21-22)
2. Israel's condition is in contradiction to God's grace (5.23-30)
3. The inadequacy of human understanding (5.31-40)
4. Why could God not have acted differently? (5.41-55)
5. Through whom will the end come? (5.56–6.6)
6. How much time will divide the ages? (6.7-10)
7. The signs of the end of the age (6.11-28)
8. Final exhortations (6.29-34)

4.1. *Analysis of Episode II*

4.1.1. *The occasion of Ezra's reflection (5.21-22).* After several days of fasting, Ezra says: 'the thoughts of my heart were very grievous to me again. Then my soul recovered the spirit of understanding' (5.21-22). Subsequently, he puts forward his opening speech, which is again an appeal to God on behalf of Israel (5.23-30).

Already, one point needs to be observed: Ezra is back to where he started in I. Again his heart is troubled by the thoughts which grieved him, as in 3.1-3. As Ezra's appeal in 5.23-30 will reveal, Uriel's words of seven days earlier have receded in Ezra's mind and are no longer pressing. The eschatological orientation of the latter half of I has been replaced by a concern for Israel in the present, a concern which Ezra initially exhibited in his first speech of I (3.4-36). It is almost as if the week-old dialogue had never taken place. Certainly,

---

1. 1979: 135. Lebram finds the extensive overlap of material in I and II 'somewhat monotonous' (1983: 201).

Uriel's two-age scheme did not have much staying power, despite its initial powerful effect.[1]

The same point is evident from Ezra's statements that his soul 'recovered the spirit of understanding'. W. Bousset understands this as a description of divine inspiration, in parallel with *2 Bar.* 10.1 ('the word of God came to me') and *Jub.* 12.17 ('and a word came into his heart, saying. . .'). He compares it with the description in *4 Ezra* 14.37-44 wherein Ezra opens his mouth to drink a potion of understanding from God in order that he might write the words of God.[2] But rather than describing a 'pneumatische Erfahrung', as Bousset thinks, this passage plays a subtler role in the development of the dialogues. Knibb's free translation captures the sense of Ezra's words well: 'I recovered the power of thought'.[3] The point is simply that Ezra has regained his composure and is able and willing to put his inquiry before God once again. Whereas his soul was troubled and fainted after being shown the signs of the end of the age (5.14), here it has recovered, allowing Ezra to resume the enquiry which he began in I. This is a curious phenomenon in view of Uriel's insistence in I that human understanding trespasses its bounds when it undertakes to discern the ways of God. Ezra is confident once again of his 'power of thought'. The Ezra of 3.1-36 has reappeared here in the opening of II. Accordingly, his complaint of 5.23-30 follows similar lines.

4.1.2. *Israel's condition is in contradiction to God's grace (5.23-30).* This speech is relatively simple. In it, Ezra employs a variety of scriptural symbols to highlight the fact that God has chosen the people of Israel from the multitude of nations and has bestowed his favour upon them alone (5.23-27)—a typical expression of Jewish ethnocentrism.[4] God's way has been to choose one thing over many—from the trees, one vine; from the lands, one region; from the birds, one dove; from the flocks, one sheep; and from the multitude, one people. Moreover, Ezra says, 'to this people, whom you have loved, you have

---

1. Cf. Willett: 'Ezra again takes up his complaint showing that the talk of the eschaton has not completely satisfied his curiosity' (1989: 67).

2. Bousset, 1926: 396.

3. 1979: 135.

4. Mundle observes that we hear from the author 'den ganzen Stolz, das ganze hohe Selbstbewusstsein des Juden wiederklingen, wenn er auf die Erwählung Israels zu sprechen kommt' (1929: 233; cf. 233-34).

given the Law which is approved by all' (5.27)[1]. As in 3.19-22, so here Ezra points to the giving of the law as the means whereby God intended to bring about Israel's salvation. It is the symbol of his electing grace upon them. But for precisely this reason, the present state of Israel is inexplicable:

> O Lord, why have you given over the one to the many?. . . And those who opposed your promises have trodden down those who believed [i.e. trusted in[2]] your covenants (5.28-29).

Here, Israel is favourably compared to the other nations on the basis of its confidence in God's covenant grace, an argument which has already been advanced in 3.28-36. This comparison serves to point out the apparent inconsistency of God's ways: He chose the people of Israel who have trusted him, but now he allows 'the many' to dominate them. Ezra does not extol God for his great blessings of the past but petitions him to conduct himself as he ought in view of his previous conduct. Ezra closes his complaint by bidding that, if God's people deserve punishment, they should be punished at God's own hand (5.30). In this way, Ezra illustrates that he is not questioning God simply because the people are suffering; suffering can be contained within a covenantal perspective. Instead, Ezra's questions arise because the manner in which God's people have been treated is so extreme as to fall beyond such an explanation, calling into question the covenantal basis of Jewish self-definition itself.

Throughout his opening speech in II, therefore, Ezra illustrates his wholly nationalistic concern by concentrating completely on the discrepancy between the people's chosen status and their present condition. In many ways, this is simply a truncated version of his opening speech of I, being less sophisticated and complicated perhaps, but producing the same effect.

---

1. Whereas the Latin speaks of the law as being 'approved by all [i.e. all peoples]' (*ab omnibus probatam*), the Ethiopic says of it, 'which you approved out of all [i.e. all laws]'. The Syriac is somewhat ambiguous (*nmws' hw d'tbhr mn kl*), the preposition *mn* expressing either the idea of agent ('the law which is tested to be sure *by* all *peoples*') or of partition ('the law which is tested to be sure *out of* all *laws*'). It is also possible, we think, that the Syriac refers to the law as that 'which is tested to be sure *in* every *thing/way*' (*kl mdm*).

2. Cf. J. Schreiner, 1981: 327; Knibb, 1979: 136.

4.1.3. *The inadequacy of human understanding (5.31-40)*. Uriel returns to Ezra to instruct him through dialogue. He asks: 'Are you greatly disturbed in mind over Israel? Or do you love him more than your Maker does?' (5.33). Ezra answers negatively. Obviously, however, he *is* greatly disturbed over Israel and has readily spoken so much before, so his denial must apply to Uriel's second query.[1] Both Uriel and Ezra accept that God loves Israel (although, as we will see, this is open to definition). Rather than being 'a source of supreme consolation', as G.H. Box thinks,[2] this fact promotes Ezra's turmoil as he strives 'to understand the way of the Most High' (5.34). Uriel replies that Ezra cannot comprehend God's ways (5.35). After Ezra's complaints ('Why then was I born?'), Uriel reinforces his point concerning the failure of human reason by relating a series of puzzles which, if Ezra can answer them, will prove him worthy of an answer. But Ezra admits his inadequacy ('I am without wisdom', 5.39). In 5.40 Uriel, speaking for God,[3] says: 'You cannot discover my judgment, or the goal of love that I have promised my people' (5.40). The word 'goal' (*finem*) contains the idea of a purpose yet to be manifest. Its temporal sense couples well with the sense of the verb 'I have promised' (*promisi*). The Ethiopic text augments the author's meaning when it reads, 'the goal of love which I await (or delay) for my people'.[4] In this way, the temporal sense of 5.40 is reminiscent of that of 4.26. There, after Ezra had complained about Israel's fate and asked what God intended to do to remedy the situation, Uriel's reply was 'live long and you will see'. In both passages, whereas Ezra's complaint concerns the ways of God, Uriel replies that the events of the future contain the solution to the matter. Once again, then, Uriel subordinates the understanding of God's ways to a temporal condition in which the future events hold the key for understanding.

---

1. But this is a peculiar denial, because Ezra has just called God's love for Israel into question. That was the point of his opening speech in 5.23-30: God has shown his love for Israel in the past, but now he acts in ways that contradict that. In 5.30, in fact, Ezra entertains the idea that God now hates Israel.

2. 1912: 56.

3. Or is it God speaking? J. Schreiner writes: 'Die Rede des Engels geht in die Gottesrede über' (1981: 329). Cf. Box, who calls it an inconsistency (1912: 58). This sort of 'inconsistency' appears often in *4 Ezra* where it is almost impossible to determine whether Uriel or God is speaking. For this phenomenon discussed, see Thompson, 1977: 141-42, 330-31; Knibb, 1979: 140.

4. See Box's discussion, 1912: 58.

Uriel's words in 5.40 not only reiterate the point of the inaccessibility of God's ways to human inquiry but also give some assurance of God's love for Israel, although it has yet to be manifested. Accordingly, Myers's comments on 5.40 must be ruled out. He says, 'The whole passage [5.31-40] ends on a pessimistic note'.[1] Although God's ways are beyond human comprehension, it is not this point that the author wants his readers to hear so much as the fact that the God whose ways are obscure will be shown to be just in the end of this age. Uriel lifts the 'incomprehensibility' theme out of the depths of pessimism and gives it a more positive character by insisting that, although God transcends the bounds of reason, he is nonetheless a righteous God, and can be recognized as such when judged from the proper (eschatological) frame of reference. For the most part, then, this section revives the dialogue already heard in 4.1-25 concerning the limits of human understanding, while punctuating it with Uriel's confidence in God whose justice will be revealed in the end.

4.1.4. *Why could God not have acted differently? (5.41-55)*. Ezra makes no complaint about the limits of human reason, but asks why God's ways could not have been different. First, following up on Uriel's future-oriented assurances of 5.40, Ezra points out that God's promised love may benefit those who are alive at the end, but what benefit is it to those who are alive before that time (5.41)? Uriel replies that God's eschatological judgment will affect all the generations evenly (5.42). Secondly, Ezra suggests that God could have done things differently (that is, better). He could have created everyone at once so that the judgment might come sooner (5.43). In what follows (5.44-49), Uriel states that God's plan must be allowed to run its course and, anyway, the earth could not support all the generations at once. Third, Ezra then asks how old the earth is in order to discover how much time is left (5.50). Uriel only says that the generations get weaker as the age of the earth increases (5.51-55).

Judging by the nature of these three queries, Ezra seems to have been influenced by Uriel's eschatological orientation (or at least he neglects to challenge it), as his questions are all concerned not with Israel's present situation in the light of their covenant status but with the coming judgment. The same is true of his next three questions, which carry the reader to the end of the dialogue: (1) Through whom

1. 1974: 200.

will the end come? (2) How much time will divide the ages? (3) What are the signs of the end?

4.1.5. *Through whom will the end come? (5.56–6.6).* To this question, Uriel replies by assuring Ezra that the one who alone set it all in motion will be the one who alone brings it to an end (6.1-6). After cataloguing the events of creation, Uriel says: 'I planned these things, and they were made through me and not through another, just as the end shall come through me and not through another' (6.6). While God is portrayed primarily by Uriel as the creator of the world, there are two significant features which maintain something of a particularistic note to it all. First, the creator is also portrayed as the one who established Zion as his footstool (6.4). Second, he is the one who sealed all those who have stored up treasures of faith, or better, faithfulness (6.5). Box clarifies this last verse: '"Faith" in this passage seems to mean the righteousness which comes from fidelity to the law'[1] (just as in 5.1; 6.5, 28; 7.34; 9.7; 13.23, and just as its opposite [*incredulitas*] appears in 7.114 to signify disloyalty to the law). Thus, whereas Ezra calls into question the righteousness of God in view of his pr⸱sent disregard for his people, this passage acts in vindication of God. The one who will bring this age to a close has both Jerusalem and the faithful (upon whom he has put his seal) in mind. Just as in 4.26-27 and 5.40, so here the rightness of God's ways will be proven on the other side of the eschatological boundary dividing the ages.

4.1.6. *How much time will divide the ages? (6.7-10).* To this question, Uriel answers with an allusion to the birth of Esau and Jacob—the hand of one clutching the heel of the other. So shall the ages give way. While the imagery of this allusion serves primarily to show that there will be no interval between the ages,[2] it is possible that an underlying symbolism also plays a part in this passage. In rabbinic literature, for

---

1. 1912: 67. Cf. Knibb, 1979: 182; Myers, 1974: 196-98; J. Schreiner, 1981: 333. Box points out that some good Latin codices make the 'sealing' refer to the *merits* of those who stored up *fidem* for a treasure, which would strengthen this understanding of *fidem* as 'faithfulness to the law'.

2. This periodization does not fit well with others given by Uriel (7.26-44); see Knibb, 1979: 147. As Stone has pointed out, using 6.7-10 as evidence, the author's presentation of the end times should not be forced into harmony but is flexible according to the purpose it serves in particular contexts (1983). Cf. Ferch, 1977: 146.

instance, Rome is commonly symbolized by Esau and Israel by Jacob.[1] If the same comparison is intended here, the import of Uriel's words would be to assure Ezra not only that the second age will immediately succeed the first, but also that while the unrighteous rule in this age, the next age is set apart for Israel.[2] One cannot be sure of this symbolism, however, and it would not seem to be Uriel's main point. Nonetheless, it would be wholly consistent with Uriel's words elsewhere wherein the righteous are promised the hope of future blessings in the new age (cf. 4.26; 5.40; 6.1-6; 25-28).

4.1.7. The signs of the end (6.11-28). Uriel describes the horrendous conditions of the end times throughout 6.11-24. This section is a continuation of the signs of the end given at the conclusion of I (4.51– 5.13; see 6.11-12).[3] But, whereas the 'theoretical' optimism of Uriel's words in I was somewhat muted by the wholly pessimistic description of the end at the conclusion of that dialogue, the present telling of the signs in 6.11-24 leads right into a description of the glorious new age: 'whoever remains after all that I have foretold to you shall be saved and shall see my salvation and the end of my world' (6.25). In that time, the earth's inhabitants will be converted to a different spirit (a new heart),[4] evil will be blotted out, and faithfulness to the law will flourish. What Uriel portrays here is the reversal of the Adamic condition portrayed by Ezra in I. It is the elimination of the evil heart which Ezra, in 3.20-27, sought for Israel in the *present* age; since God has not rooted out the evil heart in Israel, Ezra considered him not to have done enough for his people. Here, however, Uriel gives the assurance that salvation will come to the righteous, but he includes a temporal qualification that rules out Ezra's plea for God's intervention in the present age.

---

1. See Schechter, 1909: 99-100, 108. The Israel–Jacob connection was evident already in *4 Ezra* 3.16, 19.
2. See Thompson, 1977: 182-83; Knibb, 1979: 147; Gunkel, 1900: 365; Myers, 1974: 201-202; Bousset, 1926: 218; Buchanan, 1970: 29-30; Klausner, 1956: 352. Oesterley thinks the passage to speak only of the immediate succession of the ages, the Israel–Rome symbolism playing no part in the author's mind (1933: 52). Cf. Schürer, 1973: 3.298.
3. Harnisch considers 5.1-13 and 6.18-28 to be traditional material, both appearing in *4 Ezra* completely unaltered (1969: 151 n. 2). Box thinks these sections to be traditional but fragmentary (1912: 72).
4. Note the Ethiopic at this point: 'another heart shall be given to them'.

4.1.8. *Final exhortations (6.29-34)*. The dialogue concludes, as did I, as Uriel commands Ezra to pray and fast another seven days in order that he might be shown even greater things (6.30-31). Moreover, Uriel points out that it is Ezra's uprightness and purity which have allowed him to be shown these things (6.32-33). Uriel then exhorts Ezra in the following manner: 'Do not be overanxious to speculate uselessly about former times, that you may not be taken by surprise' (6.34)[1]. By this, Uriel is again encouraging Ezra to put behind him his covenantal outlook (his useless speculation concerning the former times) which fuels his complaints concerning God's ways. In Uriel's estimation, an eschatological orientation must be maintained lest Ezra jump to hasty conclusions concerning what God must do to vindicate himself. Uriel has good reason to be concerned about this, for the last time he left for a seven day period he returned to find that Ezra had reverted from an eschatological to an historical perspective concerning the ways of God. Accordingly, with his last word in II, Uriel insists that Ezra should not regress once again from the understanding he has gained through divine revelation to the idle thoughts which provoked his complaint in the first place.

4.2. *Summary of Episode II*

It is of primary importance to recognize that the thread which unites the whole of II is Ezra's concern for Israel. Initially he pleads the people's case in the light of their despair and, in return, is assured of God's love for his people. However, with this assurance comes a temporal modification: God's love for Israel will be revealed only in the age to come. Accordingly, Ezra's interests turn to the end of the age. His sights turn from Israel's covenantal history (5.21-30) to the future changing of the ages (5.41–6.28), and in this way he appears to have resigned himself to Uriel's two-age doctrine (introduced in vague terms in 5.40, but the basis of the dialogue from then on). Although his perspective has changed, his motivation has not; his eschatological interests are due only to his national interests, and the apocalyptic character of II arises only in connection with Israel's cause. Ezra's turn from Israel's condition to a broader perspective and interest in the end times should not be viewed as a diversion from Israel's interests but as an advancement of his case for Israel.

---

1. The translation is Collins's, 1984a: 162.

It does not take much to notice the structural similarity of I and II. In view of this similarity, a claim made by A.L. Thompson needs evaluation. He observes that, in II, 'essentially the same ground is covered as in I, but with the universalistic implications for the most part deleted'.[1] In his interpretation of I, Thompson thinks Ezra's interests to be largely universalistic.[2] He considers Ezra's review of universal sinfulness to illustrate his concern for the salvation not only of God's own people but of the whole of creation. This universalistic concern was not evident in our reading of I. As was stated above in Chapter 3, Ezra used the issue of the evil heart only to blame God for not doing enough for his own people who shared it with the rest of humanity. Any broader aspect of Ezra's case served only to aid his case for Israel, and was not a matter of interest in its own right. This conclusion is supported by the fact that 'universalism' is not even hinted at anywhere in II (especially in view of the fact that II parallels the structure and content of I significantly). Had universalistic concerns been of major importance to Ezra's inquiry in I, one would have expected them to appear here, where Ezra reiterates his position in I. Their failure to make an appearance in II reinforces the fact that the human condition served only a supporting role in Ezra's case for Israel in I.

Despite the similarities of structure between I and II, the second dialogue does make some advances over I. Uriel is much more assuring in II concerning salvation in the coming age. In I, Uriel said relatively little on this matter (see 4.27, 36), whereas in II there is noticeable interest on his part to establish the fact beyond question that God loves Israel and that those whom he loves will survive this age and enter into the glories of the next age. It is then, Uriel insists, that the Adamic condition will be destroyed and God's righteousness will be vindicated.

A word of caution needs to be registered at this point concerning the identity of Israel. Although Uriel assures Ezra of an eschatological salvation for Israel, the term 'Israel' is itself open to definition, as we will see from Episode III.

---

1. 1977: 181.
2. According to Thompson, in I, concern 'for Israel is overt, but there is a strong undercurrent of concern about all mankind' (1977: 187).

Chapter 5

EPISODE III

The third dialogue (III) deviates somewhat from the general outline of the first two dialogues (although obvious similarities in structure remain). Moreover, the main topic of discussion in III differs greatly from that of I and II, and the position Ezra holds here takes on a new dimension from that which he advocated previously. That is to say, in Episode III Ezra does not keep to his role as the ambassador of Israel in particular, but supplements that duty with a concern for humanity in general. Despite this advancement in Ezra's case in III, however, the point which underlies both his particularistic and universalistic interests is the same as that of I and II: the mercy of God should be effective. Uriel's position throughout III remains unchanged, but it is embellished and more revealing.

III is an extremely long dialogue, but its length itself plays a subtle role in the author's purposes, and the dialogue contributes in important ways to the development of the issues with which he is struggling. As such, it is worthy of close examination, and is outlined as follows:

1. The occasion of Ezra's reflections (6.35-37)
2. God's faithfulness and sovereignty are questioned (6.38-59)
3. Salvation belongs to the world to come (7.1-16)
4. Are the unworthy dealt with fairly? (7.17-25)
5. The messianic reign and the end of this world (7.26-44)
6. Only a few will be saved (7.45-61)
7. Two attitudes towards the human situation (i) (7.62-74)
8. The qualifications of the righteous and the unrighteous (7.75-101)
9. There will be no intercession for the unrighteous (7.102-15)
10. Two attitudes towards the human situation (ii) (7.116-31)
11. A first appeal to God's mercy, and a response (7.132–8.3)
12. A second appeal to God's mercy, and a response (8.4-41)

13. A third appeal to God's mercy, and a response (8.42-62)
14. The signs of the end of the age (8.63–9.13)
15. Ezra and Uriel recapitulate their respective points (9.14-22)
16. Transition to IV (9.23-25)

5.1. *Analysis of Episode III*

5.1.1. *The occasion of Ezra's reflections (6.35-37).* As in II, so here
Ezra—weeping after the previous dialogue—fasts as Uriel commanded him, 'in order to complete the three weeks'. This is somewhat odd, however, for the reader has been told of only one seven-day fast previous to this one (5.20). Apparently, the author considered a seven-day fast to have preceded the first vision, although it is not recorded there. It would appear that the author has styled this on Dan. 10.2-3: 'At that time I, Daniel, mourned for three weeks. I ate no choice food; no meat or wine touched my lips'.

5.1.2. *God's faithfulness and sovereignty are questioned (6.38-59).*
Ezra's initial words of III constitute an extensive recounting of the seven days in which God created the world, as recorded in Genesis 1 (6.38-54). The point of this speech is given in 6.55-59, where Ezra reminds God that he himself said that this world has been created for Israel (6.55, 59). Ezra, calling to mind how Adam is described in Scripture as the one for whom the world was created, contends that the nation of Israel is to inherit Adam's position of lordship, and yet it does not. Instead, the other nations (who are nothing, like spittle, whose abundance is as significant as a drop in a bucket) have dominion over the world, while God's own people (his firstborn, his only begotten, those zealous for him and most dear to him) are being devoured by a foreign people. Ezra concludes, 'Why do we not possess our world as an inheritance? How long will this be so?' Ezra's point is that 'the promise of Scripture as set out in Gen. 1.26 concerning man's dominion, and applied in particular to Israel, has not been fulfilled'.[1]

Once again, Ezra begins the dialogue in defence of Israel's interests. Just as in his initial speeches of I and II, so also here his complaint arises out of the incompatibility which he sees between Israel's favoured status and its present situation, hoping to indict God. The things God 'commanded' (*imperasti/pqdt*, 6.41, 42, 45, 46, 53) and

---

1. Rowland, 1982: 216. Cf. Levison, 1988: 223 n. 22.

'said' (*dixisti/'mrt*, 6.38, 40, 47) *in the events of creation* came to be, but the things he 'said' (*dixisti/'mrt*, 6.55, 56) *concerning Israel* have failed to take place. Ezra juxtaposes God's powerful creative word with his feeble assurances to Israel,[1] thereby voicing 'the basic dilemma of the covenantal tradition'.[2]

It should be pointed out, however, that there is more in Ezra's words than just a nationalistic concern. He seems to be calling into question not only God's faithfulness to Israel but also his sovereignty over humanity. The incongruity between Israel's present situation and God's promises to Israel would seem to indicate that God is impotent in his dealings with humanity. This is evident in the way Ezra plays with the relationship between God's authoring word and his resulting work. With regard to the ordering of nature, Ezra proclaims, 'Your word accomplished the work' (6.38), and 'Your word went forth, and at once the work was done' (6.43). However, when God stated that the world was created for Israel and his word produced nothing, his authority in his dealings with humanity—both the chosen people (6.54, 58) and the 'spittle'—is undermined directly. Thus, Ezra's complaint is not simply an appeal on Israel's behalf (although it is certainly that) but an indictment against the sovereignty of God in human affairs. If Israel's God fails to act on their behalf, might he not be altogether impotent in the affairs of humanity?[3] The test case of his sovereignty is that of Israel, a test which he appears to have failed.[4]

5.1.3. *Salvation belongs to the world to come (7.1-16)*. Uriel appears again in order to respond to Ezra. He first gives two analogies, both with the point that, although the goal is much to be desired, the means by which one attains to that goal is enormously difficult (7.1-9). These analogies provide the background for much of what Uriel will go on to state throughout III. In them, he emphasizes the necessity of great human effort and endurance in attaining to the goal. The same condition applies to Israel, says Uriel (7.10), now in direct response to

1. Cf. Steck, 1977.
2. Collins, 1984a: 162.
3. This is not to say that Ezra is defending the interests of humanity at this point; contra Harrelson, 1980: 33.
4. So Harnisch writes of 6.38-59 (as of 5.23-27): 'die kritische Frage nach der Macht Gottes [erhebt sich] als Frage nach der geschichtlichen Evidenz seines Erwählungswortes' (1969: 31, his emphasis removed; cf. 26). Cf. Brandenburger, 1981: 174.

Ezra's complaint. He agrees with Ezra's comment that the world was created for Israel, but goes on to say, however, that when Adam sinned the order of the world changed and came under God's judgment.[1] Now, the ways[2] of the present world are filled with many hardships, while only those of the 'greater' world are 'broad and safe, and really yield the fruit of immortality' (7.13). To get to that greater world, however, everyone must first pass through the difficulties of this world (7.14).

Here, Uriel's point is that God's original intention has been revised. Whatever was promised to Israel has now been emended by a temporal condition. The question, in effect, is not, 'Why has Israel yet to "possess" the world?', but rather, 'Which world will Israel possess?' (and, as we will see, 'Who will constitute Israel?'). Thus, just as Uriel has modified Ezra's quest for understanding in I–II by introducing a temporal (eschatological) condition, so here he encourages Ezra to turn his attention to 'what is to come, rather than what is now present' (7.16),[3] for Adam's sin has caused salvation to be withdrawn from this age, only to be transferred to the age to come. In this way, Uriel answers Ezra's charges against God's faithfulness to Israel and his sovereignty over humanity.

Uriel's case in 7.1-16 can be easily contrasted with Ezra's case in 3.1-36. In I, Ezra portrayed the desperate situation of sinful humanity in order to underline God's salvific initiative on behalf of Israel in particular (3.4-27); it is *God's mercy alone* which is able to overcome the Adamic condition. In III, Uriel argues that, in fact, Adam's sin caused the order of the created world to be replaced by a new order. Accordingly, the present world is despaired of and deliverance is expected only with the coming of the future age. Uriel holds that the effects of Adam's sin were so destructive that, in the present order, God's mercy cannot be appealed to and ethnic particularism cannot be maintained. Instead, *human persistence* is upheld as the vehicle to salvation in the next age (7.3-9, 10-14). Thus, whereas Ezra pled for God's covenant mercy despite the human predicament, Uriel dis-

1. Cf. Myers: 'The world was indeed made for Israel but Adam's violation of the divine stipulations brought about *another world* which was judged' (1974: 252, emphasis added).

2. For a defence of the translation 'ways', see Stone, 1989: 55; Knibb, 1970: 162.

3. Cf. Myers: 'The affairs of this world. . . must be placed in proper perspective. The direction of one's thoughts is important for the writer' (1974: 252).

qualifies the mercy of God altogether in the light of the pervasiveness of evil. In this way, the temporal clause inherent in Uriel's definition of the ways of God overrules any ethnocentric clause which Ezra expects to be operative in this age. Accordingly, Collins appropriately notes that, because the 'basis of salvation is individual merit, not membership of a covenant people', so in what follows 'the focus shifts from the specific destiny of Israel to the more general problem of human inability to satisfy the law'.[1]

5.1.4. *Are the unworthy dealt with fairly? (7.17-25).* Uriel has already directed the focus of attention away from Israel's present predicament to the future state of salvation in the next age. In the process, his two-age doctrine has deflated the uniqueness of Israel in the present age. The effects of this change of agenda are immediately recognizable in Ezra's words. To Uriel's scheme of the two worlds, Ezra has this objection: The situation is not fair to the many who are wicked for they suffer the toils of the present world and will not live to see the easier days of the next world (7.17-18). This prefigures much of the discussion that follows, in which Ezra tries to reconcile the punishment of the vast number of wicked with the justice of God. Here, Ezra is not functioning as Israel's own representative. Instead, he has become the spokesperson for the many, the nations. It is not the desperate situation of Israel that Ezra pleads for but that of the wicked.[2] This is unparalleled in all that has gone before in the dialogues.

Uriel reproaches Ezra for his objection (7.19-25), for can he claim to be a better judge of things than God? It is better in God's sight, Uriel says, to cause the many to perish than to allow his law to be disregarded (7.20). The next few verses all uphold obedience to the law as the means whereby punishment can be avoided. God commanded 'what they should do to live' (7.21), but the ungodly were disobedient.

---

1. 1984a: 162.
2. Box thinks 7.17-18 to refer to Israel (1912: 98); cf. Myers, 1974: 252. But this view is problematic. Box must postulate that, whereas Ezra made a distinction between the righteous and the wicked in general (7.17-18), Uriel changes the distinction to identify Israel and the gentile nations in particular. But this does not fit well with Uriel's emphasis already in 7.10-16 on all the 'living' and the condition of humanity which provokes Ezra's rebuttal. Others who also think that Ezra here has abandoned his nationalistic tone include Thompson (1977: 193), Russell (1964: 300, 302), Knibb (1979: 162).

The answer to Ezra's objection, then, is that the wicked do not deserve to see easier days, since they 'ignored his ways', 'scorned his law', 'denied his covenants', 'have been unfaithful to his statutes', and 'have not performed his works' (7.23-24). Many commentators think that Uriel's point is founded upon the idea that the law was offered by God to other nations of the world but was accepted by none except Israel. Although this may be so, Uriel does not make his case here in Israel's favour. He merely makes the point that the observance of the law is the only corrective to the anthropological condition of sin. God's law is the bridge from this world to the next,[1] and those who have disobeyed God's commandments will not arrive at his salvation.

Once again, a contrast between Uriel's case in III and Ezra's in I is revealing. As 7.19-25 and 3.4-27 illustrate, both characters agree that the law is the way out of the desperate condition of the human race and that the law is not well obeyed. Nonetheless, Uriel's speech in III differs from Ezra's in I in the determination of where the blame for the neglect of the law is to be placed. Uriel places the blame directly on those who do not live by the law.[2] Ezra, on the other hand, placed the blame on God for not removing the evil heart, thereby rendering it nearly impossible to obey the law. He argued that there is more to the issue than obedience to the law, for God's mercy to Israel is a more fundamental matter. In Uriel's words, however, there is no such clause to fall back on. Obedience to the law is the all-important factor.

5.1.5. *The messianic reign and the end of this world (7.26-44)*. Uriel then gives an elaborate description of the coming of the Messiah, his 400-year reign, and the judgment that follows in the age to come (7.26-44). In that time, a city which at present remains hidden shall be revealed (7.26; cf. IV), 'the world, which is not yet awake, shall be aroused' (7.31), and righteousness will replace unfaithfulness (7.35-36). Judgment will be meted out, recompense and reward being determined on the basis of righteous and unrighteous deeds.[3] This section does not contribute much to the dialogue itself but supplies more details about the end, the time with which the argument is now

---

1. Cf. Harnisch, 1969: 146-55; Mundle, 1929: 227-29, 232-33.
2. Cf. Harnisch, 1969: 149; Knibb, 1979: 164.
3. Cf. Nickelsburg and Stone: 'Here the testimonies of righteous and unrighteous deeds function as defense and prosecuting attorneys' (1983: 143). Cf. Münchow, 1981: 93-95.

primarily concerned.[1] It fills out Uriel's case by interweaving 'argument and information about the end'.[2] In both Uriel's 'argument' and 'information', works are said to be the prerequisite for salvation (7.37), and the mercy of God is nowhere mentioned. Instead, Uriel defends God's intention to destroy the wicked and to judge according to one's works apart from mercy.

5.1.6. *Only a few will be saved (7.45-61)*. Ezra is disturbed by what Uriel has predicted. He ponders once again the effect of the evil heart on humanity: 'For who among the living is there that has not sinned, or who among men that has not transgressed your covenant?' (7.46). The evil heart has alienated almost everyone from God and has brought them into the ways of death (7.48-49). Ezra said the same in his opening statement of I (3.4-12). There, however, he went on to cite God's gracious initiative on Israel's behalf as the corrective to the problem (3.13-19). Nothing of the sort appears here. Ezra is upset about the destruction of the many wicked, and he seems unable to reconcile this with his understanding of God's justice.

After giving something of a prefatory remark (which is most often cited as the centerpiece of Uriel's two-age scheme: 'The Most High has made not one world but two', 7.50[3]), Uriel gives two responses: (1) It would be unjust to add the wicked to the number of righteous (7.51-52);[4] (2) What is rare is more precious than what is plentiful (7.54-58). As a result, there is no reason to question the fact that only a few will be saved (7.59-61), for, Uriel says, 'I will rejoice over the few who shall be saved' (7.60), and 'I will not grieve over the multitude of those who perish' (7.61).

5.1.7. *Two attitudes towards the human situation (i) (7.62-74)*. Ezra's agitation is not dispelled and he replies with a profound lament on behalf of all humanity (7.62-69): 'Let the human race lament. . . For all who have been born are involved in iniquities, and are full of sins and burdened with transgressions' (7.65, 68). Ezra's anthropology is

---

1. This section may be seen as a continuation of the description of the end that brought II to a close (6.11-28; cf. the similarities between 6.25 and 7.27).

2. Knibb, 1979: 166. Cf. Myers, 1974: 253; Oesterley, 1935: 158; Stone, 1983.

3. Koch, citing the two-age scheme as '*das* wesentliche Thema des 4. Esrabuches', goes on to say: 'Der Satz 7,50. . . gilt weithin als der 'Grundsatz,' mit dem die Argumentationen des Verfassers stehen und fallen' (1978: 46).

4. Most texts, however, are corrupt at this point.

wholly in line with traditional Jewish views concerning the condition
of sin which engulfs the whole of humanity. Israel as a subset of
humanity, however, is nowhere in view. The predicament is pathetic
because (1) humanity knows its condition (7.62-67),[1] and (2) no one is
capable of correcting that condition (7.68-69). The angel, however,
turns Ezra's case on its head. The predicament of the wicked is certainly pathetic, but not for the reasons Ezra has given. Instead, it is
precisely because they have understood God's ways but have failed to
live by the law (7.72) that the many are in a desperate situation. The
responsibility of their condition is wholly theirs. God is, in fact, very
patient with them in this age—not for their own sake, but because he
has ordained the ages to be so (7.70-74). Uriel's remarks here make
no significant gains over that of 7.17-25.

5.1.8. *The qualifications of the righteous and the unrighteous (7.75-
101).* Because almost all humanity is destined to undergo severe judgment, Ezra's thoughts turn to the issue of the soul's condition between
death and the new age when judgment awaits (cf. 4.35; 7.32, 121).
This provides Uriel with the opportunity to describe in vivid detail (1)
how the righteous and unrighteous will be recompensed, and (2) what
distinguishes the righteous from the unrighteous. Uriel first tells Ezra
that he should not number himself among those who will be tortured
(7.76). What has allowed Ezra to escape the fate of the majority of
humanity? The answer is immediately supplied: 'You have a treasure
of works laid up with the Most High' (7.77), thereby escaping the
anthropological condition of sin. Uriel describes two groups (those
who will be tormented and those who will be blessed) in terms of their
faithfulness to the law. The former have scorned the law of God and
failed to keep it (7.79, 81). They will grieve because, seeing 'the
reward laid up for those who have trusted the covenants of the Most
High' (7.83; cf. 7.85), they await their torment without the possibility
of repentance (7.84, 86-87). The latter have 'kept the ways of the
Most High' (7.88). If Uriel's words to Ezra in 7.76 have raised the

---

1. In 7.62-63, Ezra speaks of the human mind having been created out of dust.
Harnisch thinks this to be an indication of Ezra's gnostic allegiance, whereby he
blames the material world for the presence of the evil impulse (1969: 156-69). But
Ezra's speech does not support such a thesis; the mind is problematic for Ezra not
because it is the origin of sin, but because it is able to foresee the result of sin. Cf.
Levison, 1988: 225 n.39.

reader's hopes for salvation, here he elaborates on what keeping the ways of God entails:

> During the time that they lived in it [the mortal body], they laboriously (*cum labore*) served the Most High, and withstood danger every hour, that they might keep the Law of the Lawgiver perfectly (*perfecte*). . . they have striven with great effort (*cum labore multo*) to overcome the evil thought. . . they faithfully (*per fidem*) kept the law which was given to them[1] (7.89, 92, 94).

Two things need mentioning at this point. First, it is by keeping the law 'perfectly' that the few are saved, just as it was said that Ezra has 'a treasure of works laid up with the Most High'. In both statements, salvation has nothing to do with membership in a particular community but is determined wholly by one's merits. The responsibility is entirely on the individual to show strict, laborious observance to the law and thereby store up treasures with God. As M. Knibb well writes, Uriel holds that

> by the strict observance of the law it was possible for an individual to acquire, as it were, a credit balance of good works and to earn thereby the reward in the world to come of life.[2]

No mention is made of God's mercy or initiative in the process of salvation, whether on behalf of humanity, Israel or the individual. In Uriel's eyes, the way of God includes not only a temporal aspect (God has made not one age but two) but a specific object of his 'affection'— that is, the few who will be saved according to their own achievements.

---

1. The translation of 7.94 is mine; cf. Box, 1912: 149-50. It is often translated, 'they kept the law which was given them in trust (*per fidem*)'. Whether *per fidem* modifies the keeping or the giving of the law is ambiguous. The Armenian text leaves no doubt in this regard: 'with great faith he observed the Law which was given to him' (Stone, 1979: 121). Moreover, in the Armenian text, Uriel promises 'a treasury full of goodnesses' (7.77) to those who are 'full of good deeds' (7.89) (Stone, 1979: 119).

2. 1979: 182. Oesterley argues, however, that despite the emphasis on works in 7.77 and elsewhere, the author of *4 Ezra* did not consider good deeds to be essential for salvation. He finds the proof of this is in 8.36, where God's mercy is emphasized (1933: 87). But Oesterley has paid no attention to the speakers of these respective passages; 7.77 is spoken by Uriel, whereas 8.36 is a plea for God's mercy by Ezra. In the voices of Ezra and Uriel, one witnesses the struggle between two incompatible understandings of God's ways. These two voices cannot simply be combined, as Oesterley does here, without doing great injustice to the text.

Second, those who keep the law perfectly are said to have overcome the evil heart which was formed in them. In Ezra's opening complaint in I, he had stated that the evil heart had not been removed by God and therefore the law was of no avail (3.20-27). Here Uriel agrees that the evil heart is the problem to be overcome, but he states that doing the law perfectly is still a possibility despite the human predicament, thereby undermining Ezra's complaint against God uttered in I. There, the problem was humanly insurmountable in Ezra's eyes and, therefore, the solution could only come from God. In Uriel's handling of the same theme in III, however, the problem is not insurmountable and the individual himself has it within his own means to ensure his own solution. Although the evil heart remains, God is not to blame, for he has given the law as a corrective measure which can, in fact, be kept by diligent effort. The responsibility is placed firmly on the individual to accord himself strictly with God's law.[1]

5.1.9. *There will be no intercession for the unrighteous (7.102-15).* Ezra, seemingly unsatisfied with Uriel's brute individualism, asks if the righteous will be able to intercede for the unrighteous (7.102-103). The answer is definite: No, for everyone is responsible for his own actions (7.104) and in the day of judgment 'everyone shall bear his own righteousness or unrighteousness' (7.105). But Ezra cannot justify this with what has been allowed in the past, as the Scriptures illustrate, when righteous men (Abraham, Moses, Joshua, Samuel, David, Solomon, Elijah, Hezekiah, 'and many others') made intercession for the ungodly. Will this not be the case in the judgment as well (7.106-11)? Uriel, however, does not allow Ezra to abstract principles from the past and expect them to apply in the future (7.112). There is another age to come—an age when infidelity to the law will be cut off (7.114), and mercy will not be shown to anyone who is condemned (7.115). As W. Harnisch states, Uriel maintains 'daß. . . nicht die Zugehörigkeit zum erwählten Volk, sondern allein die auf Grund des Gehorsams gegenüber dem Gesetz erworbene Gerechtigkeit die Bedingung für die Heilsteilnahme darstellt'.[2]

---

1. Uriel's position accords with the rabbinic view that the evil *yetzer* could be overcome by adherence to the law: 'The Law wears away the *yetzer ha-ra'* as water wears away stone' (*Sukk.* 52b).

2. 1969: 246.

5.1.10. *Two attitudes towards the human situation (ii) (7.116-31)*. In what follows Ezra, in ways not unlike that of 7.62-69, offers up a sympathetic lament for the race of Adam. It would have been better for the multitude of sinners never to have lived at all than to live in the shadow of torment, all the while knowing that the glories which are offered to the few are out of their (the sinners') reach (7.116-26). As in his response in 7.70-74 (cf. 7.19-25), Uriel states that that is simply the way things are. There will be great joy over the salvation of the few, but no grief will be shown over the damnation of the many (7.126-31). Uriel stresses, in contrast to Ezra, that it is within one's capabilities to secure salvation. Although it is a difficult struggle ('a contest'), if we are victorious (i.e. by living according to the law) we will inherit life (in the next age). The responsibility is one's own.

Uriel's remarks are not surprising. He has said it all before. What is novel, however, is Uriel's appeal to Moses and the prophets in support of his position. After stating that one's reward is determined by one's effort in the contest, Uriel claims:

> For this is the way of which Moses, while he was alive, spoke to the people, saying, 'Choose for yourself life, that you may live!' But they did not believe him, or the prophets after him, or even myself who have spoken to them (7.129-30).

Throughout the dialogues, Uriel has consistently urged Ezra to look to the events of the future to understand the ways of God properly. The interpretation and application of Scripture in answer to Ezra have not entered into Uriel's presentation or defence. Here, however, the message of Moses and the prophets is claimed as the precedent to Uriel's own (perhaps in response to Ezra's appeal to Moses as one scriptural example of how the righteous can intercede for the ungodly; cf. 7.106), and the proof of his allegation is found in Deut. 30.19, or so he claims.

In Deut. 30.11-20, Moses called the people of Israel to be faithful to the law of the covenant in order that they might live, increase and possess the land which God promised to Abraham's descendants. He affirmed that the law is not too difficult to keep nor is it beyond one's capabilities. The people are commanded to keep the law 'in order that you and your descendants might live' (Deut. 30.19).

Uriel is probably using the proof text of Deut. 30.19 to refer to Moses' assurances to the people that the law is not too difficult to keep (cf. especially Deut. 30.12-14), as he himself has argued (7.92). The rest of Uriel's case is not evident from the original context of Deut. 30.19. Uriel has denied anything other than a stringent individualism (which explains his omission of the guarantee in Deut. 30.19 that life will be bestowed upon one's descendants along with one's self[1]). Moreover, used in support of Uriel's position, the quotation is extracted from its covenantal environment. Uriel infuses it with the promise of an *eschatological* life to those who choose correctly to live by the law in order to be granted the reward of life in the next age. Uriel reads this verse, therefore, as confirmation of his two-age schematization, and so he aligns Moses and the prophets with himself.

5.1.11. *A first appeal to God's mercy, and a response (7.132–8.3).* Ezra is not satisfied with Uriel's glib lack of concern for the perishing, since such an attitude does not square with what he knows of God's merciful character, demonstrated in Scripture. Perhaps in reaction to the way Uriel legitimated his position by appealing to Moses and the prophets, Ezra reflects on God's merciful and compassionate nature in words which appear indebted to Exod. 34.6-7, a passage which fuelled much of this sort of reflection.[2] Ezra's comprehension of God's ways, which is rooted in the scriptural accounts of God's merciful dealings with Israel, is incompatible with Uriel's flippant disregard for the unrighteous. His speech in 7.132-40 is not merely an implicit rebuttal of Uriel's position but an appeal to God to live up to the qualities which Ezra catalogues. But Ezra is answered quite briefly: This world is for the many, the next is for the few; many have been created but few will be saved (8.1-3). There is nothing here which advances beyond Uriel's words in 7.49-61.

5.1.12. *A second appeal to God's mercy, and a response (8.4-41).* In a long speech, Ezra's words exhibit an intriguing transition from an appeal to God to have mercy on humanity (8.4-14), to a request for God to save his people (8.15-33), back to an appeal for humanity (8.34-36).

In the first section where he appeals on behalf of all humanity (8.4-14), Ezra traces the stages of human development and cites God as the

---

1. This clause is reintroduced into the Syriac text under the influence of the scriptural passage.

2. See Num. 14.17-18; Neh. 9.17; Joel 2.13; Jon. 4.2; Pss. 86.15; 103.8; 145.8; Eccl. 2.11; Wis. 15.1. Ezra's words share many features of penitential liturgies of traditional Judaism. See Boyarin, 1972; Simonsen, 1911.

director of the entire process. God is present at every point. He wonders, therefore, what purpose there could be in the destruction of
humanity. Uriel's pronouncement in 8.1-3 that only a few will be
saved is not acceptable to Ezra, who once again pleads humanity's
case.[1] But he resolves to leave humanity in God's hands while he
pleads especially for Israel. Thus, Ezra says:

> About mankind you know best; but I will speak about your people, for whom
> I am grieved, and about your inheritance, for whom I lament, and about
> Israel, for whom I am sad, and about the seed of Jacob, for whom I am
> troubled (8.15-16).

In his prayer for Israel's salvation (8.20-33, after the transition of
8.15-19), Ezra returns to a nationalistic frame of mind which has not
played any part in the dialogue since the early paragraphs of III (6.55-
59). Ezra's appeal works in two parts. First, he asks God not to look
upon the sinners of the nation, but to be merciful by allowing the
righteousness of the few within Israel to benefit the whole people
(8.20-30). In 8.31-33, however, Ezra does not continue with this same
argument. This second section includes no reference to the existence
of a righteous few who can act for the benefit of Israel's many
unrighteous. Instead, changing the nature of his logic, Ezra appeals
directly to the mercy of God without mention of the merit of the few.
God is simply requested to ignore Israel's sin. Although the deeds of
the righteous have salvific import only for the righteous few (that is,
their many works are laid up in heaven 'and they shall be rewarded
according to their own deeds', 8.33), Ezra responds to Uriel's conviction that works are the basis of salvation apart from divine grace, not
by pleading that the redemptive value of works be applied to sinners
as well as the righteous, but by invoking God to be merciful to sinners
for no reason other than that he should be merciful:

> For we and our fathers have passed our lives in ways that bring death, but
> you, because of us sinners, are called merciful. If you desire to have pity on
> us, who have no works of righteousness, then you will be called merciful
> (8.31-32).

---

1. Myers's contention that Ezra is really thinking of God's nurturing of Israel
(rather than all humanity) is not convincing (1974: 258). It fails to take account of
Ezra's concern for 'every mortal who bears the likeness of a human being' (8.6).
Thompson's handling is much better (1977: 202-204).

Thus, although Ezra's logic in 8.20-30 and in 8.31-33 may run along somewhat different lines, the constant in them both is the call upon God's mercy on behalf of Israel.

The first two sections of Ezra's speech may appear to be quite unrelated—the first pleading humanity's case (8.4-14), the second pleading Israel's case (8.15-33). In fact, however, their relationship is that of two parts of a *qal waḥomer* argument: If God can be said to be responsible for the salvation of humanity (8.4-14), how much more responsible is he to effect the salvation of Israel (8.15-33). One would expect God to be merciful to humanity (his creation) and, therefore, all the more so to Israel, his own people. Although he might refuse to do the former, he cannot refuse the latter. Of course, Ezra has already learned from Uriel that God is not responsible to save anyone, but the rhetorical argument is strong in his eyes. And so he proceeds to suggest two ways in which God might save his people: (1) by his mercy, he could allow the merits of the righteous to benefit the rest (8.20-30), or (2) by his mercy he could simply pity the sinners for their own sake, despite their lack of 'works of righteousness' (*opera iusticiae*) (8.31-33).

In 8.34-36, however, Ezra pushes his plea for Israel into the service of yet another plea for humanity:

> [T]here is no one among those who have been born who has not acted wickedly, and among those who have existed there is no one who has not transgressed. For in this, O Lord, your righteousness and goodness will be declared, when you are merciful to those who have no store of good works (8.35-36).

Ezra seems to be making the point that, if God can be merciful to the unrighteous within Israel, he can surely find it in himself to be merciful to all sinners, regardless of ethnic status. He can argue this because, when the anthropological condition of sin is in view, ethnic distinctions are illegitimate.

Ezra's whole speech in 8.4-36, although marked by noticeable shifts in logic and perspective, works towards his plea for God's mercy upon all sinners in 8.34-36, and the nationalism that appears in the middle of the speech serves that universal interest. The Ezra of III is not the Ezra of I and II. Israel's defender has become the defender of the human race. Israel is still a part of the picture, and holds a unique place in Ezra's concern, but the human condition has taken centre stage in Ezra's prosecution. Nonetheless, the ground of his case has not changed; he expects God to be merciful to sinners, for that is God's reputation, and his justice and goodness are at stake.[1]

The reader is not surprised to hear Uriel's response to Ezra. Whereas Ezra asked God not to regard *the sin* of the unrighteous (8.26-30), Uriel rather coldly replies that, in fact, God will not regard *the unrighteous* at all, because of their sin;[2] God is not concerned with the sinners, but rejoices over the salvation of the righteous (8.38-39). A parable follows to prove this point: Although many seeds are sown, only a few grow (8.41). In essence, Ezra's appeal has fallen on deaf ears. His prayer was for mercy when dealing with sinners, but in response he is told that God is concerned solely with the righteous, who are distinguished from the rest of humanity by the absence of sin.

5.1.13. A third appeal to God's mercy, and a response (8.42-62). Ezra once again objects (8.42-45). He is not convinced by Uriel's parable of the seed (8.41), and thinks it to be a faulty analogy. First, seed is dependent upon the proper amount of rainfall, which is in God's control. Evidently Ezra thinks that Uriel's analogy proves his very point: creation needs its creator in order to survive. In effect, Ezra again implies that God should be merciful lest he be unjust. Second, Ezra does not think that seed can be compared to humanity, since God created the latter in his own image. If God nourishes seed, how much more will he save humanity.[3] Both points spring from the fact that the creature is wholly dependent upon the creator and is not able to sustain itself.[4]

---

1. Cf. Cook, 1988: 96-97. Broyles demonstrates that in many Psalms of personal or communal distress, praises to God are meant to encourage God to live up to his reputation in order that the psalmist might continue to praise him (1989: 112). He cites Pss. 22, 39, 42–43, 44, 60, 80, 88, 89, 90, 102, 108.

2. Cf. Knibb: 'the words of Ezra's petition in verses 26-30 are used against him in a contrary sense to that intended' (1979: 206). The same device appears in 7.71-72 (cf. 7.64).

3. Earlier, Ezra had belittled humanity as insignificant before God, with the hopes of restraining God's anger against them (8.34); here, Ezra argues the opposite with the hopes of invoking God's mercy upon them. Moreover, Ezra does not miss the chance to put in a good word for Israel at this point: If you have mercy on your creation, then spare your people (8.45)—an argument similar to that of 8.4-19.

4. Cf. Levison: 'Since Ezra cannot plead the human or Israelite cause on the basis of their righteousness, he pleads their cause on the basis of their creatureliness' (1988: 115).

By now, the reader of this dialogue will not be surprised that Uriel's reply follows the same lines as his previous replies, and that the reply itself does not quite 'connect' with Ezra's point. He says: 'Things that are present are for those who live now and things that are future are for those who will live hereafter' (8.46). For the most part, that is his answer—a simple restatement of the two-age scheme. The assurance is given that God loves his creation (8.47), and Ezra is said to be numbered among the righteous, while the wicked are assured of future punishment for their contempt of God and his law (8.56; cf. 7.127-31). Although it was not God's intention to destroy humanity, those who have defiled his name have decided their own fate (8.48-61). Ezra is explicitly told to ask nothing further about the fate of sinners (8.55).

5.1.14. *The signs of the end of the age (8.63–9.13)*. As in I and II, a series of signs of the end times is given near the end of the dialogue. Here again there appears a description of the righteous and the sinners, and here again it is the law that determines the fate of individuals. The righteous one will be saved on account of his works or 'on account of the faithfulness (*fidem*) in which he has put his trust (*in qua credidit*)'[1] (9.7). The wicked, conversely, have scorned the law (9.11). Once again, Ezra is told not to inquire about the ungodly, but to consider the salvation of the righteous (9.13).

5.1.15. *Ezra and Uriel recapitulate their respective points (9.14-22)*. Ezra does not heed the call to concern himself exclusively with the righteous. Instead, he makes his last appeal, which is less an appeal than a statement of non-satisfaction. He declares, 'I said it before, and I say it now, and will say it again',[2] and then complains, 'There are more who perish than those who will be saved' (9.15). Evidently Ezra remains unconvinced by Uriel's case, which he cannot reconcile with God's mercy.

In reply, Uriel holds that those who will be destroyed are deserving of their fate. The world is lost and those in it are lost (9.17-20). And yet God has spared some 'with great difficulty' (*vix valde*) (9.21) and

1. My translation; cf. Box, 1912: 203. That *fidem* here has the sense of 'faithfulness' is also suggested by Thompson, 1977: 313. But see Mundle, 1929: 229-31.

2. Thompson calls this 'the seer's final thrust at God before the transition episode IV begins' (1977: 127).

has perfected them 'with much labour' (*cum multo labore*) (9.22).
Here it is *God* who has worked hard for the salvation of the righteous.
We should not think that Uriel has surrendered his earlier conviction
that salvation is granted to those who laboriously (*cum labore*) and
perfectly (*perfecte*) served God in order to overcome evil and complete the contest victoriously (7.89, 92, 127-28). Uriel has not suddenly changed his tone to affirm that salvation will be granted on the
basis of God's grace. He seems, instead, to be wrapping his position in
language which affirms God's sovereignty and justice. This is not
unjustifiable on his part for, as the three visions which follow will
reveal, God will show himself to be the deliverer of those who have
made themselves worthy and acceptable to him. Whatever effort God
may expend is not 'grace' in its traditional sense, however. He will
'save' some, no doubt, but they are those *who have merited his effort*
which he will exercise only at the end of the age. Uriel's attention is
towards this eschatological aspect of salvation, addressed in IV–VI,
wherein God acts decisively for the sake of the remnant who are
deserving of salvation. In this way, he can talk about God's own participation in eschatological salvation. Otherwise Uriel's position
remains unchanged: those who will be saved are few in number. They
are not humanity, nor Israel, but only one grape out of a cluster
(9.21-22)—a remnant. Let the multitude perish, for there is a precious
remnant who will be saved.

That the 'grape' and 'plant' imagery in 9.21-22 symbolize *the remnant* is an assertion which will need some support in the light of
Thompson's contention that these symbols do not represent the few
who are righteous but the nation Israel. He supports this by noting that
the 'use of national election terminology is unmistakable' and
'obvious'.[1] But is it? First, it must be noticed that Thompson's suggestion makes for a very disjointed reading. Thompson is forced to
see here 'a partial merging of the concepts of national and personal
salvation'.[2] This is because the phrase 'I spared some with great
difficulty' refers (as he recognizes) to individuals, while the 'one
grape out of a cluster' he thinks to refer to the nation of Israel. This
important switch in the object of God's salvation would seem clumsy,
and there are no indicators to suggest that such a reading is appropriate in 9.21. Second, it would seem unnecessarily awkward, even

1. 1977: 192; cf. 210-11, 264.
2. 1977: 192.

problematic, for Uriel to resort to some sort of nationalistic particularism at this point. His 'two-age doctrine' has been unpacked in III to reveal that it is not Israel who will be blessed in the next age but only a very few by means of their perfect and laborious fulfilment of the law. That he should suddenly defend the position he has all along attempted to negate is not to be expected, nor can it be properly defended from the text.

This is confirmed, most significantly, when the imagery Uriel uses is compared with popular nationalistic symbolism of the author's day, which Ezra draws upon in 5.23 when he begins his first complaint of II: 'O sovereign Lord, from every forest of the earth and from all its trees you have chosen one vine'. Recent studies have reinforced the significance of the vine and the grape cluster as vital and potent nationalistic symbols,

> full of meaning for a time of national crisis and emerging when high hopes of military victory over Rome, Messiah's coming, eschatological salvation, and political freedom were entertained.[1]

Jewish coins of the Roman period commonly bore the symbols of the vine or grape cluster—symbols apparently easily appropriated to support the nationalistic tendencies which arose in Jewish circles especially in times of foreign domination. Significant also are the descriptions recorded in Josephus and the Mishnah of the golden vines which stood above the golden gate into the sanctuary of the Herodian Temple, 'from which hung branches as big as a man' (Josephus, *War* 5.210-11; cf. Josephus, *Ant.* 15.395; m. *Mid.* 3.8). The vine as the symbol of the nation Israel is also apparent in various Jewish literary works of the author's time, including the targums, *Pseudo-Philo* (in which it occurs seven times in extended imagery; cf. especially 12.8-9; 18.10-11; 23.12-13; 28.4; 30.4; 39.7) and in *2 Baruch* (in which it represents the messiah who acts as Israel's representative to overthrow the forest of God's enemies; cf. 36.1–40.3).[2] After examining the textual evidence of the vine imagery of first-century Judaism, R. Hayward appropriately concludes that the vine symbolizes

---

1. Hayward, 1990: 7. Hayward, following Porton (1976) suggests that, especially after the first Jewish revolt of 66–70 CE, this imagery took on nationalistic significance.
2. For a good discussion of the vine and grape cluster imagery of these documents, see Hayward, 1990.

Israel as God's never-to-be-destroyed people, on whose existence the creation depends and for whose sake it has come into being; Israel as the one
people who glorify God and are promised eternal life.[1]

It comes as no surprise, then, that Ezra begins his thoroughly
nationalistic complaint in II by likening Israel to the vine which God
selected from all of the trees in the forest (5.23). What is significant,
however, is Uriel's recasting of this imagery in diminutive terms in
9.21-22. Out of the forest, God has chosen one plant, says Uriel. This
is not the great 'cosmic vine, reaching from the underworld to heaven,
linking the Abyss with God's Throne of Glory',[2] as it is commonly
portrayed. And if this is not enough, what Uriel identifies as the object
of God's salvation is not a cluster of grapes (a popular symbol of
Israel) but one single grape from the whole cluster of grapes. Certainly, when the significance of the vine and the grape cluster as established nationalistic symbols are reduced to the image of one single
grape, one can hardly suppose, in the light of Jewish symbolism evident in the first century CE, that Uriel intended the one grape to signify the nation Israel. Of course, Uriel's contrasts between the cluster
and the grape and between the plant and the forest[3] work along the
same lines as affirmations found elsewhere in Judaism concerning the
uniqueness of Israel in distinction from the gentiles, but Uriel trans-
forms this nationalistic contrast and reduces the scope of its boundaries significantly to include only the few (cf. 7.60).[4] This seems to be
conclusive evidence that, despite Thompson's claims to the contrary,
Uriel exhibits no nationalistic interest at this point. (It may also be
noted that, in structural terms, Uriel gets the final word, without
rejoinder from Ezra. This has been true of each dialogue.)

5.1.16. *Transition to IV (9.23-25)*. Before the dialogue ends, Uriel
tells Ezra to prepare for yet another divine visitation after a seven-day
interval. This time, however, Ezra is not told to fast as he was at the
conclusion of I and II (5.20; 6.31, 35) but to move out to an open field
and eat the flowers therein: 'taste no meat and drink no wine, but eat

1. 1990: 12; cf. Rowland, 1982: 61.
2. Hayward, 1990: 4.
3. The Latin reads 'tribe' (*tribu*), evidently reading the Greek ὕλη ('forest') as if it
were φυλή ('tribe').
4. Cf. J. Schreiner: 'Von der Terminologie. . . scheint auf die Erwählung Israels
verwiesen zu werden'; but Schreiner adds: 'In V.22 jedoch dürfte die Rettung
weniger Menschen in Endgericht angesprochen sein' (1981: 373).

only flowers' (9.24). This change of situation (from Ezra's room to an open field) and of instruction (from fasting to feasting on flowers) foreshadows a significant transformation in the tone of the book, as Ezra moves from anxiety to consolation in what follows.[1]

5.2. *Summary of Episode III*

Uriel has had the last word and has maintained his position unswervingly: only a few will be saved. This is the very point which Ezra has tried to amend throughout this dialogue. Uriel's position falls outside Ezra's conviction that God is merciful. Yet, despite his various attempts, Ezra has not received an explanation suitable to him. In spite of his lengthy exchanges with Uriel, Ezra remains unconvinced at the end of III ('I said before, and I say now, and will say it again'). In our estimation, the sheer length of III looks to be a device used by the author to break Ezra's (and the reader's) bold and enquiring spirit to understand God's ways, leaving only discontentment behind. Ezra's queries are never answered to his satisfaction and much of his frustration is sustained by what he would consider to be superfluous and repetitive responses on Uriel's part. It is almost as if, once the respective positions are defined, the content of those positions is secondary. In one sense, more important is the reader's recognition of the impasse which the two characters can never get beyond and of the despair which Ezra feels accordingly. Their cases are so mismatched that their incompatibility precludes real dialogue and progress. But perhaps there is method in the author's apparent madness. He sustains a dialogue which has the appearance of a potentially productive debate but which never develops into much of anything, the purpose being to provoke in the audience an emotional response; the longer the dialogue remains at a standstill, the more the reader is to be drawn into Ezra's own frustration.

In the process of this dialogue, Ezra has adopted a concern for all humanity. In I and II, Israel's own situation predominated. In III, however, that particularistic concern has given way to a more fundamental one of the anthropological condition. After his opening remarks, Ezra rarely focuses on Israel's situation (except in 8.15-33, 45). Although Ezra has not abandoned Israel's cause completely, it must be recognized that his plea on Israel's behalf (8.15-33) is brought

---

1. Cf. Gunkel, 1900: 347ff.; Knibb, 1979: 218; and Breech, 1973: 272.

into the service of his defence for all humanity (which surrounds it on both sides; 8.4-14, 34-36). He may be Israel's spokesman, but he has become more than that, for he has taken on humanity's case in the process. There is progress in III, then, since Ezra's agenda has changed, and nationalistic complaints have been deferred in the light of the anthropological problem.

Nonetheless, although in Episode III Ezra pleads for the whole of humanity rather than for Israel alone, his line of defence is along the same lines as it was in I and II: God should be merciful (whether to Israel or to humanity). Uriel's position is just as consistent: God cannot be held responsible for the fate of sinners since that responsibility lies solely with the individual. The righteous are those few people who, through strenuous effort, keep the law perfectly, thereby laying up treasures of deeds by which they merit salvation.[1]

Several other points need to be made in reflection upon this dialogue and the dialogues as a whole. First, it should be noted that when Uriel's words in 9.21-22 are understood aright, Thompson's evaluation of the author's project cannot be easily maintained. It has already been pointed out that Thompson considers the imagery of the grape in 9.21-22 to symbolize the nation Israel. With this as evidence, Thompson thinks that the dialogues, and *4 Ezra* itself, to move from nationalistic to universalistic and finally back to nationalistic concerns. Episode III is thought to exhibit this same structure—the first and final speeches in III enunciating nationalistic interests while the dialogue which transpires between them dares to investigate the anthropological condition. In this way, 'the author gives himself, by means of the dialogue, plenty of leeway to explore the fringes of faith and doubt, but he is safely in the fold at the beginning and at the end'.[2] But III does not end on this nationalistic note, and so neither do the dialogues as a whole. III concludes without a nationalistic resolution, and one must look beyond Thompson's explanation to understand the author's intention.

Second, it is necessary to determine the identification of 'Israel', since it appears to have a different reference for Ezra than for Uriel. Those with whom Ezra concerned himself initially could be defended collectively since they were united by the covenant of God's mercy.

---

1. It is not correct to say, with Harnisch (1983: 477-78) and Münchow (1981: 77), that Ezra is progressively won over to Uriel's position.
2. Thompson, 1977: 209.

As such, when Ezra uses the title 'Israel', it designates a distinctive ethnic group. The case is different for Uriel. He rules out the idea of God's mercy in the present age, and, with his rigid individualism, undermines the basis of a covenantal conception of Israel. If the designation 'Israel' is meaningful at all for Uriel, it is as a reference to the few who earn their way into the next age through their faultless obedience to the law. W. Schmithals's analysis of apocalyptic literature corroborates these results:

> The fact that. . . in apocalyptic thought Israel as a nation recedes in comparison with the true Israel is due to the loss of the sense of history by apocalyptic, which can no longer do anything with the historical nation of the Old Testament. . . How could one historical entity be chosen, when in fact history in its entirety stands under God's 'No'?[1]

This position is given voice in *4 Ezra* by Uriel, in contrast with Ezra's ethnocentric conception of Israel as the historical people of God.

Third, we must remark on W. Harnisch's portrayal of Ezra as one who voices a type of gnostic scepticism, maintaining that all of human existence is under the control of fate and that the individual is a pawn whose life is wholly determined by the powers which lie outside of his control. There is some truth to Harnisch's characterization, for Ezra does portray a sceptical attitude towards human ability to keep the law on account of the pervasiveness of sin throughout humanity. But to say that Ezra propagates a gnostic determinism is a misjudgment on Harnisch's part, especially in view of the commonplace in Early Judaism concerning human inadequacy before God and the recognition that, if God's salvation is to be enjoyed, it must result from God's merciful initiative alone. We saw this in §1.2.1, and recall one passage from 1QH to reinforce the point:

> Righteousness, I know, is not of man, nor is perfection of way of the son of man; to the Most High God belong all righteous deeds. The way of man is not established except by the Spirit which God created for him to make perfect a way for the children of men (1QH 7.29-32).

It is precisely this point (namely that salvation comes only by means of divine mercy) which Ezra articulates throughout I–III. There is nothing characteristically gnostic in Ezra's conviction that (almost) all are guilty of sin. That this conviction arises out of an awareness of the inescapable grasp of fate which determines one's destiny and from

---

1. 1975a: 87, his emphasis removed.

which no one can break loose is not evident from the text. Instead, Ezra's conviction—that 'there is no person who does not go astray' (1 Kgs 8.46)—has strong parallels in the literature of Jewish religious expression.[1]

It is precisely when this Jewish conviction is in view that Ezra's progression from the concerns of Israel to those of humanity can be explained. In Jewish literature, the fact that no one is righteous before God is offset by the recognition that God has established his covenant with Israel. In his opening speech of Episode I, Ezra makes this point exactly; although the human situation is hopeless, God has initiated a covenant relationship with Israel as the corrective to the anthropological situation. Throughout the dialogues, however, Uriel takes the opposite position, denying that God's mercy can be experienced at all in the present age. On this point he is insistent. Moreover, in III, Uriel goes further than he does in I and II, unpacking the practical aspect of his temporal qualification of God's ways. That is, he defines the objects of God's affections to include only the few who have laboriously overcome the evil heart and keep the law perfectly. This excludes all ethnocentric groups altogether and introduces a rigid individualism. Had Uriel promised that God's mercy would fall upon Israel, *even if only in the next age*, Ezra would not have needed to expand his defence to include all humanity, for his ethnocentric perspective would have remained intact with only a temporal emendation, and his concerns would have been answered. But Uriel makes no such pronouncement. Consequently, for Ezra, Israel's own interests fail to be of particular significance; without God's covenantal mercy, the people of Israel stand alongside the rest of humanity. Whereas in I and II, Ezra questioned why the covenant has been ineffective, in III he laments the human condition since, apart from God's mercy, the whole of humanity stands together in a desperate state.

There is no reason, then, to think that human sinfulness has motivated Ezra's troubled heart. It comes up on his agenda only as a con-

---

1. Cf. Hayman: 'The views presented by Ezra in the dialogue seem to me to be perfectly acceptable in the mouth of an orthodox Jew. They are neither heretical nor gnostic' (1975: 52). So Hayman disputes Harnisch's position: '[I]t is difficult to understand why the author should choose as the mouthpiece of an heretical viewpoint the venerable Ezra, the great restorer of the Law, and founder of the Synagogue' (1975: 50). Mundle shows well '[d]en allgemeinen jüdischen Horizont' of Ezra's complaints (1929: 224).

sequence of the fact that God's covenant mercies are ruled out as the corrective to human sinfulness. Collins rightly states in this regard:

> The basis of salvation is individual merit, not membership of a covenant people. Accordingly, the focus shifts from the specific destiny of Israel to the more general problem of human inability to satisfy the law.[1]

The sinful condition of humanity was recognized in the broader circles of Early Judaism and is nothing unique to Ezra. His case is unique only in that he has learned that there is no redemptive corrective in the covenant.

In this way, Ezra cannot be properly understood as a gnosticizing sceptic (Harnisch), nor as one attempting to break through the boundaries of Jewish exclusivism to examine the desperate situation of all humanity (Thompson). Instead, his position represents the inevitable collapse of Jewish covenantalism when the foundation upon which it was established (the mercy of God) is removed.

Lastly, it should be noted that many of Uriel's statements concerning obedience to the law approximate similar statements made elsewhere in Jewish scripture and in the literature of Early Judaism. Nonetheless, Uriel's pronouncements on this issue are made in a different theological context or system of thought than most of those which they parallel. Uriel removes obedience to the law from its traditional context, so that it no longer symbolizes the response to God's love by one who has already experienced grace within the covenant community. Instead, for Uriel, obedience to the law is initiated by the individual whose interest is to secure God's eschatological favour through his own efforts. Thus, Uriel replaces Ezra's 'reacting nomism' with his own 'acting legalism'[2] or 'individualistic legalism', thereby removing the law from the context of God's covenant mercy.

---

1. 1984a: 162.
2. To use R.N. Longenecker's terminology (1964: 78).

Chapter 6

Episode IV

As this Episode (IV) commences, it has the appearance of yet another dialogue between Ezra and Uriel. As it progresses, however, the dialogue format disappears and is replaced by the first in the series of visions. With this vision, Ezra enjoys the first increment of satisfactory assurance concerning God's ways. Accordingly, IV is something of a transitional episode, initially taking its cues from the debates of I–III while going beyond them. It will be analysed according to the following outline:

1. The occasion of Ezra's reflection (9.26-28)
2. Ezra blames the people and honours the law (9.29-37)
3. Ezra affirms God's justice, despite his sorrow (9.38–10.24)
4. A vision of the heavenly city, and Ezra's distress (10.25-37)
5. The interpretation of the vision (10.38-60)

6.1. *Analysis of Episode IV*

6.1.1. *The occasion of Ezra's reflection (9.26-28)*. As Uriel had commanded, Ezra went into a field and 'ate the plants of the field'. Another seven days passed while he remained in this condition, after which his heart 'was troubled as it was before', prompting his words to God.

The mention of Ezra's diet seems significant. D.S. Russell notes that divine revelation 'is sometimes associated with a special food or diet'.[1] The change in his diet from fasting (5.13, 20; 6.31, 35) to eating flowers of the field (9.24, 26) would seem to signal that the events of this episode will take on a different character from those of the previous three dialogues. This will be confirmed as the episode progresses. The change of location—from Ezra's room to the open field—serves

---

1. Russell, 1967: 226.

the same function. Nonetheless, at present Ezra's heart remains troubled, as it was at the beginning of each episode heretofore (3.1-3; 5.21; 6.36).

6.1.2. *Ezra blames the people and honours the law (9.29-37).* In his opening words of IV, Ezra begins by recounting God's appearance to Israel's forefathers and his giving of the law to Israel in order to glorify them. Ezra's historical review in 9.29-31 in many ways parallels his historical review of 3.16-19. The similarities between these pasages are so apparent that the two could easily be interchanged without interrupting the flow of Ezra's words on either occasion. Thus, one wonders whether Ezra is back where he began. Has nothing which transpired in I–III had any effect upon him? Is IV to be yet another sustained dialogue between two ill-matched rhetoricians?

The answer is given immediately as Ezra continues in 9.32-37. There, the problem is cited: the people failed to keep the law. In 3.20-27, this problem functioned in precisely the same way: the people's failure to keep the law has frustrated the salvific potential of the law. Nonetheless, something radically new appears in Ezra's words of IV which contradicts his point in I. In 3.20-36, Ezra argued that, in fact, God is to blame for the inefficiency of the law. In 9.32-37, however, the point is made repeatedly that the failure of the law's potential is due solely to the people's disobedience, and there is no recourse to blame God. The responsibility falls directly upon the sinner; 'complaint has vanished and the blame is shifted. Now it is man who simply must perish because he sins.'[1]

In 9.34-37, Ezra illustrates his point. There, he gives a general rule which is learned from experience and evident in nature. A container is not spoiled when its contents spoil. Although this is 'the rule',

> yet with us it has not been so. For we who have received the Law and sinned
> will perish, as well as our heart which received it; the Law, however, does
> not perish but remains in its glory (9.36-37).

Is this another complaint against God? Is Ezra indicating that God has broken a general rule to Israel's detriment?[2] Or, conversely, is Ezra simply stating the fact that, although the rule involved in Israel's case

---

1. Thompson, 1977: 125.
2. As Knibb thinks (1979: 221). Cf. Collins, 1984a: 164.

is contrary to the general principle observable in nature, it is nonetheless applicable in this instance?[1]

It would seem that the latter is more appropriate. Ezra's initial complaints have never been subtle. He has always confronted God directly, calling on him to take account of his ways. But nothing of the sort appears here, thereby suggesting that Ezra's words in 9.34-37 should not be considered as a somewhat vague indictment of God.[2] Ezra is stating a general principle learned from nature and experience: the container is greater than that which it contains. Yet this principle cannot be applied to the people (the container) and the law (that which is contained). The law does not conform to the general categories of life for, in fact, it is God's law (9.31-32), and, unlike the people themselves, it is imperishable and glorious (9.32, 37). As G.H. Box says, Ezra is making a contrast

> between what belongs to the corruptible present Age and that which belongs to the eternal order. The Law belongs to the latter; it has been sown in the corruptible vessel of the human heart of Israel, which perishes.[3]

Accordingly, the law cannot be held within the confines of human judgment and principles abstracted from ordinary human existence.

This, of course, is reminiscent of Uriel's point (in response to Ezra's initial speeches of I and II) that God's ways transcend the limits of human reckoning (4.1-21; 5.31-40). On Ezra's lips, this point is completely unprecedented, and involves a change in priorities on his part. Throughout I–III, Ezra plead for the people of Israel and for humanity (the container), but nowhere was he concerned to affirm the honour of the law at their expense. Here, however, he acknowledges the glory of the law at the expense of the people; the latter are subordinate to the former. This has been Uriel's point throughout the dialogues, as is most evident in his words of 7.20: 'Let the many perish who are now living, rather than that the law of God which is set

---

1. As Myers thinks (1974: 277).

2. The argument that the indictment against God is *implied* (cf. Harrelson, 1980: 28-29) runs against the structural grain of *4 Ezra*; if Ezra has *not* undergone a transformation at this stage, one expects an *explicit* opening indictment against God, as in I, II and III. Only if Ezra has been transformed, as we will argue, can his opening statement be an explicit indictment (as in I, II and III), but the target of the indictment has changed with his transformation. That is, it is no longer God but the people who are charged, and charged explicitly.

3. 1912: 214. Box appropriately labels this section 'The Abiding Glory of the Law, and Israel: A Contrast'.

before them be disregarded'. As such, Ezra's illustration in 9.34-37 does not constitute a subtle complaint against God. Instead, it amounts to nothing other than an implicit affirmation that the ways of God are just. Although Ezra has admitted that he is troubled by his people's condition, he nonetheless accepts that all is in order and that God is above reproach since the people themselves are to blame. As A.L. Thompson well writes:

> Israel has neither kept the law nor observed God's statutes (9:32, cf. 9:36). Presumably, Israel deserves to perish. There is no mention of the evil root or of any other element which might implicate God in Israel's disobedience and resultant demise.[1]

Ezra's opening statement of IV, therefore, is somewhat shocking in view of the three previous speeches which initiate the dialogues in I–III. Episode IV begins, as did the three previous sections, with the statement that Ezra's heart is troubled. But in I–III, because of his troubled heart, Ezra lodges an explicit complaint before God, demanding an explanation or stating that things should be otherwise. The pattern has been established that, whenever Ezra initiates a new dialogue, he begins with a covenantally motivated appeal to God on behalf of Israel. In IV, however, no such appeal appears. Instead, Ezra simply reflects on the situation without appeal to a solution or an explanation from God; those who do not keep the law will perish. He has no expectation that things might be changed.

Evidently, then, during the seven-day interval between III and IV, Ezra has resigned himself (offstage) to Uriel's insistence that there can be no recourse to divine grace, except for the fact that God has given the law to Israel. Ezra is still troubled, but appears to have accepted that the situation is as Uriel described it. At the conclusion of III, Ezra was unconvinced by Uriel's argument. His perspective may have expanded in III beyond a nationalistic to a universalistic scope, but his line of argument remained consistent: salvation cannot come except by God's grace. Here in IV, however, Ezra has relinquished his own case, has assented to Uriel's, and does not plead for God's mercy.[2] Despite the significant events of Israel's history, Ezra does not argue, as he

---

1. Thompson, 1977: 219; cf. 125, 218, 258. See also Rowland, 1982: 130; Harnisch, 1969: 173; *idem*, 1981: 96; *idem*, 1983: 478; Willett, 1989: 71, 143 n. 75.
2. Cf. Harnisch: 'Der Appell an die göttliche Gnade ist aussichtslos. Das unheilvolles Geschick, das den Sündern am Ende dieses Äons widerfährt, ist die zwangsläufige Konsequenz ihres geschichtlichen Verhaltens' (1969: 174).

had previously, that the honour of their forefathers or the giving of the law should enable Israel to have special consideration. Moreover, not only are Ezra's words in IV unlike his words in I–III, they could easily have been expressed by Uriel at many places throughout the previous dialogues. Ezra's words in 9.36-37 are almost identical to those of Uriel in 7.20, and his speech parallels Uriel's in 7.20-25, 70-74 and 127-31.[1] If those whose hopes rested with Ezra were to know of this metamorphosis, they could not help but feel disheartened. Not only has Ezra made no progress on their behalf in the dialogues with Uriel, he now appears to have forsaken his task altogether by conceding Uriel's position.

6.1.3. *Ezra affirms God's justice, despite his sorrow (9.38–10.24).*

After his opening speech, Ezra encounters a woman who is mourning for her deceased son. She tells him that although she had been barren, she sought out God, who pitied her condition and gave her a son. In return, she gave God glory. On the day of the son's wedding, however, he died. Consequently, the woman mourns and longs to die herself (9.38–10.4).

Although the woman in this vision will later be transformed into a heavenly city (10.25-27) and plays a symbolic role in Uriel's interpretation (10.38-55), at this point she functions in a different role. In the descriptions of the mourning woman, there is a striking resemblance between her condition and that of Ezra in I–III: she is 'mourning and weeping with a loud voice', 'deeply grieved at heart' (9.38), 'embittered in spirit and deeply afflicted' (9.41); although she previously sought out God and gave him great glory for his graciousness (9.44-45), she now refuses to be consoled; although others had tried to soothe her troubled heart (10.2-3), she would not be comforted; instead, she intends to 'neither eat nor drink, but without ceasing mourn and fast until I die' (10.4).

So Ezra, too, has repeatedly announced the fact of his troubled heart (3.1; 5.34; 6.36; 9.27), his distress (6.37), his agitation (3.3) and his grief (5.21, 34). In the light of the destruction of Jerusalem and God's apparent betrayal of his people, Ezra, like the woman, could give no

---

1. Cf. Harnisch: 'Was der Seher 9,29-37 im Stil der Klage vorträgt, steht sachlich durchaus im Einklang mit der Position, die der Offenbarungsengel ihm gegenüber zur Geltung bringt. . . Wenn er nun zu Beginn der 4. Vision konzediert, dass niemand schuldlos ins Verderben geht, so ist offenbar auch dies eine Folge der Belehrungen des Engels' (1969: 173).

glory to God and found no comfort or consolation in Uriel's explanations of God's ways; just as the woman now fasts, so too did Ezra in I–
III. Although the woman is fasting since she would prefer to die, her
fast symbolizes her single-mindedness with regard to the issue which
torments her. Without relief from her troubles, there is no reason to
carry on with life. This sounds much like Ezra's great lament over
humanity in 7.116-26, where his point is made repeatedly, What good
is it to live? He voices exactly the same attitude on at least two other
occasions as well. On the first occasion, Ezra cries out: 'It would be
better that we had never come into existence than to come and live in
ungodliness, and to suffer and not understand why we suffer' (4.12).[1]
The second occurs, like the first, immediately after Ezra is told that he
cannot comprehend the ways of God. He complains: 'Why then was I
born? Or why did not my mother's womb become my grave, that I
might not see the travail of Jacob and the exhaustion of the people of
Israel?' (5.35). With a few substitutions of terms, what Ezra mouths in
these two passages could easily have been recited by the woman in her
initial condition depicted in Episode IV.

How then is Ezra portrayed in this episode? We have already seen
from 9.29-37 that he is no longer the man he was in I–III. So, as A.P.
Hayman says, 9.29-37, 'in the mouth of Ezra, represents the view
elsewhere expressed by the angel'.[2] The same characterization holds
true in 9.38–10.24. Whereas the woman in this section assumes the
position held by Ezra in I–III, Ezra now takes the place held there by
Uriel. The two injunctions at the end of Ezra's two speeches of rebuke
(10.6-17, 19-24) illustrate this again. In the first instance, Ezra
instructs the woman:

> Now, therefore, keep your sorrow to yourself, and bear bravely the troubles
> that have come upon you. For if you acknowledge the decree of God to be
> just, you will receive your son back in due time and be praised among women
> (10.15-16).[3]

In the second instance, Ezra exhorts the woman in this way:

---

1. The translation is mine. Metzger's translation of 4.12a ('It would be better for
us not to be here [namely in exile]') loses the point, which most think the Ethiopic
text rightly embodies when it speaks of being 'created' or 'born'. See, for instance,
Oesterley, 1933: 33.

2. 1975: 51.

3. The final phrase has been omitted from Metzger, 1983.

> Therefore shake off your great sadness and lay aside your many sorrows, so
> that the Mighty One may be merciful to you again, and the Most High may
> give you rest, a relief from your troubles (10.24).

What Ezra means in 10.16 by 'you will receive your son back in due
time' is best understood as an affirmation that she will find the consolation which eludes her. He does not expect a return of the dead, but a
return of her emotional health, as 10.24 confirms with its promise
only of 'relief from your troubles'. The road to recovery, says Ezra,
involves bearing bravely the sorrow which had caused her to glorify
God no longer. Evidently, as 10.16 implies, her troubled heart had
undermined her confidence in God's justice. In I–III, Ezra has already
exhibited the same attitude as the woman of IV. And in response to
him, Uriel portrayed the future age as the proof of God's justice.
Uriel could give the assurance that Ezra's distress will be relieved
only by looking to the future age since he was convinced that God's
justice will be exhibited in the events of that age.[1] The connection,
therefore, between affirming God's justice and enjoying relief from
distress is obvious in Uriel's case in I–III, just as it is in Ezra's assurance to the woman.

It has been suggested that the mourning woman and the reassuring
Ezra of IV parody the mourning Ezra and the reassuring Uriel of I–
III,[2] thereby capturing in narrative drama the fact of Ezra's conversion to Uriel's perspective, as was illustrated in 9.29-37. Three other
characteristics of 9.38–10.24 would seem to support this conclusion.
First, the manner in which Ezra rebukes the woman should be
observed. When he contrasts the woman's loss of her son with Zion's
tragedy and with the destruction of the multitude (10.6-14), in spite of
his lament there is no sense here that Ezra is pleading for the case of
Israel or of humanity. Instead, he is simply putting the woman's
mourning into a broader perspective. In a way similar to Uriel's case
in I–III, Ezra states that the woman's focus is too limited, and he
attempts to expand the horizons of her vision. His words function
along the same lines as Uriel's claim that Ezra's perception in I–III
was out of focus.[3] Second, Ezra seems aware that his response fails to
penetrate to the level of the woman's sorrow, as evidenced by his

---

1. Cf. 4.26; 5.40; 5.56–6.6; 6.25-28; 33-34; 7.15-16; etc.
2. Cf. Brandenburger, 1981: 75; Harnisch, 1983: 478-79; Knowles, 1989: 271-
72.
3. Cf. Collins, 1984a: 165.

words in 10.12-14.[1] After stating that the earth (which has lost a
multitude of offspring) has more to grieve over than the woman (who
has lost only one son), Ezra recognizes that she will not accept his
argument as valid, since the real issue cannot be reduced to numerical
comparisons. She will say that her one son is more precious to her
than the multitude is to the earth (cf. 7.54-58). In reply to this possible
objection, Ezra simply states that this is not true. Third, the woman's
response to Ezra is the same as that of Ezra to Uriel in I–III. After
Ezra's first speech to her, the woman defiantly ignores Ezra's assurances and refuses to see things his way, just as Ezra's last statement of
III began 'I said it before, and I say now, and will say it again' (9.15;
cf. 7.45, 116). Ezra's case has been as unpersuasive for the woman as
Uriel's was for Ezra in I–III. These three points support the view that
Ezra, from the beginning of IV, has been transformed and now stands
in the position held by Uriel in I–III.

Moreover, this encounter scene introduces a distinction between
proper and improper modes of mourning and grief. Before his opening speech of IV, Ezra admits his troubled heart, but he goes on to
affirm in 9.29-37 that it is proper for the sinners to be destroyed
because of their disobedience to God's law. Although he is disturbed,
he does nothing to doubt God's justice. Similarly, in 10.6-24, where
Ezra portrays the woman's loss as insignificant when compared to the
loss of Zion (10.6-8) or to the loss of 'almost all' who go to perdition
(10.8-15), Ezra's sorrow for Israel and humanity is evident, but he
does not allow his remorse to degenerate into an accusation against
God, as he had in I–III.[2] Whereas Ezra insisted in 4.12 that suffering
is unbearable when there is no understanding of God's ways, now he
understands God's ways and is able to bear his sorrow and be comforted. In contrast, however, the woman's mourning stifles her ability
to affirm that God is just. It is only because her grief has undermined
her confidence in God that Ezra rebukes her. There is nothing wrong
with mourning itself, as he himself states (9.27; 10.8). In fact, in
10.39 (cf. 10.50) we hear that God looks favourably upon Ezra precisely because he has 'sorrowed continually' for Israel, and 'mourned
greatly over Zion'. Grief is acceptable when it does not trespass the
certainty of God's righteousness.

---

1. Cf. Myers, 1974: 278.
2. Cf. Knibb: 'It is important to observe. . . that despite his continued grief, Ezra
no longer blames God for these events (contrast 3:28-36)' (1979: 226).

Before moving beyond this section, it is important to explain the significance of Ezra's statements in 9.39 and 10.5. When he first encountered the distraught woman, Ezra said: 'Then I dismissed the thoughts with which I had been engaged' (9.39). After she explains her sorrow, Ezra makes the same point: 'Then I broke off the reflections with which I was still engaged' (10.5). These transitional indicators do more than signal a thematic change. They signal a significant development in Ezra's character and perspective. As we have seen in 9.29-37, Ezra, despite his troubled heart, accepted that Israel's sinfulness necessitated their destruction. The reader is prepared to hear from him a complaint concerning God's ways, or an appeal to God's mercy on their behalf, as has been his practice in his opening speeches of I–III. Ezra has consistently cited a problem and held God responsible for solving it by means of his mercy. Since no such appeal to God's intervention appears in 9.29-37, the implication is clear: God's ways are above reproach, for things are as they should be. When Ezra says that he has dismissed his thoughts with which he had been engaged (9.39), he is making his point explicitly by announcing that he has ended his words to the Most High (9.29-37). In them, contrary to the precedent he has set, no complaint or appeal appears.[1] And none is to follow. Ezra has spoken his mind in 9.29-37, and there is nothing more to come; sinners perish in order that the law might retain its glory. He sees no reason to amend this situation.

The same motivation lies behind the second occurrence of this phrase in 10.5 ('Then I broke off the reflections with which I was still engaged'). After hearing the whole of the woman's case (which imitates his own in I–III), Ezra stands firm in his resolve that complaints and appeals are inappropriate. Rather than empathizing with the distraught woman, as he might have done in I–III, Ezra does not waver from his new-found acceptance of God's ways. He fails to petition God on her behalf or to join in her resentment. Instead, he answers her 'in anger', and instructs her to affirm God's justice. Once again, then, Ezra's position is clear: no appeals to God are appropriate. There is no complaint to follow his opening speech and, unlike the woman, Ezra has resolved that God's ways are not to be questioned.

---

1. Cf. Thompson: 'On the analogy of the previous episodes, this would be the place for the lament and complaint, but here, Ezra dismisses his thoughts' (1977: 220-21).

In effect, then, when he states that he has dismissed the thoughts that had engaged him, Ezra is affirming that he will entertain no indictment of God. What he has dismissed are the complaints against God and appeals for change which constitute the main thrust of his opening statements in I–III.

Throughout 9.38–10.24, therefore, one witnesses an Ezra radically different from the Ezra of I–III. Whereas two positions were defined in I–III, the one he advocated there is the one he abandons in IV. The Ezra of IV has accepted the general outline of Uriel's position (9.26-37), has put aside his indictments of God (9.39; 10.5) and now preaches what he had not allowed himself to affirm: that God's ways are just. He assures the woman that, if she too will affirm this, God will be merciful to her and she will be comforted. Here the patient has become the doctor, and the medicine he prescribes is that which he himself had earlier refused. And by his own prescription, because he now recognizes that God is just, so can he now expect to be consoled.

6.1.4. *A vision of the heavenly city, and Ezra's distress (10.25-37).* As soon as Ezra instructed the woman to put aside her sorrow, to his amazement, her face shone and 'flashed like lightning' (10.25). At this, Ezra was frightened ('my heart was terrified') and he did not understand what had happened. Then the woman gave a 'loud and fearful cry' (10.26) and was transformed into a great city, 'a place of huge foundations' (10.27). Ezra, again afraid, cries out with a loud voice:

> Where is the angel Uriel, who came to me at first? For it was he who brought me into this overpowering bewilderment; my intention has been destroyed [or 'come to nothing'] and my plea has become shame (10.28).[1]

Throughout 10.29-37, Ezra continues in this frame of mind. He blames Uriel for his condition (10.28, 32), begs him not to forsake

---

1. The last two phrases (28c, 28d) are my translation. Two points need mention concerning 10.28c. First, *finis/ḥrt'* is taken to mean not so much 'end' (cf. Metzger) as 'purpose', 'goal', 'aim', 'intention'. So it is translated by Gunkel as 'Absicht' (1900: 388). Second, whereas the Latin reads *factus est. . . in corruptionem*, the Syriac reads *hwt. . .lhbl* which, as will be seen, captures Ezra's sense well when read as 'became ruin' (cf. חבל, 'destruction', 'annihilation', Mic. 2.10; Job 21.17; הבל, 'void', Jer. 10.3, 15; Eccl. 1.2; 6.12; Job 27.12; 35.16). Despite various proposals for textual emendation, the point seems to be simply that Ezra's intentions have been frustrated. Concerning 10.28d, the Syriac *hsd'* has the sense of 'shame' or 'disappointment', which well suits the context, as we will see.

him (10.34) and asks for an explanation of what he does not understand (10.32, 35-37).

This characterization of Ezra is intriguing, and is marked by dramatic irony. He has been proclaiming that, by affirming God's justice, one will find relief from sorrow. Ezra has already affirmed God's justice in this episode; what is still to come, then, is his consolation. But instead of being consoled, Ezra sees a vision which he cannot comprehend and which frightens and troubles him more than ever. Despite all his complaints of I–III, Ezra has taken the only option open to him and appropriated Uriel's understanding of God's ways in order to find comfort. Nonetheless, he feels himself to have been abandoned by Uriel.

Ezra's play on words highlights this point. Whereas he earlier claimed to have 'forsaken' (Lat. *dereliqui*; Syr. *šbqt*) his attitude of complaint against God (10.5; cf. the Syriac of 9.39) and then proceeded to affirm God's justice in order that he might find relief from his sorrow, he now finds himself even more upset than previously and thinks, therefore, that Uriel has 'forsaken' him (Lat. *dereliquisti me*; Syr. *šbqtny*; 10.32; cf. 10.34). He believes that he has been made the fool, feeling that the joke is on him. For this reason he cries out, 'my intention has been destroyed [or 'come to nothing'] and my plea has become shame' (10.28). Understandably, therefore, he blames Uriel for his present distress, for when he conceded Uriel's position he did not expect to experience further frustration, but reward through consolation. What he fails to realize, however, is that the vision which now troubles him greatly is, in fact, the first step in the process whereby he finds his consolation, as will become apparent to him from the interpretation to follow (10.38-60).

This irony has been noted by many scholars who recognize that what Ezra had hoped for was granted to him in the vision, although he failed to understand the significance of that vision.[1] Yet what it was that Ezra eagerly expected has often been misunderstood. Several scholars have found in Ezra's words of 9.29-37 an expectation that, despite Israel's present destruction, the people of Israel will nevertheless enjoy a eschatological salvation. For instance, Box considers Ezra's point of 9.29-37 to be that

---

1. Cf. Gunkel, 1900: 388-89; Box, 1912: 232; Oesterley, 1933: 124; Knibb, 1979: 230.

after the body and heart have perished—belonging as they do to the present corruptible order—the result of the acceptance of the Law by Israel will be realised in a blessed immortality in the incorruptible world—and this, in spite of the shortcomings of the fathers, and the failure of the chosen people to live up to the divine command.[1]

None of this is evident from the text, however, and Box's view necessitates some degree of imagination. Instead, in 9.29-37 Ezra simply juxtaposed the sinners and the law, attributing destruction to the former without recourse to any future correction to this situation. Accordingly, Ezra's frustration is not due to the fact that the vision in 10.25-28 gives him no assurance of Israel's future glorification, for surely he expected nothing of the sort. Instead, what he expected was relief from his troubled heart, in return for his acceptance of Uriel's perspective. A heart free from distress would be the proof he needed to consolidate the fact that his acceptance of Uriel's position was appropriate to comprehend God's ways. But his augmented bewilderment and fear suggests to him that his new-found understanding has failed him. Accordingly, he pleads with Uriel to explain how this vision *confirms* his new demeanour, lest he should die. Uriel obliges him in the interpretation which follows.

6.1.5. The interpretation of the vision (10.38-60).[2] In his role as angelic interpreter of the visions, Uriel is no longer Ezra's dialogical opponent, as in I–III, but now functions as Ezra's partner, an ally who lends assistance to Ezra's quest.[3] Accordingly, he interprets the vision so that Ezra, who has constantly mourned over Zion (10.39, 50), now can understand and be comforted. It comes as no surprise, then, when Uriel concludes his interpretation with the words, 'Therefore do not be afraid, and do not let your heart be terrified' (10.55).

Not all the details of what Ezra has seen are explained in the interpretation,[4] but the basic point is this: the woman represents the heav-

---

1. 1912: 214.
2. 10.38-59 in Metzger, 1983.
3. Cf. Harnisch, 1983: 468; Brandenburger, 1981: 68. This change of roles is not surprising in view of the fact that Ezra stands in the place held by Uriel in I–III.
4. Because the interpretation does not fit all the points of the vision (for details, see Knibb, 1979: 226; Oesterley, 1933: 115-16), most scholars suspect that the author is drawing upon a traditional folk-tale (cf. Tob. 6–8). This hypothesis also explains the fact that Jerusalem is represented in 9.38–10.24 as a son, whereas it is usually depicted as a daughter or woman.

enly Jerusalem who is mourning for the destruction of Jerusalem, but who herself remains great and splendid (10.38-59). Ezra is shown 'the brightness of her glory, and the loveliness of her beauty' (10.50), and is commanded to go into the city 'and see the splendor and vastness' (10.55). (Notice that the temple is unmentioned in this vision of the eschatological Jerusalem.) In the process, Uriel expects Ezra to leave behind his troubled heart.

It should be pointed out that twice in III Uriel has spoken of this great city (7.26; 8.52). In each case, this heavenly city is a benefit to be enjoyed in the age to come by the righteous few who are faithful to the law. Here then is the first confirmation of Uriel's descriptions in I–III of the age to come; the heavenly Zion is in existence now and will be revealed to those who are deserving in the age to come.[1] It serves as proof that Ezra was right to exchange his own perception for Uriel's. Whereas comfort eluded him while he held to the former, now that the substitution of the latter has taken place he is shown a vision and finds in its interpretation the satisfaction that he desired.[2] His conversion is not mocked, as Ezra initially thought, but is honoured; that a glorious Zion has been preserved serves both to give Ezra comfort and hope, and to certify that he was right to accept Uriel's understanding as his own.

The two visions that follow (V, VI) also confirm Uriel's views of I–III, while expanding upon what Ezra has already seen. Thus, Uriel concludes: 'tomorrow night you shall remain here, and the Most High will show you in those dream visions what the Most High will do to those who dwell on earth in the last days' (10.59). That is, the next two visions will reinforce Ezra's eschatological perspective by describing how God deals with humanity in the last days.

6.2. *Summary of Episode IV*

Episode IV has been shown to represent the dramatic turning point in Ezra's pilgrimage. The comfort that eluded him in I–III has now been awarded to him. The prerequisite of this comfort and hope was twofold. First, Ezra surrendered his complaint against God and his appeals to God's mercy. The reader has come to expect these at the

---

1. Willett's comment is very peculiar: 'Section IV introduces the heavenly Jerusalem, but its mention is not concerned with eschatological thought' (1989: 74).

2. Cf. Brandenburger: 'Erst muß die Wandlung Esras sich vollziehen, bevor das Offenbarungsgeschehen voranschreiten kann' (1981: 87).

beginning of each episode, and their absence here cannot be overstated in importance. Second, although he was still disturbed, he put his concerns behind him and, accepting Uriel's description of God's ways, acknowledged God's decree to be just. As a result, comfort and hope are his recompense, and his new perspective is affirmed.[1]

It must be noted that there is nothing in this episode which assures Ezra of Israel's eschatological salvation. Ezra finds comfort from the vision not because he sees in it the depiction of God's future vindication of Israel, but solely because it consolidates his new understanding, thereby proving God's justice and giving him hope. In I–III, Ezra sought understanding in order to dispel his misery (cf. 4.12); Uriel insisted that true understanding could be gained by dropping his covenantal perspective and adhering to an eschatological perspective in which the individual is stripped of all allegiances and judged according to personal merit without recourse to divine mercy. After Ezra's conversion in IV, the vision in the latter half of that episode provides the eschatological verification that he was right to accept Uriel's description of God's ways. This vision is the first of three which lead him out of his misery (perpetrated by his previous understanding) to praise and glorify God (13.57). Ezra's conversion is evidenced in 9.29–10.24, and the confirmation of the validity of his new perspective is granted in 10.25-60. Confirmation of the same sort continues in the next two episodes.

---

1. It is not enough, then, to say simply that in IV 'Ezra becomes cautiously optimistic' (Levison, 1988: 113). The real issue is *why* Ezra's demeanour is transformed in IV; the answer lies in his change of perspective.

Chapter 7

EPISODE V

In this Episode (V), Ezra is given further evidence to consolidate his new understanding. What began with the vision of IV is expanded upon here. This episode will be analysed according to the following outline:

1. The eagle vision (11.1–12.3a)
2. Ezra pleads for an explanation (12.3b-9)
3. The interpretation of the vision: a remnant will be saved (12.10-34)
4. A distinction between the worthy few and the collective people (12.35-51)

7.1. *Analysis of Episode V*

7.1.1. The eagle vision (11.1–12.3a). As V begins, Ezra is shown a vision of an eagle rising up from the sea (cf. Dan. 7.3) with three heads and twelve wings. The imagery is detailed and need not detain us. In brief, the eagle is said to have an oppressive reign which engulfs the whole world. At the end of the age, however, a lion arises and roars accusations at the eagle. He announces that 'the Most High has looked upon his times, and behold, they are ended, and his ages are completed' (11.44). Meanwhile, the last of the eagle's heads and wings disappear and its body is burned.

For our purposes, two things should be noted. First, it is readily apparent that the eschatological expectations present in this vision do not square perfectly with the eschatological expectations found elsewhere in *4 Ezra*. In particular, both the problem and the solution seem to be cast wholly in political terms.[1] Scholars usually attribute this to

---

1. Moreover, here the messiah figure actively campaigns against the political oppressors, whereas his appearance in 7.28 is wholly passive.

the fact that the author seems to be drawing upon an already established tradition. Apparently, the author found at his disposal a contemporary symbolic tale about an eagle (Rome) and its demise which is brought about by a great lion (the Messiah of Israel). G.H. Box says of the author of this tradition:

> [He] is no cosmopolitan philosopher, but. . . a Jewish particularist. The unit of his conception is not the individual man, but the people, the nation; it is the divinely chosen nation of Israel that is confronted by the panoplied wickedness and godlessness of imperial Rome.[1]

While the extremes of Box's source-critical research are to be avoided, his source-critical sensitivities allow him to make a good point here. The vision is marked by a national particularism, and the hope of a political salvation is held out for the oppressed nation of Israel, whose political (Davidic) Messiah destroys the evil empire. These nationalistic expectations are not what we have come to expect to hear within *4 Ezra*, and the distinctiveness of the tradition easily shows through the pages.

Second, and more importantly, it must be asked how the author used this tradition, which seems so unrepresentative of his thought. What did he do with it, and where did he leave his own impression on the tradition? All too often, in analyses of *4 Ezra,* this issue has been left largely unprobed and, accordingly, the author's purposes have gone unrecognized. In our estimation, the author wants to give little import to the vision itself. In fact, in the interpretation which follows, he edits it significantly to suit his overall project. Thus, the author's position must be extracted not from the details of the nationalistic vision but from the interpretation that he gives to the vision (or better, the point within the interpretation where his reworking is evident).[2] Where

---

1. 1912: 246.
2. Stone argues that the author is himself the creator of the vision and its interpretation in V (1968; 1989: 118-19). Better, however, is Collins's apparent rebuttal of Stone on this point. Collins notes that both the eagle vision of V and the man from the sea vision of VI are indebted to the vision of Dan. 7. Accordingly, 'we should expect that the author would have combined them in a single vision if he were working *de novo*'. It would seem, therefore, that in both visions 'the author is working with traditional material, for which he has supplied new interpretations' (1984a: 166). For Danielic dependency in episodes V and VI, see Lacocque, 1981; Kee, 1981; and esp. Beale, 1984: 112-39. Contrary to Stone's position, Harnisch postulates that V and VI are not integral to the original form of *4 Ezra* (1983). For criti-

there are differences or incongruities between the two, it is the interpretation of the vision, not the vision itself, which should inform our
understanding of the author's purpose.

7.1.2. *Ezra pleads for an explanation (12.3b-9)*. At the sight of this
vision, Ezra awakes 'terrified' (12.5) and 'in great perplexity of mind
and great fear' (12.3b; cf. 12.5). As in IV, so here the vision does not
immediately bring about the comfort for which he had hoped. He
blames his own spirit for his condition because, in its inquisitive manner, it 'searched out the ways of the Most High' (12.4). Because he is
afraid, he calls upon God to show him 'the interpretation and meaning
of this terrifying vision, that you might comfort my soul' (12.8). Evidently he has learned from his experiences of the previous night that
comfort will be granted him by means of divine explanation. As such,
the vision's import remains ambiguous until the interpretation which
follows. It is the interpretation that the author wants his readers to
hear and understand, just as Ezra now longs for it himself.

7.1.3. *The interpretation of the vision: a remnant will be saved
(12.10-34)*. The explanation is complicated and not easily understand-
able.[1] It is quite possible, in fact, that the interpretation (itself largely
traditional) has been updated on occasion in order to renew the
significance of the original vision.[2] In its present state, the interpretation is permeated with allusions to the political rule of Rome's successive leaders (12.10-30). The lion is identified as the Messiah (cf. Rev.
5.5) of the tribe of David who will destroy the evil reign of the eagle
(12.31-33), and save a remnant of God's people (12.34).

This last feature of the interpretation (the fact that a remnant will be
saved) is most significant for two reasons: (1) it is both extraneous to
the vision itself, and (2) it has precedents earlier in *4 Ezra*. Concerning this first point, it is obvious that the tone of the vision itself was
vindictive: those who have put down Israel will themselves be put
down by Israel's representative. In the interpretation, this same politi-

cisms of his view, see Lebram, 1983: 199 n. 110. As we shall see, V and VI are of
central importance to the author of I–III.
    1. For a review of possible historical counterparts to each of the eagle's features,
see Myers, 1974: 299-302. But see the cautions by Gruenwald, 1979: 115; Box,
1912: 281; Torrey, 1945: 118-20.
    2. Cf. Torrey, 1945: 118-120; Box, 1912: 248. A similar phenomenon is evident
in Lk. 21 which reworks the earlier tradition of Mk 13; cf. Dunn, 1977: 346-47.

cal flavour is, to some extent, maintained. The Messiah, for instance, bring about the demise of Rome. Nonetheless, those whom he saves are not the nation Israel, but 'the remnant of my people' (12.34), which includes members of Israel, but (and here is the point) *not all of Israel are delivered.* It is precisely at this point that the author's reworking of the tradition is most apparent. The divine interpretation has introduced the concept of a remnant into what originally constituted a vision confident of the whole nation's future salvation. The tradition had Israel in its sight, whereas the divine interpretation discards the nation for 'the remnant of my people' (Lat. *residuum populum meum*; Syr. *l'my dyn d'šthr*), those who have been saved 'throughout my borders' (Lat. *super fines meos*; Syr. *bthwmy*).

Concerning the second point, it is of utmost importance to recognize that, here again, it is Uriel's position of I–III that is being endorsed, for it was he who introduced into the dialogues the idea of a remnant who will be saved (6.25; 7.27-28; 9.7-8).[1] In 6.25, Uriel speaks of those who will survive the messianic woes (Lat. *omnis qui derelictus fuerit*; Syr. *kl m' dmšthr*) and who will see salvation and the end of the world because of their 'treasures of faithfulness' stored up in heaven (6.5). Similarly in 7.27-28, he mentions a group who will be delivered from the messianic woes and who remain (Lat. *qui relicti sunt*; Syr. *'ylyn d'šthrw*) to enjoy the 400-year reign of the Messiah. This group is contrasted with the many who disregard the law and who have no righteous deeds in their favour (cf. 7.19-25)—that is, they are the collection of the few individuals who have 'laboriously served the Most High, and withstood every danger every hour that they might keep the Law of the Lawgiver perfectly' (7.89). In 9.7-8, Uriel again speaks of those who will survive the messianic woes (Lat. *omnis qui salvus factus fuerit*; Syr. *kl mnw dnh'*). They constitute a group of individuals, each one having merited salvation on his own, 'on account of his works, or on account of the faithfulness in which he has put his trust' (9.7). That one will remain (Lat. *is relinquetur*; Syr. *hw nšthr*) to enjoy salvation 'within my borders' (Lat. *in finibus meis*; Syr. *bthwmy*).

---

1. The mention of God's mercy in 12.34 does not preclude this interpretation. Again, this is the eschatological 'grace' which Uriel pronounced in 9.21-22 in terms of God's great labour on behalf of the remnant. God is gracious to the remnant, the few who have earned his saving grace by their efforts and stored treasures of good works.

Thus, throughout II and III, there is a noticeable consistency in the author's handling of the concept of the remnant; it is applied to the group of individuals who have stringently kept the law and who have accrued works before God. There is little reason to think that anything different is meant by the same concept in V. When this evidence is used in conjunction with the first point (that the remnant idea is completely foreign to the vision) the obvious conclusion is that, specifically at 12.34, the author has left his own fingerprint on the tradition which had originally been used to encourage the collective people by assuring them of their future salvation. The divine interpretation of this traditional vision states that, although the evil empire will be crushed by the Messiah of Israel, the 'merciful' salvation he effects will be only for the few who have gained the eschatological favour of God by their strict adherence to the law. In this way, what was originally an apocalyptic vision concerning the vindication of the nation of Israel in the face of its enemies is turned to the service of the author's case for an individualistic legalism, apart from any ethnocentric context.[1] These unique individuals are cited collectively as 'the remnant of my people'. Within the confines of *4 Ezra* 'the remnant' represents the puny number of those who have merited salvation apart from ethnic consideration.

There is another point which combines with the two already mentioned in suggesting that the remnant theme is itself the *crux* of the author's interpretation of the eagle vision. Not only does this theme (1) fail to have a counterpart in the vision itself and (2) have strong parallels with the position advanced by Uriel throughout *4 Ezra*, it also is the final point of the interpretation. After this point is made, the divine interpretation breaks off. Only when this extraneous aspect has been incorporated into the interpretation is the divine explanation allowed to conclude. These three factors would suggest that the author's hand is most evident in the interpretation of the vision specifically at 12.34.

7.1.4. A distinction between the worthy few and the collective people (12.35-51). 4 Ezra 12.35-51 is an important passage for two reasons. First, in 12.36, Ezra is said to be the only one worthy to learn 'this

---

1. Contra Thompson: 'the interpretation continues this same [nationalistic] approach with some elaboration' (1977: 236). Cf. similar errors by Gruenwald (1979: 113) and Schoeps (1950: 157).

secret' of God. This is reminiscent of Ezra's words in 12.4 where he
recognized that these things had been shown to him specifically
because he has 'searched out the ways of the Most High'. Apparently,
then, Ezra's worthiness is due to the fact that he has converted his perspective in his quest to understand the ways of God. In the process, he
is considered to be unique in relation to the rest of the people, a distinction which will become progressively important in the remainder
of the book.

More important for the present discussion are the author's words in
12.37-39. Here again the concept of the remnant makes an appearance
of a different kind, for in these verses Uriel makes a distinction
between the few and the many *within Israel*. Ezra is commanded to
write what he has seen in a book and keep the book hidden, revealing
its teachings not to all the people but only to the wise who can understand them and keep them hidden (12.37-38). Only the few who are
wise are worthy, as was Ezra (12.37), to learn the secret ways of the
Most High. The collective people, however, are not able to understand, and so remain ignorant of God's secret ways.

The very next event which is narrated, however, is Ezra's encounter
with *all* the people of Israel (12.40). The technique employed by the
author is dramatic irony. Ezra is first instructed to reveal the secret
only to the wise, not to the whole nation (12.37-39), and then he finds
himself surrounded by all the people, who urge him not to forsake
their cause since he is their only representative (12.40-45). They all
voice, in strains reminiscent of those of Ezra in I–III and of the
woman in IV, the sentiment that, without hope, life itself is meaning-
less: 'If you forsake us, how much better it would have been for us if
we also had been consumed in the burning of Zion' (12.44). One
senses that the author intended to heighten the dramatic irony by such
qualitative descriptions as '*all* the people', 'they *all* gathered together',
'*from the least to the greatest*'. The effect of all this is to underline the
fact that Ezra's news, while encouraging to the few individuals within
Israel, is hardly positive for the majority of the nation. Now Ezra is
faced with a problem. There is comfort in knowing that Israel will be
avenged, but this translates into a salvific hope for only the very few.
The reader is drawn into the tension of the moment when all Israel
gathers around him to discover how the deliberations were proceeding. Ezra simply does as God has just commanded him to do—that is,
he does not reveal the secret of how things really are, but assures them
that God has them in remembrance. The same advice which was given

to the mourning woman of IV is given here to all Israel in their sorrow: 'Take courage, O Israel, and do not be sorrowful, O house of Jacob'. Ezra affirms that he has not failed Israel but is actively pursuing its interests:

> I have neither forsaken you nor withdrawn from you; but I have come to this place to pray on account of the desolation of Zion and to seek mercy on account of the humiliation of our sanctuary (12.48).

It must be admitted that what Ezra proclaims to the people is somewhat misleading. Ezra has long given up representing the concerns of the people of Israel, and he has long put aside arguments and pleas for mercy. In the process of his own development, such interests have been discarded. He has learned much and been shown the secrets of God which must be kept hidden from the masses—even the nation Israel—and which can be revealed only to the wise.[1] This theme will become of major importance in VII. Here in V, it makes its first appearance in dramatic fashion.

7.2. *Summary of Episode V*

At present, it is necessary to indicate how the interpretation advanced here differs from most. M. Knibb's interpretation is representative of many and will be used here to illustrate the important differences. Most fundamentally, Knibb fails to recognize the significance of the remnant theme, mentioned in 12.34. He identifies them simply as 'those who survive the woes which will occur at the end of this age'.[2] This is certainly correct, but it is not enough. For although Knibb notes the parallels with 6.25, 7.27-28 and 9.7-8, he fails to take account of the fact that in each instance the speaker is Uriel who argues *against* Ezra's nationalistic hope,[3] insisting instead that only a very few will be saved. Uriel has propagated a rigid legalistic individualism to counter Ezra's appeals to God's mercy and has used the concept of a remnant to identify the righteous few with one designation.

---

1. The subtlety of this section (12.35-50) is extremely important and has not had the recognition in *4 Ezra* scholarship which it deserves. Most scholars find here the occasion of Ezra's comforting the people (cf. Willett, 1989: 63, 72). But this is a far too simplistic understanding of the subtlety which the author creates by means of his distinction between the few who are wise and all the people.

2. 1979: 252.

3. Contra also Willett, who argues that Ezra's 'complaints are replaced by the confident assurances that God remembers his people' (1989: 72).

If there is a parallel in 12.34, the significance of Uriel's statements within the context of the debate must be taken into account, which Knibb fails to do.

Because of this error, others follow. Knibb misses the irony of Ezra's words to the people in 12.46-49, considering them to be a sober assurance to Israel that God has them in mind. This is possible, Knibb thinks, because Ezra has been satisfied in IV that Israel will experience an eschatological salvation.[1] But as we have seen, there is no reason to think that Ezra considered the vision of the heavenly Jerusalem in IV to imply the eschatological salvation of Israel. In fact, just the opposite is closer to the truth, for Ezra finds in it the confirmation of the position defended by Uriel in I–III. Moreover, although Ezra assures the people that God has them collectively in mind, he has learned privately in V that such is not the case, for, rather than the nation, only a remnant will be saved. Here again is confirmation of Uriel's position in I–III.[2] Therefore one cannot accept Ezra's words to the people as sincere.

This leads to another problem in Knibb's (and others') interpretation, this time relating to 12.36-38. Knibb explains these verses in this way:

> The command to write down an account of the vision and to hide it in a secret place is part of the apocalyptic technique; it is intended to explain how Ezra's revelation, which supposedly dated from the period of the exile, only became known at a much later date, i.e. at the end of the first century AD.[3]

Knibb thinks that the book to be concealed contains the interpretation of the end time events (an explanation which is shared by most commentators). But to identify the secret *merely* with the end time events is to miss the real point of the secrecy motif. Knibb is right to call the secrecy motif an 'apocalyptic technique', but this common technique has been utilized in *4 Ezra* for a purpose which Knibb's explanation misses, as will be shown from the following paragraph.

In 12.36-38, Uriel commanded Ezra to reveal the secrets only to the wise among the people who will understand them. As we have seen, it is this which prepares the stage for the encounter between Ezra and the whole people in 12.40-50. Uriel has already made a distinction between the many and the few within the nation Israel itself, and

---

1. 1979: 255. Cf. Buchanan, 1970: 30.
2. Properly, Collins, 1984a: 167; Rowland, 1982: 131, 168.
3. 1979: 253.

determined that the secret which Ezra has learned is to be restricted only to the few. Thus, when Ezra meets with 'all the people', he cannot reveal, under divine command, what he has learned. What, then, does he tell the people? That God has not forgotten them. But what has he learned in the vision? Something quite different: that only a remnant will be saved. There is, then, noticeable incongruity between Ezra's speech to the people and his real belief. What Ezra does not reveal to them are not mere details about the end times but, in fact, the knowledge that only a remnant will be saved. First and foremost, it is Ezra's new-found perspective, which strikes right at the heart of traditional Jewish covenantalism, that is consigned to secrecy, under divine orders. To bring this point out in full view, the author has the people ask, not about the events of the end times, but, ironically, about their own well-being before God.

Although the secrecy motif is a common technique in apocalyptic literature, its appearance in V is of great consequence. In 12.36-38, it represents the first serious attempt by the author to explain why the view first propagated by Uriel and now assented to by Ezra has little currency among the people. In VII, this motif appears again, and functions to explain why Ezra's new understanding has little grounding in the Jewish scriptures in which God's ways are depicted in completely different terms. These attempts at authentication will be analysed in more detail below. For now it is enough to note the significance of the secrecy motif for Episode V. Although the people carry on collectively under the impression that their covenantal expectations will be satisfied in time, the reader knows the 'inside story' and watches as Ezra, who was commanded by God to keep the inside story to himself and to the wise, shields the people from the truth that he has learned.[1] He assures them of his commitment, but the reader knows enough to realize that this is only lip service.[2] Such are the secret ways of the just God.

---

1. For similar dramatic technique, see Gen. 22.8, where Abraham assures Isaac that 'God will see to the lamb for himself'. Berlin makes the comment: '[t]he irony is great, for although Abraham speaks from his point of view and means one thing, the reader interprets it from a different point of view with a significance that is quite different. Actually the irony here is double. Abraham himself is being ironic, because he means the phrase one way but knows that Isaac will understand it another way' (1983: 52). The parallels with *4 Ezra* 12 are almost exact.

2. Sayler notes that Ezra's response is only superficial (1984: 132). Similarly, Thompson states that Ezra's reassurance that he is continuing to pray for Jerusalem

By way of summary, then, whereas IV began an upward turn in Ezra's progress, it is continued in V where a description is given of a messianic revenge on the culprit who destroyed Israel. But, unlike the traditional expectation, the divine interpretation of the vision does not give the assurance that all of Israel can rejoice in the hope of a future salvation, for only a remnant will be saved from among them. In the broader context of *4 Ezra*, this refers to the few spoken of by Uriel who, by their own means, have gained the privilege. It might be that what the author does in 12.34 is illustrative of his whole project—that is, he reworks a traditional nationalistic vision of the end times, sanitizing it of its ethnocentrism and utilizing it in support of his individualism, with its emphasis on merit by works.

Of equal significance is the first appearance of Ezra's new dilemma. He himself knows the mysteries of God's ways. He has long ago left behind his nationalistic perspective and has acquired a perspective shaded by individualism and legalism. His dilemma is that he is not permitted to reveal this truth to the people, who therefore remain in ignorance. Although he is both the spokesman *for* the people and *to* the people, he is no longer well suited for the former role, and is forbidden to reveal God's true ways in the latter role.

and for the temple has nothing to do with the author's argument but 'is simply a literary device to maintain the proper staging of the book as a spontaneous lament from the midst of the ruined city' (1977: 266).

Chapter 8

EPISODE VI

In this Episode (VI), Ezra receives further consolidation of his new perception of God and his ways, just as he had in IV and V. This episode will be analysed according to the following outline:

1. The vision of the man from the sea (13.1-13a)
2. Ezra pleads for an explanation (13.13b-20)
3. The interpretation of the vision: a remnant and a multitude will be saved (13.21-52)
4. Ezra is commended for forsaking his ways (13.53-58)

8.1. *Analysis of Episode VI*

8.1.1. *The vision of the man from the sea (13.1-13a)*. After a seven-day interlude, Ezra experiences another vision. This time, he sees 'the figure of a man come up out of the heart of the sea' (13.3) and rising up with the clouds of heaven (cf. Dan. 7.13). A multitude of men gather to war against him, but he carves out a mountain upon which he stands. From there, he destroys the multitudes with a stream of fire from his mouth. After this, he descends the mountain and calls to himself another multitude, a peaceable one.

As all commentators agree, this vision and the interpretation which follows it (13.25-53) most probably consist of traditional material which the author has utilized.[1] Here the culprit is not a specific political entity (i.e. Rome) as in V. Instead, all the nations of the world are the villains whom the messianic figure destroys at the end of the age. Both the vision and its interpretation give evidence of the vitality of

---

1. Cf. Box: the source 'included not only the Vision proper (vv. 1-13a), but also its interpretation (vv. 25-53)', although the latter has undergone some redaction by the author (1912: 284).

Jewish nationalistic fervour in the author's day.[1] As we saw in V, however, it should not be assumed that the author is using this tradition in the same manner. One must determine where the author's own distinctive impression has been left upon the tradition lest his purposes be misunderstood. As we shall see from the interpretation of the vision, the author has redacted the tradition so substantially as to give it a dynamic completely at odds with its traditional purpose.

8.1.2. *Ezra pleads for an explanation (13.13b-20).* Again Ezra is afraid (13.13b) and asks for an interpretation of the vision. He includes in his request the observation that, while those who survive the messianic woes have to witness great dangers and distress, those who do not survive are much worse off since they 'pass from the world like a cloud' (13.20). Although this is not a brilliantly perceptive observation, Ezra's words are important for the development of the author's case. Because Ezra does not simply make a request for an interpretation but comments on those who do and do not survive the messianic woes, Uriel is able to preface the interpretation with his remarks on 'those who survive', which is precisely the point on which Uriel's interpretation diverges from the original intent of the nationalistic vision.

8.1.3. *The interpretation of the vision: a remnant and a multitude will be saved (13.21-52).* Having made mention of two groups in 13.16-19—those who do survive the perils of the last day (Lat. *qui derelicti fuerint*; Syr. *l'ylyn dmšthryn*) and those who do not survive them (Lat. *qui non sunt derelicti*; Syr. *l'ylyn dl' mšthryn*)—Ezra is answered, 'As for what you said about those who are left (Lat. *qui derelicti sunt*; Syr. *'ylyn mšthryn*), this is the interpretation' (13.22).[2] Uriel, first interpreting Ezra's words before interpreting the vision, says that the Messiah will protect some who will survive the perils

---

1. In all probability, the gathering of the peaceable multitude (13.12) was originally a reference to the salvation of the Judaean Jews, while the gathering of those who come from afar (13.13a) represented the return of the diaspora Jews who, upon their return to the holy land of Israel, share in glory of the messianic age. See Klausner, 1956: 360-61; Gunkel, 1900: 395.

2. There is a textual discrepancy here. The Latin text speaks only of 'those who survive', while the Syriac and Arabic [I] speak of 'those who survive' and 'those who do not survive'. We have followed the Latin since it is 'those who survive' with whom Uriel is concerned in 13.21-24.

(13.23). He describes them as those 'who have works and faithfulness (*fidem*) before the Almighty' (13.23).[1] We have heard of these people throughout I–III from Uriel. They are the righteous few who will inherit eschatological salvation because they have 'stored up treasures of faithfulness' (6.5), 'a treasure of works laid up with the Most High' (7.77) by their laborious and perfect effort (7.89). Uriel has declared that everyone who will be saved from the messianic woes 'will be able to escape on account of his works, or on account of the faithfulness in which he has put his trust' (9.7; cf. also 7.24, 35, 114 and Ezra's understanding of Uriel's position in 8.33). His words in 13.23 are no different whatsoever, leading to the conclusion that when Uriel talks of 'those who are left', he has in mind the same group of which he spoke in 6.25, 7.27-28, 9.7-8, and 12.34—the remnant, the collection of the few individuals who are deserving of salvation by reason of their merits.

Two things need mention. First, it is important to notice that the vision itself made no mention of a remnant. The author has introduced this idea into the discussion by having Ezra, between the vision and the interpretation, make mention of those who survive and those who do not survive the messianic woes. Second, because it had no part in the vision itself, the remnant motif is treated initially as an additional concern. Uriel makes a distinction between the interpretation of the vision and his comments concerning the remnant (13.21-25). This distinction does not last long, however, and, when the interpretation itself begins, the remnant motif appears right alongside elements essential to the vision. In this way, the author has doctored the original import of the vision by introducing into the interpretation an element which is foreign to the vision itself.

In the interpretation of the man from the sea vision, beginning at 13.25, the Messiah is said to deliver his creation and to direct 'those who are left' (Lat. *qui derelicti sunt*; Syr. *l'ylyn d'šthrw*, 13.26). Here, then, is the first instance in VI in which the remnant motif is interwoven into the interpretation of the vision. The interpretation continues, describing how the Messiah stands on the top of Mt Zion, from where he makes war on the multitudes. There on Mt Zion, the

---

1. My translation. Thompson also recommends reading *fidem* here as 'faithfulness' (1977: 313). Knibb translates 13.23b as 'who have works and fidelity laid up to their credit with the Most High' and notes that what is intended here is 'faithfulness to the law' (1979: 261, 182).

great city Zion (which was first revealed to Ezra in IV) will be
established (13.36), and from there God's Messiah will destroy his
enemies 'with the law' (13.38).[1]

The interpretation then identifies the peaceable multitude (in distinction from those who survive the perilous end times) as the ten
tribes of Israel who had been led into exile in another land (13.40-41),
a reference to the events of 2 Kgs 17.1-6. These ten tribes, we are
told, left that land of their own accord to go to a more distant region
'where humanity had never lived' (13.41) in order that they might
keep the statutes of the law 'which they had not kept in their own land'
(13.42).[2] Uriel, assured of both their existence and their inaccessibility, describes their crossing of the Euphrates River by means of divine
intervention. Because they kept the statutes of the law in a distant land,
God will again intervene on their behalf and lead them back, gathering
them in peace to enjoy the eschatological salvation (13.47).

After this, the interpretation focuses once again on the remnant,
those who are left who are found 'within my holy borders' (Lat. *intra
terminum meum sanctum*, Syr. *bthwmy qdyš'*, 13.48; cf. 13.49).[3]
Here the remnant motif makes yet another appearance, despite the fact
that it has no precedent in the vision itself. Accordingly, it would seem
to be of utmost importance to the author, who has woven it into the
nationalistic fabric of the vision by means of the interpretation (13.21-
24, 26, 48-50). This is not surprising in view of the fact that the same
phenomenon was evident in the interpretation of the eagle vision in V.
The interpretation of the man from the sea picks up the remnant motif
of 12.34 and elaborates it. The two interpretations, therefore, overlap
on the remnant motif and reinforce each other, although the motif has
no correspondence in either of the visions. Where the interpretation of

---

1. The Latin 'and the law' (*et legem*) is almost certainly corrupt.

2. In all probability, the ten tribes assimilated the ways of their captors and lost
their Jewish identity, but the belief that the ten tribes still existed 'beyond the
Euphrates—countless myriads whose number cannot be ascertained' is evident from
several Jewish writings (Josephus, *Ant.* 11.133; cf. 2 *Bar.* 77.22, 78.1; m. *Sanh.*
10.3).

3. The mention of 'those who are left' in 13.49 has sometimes been identified
with both those who survived the messianic woes in the land and those who return
from a distant land. See e.g. Myers, 1974: 312; Knibb, 1979: 270. But this position
cannot be maintained when it is recognized that the phrase is used consistently to
refer solely to the collective group of individuals who are worthy of salvation due to
their merit. The phrase 'within my holy borders' supports this identification (cf. 9.8;
12.34).

V ends, the interpretation of VI begins. It is as if the visions themselves matter little to the author's case. Perhaps all that is really necessary are the interpretations of the visions—specifically, the remnant motif which completes the interpretation of the eagle vision and which runs throughout the interpretation of the man from the sea vision. Accordingly, the nationalistic interest of each vision is deflated when Uriel introduces the concept into his explanations of the visions. As C. Rowland writes, in the interpretations of V and VI the promise of salvation

> is reserved for the righteous alone. *There is no relaxation of the rigorous atti-tude taken by the angel in the dialogues.* The great multitude which assembles on Mount Zion (*4 Ezra* 13.40ff) is there, not because it happens to be the elect people but because it has kept the statutes of God. The future glory is for the righteous alone, and no one who has acted impiously, *whatever his religious affiliation,* can escape the coming wrath.[1]

Whereas Ezra distinguished between two groups—(1) those who perish, and (2) those who survive—Uriel has a threefold distinction between (1) those who perish, (2) the ten tribes who return, and (3) the remnant who survive the messianic woes. The third group are those who have what is required for salvation: works and faithfulness to the law. The second group also are said to have kept the law, but they kept it in a distant land. This is peculiar since, in traditional expressions of Jewish covenantalism, 'doing the law' included the offering of sacrifices, thereby making atonement for sin. Those sacrifices were to be offered at the temple in Jerusalem. Uriel, how-ever, describes the ten tribes as keeping the law, but they are said to have kept it *in a distant land although they had not kept it in their own land* (13.42). While on one level this provides for a tidy explanation of an awkward event of Israel's past (the exile of the northern king-dom), it certainly plays a far more significant role within the context of *4 Ezra.* The author is not concerned to sew together the rips in Israel's history; if the reader has been listening to the author's case throughout I–VI and keeps in mind both his argument and his post-70 CE situation, the account of the ten tribes is a well-crafted narrative employed to substantiate the author's main point, as will be illustrated below.

We noticed in Part I that in Early Judaism God's covenantal mercy was thought to be the corrective for the anthropological condition of

---

1. 1982: 131, emphasis mine. Cf. Collins, 1984a: 167.

sin: although everyone is a sinner before God, those who are members of God's covenant people enjoy God's mercy and, thereby, take on a new identity as the righteous. It was a commonplace recognition that, inevitably, even the righteous sin. Nonetheless, the righteous maintain their status by 'keeping the law' of the covenant, which included making atonement for sin by means of sacrifice and repentance. In this way, they are renewed in the covenant of God's mercy. 'Doing the law', in this scheme, includes the practice of making atonement for sin.

In contrast to this, we have seen repeatedly how, in *4 Ezra*, Uriel has ruled out at every step an ethnocentric covenantalism, arguing that God's mercy is not available to any except those few who, in contrast to the sinners, have 'a treasure of works laid up with the Most High' (7.77). Uriel, unlike most Jews of the first century CE, does not posit that the sinner can become righteous by means of God's mercy. For Uriel, the only corrective to the anthropological state of sinfulness is personal persistence in amassing works for one's own benefit. In contradistinction with traditional Jewish covenantalism, 'doing the law' means being free from sin altogether, without having need of atonement. This goes beyond the anthropological view common throughout Early Judaism and explains the significance of the great multitude who kept the law outside Israel. This is more than just a pious rereading and explanation of embarrassing historical events. It serves to fill out the author's portrayal of what 'doing the law' does *not* entail. Having come to the conclusion that it is not God's mercy which rescues one from the desperate human situation but being wholly free from sin, the author came to regard the destruction of the temple as being of little consequence. Or perhaps it is more accurate to say that the author, struggling with the fact of the destruction of the temple, came to the conclusion that one must now be wholly free from sin in order to enjoy salvation. Either way, keeping the law does *not* depend on the existence of the temple, the priesthood or any sacrificial offerings. This point is made in the portrayal of the lifestyle of the ten tribes, a (negative) model of religious practice in a post-destruction setting; keeping the law does *not* entail temple sacrifices. In fact, keeping the law has never depended upon sacrificial offerings, as is illustrated by the saving of the few who have stored up works to their own credit before God (13.23). Thus, whereas the ten tribes illustrate what is *not* necessary to keep the law (temple sacrifices), the remnant illustrates what *is* necessary (works). If some Jewish groups found means to complement (the Pharisees)[1] or substitute for (Qumran)[2] the temple sacrifices, the author of *4 Ezra* finds no need to replace temple sacrifices with another means of atonement since the need for atonement itself indicates one's unsuitability for eschatological salvation.

Together, these two groups—the ten tribes and the remnant—enable the author's innovative case to be authenticated in the light of traditional Jewish expections. Despite the fact that the exiles of the northern (722 BCE) and southern kingdoms (587 BCE) wreaked havoc upon the tribal ordering of the Hebrew people, the concept of a twelve-tribe structure outlasted the reality (as is evident from the *Testament of the Twelve Patriarchs*). So, after reviewing the pertinent literature of Early Judaism, E.P. Sanders writes, 'in the first century Jewish hopes for the future would have included the restoration of the twelve tribes of Israel'.[3] The same hope is evident in *4 Ezra* 13, the ten tribes and the remnant embodying the two components of this twelve-tribel structure; whereas the ten tribes represent the northern kingdom of Israel who were exiled from the land,[4] the remnant who are saved 'within my holy borders' almost certainly represent the two tribes of the southern kingdom.[5] Apparently, then, the author considered those who will be saved to constitute a twelve-tribe entity. In this way he maintains the traditional tribal composition of Jewish patriarchal history in his depiction of eschatological salvation. Although Jewish covenantalism has been disqualified, and with it the hope of salvation for the ethnic people of Israel, the group to enjoy the eschatological blessings are themselves members of that ethnic group and representatives of its whole constituency. Thus, to some extent, despite the innovations of his perspective, the author hopes to keep his case within traditional lines.

The appearance of the ten tribes is, in some ways, the author's 'ace up the sleeve'. As A.L. Thompson says, only in VI is it revealed that 'the number of the saved constitute an innumerable multitude, rather

1. Neusner, 1973: 81-96.
2. Klinzing, 1971; Sanders, 1977: 299-305; Newton, 1985: 10-51.
3. 1985b: 98; see his discussion, 1985b: 95-98.
4. The Syriac, Ethiopic, Armenian and Arabic [I] all read 'nine and a half' (cf. *2 Bar.* 62.5; 77.19; 78.1) rather than 'ten', as the Latin reads (cf. *2 Bar.* 1.2). The discrepancy seems to have arisen from confusion with the identity of the tribes who lived beyond the Jordan (cf. Josh. 22.7-10). For a review of the issue, see Box, 1912: 296.
5. Cf. Box, 1912: 300.

than the paltry few over which Ezra and Uriel debate in the earlier episodes'.[1] Nevertheless, the assurance that a multitude will be saved is not intended to encourage the nation Israel, for of their numbers only a remnant will be saved. Instead, it is meant to satisfy any lingering hesitations concerning the justice of God. Lest there still be some doubt over the justice of the fact that only a few will be saved by means of their own efforts, the ten-tribe multitude is introduced from 'offstage' in order to allay any dissatisfaction which might remain, thereby militating against anything less than complete confidence in God's justice. The appearance of the multitude does nothing to revise the situation of ethnic Israel, but strengthens Ezra's new-found certainty that God is just. As such, the episode ends with Ezra walking in the field, 'giving great glory and praise to the Most High because of his wonders' (13.57).

8.1.4. *Ezra is commended for forsaking his ways (13.53-58).* After the interpretation finishes, Uriel tells Ezra: 'you alone have been enlightened about this, because you have forsaken your own ways and have applied yourself to mine, and have searched out the things of my law' (13.53-54). It is often thought that this verse includes a commendation of Ezra's righteousness before God, just as he had earlier been commended for the same reason (6.32-33). To forsake one's own ways for God's way is, in this understanding, equivalent to being obedient to God's law.[2]

Although this is a possible reading, it does not wholly grasp the author's meaning. There is more to this particular verse than simply the acclamation of Ezra's righteousness. First, it needs to be noticed that there are others too (a remnant) who are righteous before God. Nonetheless, Ezra alone is singled out as the sole recipient of the mysteries of God.[3] He alone is deserving. This suggests, therefore, that righteousness is not the sole prerequisite for receiving the revelations; perhaps another quality is being alluded to when Uriel speaks of Ezra forsaking his ways.

1. 1977: 237.
2. Cf. Thompson, 1977: 237; Knibb, 1979: 271.
3. But see 8.62 and 10.57, where there is talk of a few others who have also been shown the end times. In 14.9, God (Uriel?) speaks of these others as 'those like you'. These few others seem to be the righteous who have already been taken up to heaven alive (6.26), just as Ezra is soon to be taken up alive (7.19; cf. the original ending in all but the Latin versions of 14.48).

There is better reason to think that the revelations which were given to Ezra were not meant as a a reward for his righteousness *per se*, but for the manner in which he, within the confines of *4 Ezra*, has undergone a metamorphosis. Ezra is commended for forsaking his own ways and applying himself to the ways of God. Although the phrase 'the way(s) of the Most High' has been used in III to refer to the divine commandments which one must obey (7.79, 88, 129; 8.56; 9.9; cf. 14.31), it has also occurred frequently in the earlier dialogues in a different sense, referring to the manner in which God himself acts in the world.[1] In Episodes I–VI, one watches as Ezra, seeking to understand 'the way of the Most High' (5.34; cf. the way this phrase is used in 3.31 [Syr.]; 4.2, 10-11, and notice 4.23-25), experiences a transformation of his perception of God's dealings. After the vision and interpretation of V, Uriel tells Ezra that he *alone* is worthy to learn the secret of the Most High (12.36)—the secret that only a remnant will be saved—just as Ezra himself acknowledged that he was shown this vision because he 'searched out the ways of the Most High' (12.4). This is not a reference to Ezra's obedience to the law or righteousness. Instead, it refers to his intellectual quest. 12.4 and 12.36 reinforce each other to demonstrate that Ezra was worthy because, seeking to understand how God's ways can be comprehended, he abandoned his own perspective for Uriel's. In recompense, he was shown the way things really are by means of a vision–interpretation sequence, which reinforced the fact that Uriel's explanation of God's ways is satisfactory after all.

The same point is intended in 13.53-54. If IV and V serve as indicators, one expects the vision of VI to reveal that Ezra's outlook and attitude are now acceptable to God. Just as it was said earlier of Ezra that he was the *only* (Lat. *solus*; Syr. *blḥwdyn*) recipient of these revelations (12.36) because he had *forsaken* (Lat. *dimissi derelinqui*; Syr. *šbqt*) his previous understanding (9.39; 10.5) and *searched out* (Lat. *scrutas*; Syr. *m'qb'*) God's ways (12.4; cf. 5.34), the same is said here in 13.53-54:

> you alone (Lat. *solus*; Syr. *blḥwdyn*) have been enlightened about this because you have forsaken (Lat. *derelinquisti*; Syr. *šbqt*) your own ways and

---

1. Cf. Brandenburger: 'Man darf dieses Leitwort nicht speculativ ausdeuten. Gedacht ist an etwas sehr Konkretes: an das Procedere, das Verfahren, das Wirken Gottes im Weltgeschehen' (1981: 166).

applied yourself to mine, and have searched out (Lat. *exquisisti*; Syr. *b'yt*) my law.

The terminology is the same (or, in one case, synonymous) because the point being made is the same as that in IV and V—the visions are Ezra's reward for accepting Uriel's explanation and are given in order to consolidate Ezra's new perspective. This interpretation finds immediate confirmation from 13.55 where the intellectual aspect of Ezra's worthiness is explained: 'for you have devoted your life to wisdom and called understanding your mother'.

The issue which runs consistently throughout I–VI is the manner in which God's ways can be properly comprehended. It is this same issue, more than any concern to highlight Ezra's personal righteousness, which should inform our reading of 13.53-54. There, Ezra is said to be worthy of observing God's mysteries not simply because he was one of the few righteous, but more specifically because he had relinquished his initial covenantal perspective (cf. 9.39; 10.5) and accepted a new understanding of God's ways.

8.2. *Summary of Episode VI*

This episode has given further evidence of the author's view of the mechanics of salvation. The law could be kept in a distant land—that is, apart from the temple and without sacrifices—by storing up works which make the individual worthy of salvation before God. The ten tribes and the remnant respectively illustrate all this. Moreover, although he is convinced that those who will be saved are themselves representatives of each of the twelve tribes of Israel, the author entertains no hope for ethnic Israel as a whole. Despite claims to the contrary,[1] there is no nationalistic optimism even at this point. The radical individualism and legalism of former episodes is not overturned but is reaffirmed in this episode. Finally, Ezra is said to have had these revelations because he relinquished his own views and came to accept God's perspective on the matter. Thus, in return for transforming his understanding of God's ways, evident throughout the book, Ezra receives in this vision compensation in full, and praises God in the confidence that he is just.

---

1. Cf. Schürer: the author sought 'to comfort the people in their distress, to revive their courage and zeal with a prospect of sure and imminent redemption' (1973: 1.527).

Chapter 9

EPISODE VII

The final Episode (VII) does not continue in the same vein as the previous episodes, but is nonetheless essential to the book. In it, the author seeks to justify the case he has made in I–VI, authenticating his innovation with regard to Jewish scriptures. This episode will be analysed according to the following outline:

1. Prepare, for the end is near (14.1-18)
2. Ezra asks to restore the law (14.19-26)
3. Ezra speaks to the people (14.27-36)
4. The ninety-four books and their distribution (14.37-48)

9.1. *Analysis of Episode VII*

9.1.1. *Prepare, for the end is near (14.1-18).* As VII begins, God reveals himself to Ezra in the same manner that he revealed himself to Moses—speaking to him from a burning bush (14.1; cf. Exod. 3). Ezra is told that, when Moses was on Mt Sinai, he was shown 'many wondrous things' and 'the secrets of the times' (14.5). But Moses did not reveal them to the people, for God commanded him, 'These words you shall publish openly, and these things you shall keep secret' (14.6). This introduces a contrast which is to run throughout VII between the things which are revealed and the things which are kept hidden—a contrast already encountered in V where Ezra was not permitted to reveal the secrets to all the people, but only to the wise. At present, this contrast indicates that what Moses revealed to the people after his encounter with God was not a complete record of what he had learned on Mt Sinai; the Mosaic law which is known to the people is not the complete revelation of God's ways for there is more in the secrets of the end times, secrets which have been kept hidden.[1]

---

1. Cf. Russell, 1987: 108; *idem*, 1964: 86.

Although Israel is here identified by God as 'my people', he does not wholly reveal himself to them.

Because the end is approaching (14.10-12, 16-18),[1] Ezra is instructed to take to heart all that he has seen (14.7-9) and to reprove his people, comfort the lowly, and instruct the wise (14.13). Moreover, the Most High takes the opportunity himself to exhort Ezra to live a righteous life, saying:

> And now renounce the life that is corruptible and put away from you mortal thoughts; cast away from you the burdens of man and divest yourself now of your weak nature, and lay to one side the thoughts that are most grievous to you, and hasten to escape from these times (14.14-15).

The author has inserted these exhortations within the context of warnings that the end is near. They represent his pastoral call for a decision: since the end is near, one should decide to live in the manner described by these verses. The verses themselves say nothing about what things should be actively done, but concentrate only on the things which should be avoided. Significantly, they include the thinking of grievous thoughts, which would seem to echo Uriel's instruction to Ezra in I–III and Ezra's instruction to the woman in IV.[2] Moreover, the description of things to avoid closely resembles Uriel's description in 7.88-99 of things avoided by those who laboriously kept the law perfectly.[3]

9.1.2. *Ezra asks to restore the law (14.19-26).* Ezra accepts God's commission to reprove the people of his generation (14.20). But since that will be to no avail for future generations, he asks for permission to write down what he has been shown so that they too might be enlightened.[4] Of course, the author is modelling his portrayal of Ezra on the historical Ezra who made accessible the Mosaic law to the post-destruction Jewish community. But one may wonder what the Ezra of

---

1. Although the future orientation of the traditional visions in V–VI substituted for a full-blown two-age scheme, that scheme holds the same place of importance in 14.10-18 that it held in Uriel's descriptions of I–III. See Brandenburger, 1981: 136.

2. Cf. Brandenburger, 1981: 137.

3. Cf. Brandenburger, 1981: 136 n. 138.

4. Ezra has already been assured that the end is near, but he has also been told that two and a half of the twelve periods of history remain. The claim that the end is near facilitates the author's pastoral exhortations; the claim that two and a half periods remain facilitates the giving of the law to the future generations, as the rest of VII describes.

4 Ezra has in mind when he speaks of wanting to restore the law? What does he mean by the law? It was his covenantal understanding of God's ways as recorded in the law which caused his problems in the first place. Is it this same law which he now wants to restore?

His words of 14.21-22 are not especially clear in this regard, and there would seem to be two possibilities. The first is that Ezra now considers the law itself to include not only the Jewish scriptures but also the account of the end-time events of which he has learned in the course of his encounters with Uriel. Ezra has been told that Moses too was shown many wondrous things, including the secrets of the end times, and that Moses was instructed to keep secret those things which Ezra has since learned by divine revelation—that is, the secret things of the end. Ezra now asks for permission to reveal both 'the things which have been done' and those things which 'will be done by you' (14.21) in order that he might reveal 'everything that has happened in the world from the beginning, the things which were written in your Law' (14.22). Does this indicate that Ezra now understands the law itself to be more than the traditional Jewish scripture, and includes the eschatological mysteries? D.S. Russell considers the 'law' here to include 'not only the "open" books of the Law, but the "secret" books as well'.[1]

A second possibility is that Ezra maintains a traditional identification of the law with the Jewish scriptures. In this case, although the concept of the law is not expanded to include the secrets which Ezra has learned in I–VI, it would seem to have taken on a different character from that which Ezra originally attributed to it in I–III. We need only remember Uriel's words of 7.129 to see how the law could be understood to substantiate the claim that the individual is responsible for, and capable of, earning entry into the eschatological life. Uriel considered his case to be validated by the message of Moses and the prophets and to be summed up by Moses' words of Deut. 30.19: 'Choose for yourself life, that you may live'. Ezra's words of 14.22 are not much different; he hopes to restore the law to the people in order that 'those who wish to live in the last days may live'. If Ezra is echoing the view of the law expressed by Uriel in 7.129, he no longer perceives the law as the account of God's merciful dealings with Israel but as the individual's guide to the 'path' towards salvation.

1. 1987: 109.

The issue, therefore, is the manner in which Ezra, after abandoning his covenantal perspective, modifies his understanding of the law. Is it modified in extent or in character? In the former case, the law would come to include the secrets of the end times, which rule out a Jewish covenantalism. In the latter case, the law would become a sourcebook for personal piety—again ruling out Jewish covenantalism. Either, or perhaps both, can be understood from Ezra's rather vague words in 14.21-22.[1]

The divine reply in 14.23-26 clarifies the issue somewhat. Ezra is commanded to leave the people for forty days, during which time he will be given 'the lamp of understanding' in order to write many tablets. But one significant condition goes with the task. Ezra is told, 'Some things you shall make public, and some you shall deliver in secret to the wise' (14.26). By renewing the contrast between the things which are and are not to be revealed to the people, this command helps to illuminate both the character and extent of the law. Although Ezra will write many things, only some of them will be eligible for public viewing. A distinction can easily and properly be made here between what might be called the 'public law' and the 'private law'. The extent and character of the one differ from the extent and character of the other. The public law was first given by Moses to the people, and Ezra is to reissue this law. The private law, however, was kept secret by Moses, but is now to be revealed by Ezra, even if only to the wise. If the divine command of 12.36-38 provides any kind of a precedent, the private law, no doubt, contains the details of the end times which, within *4 Ezra*, have substantiated Uriel's case of I–III, thereby perpetuating a legalistic individualism (in distinction from the public law). Accordingly, the conflicting positions of Ezra and Uriel in I–III are documented in the public law and private law respectively.

9.1.3. *Ezra speaks to the people (14.27-36).* This section records Ezra's parting words to the people. In them, his conversion-perspective is evident in two ways. First, although he reviews many of the same events of Israel's history as he did in his opening speech of I, his point here is much different. In his first speech of the book (3.4-36), Ezra charged God with injustice: the people were not able to keep the

---

1. Cf. Knibb: 'here it is quite clear that "law" is being used in a very general sense' (1979: 278).

law because God had failed to act decisively on their behalf. Here, however, Ezra puts the responsibility for the people's condition wholly on them, accusing them and their forefathers of not keeping the law (14.28-31) and charging them to 'rule over your minds and discipline your heart' (14.34), an echo, perhaps, of Uriel's description of the righteous few in 7.92 (cf. 14.14).[1]

Second, although he assures the people that there is the possibility of obtaining God's mercy after death (Lat. *misericordiam consequemini*; Syr. *nḥwwn 'lykwn dḥm'*, 'mercies shall be received by you'), what he means by 'mercy' is different from what he meant by it in 4.24, where he questioned why Israel was not worthy of obtaining God's mercy (Lat. *misericordiam consequi*; Syr. *dnḥwwn 'lyn dḥm'*, 'that mercies shall be upon us'). In 4.24, 'mercy' is a component of Ezra's ethnocentric perspective, whereas in 14.34-35 it is an eschatological reward which is granted on the basis of one's deeds,[2] much like Uriel's description in 12.34 of God's eschatological mercy upon the remnant who will be saved due to their works (cf. 9.21-22).

From these two observations, it is clear that, as A.P. Hayman puts it, 'in Ezra's parting speech to his people before his assumption (14.27-36) the standpoint espoused by Uriel in visions I–III is clearly expressed'.[3] Nonetheless, in his farewell exhortations, Ezra does not get to the point of I–VI—the overthrow of a covenantal understanding of God's ways. Although the reader recognizes that Ezra's words of VII differ from those with which he began his quest, every aspect of his speech could just as easily appear in a prophetic call for the people to be obedient to their covenant God. Although the reader is aware of Ezra's transformation, the people remain unaware of it since his speech lacks the 'bite' of Uriel's words in I–III. It is not that Ezra is an ineffective communicator, but simply that he has been charged by God to refrain from enlightening the people (14.26). According to the command of 14.26, God has willed the classified information to be withheld from the people.

---

1. Knibb calls 14.27-31 'a deliberate contrast' to Ezra's speech in 3.4-36, which gives the reader 'a clear indication of the way in which the attitude of the author has changed' (1979: 279). Cf. Münchow, 1981: 86.

2. Thompson notes that several scholars, failing to come to grips with Ezra's position in VII, identify 14.35 as a later individualizing interpolation into the text (1977: 98). Individualistic it is; an interpolation it is not.

3. 1975: 47. Cf. Brandenburger, 1981: 65, 80.

Between 14.26 and 14.27, therefore, there appears the same dramatic irony which was evident between 12.37-38 and 12.40-45. In each case, Ezra is first commanded to announce the secrets which he had been shown only to the wise (12.37-38; 14.26), and is then immediately surrounded by 'all the people' (12.40; 14.27). Without the initial command to secrecy, one would expect Ezra to instruct the people in the ways of God which he has learned throughout *4 Ezra*. But because he is charged with secrecy, no such instruction is possible. Instead, on each occasion, Ezra's words trivialize the situation.

9.1.4. The ninety-four books and their distribution (14.37-48). Herein is described the manner in which Ezra and his five scribes produce ninety-four books during a forty-day period (compare the forty-day period which Moses spent on Mt Sinai when he received the law from God, described in Exod. 24.18, 34.28 and Deut. 9.9, 11). After the completion of the ninety-four books, Ezra is commanded:

> Make public the twenty-four books that you wrote first and let the worthy and the unworthy read them; but keep the seventy that were written last, in order to give them to the wise among your people. For in them [the seventy books] is the spring of understanding, the fountain of wisdom, and the river of knowledge (14.45-47).

And Ezra comments, 'And I did so' (14.48).

The identification of the twenty-four books[1] is not controversial. They doubtless refer to the books of the Hebrew scriptures. Both the worthy and the unworthy are allowed to read them. It is the identification of the seventy books which is not as readily apparent, and which is of great importance for this project.

It needs first to be observed that, whereas the twenty-four books are available to 'the worthy and the unworthy', the seventy books are revealed only to 'the wise among your people'. On occasion it has been argued that the author understood the seventy books as being 'kept hidden away in a secret place *until the time appointed*' when they will finally be revealed to all the public.[2] Although the disclosure of the divine revelations *to the public* is evident in other passages of the

---

1. The Latin, alone, reads 'the first' books, rather than 'the twenty-four books'. The error in the Latin at 14.44 (which speaks of 904 books instead of 94) has thrown off the numerical equations which follow.

2. Russell, 1964: 114, emphasis added. Cf. Meade, 1986: 83; Gruenwald, 1973: 72; Collins, 1984b: 21-22.

apocalyptic corpus,[1] it is not to be found in *4 Ezra* 14, where it is poignantly demonstrated that those who know the divine wisdom are only the very few. That is, the author makes not a *temporal* distinction between the time of Ezra's private revelation and the time of its public proclamation, but rather a *social* distinction between those who are familiar with the books and those who are not.[2] The former are only the very few; just as in 12.37-38 and 14.26, Ezra is not permitted to reveal the secrets of God's ways to the people collectively but only to the few who are wise. This is an important observation if the seventy books are to be properly identified.

When identifying the seventy books, G.F. Moore suggested that they refer to 'the traditional law', meaning the Jewish oral law contained in the Mishnah.[3] As such, the author is seen to be attributing divine origin and authority to the oral law (contra Sadducaean and Samaritan conviction) as well as to the written law, both having been revealed to Moses on Mt Sinai (14.5-6). As we have seen, however, the seventy books are described as secret books which are restricted to the circles of the privileged few, a description which does not accord well with the oral law which was 'taught as openly as the written Law itself'.[4] Moore's suggestion, therefore, has not received much support.[5]

A second solution enjoys almost unanimous assent and identifies the seventy books as Jewish apocalyptic literature—in particular, those books which, like *4 Ezra* itself, relate the events of the end times. In this interpretation, Ezra is permitted to reveal in seventy books the eschatological happenings which Moses was commanded *not* to reveal (14.5-6). That which differentiates the seventy from the twenty-four books, then, is an interest in eschatology; whereas Ezra gave the Torah to the people, he also secretly propagated the mysteries of the end times which are the exclusive property of 'the learned, not the general public'.[6] In this way, the author is understood to be authenti-

---

1. Cf. *Jub.* 1.4-7; *1 En.* 82.1; *2 En.* 33.8-11; 35.2; 47.1-6.
2. Cf. 1QS 9.17: the master of the community 'shall conceal the teaching of the Law from men of falsehood, but shall impart true knowledge and righteous judgement to those who have chosen the Way'. So also 1QS 11.5-6.
3. Moore, 1927: 1.8 n. 4.
4. Russell, 1964: 86.
5. To my knowledge, Moore is followed only by McCullough, 1975: 206.
6. Knibb, 1979: 278.

cating the elaborate eschatological speculation evident in the majority
of Jewish apocalypses and in the visionary episodes of IV–VI.[1]

But one wonders whether a more precise identification of the seventy books is possible. It must be kept in mind that *4 Ezra* was not
written to be an exercise in eschatological prediction. The author's
quest has been to comprehend the ways of God, and, in this regard, his
commitment is ultimately to the understanding of God which Uriel
defends. He is not interested in defending some guild of eschatological
seers and their literature. Nor is he intent on propagating fanciful
descriptions of future events for their own sake. These serve primarily to verify his new beliefs concerning God's ways, human existence
and the requirements for salvation. It is the author's message which
gives his work its *raison d'être*, and the eschatological trappings serve
primarily to animate that message. As C. Rowland suggests, 'we
should endeavour to investigate *what particular message* the visionary
is wanting to communicate to his readers by means of the images
which are included in his vision'.[2] That is to say, apart from the
author's message, the eschatological framework has little significance.
This is the case, at least, for *4 Ezra* wherein eschatological descriptions serve as supports for its more fundamental message. It is only
when one has in view the central thread which runs throughout the
each episode of *4 Ezra* (namely the quest for the proper understanding
of God's ways) that the seventy books can be properly identified.

Throughout I–VI, the author has been concerned with the quest for
the proper understanding of God's ways, first by entertaining two
'competing' perceptions in I–III and then by granting the 'victory' to
Uriel's view in IV–VI. In this regard, the distinction between the two
types of books (the twenty-four and the seventy) plays a part in the
larger scheme of this quest. Ezra's complaints of I–III were rooted in
his traditional understanding and were nurtured by his reading of the
twenty-four books of the Hebrew scriptures.[3] For this reason, every
dialogue began with an appeal to God's mercy based on a covenantal
rationale. And for the same reason, III includes a developed midrash

1. This interpretation is very prevalant. A list of scholars includes Box, 1912:
304-306; Brandenburger, 1981: 134-35; Mundle, 1929: 248-29; Myers, 1974: 324,
326, 329; Cohen, 1987: 180, 187; Russell, 1964: 87-88; *idem*, 1987: 108-109;
Knibb, 1979: 272, 274; Gunkel, 1900: 401; Oesterley, 1933: 164, 166; Morris,
1972: 69; Brockington, 1961: 25 n. 3.
2. 1982: 60, emphasis added.
3. Cf. 3.13-19, 22-25; 5.21-30; 5.56–6.6; 6.55-59; 7.102-103, 132-40; 8.15-34.

of Exod. 34.6-7 which detailed the merciful and gracious character of God as revealed in the history of his dealings with Israel (7.132-40). Uriel, however, maintained a different understanding of God's ways, and assured Ezra that the events of the end would bring about God's justice. Whereas Ezra, looking back to Israel's past history, understood salvation to be wholly dependent upon the mercy of God, Uriel, looking towards the events of the end times, insisted that salvation is bestowed only upon those who merit salvation by means of works stored up with God. After his resignation to Uriel's position, Ezra was consoled by visions of the end times in IV–VI—visions which the author reworked in order to harmonize them with Uriel's case in I–III. These (reworked) visions serve to assure Ezra that by relinquishing his covenantal understanding he had come to a better understanding of God's ways.[1]

It is this theological development which transpires in the narrative of *4 Ezra*, rather than some concern to legitimate an 'apocalyptic school', that provides the best context for identifying the seventy books. By means of these seventy books, the author is concerned only to legitimate the theological innovation which he has orchestrated throughout I–VI. Ezra's quest throughout *4 Ezra* is best understood as representing the personal quest of the author as he attempted to reconcile the righteousness of God with the disastrous events of 70 CE. Ezra's solution, then, is the solution of at least one pious Jew who, having come to a new understanding of God's ways, reaffirmed once again his confidence in God. Since the covenantal perception of God did little to solve his dilemma, the author, in the guise of Ezra, replaced it with another view of God's ways. Consequently, he was faced with a new problem, for his new understanding was not evident in the traditional Jewish scriptures. Accordingly, he had little basis in which to give authority to his newly acquired solution. It is for this reason that the seventy books are introduced into the narrative. Having established his case in I–VI, the author apparently believed (and with good reason) that his new perception of the ways of God is not contained in the pages of the twenty-four books of scripture, although it is confirmed by the events of the end which were revealed in IV–VI. Accordingly, in order to justify his 'non-canonical' perspective, he

---

1. Collins, noting Ezra's transformation in IV, says: 'Ezra's conversion is now consolidated by two dream visions' in V and VI (1984a: 165). Cf. Rowland, 1982: 168.

postulated the existence of the seventy other books which God intended only the wise to see; only in them, and not in the Jewish scriptures, can one find wisdom and understanding, for they contain the secrets of God's ways which the eschatological visions have revealed.

By means of the seventy books, the author hoped to legitimate Ezra's conversion perspective, which was, in fact, his own post-destruction understanding of the ways of God. He was not concerned to legitimate apocalyptic literature in general. Instead, he was concerned only to authenticate the eschatological message of his apocalypse in particular.[1] The seventy books are not incorporated into the drama for purposes of literary structure or narrative closure. Their function is determined solely by the need of the author to guard his message against objection, a message which he legitimated through a 'secrecy' motif. With the exception of 7.129-30, an 'according to the scriptures' type of exegesis is absent from Uriel's words, which voice the author's new convictions. Instead, the author presented his case as being secretly revealed by God. Accordingly, the need for scriptural authentication is bypassed, and a prophecy–fulfilment schematization is not employed.[2]

For the author of *4 Ezra*, as for most innovators who seek to maintain their place within a religious tradition, the problem to be solved is one of continuity with religious tradition. How is it that the God who is unveiled in *4 Ezra* appears so differently from the way he has revealed himself in Israel's history and sacred books? This is all the more pressing since what the author considered to be the authoritative understanding of God's ways was not considered as such by his fellow Jews—the 'worthy and the unworthy', 'all the people'. Most of them worshipped the one whom they knew from their sacred books and who was perceived as having worked for their benefit throughout the

1. I find it significant that in 1982 Rowland regarded the seventy books as representing 'apocalyptic works' (1982: 19), whereas in 1988 he took them to be 'his [Ezra's] revelations' (1988a: 183). It is this kind of refinement which we are arguing for here, one which allows for much greater precision.

2. As we saw earlier, Uriel's appeal to Moses and the prophets in 7.129-30 is unique, even exceptional, to his argument. His attempt at scriptural authentication was not convincing to Ezra, who immediately counters Uriel's appeal to Scripture with an appeal of his own in 7.132-40, which expounds the characterization of God in Exod. 34.6-7. Never again does the author attempt to legitimate Uriel's position from Scripture, and, in fact, as 14.45-47 would suggest, he abandons the hope of scriptural support altogether.

ages. It is this twofold problem which the author addresses in 14.37-48. Although he had only recently discovered for himself the solution to his quest for understanding, the author contended that it was secretly revealed long ago to Moses and Ezra. This allowed his message the historical underpinning which it needed in order to gain a sense of continuity with Israel's past. And because this ancient revelation was made to Moses and Ezra *in secret*, the vast majority of Israel were unaware of it. Although they did not share his perception, this caused the author no angst; it was to be expected, in fact, since God intended all along for the seventy books to be revealed only to the few. In this way, the author defended (1) the *antiquity* of his message despite its relatively recent appearance, and (2) the *validity* of his message despite its minority position.[1] Here, then, we see in bold relief how 'the apocalyptic framework could offer the basis for radical steps in religion'.[2]

Now that the function of the seventy books has been recognized, we may inquire more specifically about the identity of the books themselves. Is the author making mention of actual books? What significance is there to the number 'seventy'? How are we to understand the seventy books in the light of the author's motivation for mentioning them? An investigation of these matters begins by considering the point of the number 'seventy'. G.H. Box has suggested that the number 'doubtless has a symbolic significance, denoting what is large and comprehensive',[3] meaning that the author has a sizeable collection of Jewish apocalypses in mind. But as we have seen, such a concern was not held by the author. Better is Russell's suggestion that a more subtle symbolism lies behind the number seventy. He notes that the numerical value of the letters of the Hebrew word for 'secret' (סוד) add up to seventy (ס = 60, ו = 6, ד = 4).[4] This is a tantalizing suggestion, especially since, as most scholars agree, *4 Ezra* was originally composed in Hebrew, and since numerical symbolism played a significant role in apocalyptic literature. If Russell's suggestion bears

---

1. Cf. Rowland: 'the apocalyptic framework signifies a point of view which would otherwise be looked on with some suspicion by the majority. . . In addition, the emphasis on the revelatory dimension allows those novel aspects of the teaching of the apocalypse to receive that authority which other literary forms would not have given them' (1982: 122, 134).
2. Rowland, 1988a: 182.
3. 1912: 305.
4. Russell, 1964: 114; *idem*, 1987: 109-10.

any weight, the number 'seventy' is a numerical code describing the *character* of the books themselves (that is, they are secret books) or the *contents* of the books. Probably, in fact, both aspects should be included; the secret, esoteric books contain the secrets of the Most High.

Russell's suggestion is wholly reasonable and highlights the symbolic value of the adjective 'seventy'. That is, the 'extra-canonical' books are identified not by quantity but by quality. There is little reason to think that the author actually knew of seventy books which he recognized as authoritative beyond those of Jewish scripture. Instead, he knew of *an understanding of God* which went beyond that of the twenty-four books of scripture, an understanding which he considered to be secret. We need not look any further than the recognition of the author's needs of legitimation to explain the identity of the seventy books. Since the covenantal understanding of God's ways is substantiated by the twenty-four books, the author needed to substantiate his own secret understanding of God by postulating the existence of other authoritative books. To arrive at a complementary number to twenty-four, the author simply translated the *quality* of his new understanding (viz. it is secret) into a numerical value (= seventy). The seventy books, therefore, are nothing other than a symbol of his perspective in numerical form. That is to say, *the seventy books are a numeric metaphor*. They need not be identified with any particular books, but are hypothetical books, necessary only to substantiate the author's particular message.

The argument has been presented here that the seventy books represent the author's attempt to legitimate his innovative understanding of God. His audience were to understand them to contain the secret of God's ways which Ezra has learned throughout I–VI and which are worthy only of the wise. These extra-scriptural books allow his message a revelational base which it otherwise lacks, and they infuse his case with an authoritative character. Similar techniques are employed elsewhere in Jewish literature,[1] especially in the apocalypses, wherein there is frequent mention of special books which contain divine truths specially mediated to the apocalyptic seer.[2] Often this phenomenon

---

1. See esp. Nickelsburg, 1985.
2. Cf. *Jub.* 1.4-7, 26; 4.17; 32.21-26; 45.15; Dan. 8.26; 12.4, 9; *1 En.* 82.1; 107.3; *2 En.* 22.10–23.6; 33.8-11; 35.2; 47.1-6; 48.6-8; 54.1. See Hengel's comments, 1974: 1.243.

allows an author to authenticate his own idiosyncratic views which he would otherwise have trouble legitimating. Thus, for example, the book of *Jubilees* (whether or not one considers it an apocalyptic work) professes to be the book written by Moses containing the things which God showed him on Mt Sinai concerning 'what (was) in the beginning and what will occur (in the future)'. God commanded him to 'write it in a book' (1.4-7, 26). The book itself lies open to the reader in the pages of *Jubilees*. In it, several peculiarities of the author are readily apparent. For instance, the author (1) presents the case that one can maintain the covenant only by following a solar rather than a lunar calendar (6.32-38; 50.1-13; cf. 1.14; 4.17-18; 23.19), (2) denounces Jewish intermarriage with other nations (30.7-23), and (3) argues that the patriarchs themselves kept the practices which seem to have arisen only later in Jewish history (7.3-5; 15.1-2; 16.20-31; 22.1-5; 32.4-9; 34.12-20), even to the point that they followed the solar calendar (cf. 6.17-20). Other idiosyncrasies are evident in *Jubilees*, but these are some primary concerns of the author. They need not detain us except to note that the biblical Torah ('the book of the first law', 6.22) includes very little of these concerns. Evidently, the author thought that they should be included or emphasized and he sought to reconcile this by writing a second book of the law. In this regard, I. Gruenwald writes that the author of *Jubilees* 'wants to convince his readers of the existence of two parallel versions of the biblical story. . . the one given exoterically to the whole of the People of Israel and the other given esoterically to the initiate alone'.[1]

Calendrical concerns are also evident in the Book of Heavenly Luminaries (*1 En.* 72–82) which describes Enoch's vision of the movement of the heavenly bodies. After viewing all this, Enoch gives to his son Methuselah 'the book concerning all these things' (82.1) which grants wisdom and righteousness (82.2-4), and which contains the secret that the 'year is completed in three hundred and sixty-four days' (82.6). Here again is a secret book which reveals to the wise and righteous the secret that only the solar calendar is proper to regulate one's practices—a fact which the author would no doubt have enjoyed

---

1. Gruenwald, 1980: 23. The same technique noted by Gruenwald is evident in the long version (E and T) of *Orphica*, wherein the author speaks of the 'double law'. Lafargue considers this to refer to the 'two levels of meaning (exoteric/esoteric) in Scripture' (1985: 800).

finding in the Jewish scriptures themselves, but since 'such was not the case, another book of divine revelation was necessary.

These techniques evident in *Jubilees* and *1 Enoch* barely differ from that in *4 Ezra* 14, and the motivation is precisely the same—to authenticate firmly held convictions which could not be substantiated from scripture by postulating the existence of 'extra-canonical' books, themselves being divinely inspired and approved. Once again, then, the author does not intend to legitimate apocalyptic literature in general, or eschatological descriptions of the end times *per se*, but hopes to authenticate the peculiar message of his apocalyptic book in particular.

It is significant to compare briefly the characterization of the seventy books in *4 Ezra* 14.47 with the characterization of the law in Deut. 4.6. In commanding the people to observe the law of God, Moses says in Deuteronomy: 'for this will show your wisdom and understanding to the nations, who will hear about all these decrees and say, "Surely this great nation is a wise and understanding people"'. In *4 Ezra* 14, however, God reveals to Ezra that the twenty-four books are available to the worthy and the unworthy, while the seventy are worthy only of the wise, for in them (and *not* in the twenty-four books)[1] is 'the spirit of understanding, the fountain of wisdom, and the river of knowledge'.[2] Here again, the author shows his dissatisfaction with his former comprehension of God which was rooted in the public law. Despite Moses' public declaration of Deut. 4.6, the author is convinced that only the wisdom of the secret seventy books (which are representative of Ezra's new understanding) makes sense of human experience in the light of the tragic events of 70 CE.[3] Accordingly, to label Episode VII as 'Ezra's account of his commission by God to

1.   Nickelsburg (1985: 81-82) and Silberman (1974: 196) mistakenly identify the *twenty-four* books as containing the spirit of understanding.

2.   One may compare, in this regard, the manner in which Revelation plays on the command of Deut. 4.2, 'You shall not add to the word which I shall command you, nor take from it'. John cites this in Rev. 22.18-19 while making reference not to the Mosaic law but to his own apocalypse. In this way, he considers his apocalyptic revelations to equal, at least, if not exceed, the Mosaic revelation.

3.   The distance from the author's position to a gnostic view of knowledge is not very great. Cf. Murdoch, 1967: 184; Lombard, 1981: 37. The primary difference is that the knowledge of divine mysteries is redemptive in itself in many types of gnosticism, whereas it is a precursor to proper practice in apocalypticism. See further Rowland, 1988a: 182-83.

restore *the Scriptures*'[1] is to miss the point and function of this episode completely.

One qualification remains to be made. In one sense, the author sets the public law and the private law in a hierarchical relationship, in which the latter supersedes the former in the discernment of the will of God. This is obvious from the preceding paragraphs. In another sense, however, the author cannot bring himself to do away with the public law. Although his mention of the twenty-four books being written first may simply be an indicator of the temporal distance between the revelation of the Mosaic law and the revelation of the eschatological mysteries, it may also indicate the author's desire to affirm the centrality of the Mosaic law. In that case, the relationship between the twenty-four and the seventy books would appear to be modelled on that of text and interpretation; the interpretation and application of the Mosaic law is accurate only when it is understood in the manner of the seventy books (that is, only when it is seen to demand a rigid individualism of works-righteousness). The public law may be a final law, but it is not complete in itself. It needs the commentary of the private law—the interpretative seventy books, the symbol of its individualistic key.[2]

It is evident, therefore, that the distinction between the twenty-four books, which are for the worthy and unworthy, and the seventy books, which are exclusively for the wise, plays an essential part in the author's project in that it represents his attempt to legitimate Ezra's conversion-perspective, which he himself maintains. His claim is that the seventy books, which give wisdom and understanding of God's ways to the few, contain the individualistic key which unlocks the mysterious ways of the God who is represented (although inadequately) in the twenty-four books. When the seventy books are identified in this way, the theme which provides the internal momentum and cohesion throughout I–VI (the quest for the understanding of God's ways) maintains its centrality even in VII.[3]

1. Cook, 1988: 90, emphasis added.
2. Stone characterizes apocalypticists as considering themselves to be providers of 'the real, inner meaning of scriptural revelation' (1984: 431). Lebram talks of Ezra writing a 'new Torah' which consists of ninety-four books, the seventy interpreting the twenty-four (1983: 204).
3. Or, as Brandenburger says: 'Der Verfasser von visio 1–6 und 7 ist identisch' (1981: 136). Cf. Münchow, 1981: 77.

9.2. *Summary of Episode VII*

In my estimation, Episode VII has been seriously neglected or misunderstood in *4 Ezra* scholarship. The general tendency is to regard it as secondary to the central concerns of the book. One of the most recent studies of *4 Ezra* concludes, for example, that Episode VII 'adds little to the argument and is considered an epilogue'.[1] Similarly, A.L. Thompson barely mentions this episode in his analysis of the 'Structure of IV Ezra as the Key to the Author's Argument', a section of ninety-nine pages, of which only two are dedicated to Episode VII.[2] In fact, according to the index of his book, nowhere in nearly four hundred pages does Thompson make reference to *4 Ezra* 14.37-48! Certainly there is a weakness in the approach generally taken to the text, which this project seeks to redress.

Without an awareness of the conversion theme which runs throughout I–VI, the point of VII can easily be missed. This episode contains the author's attempt to substantiate his new perception of God's ways. He seems conscious of the fact that it is not widely known or accepted by others of his day, but takes account of this by postulating that God forbade the true understanding of his ways to be revealed to the people. As such, the fact that he holds a minority view actually reaffirms the validity of that view. In conjunction with this, he then legitimates his perception with regard to the scriptures by distinguishing between the twenty-four books of Jewish scripture known by all the people and the seventy books which reveal the secret ways of God to the few who are wise. As such, VII does not function as 'einen ästhetisch gefälligen Abschluss',[3] nor as a defence of apocalyptic literature, nor can it be considered an appendix which, having been added at a later date, dislodges the original author's argument altogether.[4] In fact, this episode is fundamental to the whole of the book in that it guards the author's case where it is most susceptible, certifying it with a divine seal of approval.

1. Willett, 1989: 122.
2. See his outline, 1977: xiv.
3. Gunkel, 1900: 348.
4. Contra Torrey, 1945: 118-19; Sanders, 1977: 417-18.

Chapter 10

CONCLUSIONS TO 4 EZRA

In the course of researching this project, I have often wondered whether I was reading the same text as other interpreters. This is true on three points. Consider first the following statement, quoted at length from J.H. le Roux.

> From IV Ezra. . . it is clear that the final decision lies with God. It is the merciful and righteous God who has the last word. Although IV Ezra mentions the dealings of God with people like Noah, Abraham, Isaac, Jacob, etc. their righteousness is never the sole reason for God's intervention in their lives. Not their piety and good works but the grace of God is the most important thing. More emphasis is laid on God's love and election than on man's conduct. It is God's great love which causes Him to make a covenant with Abraham in the midst of a wicked generation. Future salvation can only be expected from God and one must rely on His grace. Certainly there are righteous men who will inherit the future glory because of their good works, but they form the minority. God is the only One who can save all other men.[1]

The problem with this statement is that it is prefaced by saying that this is a characterization of 'IV Ezra', thereby indicating the *text* rather than the central *character* within the narrative, who is the 'Ezra of *4 Ezra*'. One suspects that what le Roux is referring to, however, is not the text but the character Ezra, for this quotation is most applicable to the words of Ezra in I–III, while failing to be a description of the point of the text of *4 Ezra* as a whole.

If this be the case, there follows a resulting complication. That is, it must always be clear *which* Ezra of *4 Ezra* is being discussed: the Ezra of I–III or of IV–VII? This is of primary importance since the narrative is nothing other than a conversion story.[2] In I–III, two per-

---

1. 1981: 51.
2. Cf. Stone, 1981. Stone defines conversion as 'the radical, sudden experience of change that causes the shift of perception' (1981: 204 n. 25). Cf. Collins, 1984a: 165, 168.

spectives jostle each other for supremacy—Ezra maintains that salvation can only be by the grace of God, whether on behalf of his people (I–III) or all humanity (III), while Uriel maintains that God has done enough in giving the law, and that the responsibility now lies with the individual to overcome the common fate of humanity. In the final episodes, Ezra, having accepted Uriel's case, receives confirmation of his new perspective through the eschatological visions, which themselves conform to Uriel's descriptions of God's ways. What Ezra has learned about God's ways in the present is not left dangling, without being tied down in a new vision of the future. To have a new awareness of the demands of God for the present requires a new awareness of the ways of God in the future. The point, of course, is that the Ezra of *4 Ezra* is transformed as the narrative develops.

The second point at which we express our puzzlement at the conclusions of some picks up from this point. The text demonstrates how, as a result of his conversion, Ezra comes to a new understanding of God's relationship with Israel. Nonetheless, commentators continue to state, as does M.E. Stone for instance, that Ezra moves from despair in I–III to the comforting assurance in IV–VII that Israel will be vindicated at the end—this assurance being the outcome of 'traditional explanations' of God's relationship with Israel.[1] So also, T.W. Willett argues that the final visions offer the assurance 'that God's promises to Israel would be fulfilled'.[2] Similarly C. Münchow says that the author of *4 Ezra* is concerned 'die bezweifelte Liebe Gottes zu seinem Volk zu behaupten'.[3] Assertions such as these can be multiplied at length. But the question must be pressed: *Who is meant by Israel?* In II, Uriel affirms that God loves Israel (5.33) and that he has an eschatological blessing for his people (5.40). Following from Ezra's concern for the nation Israel, it might initially appear that Uriel too has this ethnic group in mind. As the dialogue progresses, however, eschatological salvation is described by Uriel as being for 'those who remain' (6.25)—that is, for those who have deposited treasures of faithfulness with God (6.5). In III, Uriel clarifies what he means, stating that the next age belongs to the very few who are eligible for salvation not by their membership or covenant status, but by their treasures of works which demonstrate their perfect faithfulness to the law without sin.

---

1. Stone, 1987: 215; cf. 219.
2. Willett, 1989: 75.
3. 1981: 95.

This, it must be noted, is a highly redefined sense of 'Israel'; if the term is meaningful for Uriel, it is as an eschatological concept, a collective title of those few who are saved wholly apart from their status as Jews. Ethnic considerations have less to do with the definition of 'Israel' than does the eschatological boundary. The vision of V confirms this (12.34).

Of course, in VI the eschatological Israel is shown to be an innumerable multitude. The few appear together with an entity thus far unmentioned in *4 Ezra*—the ten tribes who were led away early in the people's history. Together, these two groups form a twelve-tribe conglomerate. Nonetheless, this glorious depiction of a grand eschatological Israel is a somewhat artificial construct which offers little assurance to the ethnic people who are seeking God's mercy. The traditional expectation of God's vindication of Israel has been so radically transformed as to allow no comfort for a people convinced that *divine grace* works in *their* favour. The author's presentation in VI represents less a return to traditional beliefs than theological positioning wherein unconventional convictions are clothed in acceptable garb. To claim, then, that the author is assured of 'God's enduring purpose of covenantal election and his attendant mercy' upon ethnic Israel[1] is to miss the whole purpose of *4 Ezra*.

A third point at which we must acknowledge dissatisfaction with much of *4 Ezra* scholarship is the way in which the author's position is evaluated in terms of the character of Early Judaism and its view of the law. In contrast to the scholarly estimates concerning the certainty of God's eschatological salvation of the ethnic people Israel, other estimates are just as frequent concerning the legalistic posture of the author as the exemplar of the Judaism of his day. So, in 1929, G.R.S. Mead, recognizing Ezra's constant plea for divine mercy, commented:

> Reading it [*4 Ezra*] to-day, our sympathies are, must be, with that large-hearted and gallant old Jew of eighteen centuries or more ago. We feel with him, think with him, cheer him on; and at the end profoundly regret that *he found himself compelled to bow down his brave spirit under the weight of tradition.*[2]

1. Knowles, 1989: 266.
2. Mead, 1929: 9-10, emphasis added. Cf. the estimate of Hughes, cited above, p. 17.

In the same year that E.P. Sanders published his study on Paul and
Early Judaism, A.L. Thompson argued as Mead had done fifty years
earlier:

> Through the mouth of Ezra, the author pleads for some means of saving the
> multitude of sinners. God's righteousness would really be established if he
> would show mercy to those with no store of good works (8.36). Though he
> argues his case with great earnestness and pathos, the author apparently real-
> izes that his hopes must be disappointed, and *the closing episodes represent*
> *his acceptance of the traditional basis of salvation, namely, the merit and*
> *obedience of the individual.*[1]

Similarly we hear from M. Knibb that the author

> *in common with other Jews of his day* believed that by the strict observance
> of the law it was possible for an individual to acquire, as it were, credit bal-
> ance of good works and to earn thereby the reward in the world to come of
> life.[2]

Such characterizations of early Judaism, however, go contrary to
the characterization given within the text itself, wherein 'all the people' are confused by the absence of divine mercy on their behalf and
seek mercy once again to restore and save them (5.26-28; 12.40-45).
Similarly, the reason why Ezra cannot accept Uriel's position
throughout I–III is that it goes against the grain of the traditional
understanding of God which is rooted in the scriptural record of
God's merciful dealings with Israel in covenant relationship. If Ezra
comes eventually to another understanding of God's ways, it is not
because he has 'bowed down his brave spirit under the weight of tradition', but because he found tradition itself to be inadequate.

The author, then, is not ultimately a frustrated conservative but a
reluctant liberal (radical?) who is willing to forsake tradition where it
fails to meet experience. The author of *4 Ezra* has advanced a new
understanding of the character of Jewish existence without the temple:
salvation is not a national privilege but an individual responsibility
worked out with great effort by works of merit. Divine grace is, for
all purposes, absent in his scheme, except as an eschatological reflex to
those who have saved themselves anyway by their works.[3] He still
maintains such traditional concepts as 'law' and 'Israel' in his new

---

1. Thompson, 1977: 318, emphasis added.
2. Knibb, 1979: 182, emphasis added.
3. Cf. Collins: the author 'allows little if any place for atonement or divine mercy'
(1984a: 169).

pattern of religion, but redefines them in a way which gives them radicalized import. (See 'Thesis Conclusions', where the author's handling of these concepts is compared with that of Paul in Rom. 1–11.) In the eyes of the author, ethnocentric covenantalism could not make sense out of the destruction of Jerusalem. He found no way to maintain his intellectual integrity and to account for that definitive event within an ethnocentric perspective. Thus, he appropriated a new view which was able to make sense of that momentous event while retaining the trappings of the old view at the same time.[1]

Therefore, what we see in I–III are, first and foremost, the dialogues of the author with himself. This is not to say, however, that Ezra and Uriel represent two convictions sustained by the author simultaneously (contra Gunkel). Instead, they embody the author's case at two distinct stages in the process of his conceptual development; in the encounter between Uriel and Ezra, we overhear the author's own post-conversion self in dialogue with his pre-conversion self. The author knows the point of view of ethnocentric covenantalism all too well, and gives it a voice of its own before abandoning it for another view. This is not to say, however, that ethnocentric covenantalism has no validity. The author seems all too aware that it does. This would explain why Ezra's conversion itself is nowhere portrayed; argumentative persuasion (Episodes I–III) is not adequate to facilitate the necessary perceptual transformation. For this reason, his conversion takes place outside the context of the dialogue and in reflective solitude, off-stage. The author seems to have no argument to disqualify Ezra's initial position; he is conscious 'of the strength of the arguments which he places in Ezra's mouth'.[2] But because the author found that he could not square the arguments mouthed by Ezra with his own experience, he abandoned them altogether and appropriated another understanding, one in which he found the consolation for which he longed (or so IV–VI would have us believe). This new understanding is discovered only by the privileged few, as God intended it. The author never defended God's decision to work in this way but simply affirmed that God is just.

---

2.   It is not too far off, then, to say that traditional characterization of the degeneration of Judaism from a covenantal to a legalistic religion is played out within the single text of *4 Ezra*; if that traditional scheme misses the mark as a description of the religious history of the Jews of Early Judaism, it comes close to the mark as a description of the religious history of at least one Jew of the first century CE.

2.   Hayman, 1975: 53.

With this portrait in mind, the obvious question is: Why did the author choose Ezra, one of the great figures of Israel's convenantal history, as his pseudonym? The answer can be best illustrated by the encounter scenes wherein Ezra meets with the people of Israel. G.B. Sayler correctly notes that the 'encounters between Ezra and his people are mentioned only rarely in analyses of *4 Ezra*'.[1] She comments that 'none of the three encounters is an essential component in the development of the book; if they were omitted, their absence would hardly be noticed'.[2] In my view, however, this second estimation misses the point of what is a most telling rhetorical feature in *4 Ezra*. The encounters are not extraneous and superficial to the main body. The author places Ezra in that encounter situation at various points in his work in order to highlight Ezra's progression in the process of his conversion (from the ambassador of the national interest to the individualistic legalist) and, thereby, to authenticate his case with regard to historical anomalies.

The first encounter appears at the end of I. It serves to inform the reader that Ezra has undertaken his task in the interests of the people who feel betrayed by their God and who seek his covenant mercy. The people's hope for restoration lay with Ezra's appeals and, as Episode II especially depicts, he is well suited for this role. His characterization here is not far from that of the biblical texts.

The second encounter takes place after V, wherein the author sets up a curious situation for Ezra. No longer is Ezra the people's spokesperson; this Ezra is not the figure known from the pages of scripture, for he has learned the truth which disqualifies the people's concerns altogether. And yet, how does Ezra appear to the people when they, 'all the people', approach him at the end of V? Since God has instructed him not to reveal his new understanding to the people but only to the wise, he does as he was commissioned to do and fails to reveal the truth of God's ways to them. His only recourse is to assure the people that God has not forsaken them. This is what *the people* hear, and it is in full accord with the scriptural presentation of Ezra. *The reader*, however, knows the inside story and discerns the irony of the situation: after having learned the truth, Ezra does not disrupt the people's perspective, for this is not his task. Instead, he is to give *to the wise* the knowledge of what is required for salvation, a knowledge

1. 1984: 133 n. 28.
2. 1984: 133.

which is kept from the majority of the people. Consequently, his words to the people prove to be superficial. By means of this 'encounter motif', therefore, the author illustrates that appearances are deceiving without the proper vantage point, which the people do not have and which is not contained even in the scriptural records. (This promotes his peculiar estimate of scripture in 14.37-48.)

The third and final encounter occurs in VII. Ezra is told by God to write in books what is revealed to him, but is instructed to reveal only some things to the people, while the wise are eligible to receive the full account. Immediately after this command, Ezra gathers the people to him, thereby paralleling the situation at the end of V. Sayler states that Ezra's speech to the people in VII 'bears little, if any, relationship to the revelations he has received throughout the book'.[1] It is probably better to say, however, that the speech is (intentionally) ambiguous in its meaning. What Ezra proclaims can be understood in various ways, depending on one's prior perceptions. He ascribes Israel's desperate situation to the people's disobedience of the law, and urges them to discipline themselves in the ways of the law in order to be kept alive and obtain mercy after death. This, of course, bears striking resemblance to the prophetic voice and to traditional exhortations of Judaism. It also, of course, is the core of Ezra's new perspective. Thus, in its ambiguity, it feeds both the people's ethnocentrism and Ezra's individualistic legalism. While he points to the answer he has discovered (viz. adherence to the law), he never sinks that answer into the system of thought which he has learned from Uriel. Instead, he allows the people to remain in their ignorance and does not supplant their covenantal self-perception. Can he be blamed for this? No, for he is under orders from God himself, whose ways are just.

This 'encounter motif', then, is an early exercise in hermeneutics and epistemology, motivated by a concern to legitimate innovation in the face of historical appearances. Whereas the official Jewish history books portray Ezra in one light (the second Moses, the founder of the Great Assembly of scribes and interpreters), the author presents a different picture of Ezra, but one which incorporates the scriptural account while *reinterpreting* the historical significance of one of

---

1.   1984: 133. Cf. Hayman, 1975: 47; Brandenburger, 1981: 65, 80.

Israel's great heroes.[1] (A 'Christian' revaluing of Ezra is evidenced in *Ques. Ezra* A.32-33.) The author does not attempt to deny the covenantal *appearances* of Israel's history. His case is more subtle. In the figure of Ezra, the author has isolated a post-destruction figure of great significance in the history of Israel and of the law, but he demonstrates that behind the depiction of Ezra in the official history books of Scripture lies a motivation not explained in Scripture: underlying Ezra's actions was not a vibrant covenantalism but a stringent legalism. If the people fail to see this, such is to be expected.

A similar authenticating technique is employed by the author of Mark's Gospel in Mk 4.10-12. There Jesus is said to have spoken parables to all, but to have explained them to only a few who have 'been given the secret of the kingdom of God'; the rest hear but do not understand 'lest they might turn and be forgiven'.[2] Whether or not this is a historical account, as a literary-redactional technique it reinforces the community's christological understanding which is not shared by 'those outside'. It authenticates what was not apparent to others by virtue of the fact that those others were not privy to vital information. This distinction between public proclamation and private explanation feeds the gospel's 'messianic secret' motif.[3] A similar motivation and technique is evident in the 'encounter motif' of *4 Ezra*, promoting a 'soteriological secret' motif. If readers identified with Phaltiel and the people in I, by V and VII they are to distinguish themselves from them, identifying instead with Ezra and the few who understand the true ways of God, which are not evident to the majority.

From the text of *4 Ezra*, then, we can recognize the author to be a pious and sensitive Jew so disturbed by the events of 70 CE that his confidence in God's righteousness was fundamentally shaken. Instead of abandoning his loyalty to God, however, he arrived at a new understanding which enabled him to reaffirm once again his confidence in God. In the process, however, his beliefs took on a radical character, following on from his denial of divine grace in the pre-

---

1. Herford wonders whether the author wanted 'to connect the apparent breakdown of the religion of the Torah with the man who was mainly responsible for that form of religion' (1933: 180 note).

2. Cf. Isa. 6.9-10. For the influence of Isa. 6 in Early Jewish and Christian self-definition, see Evans, 1989, where, however, the phenomenon in *4 Ezra* goes unmentioned.

3. See, in this regard, Watson, 1985.

sent. In a very real way, then, while refusing to abandon the God of the law and of Israel, the author has had to abandon his belief in the primary quality which distinguished that God in his relationship with Israel, as presented in Scripture: the efficacy of God's grace. Consequently, he focused his expectations concerning eschatological salvation upon the works performed by the individual in this age.[1]

Throughout Part II, we have seen how the author of *4 Ezra* reacted to the destruction of Jerusalem in 70 CE, a 'crisis event' which jolted his traditional understanding of God's ways and caused him to transform his perspective in its wake. In Part III, which follows, interests turn to one other Jew of the first century CE who falls 'outside' the common covenantal pattern of Early Judaism and whose perspective was also radically transformed as a result of a 'crisis event' (namely the revelation of Jesus Christ): Paul.

---

1. Much work remains to be done in analysis of this text. Three avenues especially will be mentioned here. First, the ground is fallow for a literary reading of *4 Ezra*; the results of such a project would, I think, prove to be fascinating. Second, a sociological description of the author, his community and the purpose of this book in relation to the community's self-definition is necessary. This would prove to be a difficult task, by reason of the fact that social indicators within the text are not readily evident. Despite recent attempts (cf. Stone, 1987: 216; Gray, 1976; Kolenkow, 1982; Mueller, 1981), this area still remains unclear. (On the social setting of Jewish apocalypticism in general, see esp. Nickelsburg, 1983; Grabbe, 1989.) Third, a comparison of the author's position with some gnostic tendencies and ideologies would help to demonstrate the overlap of Jewish apocalypticism and gnosticism already in the late first century CE, while highlighting at the same time some of their fundamental differences.

PART III

ROMANS 1–11

Chapter 11

INTRODUCTION TO ROMANS 1–11

11.1. *Introduction to Romans 1–11*

In his classic work of 1980, J.C. Beker demonstrated decisively the 'contingent' nature of Paul's letters. Beker argued that a coherent 'apocalyptic' perspective gives substance to what are shown to be situation-bound arguments within Paul's letters. This dynamic between 'coherence' and 'contingency' is fundamental to many issues concerning Paul and his letters, and in one regard this is especially true. The contingent expressions of Paul's gospel do not always dovetail into one nicely wrapped package for the benefit of scholars and believers two millennia removed; instead, they are composed with specific situations in mind, and their content is determined by Paul's view of those situations as he attempted to address them.[1]

All this is pertinent for this project in that, since only one Pauline text is to be examined below (and that only in part), whatever transpires from that examination must be recognized not as a comprehensive treatment of Paul's view on any matter, such as 'Paul and the Law'; such is not the intention. The interest here is only in analysing one of Paul's contingent arguments in order to compare it with the case of the author of *4 Ezra*. There is no doubt that were another Pauline text chosen for evaluation, the results of the comparison would be somewhat different, because of the different situation in which Paul found himself and his audience at the time of writing.

The text chosen for this analysis in Part III is Rom. 1.18–11.36, which provides many points for comparison. Much attention has been given to analysing how one or another situation may have determined the content and argument of this letter. Is it Paul's own situation[2] (the events which confronted him in Corinth and Galatia, or his approach-

---

1. Beker, 1980: 23-131.
2. Cf. e.g. Bornkamm, 1977; Jervell, 1977.

ing visit to the Jerusalem church) or the situation of the Roman christian communities[1] which motivates Paul's presentation? Or is this a false juxtaposition altogether, with the primary motivation for the letter arising instead out of the interface between the two?[2] A few words should be said in this regard before beginning a study of the text.

First, a fairly consistent picture emerges from his other letters concerning Paul's situation: Paul was a Jew who boasted of his Jewish heritage (Phil. 3.5), who had persecuted some early believers (Phil. 3.6), who encountered the risen Messiah (Gal. 1.15-16), who involved himself in proclaiming the message of the crucified and exalted Messiah, and who undertook at some point in his career a controversial mission to the gentiles by preaching that salvation was available to them on the sole basis of their faith in Christ (cf. Galatians). For whatever reason, his mission was suspect by many believers and proved often to be a point of contention within the early christian movement, making for some tension between various groups (cf. Gal. 1–2). Moreover, Paul hoped to collect offerings from the communities which he had established in order to present them to the christian communities in Jerusalem (1 Cor. 16.1-4; Gal. 2.10). His interest in this collection seems motivated not solely by a desire to make a display of solidarity among the christian communities which were separated by distance, practice and belief; other factors may well have contributed to his interest in this regard, for if the Jerusalem congregations would accept the collection as a symbol of gentile-christian charity and of christian unity, such a scenario would no doubt help to legitimate Paul's position and mission within the movement itself. It is with this controversial reputation, this concern for the spread of his gospel, this desire for christian unity, and this need for acceptance and legitimation that Paul writes to the christian communities in Rome, which he had never visited previously.

Second, it seems possible to delineate sections of Paul's letter in terms of their relationship either to Paul's own situation or to the situation of the christian communities in Rome. It is telling that scholars usually concentrate their investigations concerning the latter on the early verses of Romans 1 or (especially) on the latter chapters of Romans (Rom. 12–16); if any passages within Paul's letter give us a

1. Cf. e.g. Minear, 1971; Wiefel, 1977.
2. Cf. esp. Wedderburn, 1988.

glimpse of what is happening in the Roman congregations, they would seem primarily to be those passages which surround Rom. 1.18–11.36.[1] What Paul says in Rom. 1.18–11.36 (a section marked by a certain degree of 'Selbständigkeit')[2] appears to be less concerned with the situation of the Roman communities than with establishing a theological rationale for Paul's provocative mission; both the nature of the chapters themselves (namely the virtual absence of situational indicators) and Paul's introduction to the 'thesis' of 1.16-17 ('I am not ashamed of the [read: 'my'] gospel') suggest that Paul's agenda herein is primarily to explain his gospel in order to authenticate it in preparation for his visit to the Roman communities.

These chapters arise primarily out of Paul's reflections on his own situation within the purposes of God; his concern is seemingly to legitimate his perception of God's ways by spelling out the theological grounds for his controversial mission. Paul evidently expected some believers in Rome to be wary of his mission, just as many others seem to have been elsewhere. Only later do we learn why Paul took precautions to allay the suspicions of the *Roman* communities in particular by sending them his theological legitimation; he wanted to seek their support and acceptance in order to establish a geographical springboard towards his envisaged Spanish ministry (Rom. 15.17-24, 28-29, 32). He also hoped, no doubt, that his gospel would be of help in alleviating some dangerous developments within the Roman communities as well (especially Rom. 14–15.13) and sought their support in return (at least through prayer) for his impending visit to Jerusalem, which he knew would involve some danger of its own (Rom. 15.30-31). Nonetheless, all of these interests are dependent upon the persuasiveness of Paul's case in Rom. 1.18–11.36, wherein he seeks to authenticate for this Roman audience in particular his controversial ministry; once done, he can then proceed with some authority to contribute towards the betterment of their situation, and they to his. We approach Rom. 1.18–11.36, then, intent on discovering how Paul presented himself to believers in Rome, most of whom he had never met and many of whom, it seems, were cautious, suspicious and perhaps even antagonistic towards him. For them, he lays out his credentials in

---

1. I remain sceptical of attempts to recreate the situation of the Romans christian communities from this material; cf. e.g. W.S. Campbell's attempt to do so from Rom. 9–11 (1981b).

2. Schmithals, 1975b: 9.

1.18–11.36 especially, before proceeding into exhortations and admonitions in Romans 12–16.

Of special concern for this project is Paul's handling of the significance of the law and the people of Israel as he seeks to authenticate his perceptions and ministry. Before beginning a new investigation into these matters, it will be helpful to call to mind something of the present scholarly debate, allowing it to serve as the backdrop for this investigation. In what follows, then, a very brief and selective survey will be set out which seeks to highlight the issues pertaining to the examination of Paul's text.

11.2. *A Selective Survey of Recent Pauline Scholarship*

Perhaps the thorniest of issues in Pauline scholarship concerns the role of the law in Paul's thought. The issue has proved to be so fundamentally problematic that several scholars have recently attributed the dilemma to Paul himself, finding his own reflections on the law to have been disjointed. This course has been steered, for instance, by H. Räisänen, who argues that inconsistency permeates Paul's reflections on the law.[1] Theories which seek to explain inconsistencies as arising out of development within Paul's thought[2] do not get to the heart of the problem, says Räisänen, since each particular letter shows within itself inconsistencies and contradictions. The problem is explained, instead, by emotive factors within Paul: Paul is 'torn in two directions, incapable of resolving the tension theologically'.[3] Those two directions are due to (1) Paul's conviction that the law has been abolished, and (2) Paul's conviction that the law, having been given by God, is incapable of being abrogated.[4] His experience forced Paul to abandon his loyalty to the law, although he also paid lip service to it for the sake of appearances.[5] As a consequence, the meaning of 'law' oscillates to fit the needs of Paul's arguments in relation to his two conflicting convictions. Although he instigated a break with the law, Paul left this implicit in his scheme, concealing it from others and, most probably, even from himself; what was implicit became explicit only in gnostic

---

1. Räisänen, 1983. Cf. Boers: 'what gives coherence to Paul's thought is contradiction at its most fundamental level' (1988: 63, emphasis removed).
2. Cf. Hübner, 1984a; Drane, 1975; Wilckens, 1982.
3. 1983: 264.
4. 1983: 264-65; cf. 1987b: 410.
5. 1983: 266.

circles where the abandonment of the law became complete.[1] Moreover, Räisänen finds Paul's case to be fundamentally ill conceived,
involving a 'misinterpretation' of the role of the law in Early Judaism;
Paul can denounce the law as he does only because he ascribes to the
law a status 'which it never had in genuine Jewish thought' and a
function 'detached from God's covenantal grace'.[2] Paul 'gives a totally
distorted picture of the Jewish religion'[3] since, as Paul presents it,
Judaism was legalism.

Although Räisänen has been accused of carrying out an 'atomistic
treatment' of Paul,[4] his work nevertheless demonstrates well that, in
the course of defending his gospel, Paul was not much concerned with
logical consistency but used various lines of argument even within a
single letter to score points in support of his case. Paul's statements on
the law, then, are performance-oriented, or as F. Watson says, Paul
'makes use of various types of theoretical legitimation, which are not
always compatible with one another as pure theory but which all contribute to the same practical goal'.[5]

In this regard, E.P. Sanders has argued that Paul's estimates concerning the law are secondary to his exclusivistic soteriology; they are
explained by his conviction that salvation is exclusively through Christ
and do not explain that conviction. Sanders, like Räisänen, sees Paul's
various estimates of the law as unable to be harmonized (they are
'unsystematic'). Nonetheless, he emphasizes that Paul's critiques of the
law are coherent in that they all arise from a common factor: the
conviction that salvation is through Christ alone and, therefore, cannot
be by any other means.[6] The exclusivism of Paul's soteriology gives
coherence to his diverse critiques of the law. Sanders also notes, however, that whereas the negative estimates of the law arise when Paul
discusses the conditions for membership within the christian community, positive estimates are given when he discusses the behavioural
norms of that community. In the latter context, Paul insists that the
law should be fulfilled, albeit by means of the Spirit.[7] Taking his cues
from Paul's comments in Philippians 3 and 2 Corinthians 3, Sanders

1. 1983: 201.
2. 1986b: 39.
3. 1986b: 38.
4. Dunn, 1988a: lxvii.
5. 1986: 22.
6. 1977: 519.
7. 1983a: 84, 105, 114.

thinks that, despite his many arguments against the law, Paul found nothing fundamentally wrong with the law except that it was not Christ. The dispensation of the law was glorious, but its glory was surpassed for Paul, and became 'loss' in comparison with the dispensation of faith in Christ: 'the only thing wrong with the old dispensation is that it is not the new one'.[1] Paul knows the function of the law in Jewish covenantalism, but he no longer accepts it to be regulative, and consequently constructs various arguments against it as a means to salvation.

Other approaches have been taken to resolve the issue of the law in Paul's presentations. Rather than 'law' being a slippery, oscillating concept, as some argue, S. Westerholm thinks that a distinction runs consistently between Paul's various estimates of the law, a distinction between (1) the Pentateuch or Jewish scriptures, which for Paul pointed to faith in Christ, and (2) the Sinaitic legislation, which prescribes 'doing' and 'works' rather than faith. While Paul puts his presentation in line with the former and, accordingly, claims to uphold the law (Rom. 3.31), he considered the Sinaitic legislation to have been abrogated by God's action in Christ, thereby ruling out 'works' and 'doing' from the sphere of proper response to God. Westerholm essentially argues a traditional line, finding, as does E. Käsemann, that for Paul 'law' and 'gospel' are 'mutually exclusive antitheses'.[2] So Westerholm proposes that 'students who want to understand Paul but feel they have nothing to learn from a Martin Luther should consider a career in metallurgy'.[3] He agrees with Sanders, however, that Early Judaism is best represented as 'covenantal nomism', and thinks, consequently, that Paul's juxtaposition of grace and works was not shared by his Jewish contemporaries:[4] 'the Jewish position could hardly be reconstructed on the basis of Paul's writings'.[5] Westerholm does not accuse Paul of distorting the issue, however; Paul's case does not involve a caricature of Judaism but is a recasting of traditional categories in which he 'moves the whole discussion onto a different level'.[6]

---

1. 1983: 140.
2. Käsemann, 1980: 282.
3. 1988: 173.
4. 1988: 148-50.
5. 1988: 150.
6. 1988: 150.

Others argue that Paul's criticisms are not against the law per se but against a misapprehension of the law and its significance; what Paul rejected was the improper view of the law as a 'law of works', for the law is properly the 'law of faith'. This approach counters the prevalent juxtaposition between 'gospel' and 'law' with its 'cavalier dismissal of the law',[1] positing instead a distinction between the proper and improper usage of the law. So N.T. Wright says: 'Whatever solution is to be found to the question of "Paul and the law". . . it will not come by treating Paul simply as a Lutheran—still less a Marcionite—born out of due time'.[2] This approach has taken two forms. First, C.E.B. Cranfield and H. Hübner argue that, for Paul, the law is misused when allowed to promote Jewish legalism: only when it promotes faith is the law properly fulfilled.[3] Like Räisänen and Westerholm, Cranfield and Hübner think that Paul charges his Jewish contemporaries with legalistic motives, in which salvation is earned apart from grace; unlike Räisänen and Westerholm, however, Cranfield and Hübner use this charge to reconstruct Early Judaism as a sterile religion of legalism. So Hübner says that, in Early Judaism, the law had been 'degraded and depraved into a means of having to assert oneself before God'.[4] Cranfield and Hübner find Paul's critique to be right on target: Paul found Jewish legalism to be an inappropriate understanding of God's ways in view of God's grace mediated through faith.

This general approach, which distinguishes between proper and improper usages of the law, is advocated also by N.T. Wright and J.D.G. Dunn, who argue, however, that it was not 'legalism', in the traditional sense, but Jewish exclusivism or nationalism which Paul regarded as an illegitimate perception of the law's significance.[5] Paul considered that 'most of Israel has misunderstood the law, by taking it as a badge of national and covenant identity'.[6] Wright and Dunn consider Paul to be interacting with, rather than misunderstanding or distorting, the covenantal character of the Judaism of his day. Instead of a sterile legalism, they think that Paul rejected the exclusivistic atti-

---

1. Wright, 1988: 424.
2. 1988: 424.
3. Cf. Cranfield, 1975a: 220; Hübner, 1984a: 138. For Hübner, Paul argues this line only in Romans.
4. 1984a: 138.
5. Wright, 1978; *idem*, 1980; Dunn, 1983; *idem*, 1988a.
6. Dunn, 1988a: 192.

tude which prevailed in Early Judaism as a result of a covenantal self-identity.

Intertwined with Paul's statements concerning the law is, of course, Paul's estimate of Israel. One dilemma which he encountered seems to be that, although the people of Israel claimed to be the covenant people of God who possess in Scripture the revelation of God's ways, the majority of them failed to believe in the Messiah of God, of whom Paul considered the scriptures to speak. This dilemma, coupled with his need to authenticate his gentile mission, forced Paul to reflect upon the relationship of the christian movement (as he perceived it) to traditional expressions of Judaism and God's dealings with Israel. In this regard, W.D. Davies has championed the case that, for Paul, the gospel of faith was not antithetical to but was 'the full flowing of Judaism, the outcome of the latter and its fulfillment'.[1] Somewhat differently, F. Watson characterizes Paul as one 'who devotes his energies to the creation and maintaining of sectarian groups hostile to all non-members, and especially to the Jewish community from which in fact they derived'.[2]

Different in all respects is L. Gaston's case that, for Paul, unbelieving Jews experience God's grace even apart from faith in Christ, since they are God's covenant people irrevocably; Paul considered God's work in Christ to be solely for the benefit of *the gentiles*, for whom salvation is now available apart from converting to Judaism.[3] One passage which Gaston cites especially in support of his case is Rom. 11.26-29, wherein Paul is convinced of Israel's salvation on the basis of their irrevocable call and election by God in love. This passage is often cited by others who do not assent to Gaston's views as springing not from the logic of Paul's gospel for salvation by faith but from his affection for his own people; he is certain that God will not abandon Israel, although his arguments throughout the rest of Romans work in the opposite direction and give no basis for this rather surprising claim (a 'mystery', as Paul calls it). At this point, it is often said that Paul wants to have his cake and eat it, or, as Sanders says, Paul 'desperately sought a formula which would keep God's promise to Israel intact, while insisting on faith in Jesus Christ'. In this regard,

---

1. 1980: 323.
2. 1986: 180-81.
3. Gaston, 1987.

says Sanders, Paul has 'more than a little difficulty reconciling his native convictions with those which he had received by revelation'.[1]

With this very brief and selective survey in view, investigation of the text of Rom. 1.18–11.36 can begin. Nonetheless, before proceeding along these lines it is necessary to examine briefly several aspects of Paul's case in Rom. 1.16-17, a section which is in many ways a summary of the contents of his particular letter. Paul unwraps and develops this 'nutshell' summary especially in the eleven chapters to follow. It is, therefore, deserving of quick mention before delving into the complexities of Paul's case. This is the purpose of the following paragraphs.

11.3. *Setting Up the Context of the Discussion: Romans 1.16-17*

Having introduced himself in the first fifteen verses of Romans 1, Paul proceeds in 1.16 to introduce his gospel, which he calls 'the power of God', a power in distinction from the powers of sin and its associates (cf. 3.9; 6.1–7.25). Unlike the power of sin, this divine power leads not to death but 'to salvation', and it does so for all those who live by πίστις. By πίστις, Paul is speaking not of 'faithfulness' in the sense of nomistic practice (its usual connotation in Jewish literature) but of 'faith', a response to God which includes no particularistic content (cf. Rom. 3.21–4.25 especially). This universalism proved, of course, to be the controversial point of Paul's gospel since it appeared to deny the effectiveness of God's election of, and dealings with, the people of Israel as the particular focus of his affection and attention. As if to address this objection, Paul adds (with what seems to have been a deliberate sense of ironic twist) one qualification to the universalism of his gospel: 'to the Jew *first* and also to the Greek'. In this way, then, we can already notice a peculiar tension in his perspective, a tension which includes an ethnic advantage or priority within his universalistic outlook. Only once does this tension arise within his argument (3.1-8) before being addressed (and resolved) finally in Romans 9–11.

Paul continues in 1.17, introducing 'the righteousness of God' as an essential aspect of his gospel. Much effort has been devoted on defining the exact nuances of this term. For the purposes of this project, however, it is enough to understand it primarily as denoting God's own 'acting to sustain his people, his loyalty to his own

---

1. 1983a: 199.

promises, and his total reliability'.[1] It pertains to God's own activity within the context of the covenant relationship between himself and his people, each of whom has responsibilities to the other in order to maintain the relationship. Synonymous with this is Paul's mention in 3.3 of God's 'faithfulness'—that is, his covenantal trustworthiness (cf. 15.8). Already, then, Paul has signalled to his readers that the presentation which follows has to do with understanding the God of the covenant and his actions.

Although Paul's gospel has to do with the God of Jewish covenantal history, Paul adds an important eschatological dynamic to his case by means of the word ἀποκαλύπτεται: the righteousness of God 'is revealed'. The revelation of God's righteousness has the eschatological 'Christ-event' as its basis, just as Paul states in parallel fashion in 3.21-26 that God's righteousness 'has been made apparent' (πεφανέρωται) through the sacrifice of Christ's death, thereby inaugurating the new eschatological age within the old. Both ἀποκαλύπτεται and πεφανέρωται highlight the way in which Paul perceives God's activity in Christ as 'the irruption of the Eschaton into the present'.[2] Paul's point is not that God's righteousness has been absent in history until Christ's coming brought in the eschatological age. Instead, Paul means to say that the eschatological event has revealed something about God's righteousness which may not have been apparent previously; in the light of the Christ-event, the covenantal faithfulness of God is to be understood in a new light, having a fuller significance than was previously appreciated. As Paul proceeds to explain his case in 1.18ff., he does so by repeating once again this eschatological foundation of his gospel, saying in 1.18 that the wrath of God 'is revealed' (ἀποκαλύπτεται) against sinners. Here again, the point is not that God's wrath was absent before the coming of Christ. Instead, Paul's point is that God's wrath is to be understood in a new way in the light of the Christ-event. Paul goes on to explain this in Rom. 1.18–3.20, wherein he argues that the 'sinners' who are deserving of God's wrath include people of all races, including the Jews collectively. One of the things that Paul intends to do in his project is to provide new definitions of terms such as 'the righteous', 'the sinners' and 'the righteousness of God' (as well as others; see especially the analysis of Rom. 2.1-11 in Chapter 12). This is precisely what has caused him so

1. Ziesler, 1989: 70. Cf. Dunn, 1988a: 40-42.
2. Hübner, 1984a: 127.

much trouble in the past with some of his contemporaries (cf. e.g. Galatians 1–2). Accordingly, Paul appeals to eschatological insight at the outset of this letter in order to assure his audience of the validity of the way in which he will redefine traditional categories in the presentation to follow.

Already a significant parallel with our results in Part II can be noted: for both Paul and the author of *4 Ezra*, traditional understandings concerning the God of Israel's history need to be informed (or corrected) by the revelation of God's eschatological ways. Despite the fact that Paul and the author of *4 Ezra* perceive the eschaton quite differently (especially since it is already inaugurated for Paul whereas it is still wholly in the future for the author of *4 Ezra*), both authors appeal to eschatological revelation as the basis for their presentations.

Complementing this revelatory aspect of Paul's claim is his insistence that his gospel has scriptural support as well. Citing as evidence Hab. 2.4, Paul is intent to root his eschatologically revealed case in the Jewish scriptures, especially since Paul will go on to argue that the God who gave the scriptures to the Jewish people is the same God that Paul announces in his gospel. This is a fundamental conviction of Paul's throughout Romans, and here it is stated quite simply. As his case continues, however, the extremes to which Paul must go to maintain and support this conviction will be observed.

Already, then, two important dynamics of Paul's case have been noted within Rom. 1.16-17, and each animates much of his case throughout Romans 1–11: (1) the relationship between eschatological insight ('innovation') and scriptural authentication (historical continuity), and (2) the tension between universal salvation and particularistic advantage. Both of these issues are subordinated under the categories of the law and the people of Israel, the focal points of the present study. At this point, then, we turn to the task of examining the main body of Paul's case throughout Rom. 1.18–11.36 with these two issues in view: Paul's handling of the law and the people of Israel.

In the remaining chapters of Part III, our examination will follow not a sequential outline *per se*, as in Part II, but a thematic outline. Chapter 12 will concern itself with Paul's description of the anthropological condition and the implications which he draws from it in Rom. 1.18–3.20; Chapter 13 investigates the solution to that problem as it is laid out in Rom. 3.21-31, 9.30–10.13 and 7.7–8.4; Chapter 14 takes note of the 'ethnic' aspect of Paul's view of salvation history as it is found in Romans 9–11 and seeks to explain it in view of his larger project concerning salvation through faith. These passages have been chosen for their direct relevance to the concerns of this study. (Unlike Part II, a summary chapter will not appear in Part III. In order to avoid unnecessary redundancy, the 'conclusions' to this analysis of Romans 1–11 appear in Part IV, where they appear in comparison with appropriate conclusions from the analysis of *4 Ezra*.)

Chapter 12

THE ANTHROPOLOGICAL CONDITION

After laying the groundwork in Rom. 1.16-17 for his presentation to the Roman christian communities, Paul proceeds to elaborate his case throughout the rest of the first eleven chapters of his letter. Structurally, he works his case in its early stages from problem to solution; initially, he exposes the dilemma (1.18–3.20) which he will later seek to address only later (3.21ff.) by means of his own understanding of the significance of God's eschatological revelation in Christ. The seven sections of this chapter will deal with the way in which Paul sets up the problem to be solved as it appears in Rom. 1.18–3.20.

12.1. *Paul's Description of the Anthropological Condition: 1.18-32*

Paul, in commencing his case that God's righteousness 'is revealed from faith unto faith' (1.17), sets out the first facet of his argument in 1.18: 'The wrath of God is revealed from heaven against all the godlessness and wickedness of men'. In 1.26-31, Paul gives a list of moral vices to illustrate the extent of human depravity which provokes God's wrath. He does not characterize these moral failings as the disease to be corrected, but as the symptoms of a more fundamental condition described in 1.19-25. His prognosis of that condition is evident especially in 1.21: 'although they knew God, they neither glorified him as God nor gave thanks to him', the point being that they failed to give rightful honour to the creator in proper response as his creation. Instead they became idolatrous (1.23, 25). Consequently, God 'gave them over' to the desires of their heart, resulting in crimes against the natural order and against others, as described in 1.24 and 1.26-31. These evil deeds are the outward expressions of an inward condition which is deserving only of death (1.32). Although 'what may be known about God' is evident in the natural order and is clearly perceived by all (1.19-20), 'they did not think it worthwhile to retain the knowledge of God' (1.28), and so 'exchanged the truth of God for a lie' (1.25), suppressing 'the truth by their wickedness' (1.18). Accordingly, they themselves are held accountable 'without excuse' (1.20).

It is sometimes held that Paul's description in 1.18-32 is intended as an indictment of the gentiles, whose sinful condition is expressed in idolatrous and sexually perverse lifestyles. So L. Gaston claims that this section deals '*exclusively* with the situation of the Gentile world'.[1] Certainly, Paul's description in 1.18-32 includes a condemnation of the gentile nations; charges of idolatry and sexual immorality (especially homosexuality) were common artillery in Jewish denunciation of the gentile nations. Nonetheless, to state, as Gaston does, that Paul's sights are focused exclusively on *gentile* deficiencies is to narrow down the dynamics of Paul's case. It is not the gentile condition alone that Paul is describing here but a more fundamental *anthropological* condition which includes in itself no ethnic differentiation.[2] That is, if what Paul is describing pertains exclusively to the gentiles, that is true only by way of the fact that, for most Jews, gentiles alone were thought to remain in the anthropological condition of sin, whereas Israel has been rescued from that condition by the covenant grace of God; Jews too are susceptible to that anthropological condition except for God's election of them. It follows, then, that Paul is painting herein a picture of humanity *in toto* before God, although such a condition was thought to have been offset for Israel by God's mercy upon them.

It should be noted that, in this initial section, overtones can be heard of the biblical account in Genesis 2–3 of the fall of Adam into sin.[3] Despite his knowledge of God and God's decree, Adam forfeited the glory of God in which he had been created by believing the lie of the serpent ('you will be like him'), thereby perverting his natural creatureliness. Accordingly, Adam entered into the perversity of sin, as is clearly evidenced by his offspring. Not surprisingly, Paul evidently chose to frame his portrayal of the *human* condition in a semi-narrative form that is indebted to the Genesis account of the fall of Adam.

It also should be pointed out that Paul's words in 1.23 are tantalizingly reminiscent of those in Ps. 106.20 which speak of Israel's own

1. Gaston, 1987: 140, emphasis added. Cf. Ziesler, 1989: 78; Räisänen, 1983: 97.
2. Cf. Wedderburn, 1980: 120; Wright, 1980: 95.
3. See Jervell, 1960: 312-31; Wedderburn, 1980; Dunn, 1980: 101-102.

fall into idolatry, as recorded in Exodus 32; their worship of the golden calf is described as their exchange (ἠλλάξαντο) of the glory (δόξαν) of God for the likeness (ὁμοιώματι) of an ox. If this echo is deliberate, as many think,[1] it is telling that the nation of Israel itself forms one obvious example of the story of the fall of Adam. As he proceeds, Paul will exploit this connection between the sinful condition of Adam and the people of Israel. Here he leaves it undeveloped.

12.2. *Paul's Initial Attack on Jewish Ethical Superiority: 2.1-11*

Scholars have long recognized, especially in the early chapters of Romans, Paul's use of the diatribe format to present his case.[2] By means of this rhetorical device, Paul allows his readers to overhear him in conversation with an imagined dialogue partner as he advances his case. Whereas in the dialogue format of *4 Ezra* both participants of the debate voiced their own views, in the diatribe format the position of each participant can be gleaned from the author's own presentation as he poses problems which he then proceeds to solve. Much like the Socratic method of instruction, diatribe was employed to engage a student (often imagined) in an exchange which, as it unravelled, led the student from an immature to a proper understanding of the issue at hand. As such, it is primarily a pedagogical tool used within a school context,[3] and 'is motivated by concern rather than contempt' for one's dialogue partner.[4]

This provides the rhetorical context for Paul's use of diatribe in Romans 2. As his argument unfolds, it becomes clear who his discussion partner is. As most scholars agree, he is 'the typical Jew'[5] who thinks that the description of 1.18-32 applies to others but not to himself by reason of the covenant privileges which he enjoys as a Jew (see especially 2.17-20). As such, the diatribe is cast as an intramural exchange between two Jews. But if the dialogue partner, whom we will refer to hereafter as 'the Jew'[6] (cf. 2.17), expects Paul's descrip-

---

1. Cf. Dunn, 1988a: 61, 72-73; Ziesler, 1989: 78; Garlington, 1990b: 144-45.
2. Cf. e.g. Bultmann, 1910; Black, 1973: 29-30.
3. Stowers, 1981; *idem*, 1984: 710-14, 722; *idem*, 1988. But see the latest survey of diatribe by Schmeller, 1987.
4. Stowers, 1988: 81-82.
5. Cranfield, 1975a: 138. See defences by Cranfield, 1975a: 137-39; Räisänen, 1983: 97-98; Watson, 1986: 109-10; Lübking, 1986: 26; Ziesler, 1989: 81.
6. This appellation can be misleading if it is thought to imply that Paul is critiquing Judaism from the outside. Similarly, the appellation 'the Jew' is not intended to be an

tion of the anthropological condition in 1.18-32 to be offset by a recital of God's grace to Israel in the covenant, he will be surprised by the argument that Paul constructs throughout 2.1–3.20.

The tone of 2.1-11 is set in 2.1, where Paul writes:

> Accordingly, you have no excuse, O man, each one of you who passes judgment on someone else, for at whatever point you judge the other, you are condemning youself, because you who pass judgment do the same things.

The word διό, 'accordingly', indicates that Paul is now ready to draw out implications or conclusions from his portrayal of the anthropological condition in 1.18-32. Rather than going on to distinguish between the sinners who remain in the anthropological condition and the righteous who are saved by God's mercy, Paul stops to draw up his conclusions already in the light of the anthropological condition described earlier without recourse to the covenant mercy of God.

Paul first portrays 'the Jew' as ὁ κρίνων, 'the one who judges'. The attitude which Paul wants to capture by means of this appellation is demonstrated well by Ezra in the first Episode of *4 Ezra*, who judges the nations to be morally inferior to Israel (3.28-36). For instance, Ezra calls the gentiles 'godless tribes' (4.23); moreover, he considers creation to belong exclusively to Israel (6.38-59) since God himself described the gentiles as 'nothing', 'like spittle', and as significant as 'a drop from a bucket' (6.56). Paul is aware of the same attitude of Jewish superiority. The difference between Paul and Ezra is that, whereas Ezra considers the judgment against the gentiles and in favour of Israel to have come from God (cf. 6.56), Paul describes this judgment as derived from 'the Jew'; as Paul goes on to say, God's judgment is different (2.2). Moreover, in Paul's view, 'the judge' is not a righteous judge. Paul describes him with the same adjective which he used of the sinner who is trapped in the anthropological condition—ἀναπολόγητος, 'without excuse' (2.1; cf. 1.20). The irony is that, when 'the Jew' judges (κρίνω) the other, he condemns (κατακρίνω) himself, for, as Paul explains, the judge has himself done the same things (τὰ αὐτά) as the one he condemns.

The charge that 'the Jew' does the same things seemingly refers to the list of vices of 1.24-31. But how can he make this claim? Did not the Jews gain the respect of many gentiles precisely because of their

all-embracing characterization of all Jews of Paul's day. It is employed here quite simply with a particular reference to the imagined interlocutor of Paul's case in Rom. 2–3 especially.

moral integrity? Were not idolatry and homosexuality shunned by pious Jews? Paul cannot be talking here only of a select group of Jews (namely their leaders),[1] since Romans 2 should not be divorced from Romans 3, where the Jewish people appear collectively (3.9, 19). Is Paul talking, then, about only some less heinous crimes, such as gossip? Or is he thinking of the manner in which the commandments may be broken without a literal transgression of them, such as adultery (cf. Mt. 5.27-28)?[2] Or is he referring to hypocrisy, wherein one sees the sin of others without noticing his own?[3] Perhaps something different occasioned Paul's charge, as is demonstrated below from other texts of Early Judaism.

It is worth noting first, however, that Ezra's initial speech in *4 Ezra* parallels to a certain extent Paul's case here and includes the same charge as that of Rom. 2.1. After reviewing the state of human sinfulness (*4 Ezra* 3.3-12), Ezra recalls the election of Abraham and his descendants (3.13-17) and the giving of the law to Israel (3.18-19). And yet, Ezra claims that Israel stands rooted firmly in the position of human sinfulness, as is evidenced by the fact that *they do in everything the things which Adam and his wicked descendants had done* (3.26). The point is that the covenant has been of no avail to them. The charge of doing the wicked things of Adam's race is not indebted to a notion of hypocrisy or to a redefined understanding of what it means to break the commandments. It simply functions as a technique to demonstrate that the covenant relationship established by God seems nonexistent, as is evidenced by the sinful behaviour of Israel who do as the gentiles do. That this is simply a rhetorical technique without empirical correspondence is demonstrated by the fact that Ezra proceeds in 3.28-36 to argue that Israel is morally superior to the gentiles. Rather than harmonizing these two arguments, the point of them both is that they lay the blame squarely on God for Israel's position; God is to blame if the people do as the other nations do, and God is to blame because the people have no benefit from him despite the fact that they do not do the things that characterize the other nations. The charge of doing the same as the outsiders of the covenant in *4 Ezra* 3.26 functions, then, to break down the covenant relationship in order to lay blame (in this case, on God).

---

1. As Watson thinks to be the case throughout Rom. 2 (1986: 113-15).
2. Cranfield, 1975a: 142.
3. Dunn, 1988a: 89-90.

Paul's charge is hardly different, except in that he does not blame God but 'the Jew'. His charge follows not from *empirical* observation but from the 'grammar' of ethical denunciation. From evidence shown below, it was often the case that, once the boundaries of the community of grace were drawn up, those who were considered outside its boundaries could all be classed together. There is no middle ground. There are no greys; everything is black and white. In the process of denunciation, the one to be denounced becomes the object of ethical criticism and slander, being accused of behaviour which is unworthy of the righteous and which equals the worst sin of all outsiders. Whether such charges are deserved or not matters little; the 'grammar' of ethical denunciation allows for denunciation of this kind.

One example of this rhetorical technique is evident in the *Psalms of Solomon* 4, which provides also a close parallel to the description of 'the judge' of Rom. 2.1. The author describes the condition of a Jewish 'profaner' whose heart is impure and who breaks the law of God while moving in the circles of the assembly of the righteous (4.1). With great ceremony and appearances, this profane Jew condemns (κατακρίνω) sinners in judgment (ἐν κρίσει, 4.2). But, like 'the Jew' of Romans 2, although he is quick to judge the sinner, he himself is guilty of all manner of sin (4.3), which is described in great detail in 4.4-5 and 4.9-13. He is accused of sexual perversity to the extent that it motivates his every action. Such charges, however, may have borne little relationship to reality at all, as R.R. Hann comments:

> Although it is most unlikely that the backsliding sectaries [the profaners] were in fact guilty of the immorality of which they were accused (they would surely have been expelled if the charges had been literally true), it is significant that they are described in the same moral terms as are the sect's opponents. Once their less rigid observance has been identified, they have lost status within the cult and are classified as the equivalent of outsiders... It is not necessary that the less strict sectaries actually committed the deeds of which they are accused.[1]

Elsewhere in the *Psalms of Solomon*, the behaviour of Jewish apostates is described as *equal to* (17.14-15) or *worse than that of the gentiles* (1.8; 8.8-13), doing wicked things which had never been done

---

1. 1988: 178. He continues: 'Once matters of morality have been conceived in such rigorous terms, the ethics of the sect must be defined in opposition to the behaviour of those of the outside'.

before (2.9) and which even the gentiles despised (2.12). Although these charges are quite trumped up, the rhetoric of ethical denunciation allows for such exaggeration; just as the covenant boundaries are drawn up rigidly, so too is a sharp distinction between the morality of the righteous and that of the sinners. As soon as a Jew is thought to have 'fallen from grace' (at least in the eyes of another Jew), so the worst of the worst can be said of him in order to reinforce that fact, whether or not those accusations correspond to reality. The author heaps up the descriptions of the sinners' perversity in order to portray their ethical standing in the bleakest of terms, thereby disqualifying their covenant membership.

Ethical denunciation of this sort not only allows for exaggeration but frequently does so in highly polemical language. So Mic. 3.3 denounces Jewish apostates, identifying them as those who 'eat the flesh of my people, strip their skin from off them, break their bones in pieces, chop them up like meat in a kettle, like flesh in a pot'. No doubt there is little correlation between this description of apostates and the actual misdemeanours that they may have committed, but the motivation for such polemic has little concern for accuracy.

The same phenomenon is evidenced in *Pseudo-Philo* 25, wherein groups of Jewish sinners confess their sinful deeds which have resulted from their disregard of the covenant. Their behaviour matches their position as apostates; they are credited with having committed idolatry, adultery, imitating the practices of the gentiles, and desiring to eat the flesh of their own children (25.9-13). The principle is clear: those Jews who are thought to be outside the boundaries of the covenant are credited with practices indistinguishable from those of the gentiles.[1]

A most significant variation of this principle is to be found in the Prayer of Manasseh, a poignant prayer of repentance to a merciful God. The speaker recounts the extent of his sinfulness: his sins 'multiplied in number more than the sand of the sea' (Pr. Man. 9a), and he finds himself with no strength to lift up his eyes to heaven 'because of the multitude of the iniquity of my wicked deeds, because I did evil things before you' (v. 10). Especially important is the way in which the confessional section of the prayer culminates in the admis-

---

1. The author's assurance of the mercy of God allows him to entertain the possibility that, after the death of these sinners, God may have mercy upon them. This does not negate the principle cited here, but demonstrates the author's confidence in God's mercy.

sion of idolatrous practices: 'I set up idols and multiplied defilement' (v. 10). If the attribution of this prayer to Manasseh is original to the prayer, the mention of idolatry seems to be a reference to the biblical portrayal of Judah's King Manasseh in 2 Chron. 33.7, wherein he is said to have placed an idol in the Jerusalem temple. But the point to be noted is that the author who crafted this prayer and any other Jews who incorporated it into their worship identified themselves as idolaters each time they recited it. To incriminate oneself in such a fashion is certainly significant. The author, citing the multitude of his iniquity, goes so far as to cap his confession with the most heinous sin imaginable—idolatry, the sin which characterizes the gentile world *par excellence*.

We may suppose, however, that the charge is overblown. There is little reason to think that such self-denunciation had a factual basis, and we are well advised against seeing the author as 'a miserable wretch, or a Jew who has committed disgusting sins'.[1] Instead, as J.H. Charlesworth describes him, he was simply 'a devout Jew'[2] whose composition serves as 'a palpable reminder of the living force of Jewish piety during the turn of the era'.[3] If he is not some heinous sinner but a typical Jew of the first century, in what way can he identify himself as an idolatrous pagan? The answer comes in the recognition that the pious Jew, in confession before God, recognized his sinful standing alongside the rest of humanity; and where there is no distinction, the sins of one may be applied to another. Once again, the principle is affirmed: in ethical denunciation, the sin of the Jewish sinner tends to be augmented in order to highlight the fact that he no longer is worthy to have a part in the covenant people. When standing outside the parameters of the covenant, he can be accused of crimes characteristic of those outside the covenant, even if such accusations are not literally true. What is so shocking is that this principle can result in *self*-denunciation when standing before God in confessional prayer.

In the Prayer of Manasseh, the speaker is not denouncing himself as one who has rejected the covenant; indeed, he appeals to the mercy of the covenant God in order that he might be cleansed. Instead, he stands before God mindful of the fact that, before God, no one living is righteous. Since it is illegitimate for him to postulate a social distinc-

---

1. Charlesworth, 1988: 48.
2. 1988: 48. Cf. *idem*, 1985b: 314.
3. 1985a: 631.

tion between the righteous Jew and the sinful gentile while standing before God in confession, he therefore humbly identifies himself with the gentile and confesses the sin which is characteristic of the sinners, thereby emphasizing all the more his need for the grace of God to restore him. He would, no doubt, have denied the charge of idolatry if anyone had applied it to him, but, in the context of humble petition for divine mercy, he accentuates his dependence upon God's grace by emphasizing the state of his sinfulness.[1] The speaker of this prayer claims for himself no right to salvation, unless it be by the grace of the covenant God of Israel. Without that, he is no different from the idolatrous gentiles.

This digression into several texts of Early Judaism is necessary to establish the proper rhetorical context of Paul's charge in 2.1, and elsewhere in his letter (2.21-24; 7.7-25). The principle is simple: where the covenant is of no avail, whether that be due to God's negligence (*4 Ezra* 3.20-27), apostasy (*Psalms of Solomon*, *Pseudo-Philo*, Micah), or confession before God (Prayer of Manasseh), the most heinous sins are said to characterize one's behaviour. Paul's charge follows the same principle. It is important to point out, moreover, that ethical denunciation of this kind follows from prior convictions concerning the boundaries of the covenant of grace (cf. sociologists' talk of 'double-faced ethics'[2]). That is, Paul's charge against 'the Jew' is arrived at in view of theological commitments already held, rather than vice versa; the charge is explained by, rather than explains, Paul's christological case. It functions at the level of polemic without necessary correspondence in fact, and it demonstrates from the outset that Paul's use of diatribe is system-dependent, being determined by his conviction that ethnocentrism is improper. Because of the revelation of God's eschatological ways (cf. 1.17-18), Paul already knows that Jews outside the boundaries of the christian community fall outside the community of grace, so he can charge 'the Jew' (the spokesman for ethnocentric Jews) with the same ethical deficiencies as those from whom 'the Jew' thought himself distinct. In this way, Paul simply follows the pattern of ethical denunciation; those outside can all be grouped as one without distinction. What one scholar has said of the

---

1. Compare Nickelsburg's distinction, when analysing the Qumran Thanksgiving Hymn scroll, between one's 'public and private sides' (1981: 139).

2. Urbach elaborates: 'This is an attitude which makes a distinction between the moral code of behaviour towards a fellow citizen or co-religionist and that towards an outsider' (1981: 282).

charges against the Jewish 'sinners' in the *Psalms of Solomon* can be said of Paul's charge in 2.1: the charge 'should not be read as an impartial and objective testimony. This is factional propaganda and polemic, with a fair degree of exaggeration.'[1]

In the light of this, it might be helpful once again to reflect briefly upon Ezra's initial case in *4 Ezra* where he argues two points in indictment of God. First, he argues that Israel's covenant status has failed to be of any benefit: God has not weeded out from them the evil heart of sin which is common to all humanity, so they do the same things as the gentiles (*4 Ezra* 3.20-27). Second, because Israel is better than the gentiles, God's covenant faithfulness is in doubt (*4 Ezra* 3.28-36). Obviously, these two cases are difficult to maintain simultaneously (is Israel as bad as, or better than, the gentiles?), but both cohere in laying the blame for Israel's position squarely on God. The point to be noticed, however, is that, whereas Ezra initially maintains both (1) the universal sinfulness of humanity and (2) the covenant status of Israel resulting in their ethical superiority, the latter is eventually disallowed in the light of the former due to the conviction that the two are incompatible. This is a significant parallel to Paul's case; Paul (like the author of *4 Ezra*) sees in these two points nothing but contradiction and, as his case proceeds, hopes to dispense with ethnocentric distinctions by means of his argument concerning the all-embracing condition of sin.

In 2.2, Paul juxtaposes 'the Jew's' judgment of ethical superiority with another judgment—that of God, whose judgment is based on truth (κατὰ ἀλήθειαν). Since God's judgment includes the condemnation of anyone who does the things described in 1.24-31, and since 'the Jew' is no different from the gentile on that score, so Paul can point out that God's judgment falls without ethnic consideration. In the light of the pervasiveness of sin, God's true and impartial judgment on the matter disqualifies ethnocentrism altogether.[2]

The same point is made in 2.3, where Paul emphasizes that the one who judges others, and yet does the same as they do, cannot escape

---

1. Dunn, 1988b: 288 n. 65. Cf. Räisänen, 1983: 96.
2. Here, then, it becomes obvious why in 1.23 Paul seems to have relied on the terminology of Ps. 106 (which describes the fall of Israel into idolatry) to illustrate the extent of human error; for him, Israel's history itself proves that the anthropological condition of sin applies just as well to the Jew as to the gentile, a point which he works to disqualify ethnocentrism. Cf. Bassler: 'already in chap. 1 Paul's argument was deliberately double-edged' (1984: 45 n. 8).

God's judgment upon sin. This verse illustrates again the manner in which Paul's case is carried out in the face of ethnocentric covenantalism. In this regard, it is significant that one can recognize in 2.3 a parallel with *Pss. Sol.* 15.8: 'Those who do lawlessness will not escape the judgment of the Lord'. It is not necessary to determine the relationship between these two texts (i.e. is Paul quoting? do both authors draw upon common parlance?). Instead, it is enough simply to note how the two authors utilize the same idea in completely different ways.

In the *Psalms of Solomon* 15, the sinners 'who do lawlessness' are distinct from the righteous who live by God's mercy (15.13). These two groups, the sinners and the righteous, equal those outside and inside the covenant respectively—that is, the gentiles (along with the Judaean sinners), and Israel. As such, the pronouncement of *Pss. Sol.* 15.8 is an expression of ethnocentric covenantalism, charging that gentile (and Judaean) sinners will not escape God's judgment against them. God's justice is distributed in line with his covenant with Israel.

When the same pronouncement is employed by Paul, however, it appears in a completely different system of thought; those who cannot escape God's judgment are all those who sin, apart from any consideration of the covenant and its people. On this score, then, this pronouncement works out in a completely different way in Paul's case than in the *Psalms of Solomon*. In the latter, divine judgment is contained within the context of ethnocentric covenantalism, whereas in the former it is not, and, in fact, critiques ethnocentrism altogether. The charge that sinners do not escape God's judgment is common to both authors, but it has a different effect in their respective works since it is employed in a different system of thought.

In 2.4, Paul continues his attack upon ethnocentric covenantalism, saying, 'Do you presume upon the riches of his kindness (χρηστότητος), tolerance and patience (μακροθυμίας)?' Paul here is polemicizing against the kind of presumption evident throughout much of the literature of Early Judaism. One example of this is Wis. 15.1-2: 'But you, our God, are kind (χρηστός) and true, patient (μακρόθυμος) and in mercy governing all things. For even if we sin, we are yours.' Paul considers this type of Jewish confidence in the mercy of God, despite their own sin, to be a false presumption. He says to 'the Jew': 'Do you not realize that God's kindness (χρηστόν) leads you to repentance' (the second 'you' probably bearing the emphasis of the sentence). Paul's statement itself is not untypical of

Jewish piety, but, again, it is used by him in an untypical fashion. For 'the Jew', the very fact that God is merciful no doubt leads him to repent of his sin in order to maintain his covenant membership. In this way, 'the Jew' would have agreed with Paul that God's kindness leads him to repentance, but by 'kindness' he would have meant God's covenant mercy upon Israel, as in Wis. 15.1. In Rom. 2.4, 'kindness' has no such significance; by relying upon his ethnic status, 'the Jew' presumes upon God's kindness. Once again, the system into which Paul drops the points of his argument is different from that of 'the Jew', although the points of argument are common to them both. Because Paul *knows* already (via eschatological revelation, 1.17-18) that the system of ethnocentrism is wrong, so he sinks the principle of divine 'kindness' into another system of thought, thereby *proving* that ethnocentrism is wrong.

Paul's rejection of ethnocentric covenantalism is reinforced in 2.6 and 2.11, wherein he twice states the principle of divine impartiality, while 2.7-10 unpacks the significance of that principle. In 2.6, Paul cites Ps. 62.12 (LXX 61.13) and Prov. 24.12: God will repay each according to his works (κατὰ τὰ ἔργα αὐτοῦ). Similar pronouncements appear elsewhere in the literature of Early Judaism. The idea of divine retribution according to works is evident in the *Psalms of Solomon*, for instance. Therein, one reads statements such as that in 2.34, which describes the purpose of God's impartial judgment to be to separate 'between the righteous and the sinner, to repay sinners forever according to their actions' (κατὰ τὰ ἔργα αὐτῶν; cf. 2.16; 17.8-9 [twice]). But in the *Psalms of Solomon*, the principle of judgment by works operates once again within a context other than that used by Paul. There, one's works are thought to indicate one's position as an outsider (= the sinner) or insider to the covenant. The latter intends to preserve his membership in the covenant by relying on God's covenant mercy (notice, God's 'kindness', ἡ χρηστότης σου, *Pss. Sol.* 9.7) to forgive the sin of which he (= the righteous) repents.[1] The

---

1. Cf. the distinction in 9.4-7 between those who do what is right (ποιῆσαι δικαιοσύνην) and those who do what is wrong (ποιῆσαι ἀδικίαν).

Bassler cites divine judgment according to works in the *Psalms of Solomon* as evidence of the theme of divine impartiality in Early Judaism (1984: 49 n. 19). But, in fact, the *Psalms of Solomon* demonstrates how the principle of judgment 'according to works' is undergirded by a covenant distinction between the righteous and the sinners; the Judaean sinners who have abandoned the covenant will be judged by their actions which have placed them outside the bounds of the righteous. Cf.

author is convinced that there is no discrimination in God's judgments, but for him God's impartial judgment works within the context of his elective mercy upon Israel. In Psalms of Solomon, then, God's standard of impartial judgment is contained within his faithfulness to his people; he will show no partiality to those who have rejected the covenant, and he will be merciful to those whose works indicate their desire to maintain the covenant relationship.

Paul's case, of course, is quite different. He finds it presumptuous to contain the principle of divine impartiality within an ethnocentric context. Such a presumption arises, says Paul from a stubborn and hardened heart and is deserving of God's wrath (2.5). Although the principle of judgment according to works is common to both Paul and the author of the *Psalms of Solomon*, the system in which that principle operates is wholly different in their two works. In his diatribe, Paul affirms the principle of judgment by works which was indispensable to ethnocentric covenantalism, but, having abstracted the principle from its traditional context, he uses it to bolster his own notion of divine impartiality, thereby negating ethnocentric covenantalism.

After extracting the principle of judgment by works from its native covenantal context, Paul is left with a system which operates solely on the basis of actions. Thus, in 2.7-10 he describes the two ways to eternal life and wrath: the one is by doing 'good work(s)', the other is by doing what is unrighteous. This is not the end of Paul's case, of course, but it is the natural result of his technique throughout this section of his diatribe, in which he extracts aspects from the ethnocentric system of covenantal perception and reworks them into a system without an ethnocentric character. The result is a case hardly different from that evident in *4 Ezra*: Paul ends up arguing that, because there is no favouritism with God (2.11), so one remains in the condition of sin unless one can free oneself from it by means of good works. This is not Uriel speaking in *4 Ezra;* this is Paul in Romans. Both, however, engineer the collapse of ethnocentric covenantalism, and maintain that the escape from the anthropological condition is by means of one's works.[1] Although Paul later hopes to ground this principle

Sanders: *'God's grace* establishes the framework within which works are required, and performing the works commanded (or atoning for transgression of them) is the condition of remaining in the elect' (1982: 401, emphasis added).

1. Many scholars exhibit particular difficulty in exegeting Rom. 2.6-11, in the light of Paul's heavy emphasis there on salvation by ethical works. Cf. Käsemann's

within the christian community (2.28-29; 8.4; 13.8-10), both Paul's and Uriel's cases are patterned along the same lines at this point.

12.3. *What Then of the Law?: 2.12-16*

Having argued that there is no favouritism with God, Paul narrows his discussion to focus upon that which provided the basis of Jewish ethnocentrism—their possession of the law. The typical Jewish distinction between the righteous of Israel and the sinners of the heathen nations is rooted in the fact that Israel has been given the law. Paul works his case in the same way, making a distinction between those who are 'without the law' (ἀνόμως) and those who are 'in the law' (ἐν νόμῳ). As he begins in 2.12a, Paul states that for those 'without the law' (the gentiles) sin is rewarded with destruction. No doubt 'the Jew' would have heartily agreed. In 2.12b, however, Paul again turns the tables on 'the Jew' by applying the same connection between sin and condemnation to those 'in the law'. Moreover, he affirms that to the one who is ἐν νόμῳ condemnation is, in fact, distributed διὰ νόμου. The point seems to be that, rather than being a sign of ethnic superiority (2.17-20), the law acts as the standard of judgment which actually condemns those 'in the law' who sin. Paul here is not referring to Jewish apostates but to every Jew who considered his being 'in the law' as a privilege which offset his place in the condition of universal sinfulness. Paul's point is that, although Israel has possession of the law, the law does not offset their sinfulness but condemns them because of their sin.

Paul then makes another distinction, this time between the 'hearers of the law' and the 'doers of the law': whereas the doers will be justified, those who only hear the law are not righteous before God. This in itself is not a controversial distinction. Paul's own use of it, however, is unusual, for it carries the implication (following from 2.12) that the one 'in the law' who sins is not a doer of the law; his sin disqualifies him from doing the law. For 'the Jew', doing the law does not necessitate the absence of sin altogether but necessitates acting on the measures which the law provides for correcting that sin; for him, making atonement for sin *is* doing the law, so that sin itself does not negate one's ability to do the law. In the context of Romans 2, however, Paul has constructed a case in which sin disqualifies one from

treatment (1980: 57-58). These difficulties fall away when Paul's rhetorical technique (demonstrated above) is recognized.

being a doer of the law (cf. Uriel's case in *4 Ezra*). Both discussion partners maintain the relationship between doing the law and righteousness, but Paul removes these two components from the context which 'the Jew' would have considered their natural environment and works them against 'the Jew's' perceptions.

Paul's case in 2.14-15 has proved somewhat difficult to sort out. There, Paul makes mention of *gentiles who do the law*. He writes:

> Indeed, when gentiles, who do not have the law (τὰ μὴ νόμον ἔχοντα), do by nature (φύσει) the things of the law (τὰ τοῦ νόμου), they are a law for themselves, even though they do not have the law (2.14).

This is an awkward component of Paul's argument if we keep in mind that he is working his case from his depiction of the anthropological state of sin to the conclusion of 3.9 that 'all are under sin'; the mention of gentiles who 'do the things of the law' would seem to go against the thrust of Paul's case.[1] Various arguments have been presented to iron out the problem, and need mentioning at this point.

A good many scholars suggest that those whom Paul has in mind here are *christian* gentiles.[2] Support for this opinion comes from Paul's case in 8.4, wherein the believer is said to fulfill the righteous requirement of the law (cf. 13.8-10). However, several criticisms can be applied to this interpretation. Particularly convincing is the fact that Paul is unlikely to have referred to believing gentiles as doing the things of the law *by nature* (φύσει). For Paul, believers can be said to fulfill the law only by means of the indwelling of the Spirit (8.4; cf. Gal. 5.14 with 5.22-23).[3] What Paul has in mind must not be *christian* gentiles,[4] but simply gentiles.

Other scholars, taking this into account, attempt to solve the problem by pointing out that Paul is not claiming that gentiles do *all* the

1. To say that Paul considers 'doing the law' in 2.14-15 to be sin (cf. Gaston, 1987: 31) seems to miss Paul's point altogether. Like most, I consider 'doing the law' to be a positive phenomenon in the context of 2.1-29.

2. Cf. e.g. T.R. Schreiner, 1989: 62.

3. Cranfield argues that Paul meant φύσει to modify τὰ μὴ νόμον ἔχοντα, reading 2.14 as 'those who do not have the law by nature' (1975a: 1.156-57). But this does not explain Paul's description of these gentiles as 'a law for themselves'. Moreover, if Paul had intended what Cranfield thinks he intended, it would have been far more natural for φύσει to appear within the ἔχοντα clause; cf. Dunn, 1988a: 98.

4. Cf. Snodgrass: The 'christian gentile' interpretation 'requires a considerable stretch of the imagination' (1986: 74).

law; he does not envisage the complete fulfilment of the law but only
the *occasional* fulfilment of *some* of the law.[1] In this interpretation,
there is no incongruity with Paul's conclusions of 3.9, for the
fulfilment of some (but not all) points of the law does not undermine
Paul's basic thesis that all are under sin. There is, in this reading, a
quantitative qualification of the phrase τὰ τοῦ νόμου. The problem,
however, is that, as H. Räisänen points out, this understanding cannot
be maintained well in 2.27 where Paul utilizes the same idea once
again.[2] There, Paul says that the gentiles who fulfil (τελέω) the law
condemn the Jews who transgress the law. Since in both 2.14 and 2.27
the law is portrayed in ethical terms, it is hard to understand how the
condemnation of the Jew (who must have fulfilled at least *some* ethical
conditions of the law, despite being a transgressor of the law in general) is accomplished by the gentile who, according to this interpretation, also fulfils only *some* of the law's ethical demands. The argument
in 2.27 juxtaposes the gentile and the Jew, portraying them respectively as fulfilling (τελέω) the law and transgressing the law. They are
not equal in their ethical performance. τελέω here must have a quantitative sense signifying the *full* performance of the ethical stipulations
of the law. The same sense is evident in the phrase τὰ τοῦ νόμου of
2.14.[3] If other phrases with the same construction are any indication,[4]
the application of a quantitative qualification to the expression τὰ τοῦ
νόμου (they do *some* things of the law) would seem most unusual.

It would seem, then, that in fact Paul does suggest here that some
gentiles do fulfil the law outside of the christian community. Paul's
statements in 2.14-15 represent a strategic manoeuvre of polemic
against his Jewish dialogue partner; they are, as Räisänen states, a
'convenient weapon to hit the Jew with'.[5] Already in his argument
Paul (1) has highlighted the fact that sin is not foreign to 'the Jew',
and (2) has claimed that sin and doing the law are incompatible, intimating that 'the Jew' *ipso facto* has no claim to being a doer of the

---

1. Cf. Nygren, 1949: 123-24; Bornkamm, 1971: 123; Dunn, 1988a: 98.
2. 1983: 103.
3. It is quite permissible to read 2.14-15 in the light of 2.27 since, as Snodgrass
says, '2.25-29 is parallel to 2.13-16' (1986: 80).
4. Cf. τὰ τῆς σαρκός, Rom. 8.5; τὰ τοῦ πνεύματος, Rom. 8.5; τὰ τῆς
εἰρήνης, Rom. 14.19; τὰ τοῦ ἀνθρώπου, 1 Cor. 2.11; τὰ τοῦ πνεύματος τοῦ
θεοῦ, 1 Cor. 2.14; τὰ τοῦ κυρίου, 1 Cor. 7.32-34; τὰ τοῦ κόσμου, 1 Cor. 7.32-
24.
5. 1983: 106.

law. If 'the Jew' is not a doer of the law (as Paul has argued in 2.12-13), and if some gentiles are 'doers' of the law (as Paul now posits in 2.14-15), then how can 'the Jew's' sense of ethnic superiority be maintained?

Paul does not stop there, but takes his point one step further in the apodosis of 2.14b, where he draws a conclusion which would have been strange to 'the Jew' but which again is directed against Jewish ethnocentrism: those who do not have the law but do it anyway are 'a law for themselves'. The point seems to be this: although gentiles who keep the law are 'without the law', they are nevertheless 'defined' in some sense by law even apart from ethnic constraints. 2.15 continues this point, stating that the gentiles illustrate that the work of the law is written in their hearts. Here the privilege of possessing the written law is extended beyond the ranks of the Jews to include, in a different way, even the gentiles; they too have a law, written not on tablets but on their hearts. That they do the law is testified to not by their under-taking of ethnic rituals (contra ethnocentric covenantalism) but by their moral conscience and the thoughts which guide them in their ethical living (2.15). These are the badges which prove that the gentiles too have knowledge of the things of the law. Paul here has already set the scene for what he will do in 2.17-28, wherein he denounces ethnic badges as secondary to the fundamental ethical issue. Although the gentiles do not share the ethnic badges of the Jews, some gentiles are known to have carried out the moral requirements of the law. The badge which testifies to the fact that they too know the things of the law is not circumcision or any other ritualistic practice, but their conscience.

It is clear, then, why Paul makes his claim in 2.14-15 that gentiles do the law: he finds mileage in it for indicting the nationalist pride of 'the Jew'. It is not difficult to see that Paul, in the process of his polemic, has arrived at a position which does not coincide with his basic theological convictions.[1] Paul's method of turning the tables on 'the Jew' has caused him here to compromise his case that all are under sin and in need of redemption, the very point towards which he is working (3.9). Paul is nonetheless able to use the logic of 2.14-15 to make the charge that 'the Jew's' confidence in his favoured status

---

1. Cf. Westerholm: 'In suggesting that some Gentiles will be approved by God on the basis of their works, Paul appears to allow in Romans 2 what chapters 1 and 3 categorically deny' (1988: 160).

before God is misplaced. Although the logic of Paul's polemic in 2.14-15 may be theologically problematic for his christological perspective, it allows him to critique ethnocentric covenantalism once again, demonstrating it to be an incorrect understanding of the ways of God.[1] The claim will not be made herein that Paul's case is the paradigm of logic (it fares better as a model of polemic). Nonetheless, from what we have seen so far, his argument, which takes various turns here and there, is motivated by one constant: the overthrow of ethnocentric covenantalism.

It is important to notice that Paul has succeeded once again in portraying the law in wholly *ethical* terms. At this point in his argument, 'doing the law' cannot refer to the performance of cultic rituals or ethnic practices. Throughout 2.12-15 doing the law means acting in accordance with God's *moral* law. This is the result of Paul's argument already in 2.1-11, wherein he portrayed God's judgment as dependent upon one's ethical behaviour.[2]

Romans 2.16 has proved to be problematic for most interpreters. Paul writes there: 'on the day when God will judge the secrets of men according to my gospel through Jesus Christ'. Various theories have been suggested to interpret Paul's meaning. The fact that this verse is still being written off as a gloss,[3] despite the lack of any textual evidence for such an extreme measure, indicates the difficulty which it presents for a smooth reading of Paul. Probably, what Paul is emphasizing is that the principle of divine equality in judgment coincides with the message of the gospel that he preaches. The function of 2.16 will become clearer in the light of Paul's comments in 2.29, which will be discussed below.

---

1. Cf. Sanders: 'Even at the point at which Paul may most obviously be charged with true incoherence, the statements in Romans 2 that the sole basis of salvation is fulfillment of the law, we can see that he has been led to make use of material which is contrary to one of his central convictions (salvation by faith in Jesus Christ) by the desire to assert another one (the equality of Jew and Gentiles)' (1983a: 147).

2. Sanders makes the point that, although a Jewish author knew the law to be broad in its significance, nonetheless he may well have tended to limit its significance to one or two points for homiletical purposes (1983a: 135 n. 45). Other summaries of the law include loving one's neighbour and being charitable; see Bornkamm, 1963: 107-11.

3. Watson, 1986: 116-17; Bultmann, 1967: 282-84.

12.4. *Paul's Second Attack on Jewish Ethical Superiority: 2.17-24*

Only in 2.17 does Paul explicitly recognize the interlocutor as one who calls himself a Jew. Throughout 2.1-16, we have seen him to be a 'typical' Jew whose self-identity is rooted in his covenant status, who prides himself on being 'in the law', thinking himself to belong to the privileged people who are set apart from the heathen nations. Paul has attacked this confidence in various ways throughout 2.1-16, principally by deflating the Jewish claim of ethical superiority (2.1-11) and by recognizing that moral uprightness can be attributed even to gentiles (2.12-16). In 2.17-24, Paul's line of argument focuses again on undermining the Jewish sense of ethical superiority ('cutting the Jews down to the Gentiles' size'),[1] thereby paralleling his argument in 2.1-11. In 2.25-29 he will re-argue his point that gentiles can be said to do the law, thereby paralleling his argument in 2.12-16.

Romans 2.17-24 is fairly straightforward. Paul begins in 2.17-20 by characterizing 'the Jew's' confidence in the covenant in ways which 'the Jew' himself might have done; he is one who boasts not in his own merits but in his privileged position, who has the law, knows God's will and is, therefore, a guide to the blind and a light to those in darkness. But if 'the Jew' considers himself to be unrivalled in his position before God because of his possession of the law and its benefits, Paul again questions whether that attitude is borne out by the ethical behaviour of 'the Jew'. In 2.21-22, he sets up an incongruous relationship between the claim and the behaviour of 'the Jew': he preaches what he does not practice. The same case is made here as in 2.1 and 2.3 (there it was in terms of judgment of others, here it is in terms of instruction of others). The ethical crimes cited against 'the Jew' are robbery, adultery and sacrilege. Thus, Paul accuses 'the Jew' of disobeying the very law which he possesses and takes pride in, and denounces him as a moral degenerate—one outside the boundaries of the covenant. 'The Jew' himself boasts in God (2.17) and in the law (2.18), considering God to be the God of the Jews and the law to be the symbol of Israel's election by God. Although he considers himself to be one of the 'righteous', Paul portrays him as morally perverse; rather than pleasing God, he dishonours God (2.23). Once again, Paul has gone on the offensive against 'the Jew's' understanding of the covenant by deflating 'the Jew's' sense of ethical superiority.

1. Ziesler, 1989: 92.

Moreover, Paul goes on in 2.24 to apply this charge against not just the single exceptional Jew but against the whole of the covenant people. There he cites Isa. 52.5 (LXX) to make his point: 'The name of God is blasphemed among the gentiles because of you (ὑμᾶς)', the 'you' having a plural referent. Whereas the LXX reading of this verse accuses the whole of Israel of unfaithfulness, Paul accuses the whole Jewish community of ethical laxity in order to undermine Jewish ethnocentrism. Here, then, is the first evidence of what we have expected all along—'the Jew' is Paul's representative of the Jewish community at large.

But how can Paul make this charge against the *whole* of unbelieving Israel? Many take a view similar to that of E. Trocmé on this matter. Trocmé says:

> Paul picks out *some* fields in which *some* Jews had a *few* crimes on their conscience and claims that it is enough to disqualify *the whole Jewish people* as a Law-obedient group. A strange reasoning indeed, but colored by Paul's conviction that. . . a people is a unit which has one and the same fate.[1]

This is a possible explanation, but its premise is not altogether clear from other Jewish sources of Early Judaism. That is, it is not evident from the extant Jewish texts that 'a people is a unit which has one and the same fate'. A large number of texts rely on precisely the opposite conviction: that a people consists of both the remnant and the unfaithful, each having its own 'fate'. I think, instead, that Paul's collective denunciation of the Jews follows on from the 'grammar' of polemic and ethical denunciation, whereby the sins of the worst sinner can be applied to all those who stand outside the boundaries of the covenant of grace. Paul is simply following through on this premise, applying it to all those Jews who stand outside of the boundaries of the christian community. As was stated above, denunciation of this kind is possible only in view of a prior understanding of the boundaries of God's covenant grace.

At this point, Paul introduces his first explicit quotation of Scripture since 1.17. In that it accuses the people of Israel of moral bankruptcy, this proof-text conforms perfectly to Paul's strategy of undermining ethnocentric covenantalism by disqualifying the ethical claim of 'the Jew' who represents them. The implication is consistent with Paul's earlier point that, rather than protecting 'the Jew' within the covenant,

---

1. 1985: 153, emphasis added. Cf. Stendahl, 1976: 81.

the law condemns those 'within the law' who transgress its moral code (2.12). Once again, Paul characterizes the law not as a symbol of Israel's superior position before God but as a universal code of ethics.

12.5. *What Then of Circumcision?: 2.25-29*

Whereas Paul's case in 2.17-24 paralleled that of 2.1-11 in criticizing Jewish ethical behaviour, his case in 2.25-29 parallels that of 2.12-16;[1] that is, having charged the Jewish community with ethical laxity, he once again juxtaposes that situation with the ethical awareness demonstrated by some gentiles. And once again, this is accomplished by removing covenantal value from the law which, thereby, comes to have solely ethical significance apart from ethnic boundaries. Thus, in 2.25 Paul immediately divorces circumcision from the arena of what doing the law entails: 'For circumcision is of benefit if you practise the law' (2.25a). This would be a peculiar statement for 'the Jew'; for him, circumcision is fundamental to the performance of the law. The law which God gave Israel prescribes that every Jew must carry on his flesh the mark of circumcision as a symbol of the covenant (especially Gen. 17.9-14). Paul, however, differentiates between 'doing the law' and 'circumcision'. Thus he writes in 2.25b: 'but if you are a transgressor of the law, your circumcision has become uncircumcision', again forcing the issue of 'doing the law' beyond ethnocentric ritualism and into an ethical sphere (cf. 14.1-6).

In 2.26, the law continues to transcend ethnic boundaries, still maintaining its solely ethical character: 'If then the uncircumcised keeps the just requirements of the law, will not his uncircumcision be reckoned as circumcision?' Paul once again makes the case that gentiles do the law. This technique was evident already in 2.14-15 where the same argument was given with the same end in view—to undermine the Jewish sense of ethical superiority.

The point is then driven further in 2.27, where Paul again introduces the theme of judgment: those who are uncircumcised and fulfil the law will judge those who define themselves by their circumcision and transgress the law. Paul has already rebuked 'the Jew's' judgment

---

1. Bassler considers 2.12-19 a unit in itself, following on from 1.18–2.11 (1984: 45-53). But it seems best, despite Bassler, to take 1.18-32 as a description of the anthropological condition of sin, and 2.1-16 and 2.17-29 as two similarly constructed arguments against ethnocentric covenantalism. Cf. Lübking: 'In 2,1-16 und 2,17-29 liegen zwei parallele Gedankengänge vor' (1986: 27).

of the gentile (2.1, 3) on the basis that, in ethical terms, 'the Jew' is a *peer* of the gentile; Paul has also demonstrated that God's own judgment (2.2, 5, 12-13) is not according to race but according to one's works; finally the 'judgment' theme goes full circle as Paul draws the conclusion that it is, in fact, the moral gentile who judges the Jewish transgressor (probably in the sense that the gentile's justice brings to the fore Jewish transgression more strongly). The irony of this situation, Paul says, is that 'the Jew' is condemned while he remains within the realm of 'the letter' and of 'circumcision' (διὰ γράμματος καὶ περιτομῆς).[1] The point is made once again, therefore, that doing the law is wholly independent of ethnic considerations. Paul can make this claim because he portrays the law as an ethical guide. Furthermore, it should be noted that, as in 2.14-15, Paul's argument in 2.26-27 concerning the righteous gentile goes 'against the grain' of his broader case.

Paul rounds off his argument in 2.28-29 supplying his own definition of what it means to be a Jew; being a Jew has to do with an inner condition of the heart. The point is directed against the rite of circumcision, which was considered by most Jews of Paul's day as the indispensable marker of what being a Jew meant (cf. Gen. 17.11: circumcision is the 'sign of the covenant'). But Paul distinguishes between outward, physical circumcision and inward circumcision of the heart. He is not simply arguing that ethnic symbols should be grounded in an inner piety if they are to have covenantal significance. His point is far more radical, arguing that ethnic symbols are salvifically irrelevant, for the inner condition of the heart is all that matters. We know from Philo that there were Jews in Egypt who argued a similar line, finding circumcision and other ethnic symbols to be full of symbolic meaning without literal necessity (cf. *Migr. Abr.* 89-94). Most Jews of Paul's day would have denounced their position,[2] as did Philo, who argued that the command to circumcise was to be taken literally, no matter what symbolic significance the rite of circumcision might also contain. These same Jews would no doubt have denounced Paul's conclusion as well.

---

1. Paul uses the pejorative word γράμμα here, as in 7.6 where he contrasts living in the realm of the letter and living in the realm of the Spirit. Ethnocentric Jews have only 'the external form' of the law ('the letter') but lack what the law really requires. Cf. Westerholm, 1988: 211.

2. Borgen argues that *Migr. Abr.* 86-93 demonstrates that those Jews who disparaged circumcision were subsequently persecuted by other Jews (1983: 38).

One point especially distinguishes Paul from the Egyptian Jews mentioned by Philo: Paul makes mention of the fact that circumcision of the heart is *by the Spirit*.[1] The significance of this can hardly be overemphasized; in 2.28-29 Paul has not only rooted the ethical doing of the law in an inner condition of the heart but has illustrated how that inner condition is itself facilitated only by the presence of the Spirit. In that he later argues that the Spirit is with those who have faith in Christ, Paul is foreshadowing his solution to the anthropological condition: faith in Christ, despite ethnic standing. Moreover, his case here now throws the whole of 2.1-29 into a different light, for at this point it becomes evident that Paul understands the doing of the law to be a solely 'christian' phenomenon. This does not sit well with the point which Paul has made along the way concerning non-believing gentiles who do the law. Evidently, after employing arguments at various places which go against the grain of his own beliefs in order to score points against 'the Jew' (2.14-15, 26-27), Paul is forced in the end to 'christianize' the case which those arguments allowed him to make (2.28-29). Evidently Paul's polemical arguments do not always match his personal conviction.

The same is true of 2.14-16. There, the conviction that gentiles do the law supports Paul's sociological argument (that ethnocentric covenantalism is an inadequate understanding of the ways of God) but endangers his christological argument (that faith is the only means to righteousness). Paul has postulated a situation which he cannot envisage (the *non-christian* gentile doing the law) in order to undermine Jewish ethnocentrism. Once that sociological point is made, Paul's reflex is to sanitize his case by injecting it in 2.16 with a theological confession of confidence in God's sovereignty through Christ, thereby rescuing his christological case from being side-tracked and derailed.

We have seen, then, two cases in which Paul's personal conviction is subtly subordinated to his polemic (2.14-15, 26-27). In order to undermine 'the Jew's' position, Paul has, in the process of polemical argument, entertained a proposition which actually undermines the necessity of his own christological corrective. This is a very telling indicator of the extent to which Paul was prepared to go in order to discredit an ethnocentric understanding of God's ways. Nonetheless,

---

1. Cf. Dunn: 'it is now usually agreed by comparison with 7:6 and 2 Cor. 3:6 that in Paul's intention πνεῦμα = Holy Spirit, not the human spirit' (1988a: 124). Contra, Sanders, 1983a: 128.

once his polemic has had its desired effect, Paul then alters the thrust of that polemic by 'christianizing' it (2.16, 28-29). This can be contrasted with the situation in 3.5-6, where Paul again entertains a logic which is not his own, only to reject it altogether ('I am speaking κατὰ ἄνθρωπον'). But since he cannot retract his arguments in 2.14-15 and 2.26-27, he must infuse them finally with a christocentric focus. In this way, Paul allows his sociological polemic (*viz.* some gentiles do the law) to do its damage, only to harness it finally in conformity with his own christological convictions.

12.6. *God's Faithfulness and Impartiality: 3.1-8*

Many scholars, finding Rom. 3.1-8 to be 'one of the most puzzling passages in the epistle',[1] have appreciated (to some degree) C.H. Dodd's estimation that the argument of this section is 'weak and feeble' and that 'the argument of the epistle would go much better if this whole section were omitted'.[2] But such an estimation misses Paul's intention in these verses. In them, Paul defends his case of 2.1-29 by discrediting several charges which might be laid against it.[3]

In Romans 2, Paul's case for the impartiality of God allowed him to discredit Jewish confidence in their ethnic standing. The question which naturally arises then is that of 3.1: 'What then is the advantage of the Jew, or what is the advantage of circumcision?' No doubt, 'the Jew' would have sympathized with this question, and Paul's audience may well have expected his answer to have been 'None whatsoever' (just as Dodd expected).[4] But, instead, Paul answers, 'Much in every way', since the Jews were entrusted with the oracles (τὰ λόγια) of God (3.2); that is, their advantage is their possession of the scriptures.[5] Because Paul considers the scriptures to contain the promise that God's righteousness will be revealed through faith (cf. 1.2; 3.21), the advantage of 'the Jew' is that he stands first in line to enter into right relationship with God when that promise is fulfilled. Paul's reply in 3.2, therefore, is not as incredible as it might first have appeared; the advantage of 'the Jew' does nothing to remedy his position in the

---

1. Hall, 1983: 183.
2. Dodd, 1932: 71.
3. In his sights specifically is the objection that he has applied the maxim of divine impartiality in a manner contrary to its proper usage. Cf. Bassler, 1982: 153.
4. 1932: 168.
5. Cf. Doeve, 1953.

state of sin, but allows him to recognize the remedy (christian faith) more readily. Paul does not allow Jewish advantage to impinge upon his case for divine impartiality since, for him, possession of the divine oracles does not translate into a salvific privilege apart from faith. As we will see in 3.20, the law actually indicates the Jewish need for salvation along with the gentiles.

It is significant that the Jewish scriptures (here, τὰ λόγια) are *not* portrayed here as a tome of ethical prescriptions, as in 2.1-29. Instead, their revelatory character comes to the fore in this discussion of Jewish advantage: the Jewish scriptures reveal the ways of God for those who possess them. The irony for Paul is that the possessors of the scriptures have missed the point of God's ways, which of course culminate in Christ.

The difficulties of this section begin at 3.3. From that point, it is difficult to know whether or not the diatribe continues throughout 3.1-8,[1] and if it does, where Paul speaks for himself and where for another (whether that be 'the Jew' or a curious gentile).[2] The best solution, I think, is to consider that in 3.3, 3.5, and 3.7 Paul entertains three further queries which he expected 'the Jew' to have in mind and which, if allowed to stand, would negate his conclusion. Paul answers these possible queries in 3.4, 3.6 and 3.8.

The query of 3.3 concerns the faithfulness of God: 'if some have been unfaithful, has their unfaithfulness abolished God's faithfulness?' The 'some' (τινες) here are those many Jews who have failed to put their faith in Christ (cf. τινες in 11.17), thereby being unfaithful to the scriptural record which they held in their possession and which prophesied that God's righteousness will be revealed in Christ.

It is of great importance to note that, in 3.2, Paul *does* recognize a covenant of some sort between God and Israel. He does not elaborate on this point until Romans 9–11; until then, his allowance for some sort of a relationship between God and Israel never again resurfaces. However, as Paul's case in 3.2 shows, even within Paul's understanding of the covenant there is a clause which includes some advantage for ethnic Israel, and because of that clause, the unbelief of some (many) Jews[3] allows God's righteousness to be called into question in

---

1. Hall argues throughout his article that it does not (1983).

2. For discussion, see Stowers, 1984: 708-10; W.S. Campbell, 1981a: 31-32.

3. Because their unfaithfulness is their unbelief, ἀπιστία may here be legitimately translated by either 'unfaithfulness' or 'unbelief'. The sense of 'covenant unfaithful-

the manner of 3.3. The point of 3.3 is that, if there is an ethnic clause in Israel's favour in Paul's understanding of the covenant, and if some Jews do not enjoy any benefits from that clause, is not God's righteousness in doubt? If the covenant allows some advantage to the Jew in the process of salvation history, and if that advantage has been rendered ineffective, is God not in some way responsible? And if this is the necessary result of Paul's argument, the very fact that it is an unacceptable conclusion disproves Paul's case.

For Paul too, the idea of God being unfaithful is abhorrent, and he gives an emphatic denial to this idea in 3.4: 'May it not be. Let God be true (faithful) and every man a liar (unfaithful[1])'. What he means by this becomes clearer in 3.4b where he quotes from the LXX of Ps. 51.4 (LXX 50.6): 'so that you might be justified in your words and will be vindicated when you are judged'. The scene is of a courtroom trial with God himself under the accusation of being unrighteous, as in 3.3. The plaintiff has already been identified as one who is unfaithful. So too in the original context of Psalm 51, the author repeatedly acknowleged his lawlessness and sin (in the first five verses, ἀνόμημα [once], ἁμαρτάνω [once], ἀνομία [thrice], ἁμαρτία [thrice]). But the sinner of Psalm 51 (David) did not hold God accountable for his own sin but rather declared him (God) to be righteous. Such is the biblical precedent, says Paul: the guilty party does not hold God accountable but affirms, in his own condemnation, the righteousness of God.

By proving in 3.4 that his argument does not imply that God is unfaithful, Paul has kept his argument from being derailed. Of course, for Paul, God's faithfulness to Israel does not entail the redemption of Israel at the expense of the gentiles. That position (ethnocentric covenantalism) he has already negated. But it is not until later that Paul explains how God can be said to be faithful to Israel. At present, he is content only to preserve the momentum of his case by insulating it from attack.

Having defended his argument against a first objection, Paul is now faced with a second objection which springs from his insistence in 3.4 that God is faithful: 'But if our unrighteousness illustrates the right

ness' captures especially the point of the verse, since Paul juxtaposes it with God's own 'covenant faithfulness'.

1. According to Black, ψεύστην here has the sense not just of 'liar' but of an 'unreliable, perfidious, faithless person' (1973: 63).

eousness of God, what shall we say? Is God unjust to inflict his wrath (upon us)?' (3.5).[1] The point is this: if Paul is right that God's faithfulness is clearly demonstrated by the guilt of the unfaithful Jew (3.4), and if Paul is right that God's impartial wrath falls upon the unfaithful Jew (Romans 2), then God's wrath falls upon the very one who proves him to be righteous; but that would seem to render him unrighteous, which cannot be the case; therefore, Paul must be wrong and the case for divine impartiality presented in Romans 2 is false. But Paul does not allow such a conclusion to be drawn from his argument (μὴ γένοιτο, 3.5c), and asks in 3.6: 'How else does God judge the world?' Paul's reply seems here simply to restate the point of 2.6-11: if God were not impartial, he could not be a just judge. In effect, whereas the objection of 3.5 implies that Paul's argument concerning divine impartiality is in error, Paul's reply in 3.6 implies that divine impartiality proves his argument to be valid. There would appear to be something of an impasse between Paul and his objector, at least at this point in Paul's case.

Paul, thinking his point of 3.6 to be self-evident, then entertains in 3.7 another objection: 'But if the truth (faithfulness) of God increases his glory because of my lie (unfaithfulness), how is it that I too (κἀγώ) am judged to be a sinner?' This objection, like the first two, is concerned with the relationship between God's faithfulness and Jewish unfaithfulness, questioning whether 'the Jew' can be rightly identified as a 'sinner'. The κἀγώ points to the objector's amazement that *even he* can be considered a sinner, along with the gentiles (cf. 2.1ff.). Once again, the objection is raised against Paul's case for the impartiality of God which flattens out ethnic distinctiveness: 'how can I be judged in the same way as the gentile if God is faithful to his covenant responsibilities and, therefore, to me as a privileged Jew?' The problem for the objector is that Paul wants to maintain both God's impartiality *and* God's faithfulness to the privileged people simultaneously. 'The Jew' is no doubt puzzled, and understandably so, since in Romans 2 Paul chided 'the Jew' for thinking that divine impartiality and ethnic advantage could be maintained simultaneously. Throughout 3.1-5, however, 'the Jew' has heard Paul doing precisely that. Paul appears to have gotten himself into a muddle, which the objections of 3.1-7 highlight; after having set the terms of the discussion in 2.1-11

---

1. Cf. Räisänen: 'Das "Wir" von V.5 ist zweifellos der ungläubige Jude' (1986f: 196).

(namely divine impartiality rules out ethnic advantage), he seems to contradict those rules in 3.1ff. While Paul goes on to explain in Romans 9–11 how divine impartiality and ethnic advantage can be held in complementarity, the objector is at a disadvantage by not yet knowing Paul's understanding of how these two are related. Paul presents a fascinating argument in 11.11-36 in explanation of this.

In the meantime, however, Paul hopes to turn this objection to his own advantage in 3.8 where his words are to this effect: 'Although Jewish unfaithfulness does not impinge upon God's faithfulness, if you think that God's continued faithfulness allows you to sin without consequence, then you are guilty of boldly saying, "Let us do evil that good (the demonstration of God's faithfulness) may result". Although my opponents have accused me of taking this position, it is not my position but theirs, and their condemnation is well deserved.' This verse gives us an insight into the kind of disputes in which Paul and the opponents of his gospel were engaged. As he will later affirm, his gospel is of God's righteousness revealed through Christ *apart from the law* (χωρὶς νόμου). In the eyes of his opponents, this is a declaration of antinomianism since the law contains God's prescriptions for proper living. They accuse Paul, therefore, of promoting sin in order to prove God's righteousness, since God will remain faithful despite one's sin. Paul's perspective is the exact opposite; the one who promotes sin is 'the Jew' who thinks that, despite his sin, God will be faithful to him.[1] Paul's charge throughout 2.1-29 is here restated in the most pronounced terms: by presuming upon the faithfulness of God, ethnocentric covenantalism leads to moral laxity, and is rightly condemned as an inadequate understanding of God and his redemptive workings in history.[2]

12.7. *The Anthropological Condition Encompasses All: 3.9-20*

The conclusion that Paul wants his readers to accept before he introduces his christological corrective in 3.21ff. appears in 3.9b: 'all are under sin', the 'all' including both Jews and gentiles. He argued in 1.18–2.29 that Jews have no claim to be ethically superior to the gen-

---

1. It is evident here how necessary ethical integrity is in substantiating one's case; if the charge of antinomianism can be made to stick against one's behaviour, that charge rules out the appropriateness of one's claim to covenant membership.
2. Thus, this section cannot be considered to contain merely 'side issues', as Bassler estimates (1982: 153).

tiles, and because he has framed this point in terms of the anthropological condition of sin in 1.18-32, he draws the conclusion of 3.9 in the light of that anthropological condition. For this reason, Paul thinks he can claim to have already proven (προητιασάμεθα) that all are under sin. Although, in manoeuvring his case polemically, Paul has entertained one idea (that gentiles can do the law) which is compatible with neither his conclusion (3.9) nor with his depiction of the anthropological condition of sin (1.18-32), he now leaves that idea far behind. His case becomes quite simple: not only does 'the Jew' have no claim to superiority over the gentiles, but, moreover, both Jew and gentile share the same position in the anthropological condition under sin (described in 1.18-32) and stand in need of redemption (described explicitly in 3.21ff.).

After drawing his conclusion, Paul proceeds to support it with a catena of scriptural proof-texts. The first, a quotation from Eccl. 7.20 (or Ps. 13.1), makes his point most obviously: 'There is none righteous, not even one'. This is one example of the Jewish sense of universal sinfulness before God. But whereas Paul's contemporaries considered universal sin to be offset by God's covenant which marked Israel off as superior to the other nations, nothing of the sort is possible in the context of Paul's case. He has targeted his case against Jewish ethnocentrism, and he targets his reading of scripture in the same way. Throughout 3.10-12 runs the phrase 'there is none'—none who is righteous or understands, none who seeks God or does good; instead, all have turned away and have become worthless. Because this includes the Jew alongside the gentile in the anthropological condition (cf. 3.22), it also excludes Jewish confidence in their ethnic standing.

After the catena of verses ends, Paul drives the point home again in 3.19 by stating that what the law says, it says to those 'in the law', and what it says (to the Jews!) is that, before God, *every* mouth is to be silent and *all* the world is held accountable. Again it should be noted that the same point could well have been made by 'the Jew'. What distinguishes Paul's case, however, is that it does not proceed to outline the salvific benefits of the covenant for Israel. For Paul, the anthropological condition of sin is the whole story, encompassing the whole of humanity and leaving no room for ethnic considerations. All mouths are silenced, and thereby have no recourse to ethnic defence.

Paul makes his point one final time in 3.20, this time framing it in terms of 'works of law'. He inserts this expression into his reading of Ps. 143.2, where it was not originally: 'because *by works of the law* (ἔργων νόμου) no flesh will be justified before him'. It is of great importance to recognize what Paul has in mind by this expression, which is used here for the first time in Romans. What Paul envisages by 'works of law' are not legalistic merit points which one deposits before God in order to earn the right of salvation. Instead, the phrase signifies collectively those practices necessary to Jewish lifestyle which reinforced their self-identity as a unique and superior people—the covenant people of God.[1] Paul is referring to particularly *Jewish* practices (such as circumcision, referred to in 2.25-29) which serve to differentiate the Jews from the other nations—'the practice of the law within the Jewish community'.[2] The way Paul makes use of this phrase in Gal. 2.16 reinforces this reading especially well in the context of Paul's argument and in light of the dynamics surrounding the Antioch incident described there.[3] Thus, Paul's point is made once again, this time by his reading of Scripture itself: national status has no salvific

---

1. See especially Dunn, 1988a: 153-55; *idem*, 1983: 107-11; *idem*, 1985: 527-32; Tyson, 1973: 424-25; Sanders, 1983a: 46; Watson, 1986: 129-30; Snodgrass, 1988: 102; W.S. Campbell, 1988: 7; Barth, 1974: 1.244-48.

2. Watson, 1986: 36.

3. See e.g. Dunn, 1983. This understanding is, of course, not shared by all. Most recently, for instance, Westerholm has challenged this reading on several fronts (1988: 117-19). One of Westerholm's criticisms is directly related to Rom. 3.20. He notes that in Rom. 2.21-22 Paul has attacked 'the Jew' on moral grounds: the Jew has not met the basic moral requirements of the law contained in the Decalogue. These (ethical) practices, claims Westerholm, are what Paul has in mind by the phrase 'works of the law'; no one can be justified by moral performance ('works of law') because no one does what the law requires for ethical behaviour; the problem with 'works of the law' is, in Westerholm's opinion, that 'Jews do not do them' (p. 121).

While it is true that Paul's critique of 'the Jew' does, of course, depend upon charges of moral inadequacy, this does not necessitate identifying 'works of law' in any other way than as the Jewish practice of the law. Paul's point in Rom. 3.20 is that, because of 'the Jew's' moral inadequacy, he has no exclusive claim to divine grace, no matter what ethnic symbols or practices ('works of the law') he might demonstrate. Paul's charge here is no different from that of 2.25: 'if you break the law [the moral requirements of the law], your circumcision has become uncircumcision'. Because 'the Jew' does not keep the moral requirements of the law (demonstrated in 3.10-18; cf. 2.1-24), so Jewish 'works of the law' (3.20; cf. circumcision in 2.25-29) which 'the Jew' *does* practise (contra Westerhorm) are rendered salvifically null and void. Thus, Paul's charge against the salvific efficacy of nomistic practices in 3.20 depends upon his charge of ethical inadequacy in Rom. 2, and his scriptural charge in 3.10-18.

value in and of itself, for God's favour does not depend upon ethnic considerations.

Some scholars have cited Paul's comments in 3.20 ('by works of the law no flesh will be justified before him') in juxtaposition with his words in 2.13 ('the doers of the law will be justified') in order to indicate further contradictions in Paul's thinking about the law.[1] While I do not dispute that Paul's argument does contain contradictions, I do not accept that this is one indication of that fact. Paul has two completely different arguments running in the two cases. Whereas 'works of the law' in 3.20 makes reference primarily to particularly Jewish nomistic pratice, 'doing the law' in 2.13 is rooted in Paul ethical denunciation of 'the Jew' and, as such, refers exclusively to *moral uprightness*. Paul argues that (1) Jews have no claim to righteousness on the basis of their nationalistic 'works of law', and (2) those who do the moral requirements of the law demonstrate themselves to be the righteous ones. There is no contradiction here.

With 3.20b, Paul goes further in redefining the function of the law: the law brings the knowledge of sin. That is, instead of reinforcing the Jewish sense of national superiority, the law is intended to make those 'within the law' aware that they too stand with the gentiles under sin, thereby discrediting Jewish confidence in their ethnic identity. In Paul's eyes, Jewish possession of the law should not bolster ethnic pride but should flatten it; by the law comes the knowledge of sin, and by that knowledge one is reminded that there is no distinction, for no one is righteous before God.

Underlying the whole of Paul's case in 1.18–3.20 are two key points: (1) the principle of divine impartiality, and (2) the conviction that all are under sin. Each of these two points is commonplace within Early Judaism but Paul employs them in a completely different fashion, because of his peculiar (but eschatologically revealed) understanding of the covenant, which he lays out in its first explicit form in 3.21ff., one of the passages with which the next chapter deals.

---

1. Recently, Boers has argued that the two demonstrate a blatant contradiction (1988: 61). Conversely, see Snodgrass, 1986: 84-85.

Chapter 13

THE CHRISTOLOGICAL CORRECTIVE
AND THE COMMUNITY OF GRACE

In this chapter, three passages will be examined: Rom. 3.21-31, 9.30–
10.13, and 7.7–8.4. From these passages, a fairly consistent picture
emerges concerning Paul's reflections on the law and the people of
God as he legitimates his mission in terms of christian self-definition.
After Rom. 3.21-31 (§13.1) has been analysed, an analysis of Rom.
9.30–10.13 follows (§13.2). These two passages demonstrate the lines
of Paul's thought concerning the matters at hand, and similar themes
are evident in each. Finally, Rom. 7.7–8.4, one of the thorniest passages in the Pauline corpus, will be approached (§13.3) and an interpretation suggested in the light of the findings from Chapter 12 and
from §13.1 and §13.2.

13.1. *The Community of Grace and the Law (1): 3.21-31*

One of the central themes upon which Paul built his case in 1.18–3.20
is the impartiality of God. Accordingly, he made the claim that Jewish
ethnocentrism is a misunderstanding of the ways of the covenant God.
In Rom. 3.21-31—'the theological centre and basis of Paul's argument
in Rom. i–xi',[1] the 'heart of Paul's gospel'[2]—the same theme appears.
Once again Paul employs it to negate the idea that righteousness is
ethnically determined. Moreover, this theme underlies the solution to
the anthropological condition of sin, which Paul posits here in its first
explicit form: the corrective is faith, which is available to all in relation to the person of Jesus Christ.[3]

---

1. W.S. Campbell, 1981a: 26.
2. Scroggs, 1976: 276 n. 16.
3. The ambiguity here is intentional in light of the controversy surrounding the
phrase πίστις Ἰησοῦ Χριστοῦ, a controversy stirred up afresh by Hooker 1989;
Keck, 1989: 452-57; Williams, 1987; Hays, 1983; Stowers, 1989.

The first occurrence of the theme of divine impartiality is in 3.22, where Paul restates his point of 3.9: 'for there is no difference' between Jew and gentile. Having stated this, Paul again introduces into his discussion the problem which inflicts itself upon all humanity without distinction: 'for all sinned and fall short of God's glory' (3.23). In 3.29-30, Paul embellishes this to mean that, since all are equal in the problem, so the corrective must be the same for all. Once again, divine impartiality is the principle upon which his case rests: 'Is God the God of the Jews only? Is he not God of the gentiles also? Indeed of the gentiles as well, since God is one.'

Paul, no doubt, intends here to marshal in support of his case the basic affirmation of Jewish ethnocentric covenantalism—the affirmation that God is one. This affirmation stands as the frontispiece of the Shema ('Hear, O Israel, the Lord your God is one'), the prayer which was offered daily by the pious Jew on the basis of Deut. 6.4-9, 11.13-21, and Num. 15.37-41. In Deut. 6.4, the God who is one is identified more specifically as Israel's God: 'The Lord our God (MT אֱלֹהֵינוּ; LXX ὁ θεὸς ἡμῶν), the Lord is one'. Immediately following this in Deuteronomy, there appears the command to love God and to obey the commandments which he has given Israel in order that they might live pleasingly before him, in distinction from the other nations (Deut. 6.5ff.). Paul, however, extracts the affirmation from this ethnocentric context and works it in support of his own case *against* ethnocentrism: if God is one, he is the God not only of Israel (cf. Deut. 6.4: ὁ θεὸς ἡμῶν) but of both Jews and gentiles. Accordingly, Paul writes, 'he will justify both the circumcision by faith and the uncircumcision through faith' (3.30). Any distinction which might be made between 'the circumcision' and 'the uncircumcision' is, says Paul, salvifically irrelevant, for the basis of salvation for all is faith. In this way, Paul makes a case which disqualifies Jewish ethnocentrism by means of the central affirmation of Early Judaism. Once again, Paul's strategy evident in Romans 2 reappears: he picks up one strand of the logic of ethnocentric covenantalism and reapplies it in a new manner for his own purposes.

Paul frames his discussion of the oneness of God in terms of 'the righteousness of God', a key component of his case in 3.21-26. It refers not to an abstract metaphysical attribute of divinity, but is a relational term which denotes the saving activity of God in history 'on behalf of those to whom he has committed himself'.[1] Paul's argument is that those to whom God has committed himself (namely those who participate in a covenant relationship with him) are not the Jews *per se*, as had generally been held in Early Judaism, but all those who have faith (3.22). This, of course, is not just any kind of faith; even Jews outside the christian community could claim to have faith in God. Paul retains saving faith as the exclusive possession of the *christian* community by coupling divine grace with being 'in Christ': 'having been justified freely by his grace (τῇ αὐτοῦ χάριτι) through the redemption which is in Christ Jesus' (3.24). Although the syntax of the participle is awkward, δικαιούμενοι has direct reference to those of 3.22 who have faith (τοὺς πιστεύοντες). Their faith is met by God's grace, an interaction which takes place only ἐν Χριστῷ Ἰησοῦ.

The grace which the christian community enjoys is eschatological in character; it is grace imparted only within the boundaries of the new age which has dawned. Within 3.21-26 Paul sets his gospel of faith within this temporal context, drawing up a contrast between the former situation of sin (which permeated humanity and provoked God's wrath) and the present situation, the eschatological 'now' (3.21: νυνί; 3.26: ἐν τῷ νῦν καιρῷ). The remedy for sin (God's righteousness through faith) is itself temporally determined, being intrinsically tied to the Christ-event, described in sacrificial terms in 3.25. The problem of the power of sin could not have been solved at just any point along the way, for the corrective has become 'available' only with the change of the ages.

With the temporal shift to the 'now', it has become obvious to Paul how God's righteousness operates: his saving grace is not restricted to an ethnic people, for it is manifest in the present time within the eschatological community of believers, and only there. To think otherwise is to misunderstand God's ways and to estimate incorrectly the nature of his covenant.

This is what stands behind Paul's case in 3.21a where he says that the righteousness of God is now manifest 'apart from law' (χωρὶς νόμου). It must be clear what Paul has in mind here. His point is not, as some have suggested, that God's righteousness is apart from law

---

1. Dunn, 1988a: 166. See the way the term 'righteousness of God' is employed in Deutero-Isaiah and the Psalms, as noted by Williams, 1980: 260-63. Cf. Dahl: 'Especially in the Psalms and in Second Isaiah, God's "righteousness" means his saving righteousness, his vindication of himself and of his covenant people' (1977: 96).

because keeping the law is impossible.[1] Instead, the expression χωρὶς νόμου in 3.21a should be understood along the lines of Paul's comment regarding 'works of law' in 3.20: 'no one will be justified before him by works of law' (ἐξ ἔργων νόμου). As we saw in Chapter 12, by 'works of law' Paul has in mind the *ethnic* practices of the law which marked out the Jewish people from the other nations—the 'badges of national privilege'.[2] The same phrase, 'works of law', appears again in 3.28 where Paul writes: 'a man is justified by faith apart from works of law' (χωρὶς ἔργων νόμου). Paul means to divorce the righteousness of God from the arena of Jewish ethnocentrism and its identity markers.[3] Such a contentious move turns ethnocentric covenantalism on its head, but it follows in Paul's mind from his case which culminated in 3.20, and he has nothing else in mind by the phrase χωρὶς νόμου in 3.21a. Paul is claiming that God's righteousness is conferred without being restricted to the Jewish way of life, a way of life which he characterizes here as a life of 'law'.[4] Paul's statement in 3.21a, that 'God's righteousness has been manifest apart from the law', is simply a restatement of 3.20 wherein Paul claimed that righteousness cannot be attained by means of ethnically restrictive practices, as he argues also in 3.28.[5]

It is just as important to note that, while Paul denounces 'works of the law' (the markers of ethnic membership) as salvifically irrelevant, he does not denounce the law (= Torah) itself. In fact, after stating that God's righteousness is χωρὶς νόμου, Paul immediately adds the phrase, 'testified to by the law (ὑπὸ τοῦ νόμου) and the prophets' (3.21). Although God's righteousness has been made manifest only 'now', it was foretold in the scriptures. In this way, what might appear to others as a Pauline innovation (the claim that God's righteousness is apart from ethnic practices) is rooted in the revelation of God which the Jews (those who are 'in the law') have possessed all along (2.12, 17-20). Accordingly, Paul clothes his eschatological gospel with the

1. T.R. Schreiner has argued this case in his 1984 and 1985 articles. Cf. Westerholm, 1988: 166-67, and elsewhere.
2. Wright, 1978: 82.
3. Cf. Sanders, 1983a: 46; Wright, 1980: 72-73; Dunn, 1985: 529; *idem*, 1988a: 186. Contra Moo: 'Paul appears to criticize "works of the law" not because they are νόμου ("of the law") but because they are ἔργα ("works")' (1983: 97).
4. Cf. e.g. Williams, 1980: 271; Ziesler, 1989: 109; Watson, 1986: 132-34.
5. Cf. Cranfield: 'χωρὶς νόμου here is equivalent in significance to χωρὶς ἔργων νόμου in v.28' (1975a: 201).

garb of continuity with God's workings throughout Jewish history (cf. 1.16-17). Although God's righteousness is mediated in the 'now' by faith, this is not out of line with his previous revelations of himself. In fact, it is the fulfilment of those previous revelations.

The first two points—God's righteousness apart from ethnic consideration but testified to by the Jewish scriptures—stands behind Paul's question in 3.31: 'Therefore do we invalidate the law through faith? May it not be, but we establish the law.' Paul does, of course, intend to invalidate *the ethnic identity markers* (ἔργα νόμου in 3.20, 28) or a nomistic manner of life (νόμος in 3.21a) as salvifically effective, but he evidently did not envisage invalidating *the law*. For Paul, stripping away 'works of the law' from the concept of righteousness did not invalidate the law; in fact, faith as the sole means of appropriating God's righteousness is itself the establishment of the law, for the law and the prophets had foretold of this situation all along (3.21, as he goes on to show in Rom. 4). As S. Westerholm observes, Rom. 3.31 is a demonstration that 'according to Paul, the *true* nature and purpose of the Law come to light when it is viewed from the perspective of justification by faith'.[1]

With these aspects of Paul's case in 3.21-31 in mind, attention will now turn specifically to Rom. 3.27, a verse of utmost importance if Paul's argument is to be properly grasped. There Paul writes: 'Where then is boasting? It has been excluded. By what kind of νόμος? Of works? No, but through the νόμος of faith.' Controversial in this verse is Paul's double mention of νόμος; does he mean to refer to the Torah/Scripture or to a general principle/rule?[2] Many think the latter to be the case. So H. Räisänen remarks that

> jeder νόμος in V.27 eine 'Ordnung' meint. νόμος πίστεως ist die Heilsordnung, die auf Glauben fundiert ist; νόμος τῶν ἔργων die Ordnung, die auf Werke des Gesetzes aufgebaut wurde.[3]

This is certainly both possible and sensible within the contours of Paul's case. Nonetheless, the equation of νόμος in 3.27 with the Torah (or Scripture) fits well with what Paul has argued at four points throughout 3.19-31 wherein the same equation appears (3.19, 20, 21b,

---

1. 1988: 122 n. 47.
2. Wilckens has argued that such a translation ('principle') is impossible (1978: 2.122) but Räisänen has demonstrated otherwise (1983: 50 n. 34; 1986d; 1986e).
3. 1986d: 112. Cf. *idem*, 1983: 50-52; Barrett, 1957: 83; Sanders, 1983a: 33; Watson, 1986: 132; Ziesler, 1989: 118.

31). Of course, Paul could be playing with the term in 3.27, giving it a different meaning for effect; he seems to do so in 3.21a where νόμος refered not to the biblical text but to a nomistic manner of life. In my opinion, however, Räisänen's estimation (quoted above) does not hit the mark. This is due not only to the four occasions throughout 3.19-31 where νόμος does refer to the biblical text but, more significantly, to the context of Paul's thought in view of what has preceded 3.27. The issue of this verse is 'boasting', which Paul has made reference to in 2.17 and 2.23 when speaking of Jewish pride in their covenant relationship with God. The basis of this ethnocentric boast is *Jewish possession of the* νόμος, the Torah/scriptures. Says Paul, 'the Jew' 'relies on the law' (ἐπαναπαύῃ νόμῳ) and so boasts in God (2.17); being instructed by the law (κατηχούμενος ἐκ τοῦ νόμου, 2.18), he considers himself the better of others because he has the embodiment of knowledge and truth in the law (τῆς γνώσεως καὶ τῆς ἀληθείας ἐν τῷ νόμῳ, 2.20); accordingly, he *boasts* in the law (ὃς ἐν νόμῳ καυχᾶσαι, 2.23).

Already, then, Paul has established an intricate connection between Jewish boasting and their possession of the biblical texts—ὁ νόμος. (The Jews are, after all, ἐν νόμῳ.) When the two terms appear again in 3.27, the reference of each is presumably the same as in 2.17-23 unless otherwise clarified. But Paul does not indicate that the references have changed. Moreover, had he wished to avoid the identification of νόμος as the Torah or Scripture, he could easily have left the word out altogether without damaging his case in the least. That is, he could well have written ποῦ οὖν ἡ καύχησις; ἐξεκλείσθη. διὰ τῶν ἔργων; οὐχί, ἀλλὰ διὰ πίστεως. As soon as he introduces νόμος into this context concerned with boasting, precedent suggests that he is referring to the biblical text, rather than simply juxtaposing two 'principles'. Paul here has introduced a distinction with reference to the law through the genitives which modify it: works and faith. So C.F.D. Moule makes note of 'Paul's notoriously flexible and poignant uses of the genitive'.[1] Similarly, K. Snodgrass finds that nouns in the genitive case 'are not incidental "add-ons" for Paul, but often carry as much or more force than the noun they qualify'.[2] Such would seem to be the case here where a distinction in

1. 1974: 181.
2. 1988: 101.

Paul's concept of the law (= Torah) appears through his use of the genitives ἔργων and πίστεως.

In 3.27, then, Paul demonstrates his concern to undermine Jewish ethnocentric pride,[1] and he does so by attacking its very basis: the possession of the law. Instead of *promoting* ethnocentric boasting (as Paul demonstrates in 2.17-23), the law *excludes* such nationalistic confidence. Paul makes this claim by (re)defining the concept of Torah (νόμος) according to his own gospel of faith; the law is not one of (ethnocentric) works but of faith.[2] Because faith is the prerequisite of righteousness for both Jew and gentile (3.28-30), Paul says in 3.31 that faith *establishes* the law. Paul contends that in the 'now', the law promotes not nomistic practice but faith; for this reason, he speaks of the Torah in 3.27 as the 'law of faith'. When the law is used improperly as a badge of ethnic superiority and national security (cf. 2.17-23), the law brings condemnation (cf. 3.20; 5.20); as such, Paul speaks of it as the 'law of works' (3.27). The law in both cases is the Torah of divine revelation as it is rightly and wrongly used or perceived.

In my estimation, this interpretation of 3.27 makes the best sense of the verse within the context of Paul's argument in Romans, despite the denials of many.[3] Sanders, for instance, finds this reading 'clearly impossible' for the reason that it makes 'nonsense of Paul's view of the death of Christ'.[4] But this is a strange criticism coming from the man who popularized anew the estimate that Paul's thought proceeded from solution to plight, that Paul's 'soteriology' explains his view of the law, rather than vice versa, and that Paul's various portrayals of the

---

1. Cf. Sanders, 1983a: 33; Räisänen, 1983: 170-71; *idem*, 1986b: 34-35; Howard, 1970: 232-33; Wilckens, 1978: 1.248; Watson, 1986: 133-35; Moxnes, 1988: 71; Snodgrass, 1988: 101; Dunn, 1988a: 185; Ziesler, 1989: 43, 117.

2. Cf. Friedrich, 1954; Lohse, 1973; Hübner, 1984a: 115-16, 138, 144; Cranfield, 1975a: 220; Wilckens, 1978: 1.245; Wright, 1980: 117; Dunn, 1988a: 185-87; Rhyne, 1981: 68-70; Snodgrass, 1988: 101-103; Stuhlmacher, 1985: 97; *idem*, 1989: 62-63; von der Osten-Sacken, 1975: 226-32, 245-46; *idem*, 1989: 13-19, 23-33; Gaston, 1987: 31, 75, 131, 172. Räisänen cites others, 1983: 51 n. 37.

3. Esp. Räisänen, 1983: 42-52. Interestingly, on a related topic, Räisänen accuses others of assuming 'that *nomos* means something other that the law in the "difficult" passages' (1983: 66), which is precisely what he himself assumes of the 'difficult' passages of 3.27 and 7.22-8.2.

4. 1983a: 15 n. 26. Sanders recognizes that the 'boasting' mentioned in 3.27 must refer back to the two references of 'boasting' in 2.17-23 (1983a: 33), but he fails to apply the same method to the νόμος of 3.27, which occurs five times throughout 2.17-23, each time in reference to the Torah/scriptures.

law are contingent upon his various points of argument and cannot be systematized. The fact is that Paul is not, of course, explaining the death of Christ, but is defining in 3.27 the constituency of the eschatological covenant people. In Early Judaism, 'covenant' and 'law' went hand in hand, and the same is true for Paul's innovative definition of the covenant. Having already restricted God's covenant grace to the 'in Christ' community of faith in 3.21-26, Paul immediately makes claim to the law on behalf of that same community. To do so, Paul makes an unusual but useful distinction with regard to the law which supports his definition (it is a 'law of faith') and which includes a denunciation of other definitions of the covenant; for them, the law has nothing to do with faith (a provocative claim!) but is inferior, operating as a 'law of works'. Following on from this juxtaposition, Paul cites in 3.31 a common challenge to his gospel (it invalidates the law) in order to demonstrate how ill founded that charge is.[1] In Paul's opinion, only his gospel upholds the law in the eschatological age. Evidently, then, in his battle for the definition of the community of grace, Paul has to battle also for the definition of the law, as we see in stark terms in 3.27. Accordingly, the dangers of speaking (as some do) of 'Paul's Christ–Torah antithesis'[2] are readily apparent.

Already in this brief passage (3.21-31) we have seen something of the variety of ways in which Paul makes use of the word νόμος. First, it referred in 3.21a to the distinctively Jewish 'way of life', a life that is thoroughly 'nomistic' in orientation. So Paul says that God's righteousness is now shown to be 'apart from law' (χωρὶς νόμου). Second, νόμος was employed in 3.21b in reference to the Torah, God's revelation of himself which the Jews have possessed (3.2; cf. 2.12: they are 'in the law'). In this regard, Paul says that God's righteousness 'apart from law' is testified to by the Jewish scriptures—the law and the prophets. Third, Paul recognizes νόμος (= Torah) to be subject to two 'perspectives', one of which is improper with regard to its intentions and the other which fulfils its intentions. On the one hand, the Torah can be regarded as the 'law of works' (3.27)—that is, the law understood as prescribing ethnocentric practices as the symbols of covenant

---

1. Thus, Paul is not backtracking in 3.31, wanting to affirm the law after having already undermined it. He has developed an argument in 3.27 by which he hopes to convince others that he affirms the law. Once that is done, he asks what evidence there is that he is undermining the law (3.31). There is none, he states.

2. Donaldson, 1989.

membership, 'the law as a charter of national privilege'.[1] When understood in this way, the law does not exclude boasting (3.27) but promotes Jewish boasting in their covenant membership at the expense of the gentiles (2.17, 23). On the other hand, the law can be regarded as the 'law of faith' (3.27)—that is, the law understood as prescribing faith as the symbol of membership in the eschatological community of God's grace (cf. 1.2; 3.21b). When understood in this way, the law does not promote Jewish boasting but excludes it (3.27), for God, who is one, justifies Jew and gentile alike by faith (3.28-29). Accordingly, faith establishes the law (3.31).

S. Westerholm has recently challenged the reading of Rom. 3.21-31 which has been advocated here. Westerholm charges that Rom. 4.1-5 is 'positively fatal' for any reading which considers Paul's critique in 3.21-31 to operate on the level of an attack on Jewish ethnocentrism. Extending his case of 3.21-31 in 4.1-25, Paul refutes there not simply ethnocentrism but, according to Westerholm, the general notion of works altogether. This is evident by his denial that Abraham could have boasted before God of any 'works' which might have been to his credit. Says Westerholm: 'the "works" by which Abraham could conceivably have been justified, and of which he might have boasted (4:2), were certainly not observances of the peculiarly Jewish parts of the Mosaic code'.[2] Accordingly, Westerholm considers this to be proof that what Paul is attacking is the notion of the salvific sufficiency of 'works in general', rather than ethnocentric practices in particular.

Westerholm's criticism suffers in that it does not grapple with the manner in which the figure of Abraham functioned in Early Judaism; in Jewish self-definition, and in Jewish attempts to preserve their distinctive way of life, Abraham played an essential role. For instance, in times of national or religious persecution, the example of Abraham's faithfulness to God in times of testing (Gen. 22) helped to bolster Jewish concerns to preserve their ethnic distinctiveness in faithfulness to God.[3] Moreover, Abraham was considered to be the ideal Jew, and, in this regard, he was said to have observed the Mosaic law *in toto* even before it was revealed to Moses[4]—a fact which itself calls into

---

1. Wright, 1980: 97.
2. 1988: 119. Cf. Moo, 1983: 94-96.
3. E.g. *Jub.* 17.15-18; 21.21-22; Jdt. 8.25-27; 1 Macc. 2.52; *4 Macc.* 14.20; 16.19-20; *Ps.-Philo* 40.2-5.
4. Gen. 26.5; *Jub.* 16.28; Sir. 44.20; *2 Bar.* 57.2; Philo, *Migr. Abr.* 3-6; 60-62, 276.

question Westerholm's claim that Abraham's works 'were certainly not observances of the peculiarly Jewish parts of the Mosaic code'.[1] In fact, a central theme throughout *Jubilees* is the insistence that the patriarchs observed all the Mosaic prescriptions for ethnic distinctiveness. So, for instance, Abraham's obedience to the Mosaic law is evidenced by his participation in the feast of weeks (6.19; 14.20; 15.1-2; 22.1-9) and the feast of booths (16.20-31). Accordingly, as F. Watson puts it, in Early Judaism Abraham is depicted

> as a model of obedience to God. His function is to reflect and legitimate the self-understanding of the pious and loyal Jew of the present. He too, like Abraham, must separate himself from the ways of the Gentiles and devote himself wholly to the law of God, whatever the suffering this entails. The figure of Abraham symbolizes this sense of a unique status, privilege and responsibility.[2]

In many ways, then, the Jews of Early Judaism looked to Abraham as the model Jew and forefather of Jewish society, claiming for him what they considered to be essential to their own self-identity.

In the light of this, it seems unlikely that Paul's reference to Abraham has little to do with Jewish ethnocentrism. Instead, it more likely has everything to do with it. As N.T. Wright notes, 'Paul's critique of "works". . . functions *within* his critique of "national righteousness"'.[3] Nonetheless, it has yet to be determined *how* this critique of 'works' functions within a critique of Jewish particularism. There are two possibilities: that is, two senses can be applied to 'works' in 4.1-5 without disregarding Paul's intention to upset nationalistic definitions of the covenant, and the two are not necessarily mutually exclusive. Each will be noted presently.

First, it is arguable that by 'works' Paul is thinking in 4.1-5 specifically of ethnic practices which distinguish Jews from gentiles. This would fit well with what we know of Abraham's significance in Early Judaism. Moreover, it would be consistent with the manner in which Paul employs the term 'works' (in conjunction with 'boasting') in 3.27 and with the manner in which the 'faith–works' dichotomy is replaced in 4.9-12 by a 'faith–circumcision' dichotomy, still in reference to Abraham. Furthermore, this interpretation makes good sense

1. 1989: 199.
2. 1986: 137. See his fuller analysis on pp. 136-38. Cf. Dunn, 1988a: 200-201; R.N. Longenecker, 1977: 204-205.
3. 1980: 97.

of Paul's concern in 4.1-25 to identify Abraham as the father of those
who believe rather than of those whose self-identity is determined by
their place within the realm of the law (4.14: οἱ ἐκ νόμου; cf. 4.16)
and for whom the outward mark of circumcision is all-important. It is
this sense of ἔργα (= nomistic practice) which we suspect was uppermost in Paul's mind throughout 4.1-5. His sights are set on toppling
the salvific necessity of these practices ('works').[1]

If the 'semantic field' of Paul's argument suggests that by ἔργα Paul
has distinctively Jewish practices in mind, it is also arguable, even in
conjunction with what has just been shown in the previous paragraph,
that within 4.1-5 Paul *expands* his critique of Jewish ethnocentrism *to
include* a charge of legalism. Paul incorporates in 4.4-5 an analogy of
a worker who tries to earn a wage by his own efforts, expecting to be
rewarded according to his labours. It is not hard to hear a charge of
legalism behind this analogy.

It needs to be seen, however, that *if* Paul is charging Jews with the
attempt to *earn* their salvation by works in a legalistic sense, even this
plays a part within his case against Jewish ethnocentrism. It is necessary here to distinguish between *what* Paul is fighting against (Jewish
ethnocentrism rather than legalism) and *how* he fights against it. A
charge of legalism may well have aided Paul's larger attempt to discredit Jewish particularism. Quite simply, once Paul has argued that
God's covenant grace is restricted to the christian community, any
Jews outside of that community who expect God to look favorably
upon their ethnic practices could well be accused of attempting to earn
salvation apart from God's grace. They think that they are *reacting* to
God's grace by their ethnic practices, but, as Paul insists, the proper
response is faith. By rejecting this requirement of covenant relationship, ethnocentric Jews are seen to be *acting* by their own efforts
(their ethnic 'works of law') in order to gain God's grace. In that
sense, ethnocentric Jews are comparable to a worker who expects a
wage for his toil (4.4-5).

As we have seen, *4 Ezra* demonstrates that, when God's grace is
removed from ethnocentric definitions of the covenant, ethnocentrism
is replaced by legalism. The same would be true of Paul's charge in
Rom 4.1-5, following on from 3.21-31 where he demonstrated that
God's grace is upon the christocentric community, not upon the ethnic

1. Cf. Ziesler, 1989: 123-25; Dunn, 1988a: 200-205, 226-28; Räisänen, 1983:
171-72; *idem*, 1986c: 82; Sanders, 1983a: 34-35; Watson, 1986: 138-41.

group of the Jews *per se*. Outside the christian community of faith, any 'pursuers' (9.31) of righteousness are simply spinning their wheels, acting on their own accord, but to no avail. They are guilty, in this way, of legalism, a characteristic which most Jews would have shunned, but one which (Paul may be intimating) applies to them since they are outside the boundaries of God's covenant grace.[1] In this way Paul's case against Jewish ethnocentrism may well have included a charge of legalism: outside the christian community the Jew who thinks himself to respond to God's grace by his nomistic practice is, in Paul's eyes, attempting to earn salvation through works, thereby cutting himself off from God's promise to establish for/through Abraham a worldwide family by means of faith.

In either of these interpretations, 'Paul's critique of "works" . . . functions *within* his critique of "national righteousness"'. Paul's sights have not moved off the target of rejecting Jewish ethnocentrism. In 3.21-31, that target is attacked directly with the designations 'works of the law' and 'works' which denote practices characteristic of the Jews alone and which Paul rules out as having salvific significance. In 4.1-5 the designation 'works' may well include a connotation of legalism (4.4-5), but even if this is so, the target has not changed. And the same target remains throughout 4.1-25 wherein Abraham's significance is broadened past ethnic boundaries to include all those who believe, whether Jew or gentile. God has promised that Abraham would be the father of a great multitude, and that promise is being fulfilled in the 'now' by the faith of both Jews and gentiles, in accordance with the promises of Genesis 17, thereby demonstrating God's faithfulness to his word. The newness of the present age has unfolded in complete accord with God's previous revelations; God's present activity complies fully with his promises to Abraham, whereby covenant history was initiated. Those who consider their nomistic practice ('works of the law') to have salvific significance are deluded, their efforts are in vain, and their attempts to *respond* to God's grace are, in fact, nothing other than works of a laborer who hopes to earn a wage. This charge of legalism is the product of Paul's case that God's grace is found only within the boundaries of the christian community of faith; it is not necessarily an accurate portrayal of any sector of Early Judaism.

---

1. The same would apply to Paul's juxtaposition of works and grace in 9.11-12, 32 and 11.5-6.

Throughout 3.21-31, Paul has discussed the manner of attaining to righteousness with reference to the law. Two alternatives were juxtaposed (righteousness by faith and righteousness by national right) and Paul has insisted that ethnocentric covenantalism is a misunderstanding of the ways of the covenant God who gave the law. Although it comes much later in Paul's epistle, Rom. 9.30–10.13 restates these basic concerns in a similar fashion. It is this passage with which the next section deals.

13.2. *The Community of Grace and the Law (2): 9.30–10.13*

Paul begins this section by juxtaposing the position of gentiles (specifically those gentiles who believe) with that of unbelieving Israel. Paul characterizes the gentiles as those 'who do not pursue righteousness' (9.30a) (which is to say that they are those who traditionally have not sought after covenant relationship with God), whereas Israel is characterized as 'pursuers'; they pursue 'the law of righteousness' (9.31a).

It is not altogether clear whether Paul intended in 9.30-31 to conjure up images of pursuit,[1] or, more specifically, of a foot-race between two contestants—'the pursuers' and 'the non-pursuers'.[2] If this footrace imagery is uppermost in Paul's mind, he has set up an ironic situation in which those who win the contest did not even participate in it. The winners are 'the non-pursuers' (cf. 10.20), the gentiles who attain to righteousness by faith (9.30b). Conversely, Israel fails to finish; they have not reached the law which they pursued (9.31b). Paul refers to the Torah here as the 'law of righteousness' (νόμον δικαιοσύνης); as F. Refoulé states, 'Le contexte invite à l'identifier à la Loi mosaïque. Quelle autre loi pourrait chercher Israël?'[3] By this phrase, Paul is characterizing the Torah as that through which righteousness is conferred when it is properly 'reached'. Thus, the irony of Paul's imagery is all the more striking; although gentiles are not pursuers and Jews are, gentiles have attained

---

1. Cf. Ps. 119.32: 'I run in the paths of your command'; Isa. 51.1: 'Hear me, pursuers of righteousness and seekers of the Lord'. See Noack, 1970; Refoulé, 1985: 174-75.

2. Cf. Barrett, 1977: 106; Gaston, 1987: 126.

3. Refoulé, 1985: 179-80. This phrase (νόμον δικαιοσύνης) should not be read as 'righteousness of the law'; contra Luz, 1968: 157; Westerholm, 1988: 145; and the RSV. See Cranfield's amusing criticisms, 1975b: 36.

to righteousness while Jews have not reached their goal of the law, by which they would have attained to righteousness.

The attribution of righteousness to gentile believers is significant since the term itself is a relational one 'which here seems to mean something like "life as God's people"'.[1] Paul contends that, by their faith, gentiles have fulfilled the covenant responsibilities. The problem with Israel is not the fact that they *pursue* the law of righteousness, as if the *activity of pursuit* itself is condemned by Paul; Paul in fact commends Israel's zeal only four verses later (10.2). Nor is the *object of pursuit* (the law) the reason for their fault. Paul describes the law here as the 'law of righteousness'. Instead, in Paul's eyes, Israel's problem is the *manner of their pursuit*. If Israel has failed to 'reach' the law, it is because their attempt was off-target and failed to meet the requirement of covenantal responsibilities of which the law speaks.

Paul explains this in 9.32: Israel's pursuit has been misguided because they attempt to fulfil the law 'not by faith but as (if it were) by works'.[2] Just as in 3.27, the law is here modified by two genitives: πίστεως and ἔργων. Fulfilment of the law is the issue in 9.31, and in 9.32 Paul proposes that faith is the means to that end.[3] The problem with Israel is that they have not pursued the law by faith, as is proper. Although it is hard to understand what Paul means by 'pursuing the law', it is easy to see his dilemma; he is struggling to support his definition of the community of grace by refuting the significance of the law for others and by positioning the law squarely in his own camp. The principle is simple: those who neglect the requirement of the covenant (faith) cannot make a proper claim to the law; or conversely, those who fail to demonstrate the identity marker required by the law cannot make a claim to membership in the community of God's grace. Paul does not disparage the law; he needs the law on his side if he is to have a convincing definition of the community of grace. Accordingly, he postulates that the law rightly stands together with righteousness only when christian faith is presupposed.

---

1. Ziesler, 1989: 250; cf. 252. See Dunn's comments, 1988a: 592.

2. The issue of punctuation in 9.32 is best resolved by the position taken by Cranfield, 1975b: 38-39.

3. This conclusion can be avoided if the object of pursuit in 9.32 is not the law but righteousness, as Ziesler contends (1989: 49, 254). But such a view is hard to maintain, for the object of pursuit in 9.31 is explicitly stated as the law, and Paul does not indicate a change of object between 9.31 and 9.32.

When he talks of Jewish 'works', what Paul seeks to discredit is not self-achievement *per se*; that is not in his view. What Paul seems to have in mind by 'works' are (as in 3.27) those Jewish practices which are ethnically normative and restrictive,[1] and which were thought by most Jews and many Jewish believers to be necessary badges of covenant membership (cf. 'works of the law').[2] In Paul's mind, such a restriction is a misunderstanding of the law, and causes the unbelievers of Israel to be excluded from covenant membership altogether. As in 4.4-5, Paul's case here may well include an accusation of legalism against nonbelieving Jews: because they are outside the boundaries of the covenant, instead of *reacting* to God's grace, they are simply *acting*. If such connotations are present, however, they function wholly within Paul's attack on Jewish *ethnocentrism*.[3]

Paul supports his argument of 9.31-32 with his reading of Isa. 28.16. Therein, Isaiah prophesied that Israel would stumble over the stumbling stone, but he also gave the assurance that those who believed in the stone would not be put to shame. Paul intends this prophetic announcement to bolster his case (underway since 9.6) that God's word has not failed; his word has, in fact, been proven, for he foretold through Isaiah the stumbling of most of Israel. Citing Isaiah, Paul makes the charge that, by misunderstanding the covenant to be an ethnocentric covenant, the majority of Israel has, just as Isaiah pronounced, failed to fulfil the requirement of faith and has stumbled over the 'stone' (= Christ).[4]

Paul takes this occasion to express his deep concern for his fellow Jews. He wishes that their situation could be otherwise (10.1), for, as he testifies on their behalf, 'they have zeal for God, but (their zeal is) not according to knowledge' (10.2). It is important to note the connotations of the word 'zeal'. Jewish literature of Paul's day demonstrates clearly that 'zeal' was frequently employed in reference to Jewish

---

1. Cf. Wright, 1980: 98; Watson, 1986: 165; Dunn, 1988a: 582; W.S. Campbell, 1981b: 34-35; Räisänen, 1983: 174-75.

2. Several Greek manuscripts contain here the phrase ἔργα νόμου. While this reading is not original, it does capture precisely what Paul is meaning.

3. Contra (with others) Gundry: 'it is not pride of privilege so much as self-reliance Paul is objecting to' (1985: 18).

4. Barrett (1977: 112-13), Meyer (1980: 64), and Gaston (1987: 129) think the stone to be the Torah. See criticisms by Badenas, 1985: 106-107; Aageson, 1987: 61; Evans, 1984: 563-66. Romans 10.11 should also be read with this identification in mind. Cf. Lübking, 1986: 86.

nationalistic piety.[1] In their attempt to honour God by obeying his commandments and preserving the purity of the covenant, the Jews considered themselves to be zealous for God and his law, a quality which took on various forms of expression. On the one hand, zeal is said to have characterized those Jewish activists who, at various times in Jewish history, fought to preserve Israel's ethnic and political identity.[2] This ideal is characterized in the Maccabaean literature as 'zeal for the law'.[3] The Qumran sectarians also spoke of their 'zeal for just laws' (1QS 4.4; cf. 9.23) and of their 'zeal against all the workers of iniquity and the men of deceit' (1QH 14.14). Their 'zeal', however, led them to remove themselves from the larger society in order to preserve the covenant, a reaction quite different to that of the Maccabaeans.

Despite the diversity of zealous expression, 'zeal' was characteristic of Jewish commitment to the preservation of the covenant relationship. Paul cannot help but admire this zeal; it is a characteristic he knows all too well, since he elsewhere admits that his persecution of 'God's church' arose out of his great zeal which exceeded that of others (Gal. 1.13-14; Phil. 3.6; cf. Acts 22.3-4). But, as he implied in 9.31, zeal for God which is motivated by, or channelled into, Jewish ethnocentrism is not properly guided; it misses the target because it is 'not according to knowledge'.

In 10.3 Paul continues this point concerning the knowledge of God. Having argued that righteousness comes only by faith, Paul accuses Israel of not knowing God's righteousness (10.3a) and of not submitting to it (10.3c). This double-barrelled accusation is explained by the middle term of 10.3: 'because they seek to establish their own righteousness' (10.3b). Again, it must be said that what Paul finds wrong with unbelieving Israel is not some tendency on their part to attempt to win salvation through self-achievement; that is not in Paul's view. When he speaks of them as seeking 'to establish (στῆσαι) their own (ἰδίαν) righteousness', Paul has in mind the nationalistic understanding of God's ways which he has tried to discredit in 3.21-31; Israel has considered righteousness to be their own and theirs alone (ἰδίαν), as a

1. Cf. Dunn, 1988a: 586-87; Donaldson, 1989: 672-74.
2. Cf. Hengel, 1974: 305-309. Dunn cites the following references: Simeon and Levi (Jdt. 9.4; *Jub.* 39.5-20), Mattathias (1 Macc. 2.19-26; Josephus, *Ant.* 12.271), Phinehas (Num. 25.10-13; Sir. 45. 23-24; 1 Macc. 2.54; *4 Macc.* 18.12), Elijah (Sir. 48.2; 1 Macc. 2.58). Cf also m. *Sanh.* 9.6.
3. 1 Macc. 2.26, 27, 50, 58; 2 Macc. 4.2.

nationalistic possession.[1] They have defined the covenant along ethnic lines, thereby excluding others. Because they possessed the law, they thought of themselves as 'possessing' the covenant as well, but as Paul argues throughout this letter, a truly enlightened reading of Scripture illustrates that ethnocentric restrictions of the covenant are improper.[2] For Paul, it is precisely because of their definition of the covenant that Israel has failed to enjoy God's righteousness and has been unmindful of the true ways of God (10.3a). Accordingly, in Paul's mind, ethnocentric covenantalism disqualifies the majority of Israel from participating in God's righteousness (just as Isaiah prophesied). They are blind to God's ways and have misunderstood the nature of the covenant by misreading the scriptures which they have held in their possession.

Romans 10.4 has been the focal point of much debate in scholarly circles. There Paul writes: τέλος γὰρ νόμου Χριστὸς εἰς δικαιοσύνην παντὶ τῷ πιστεύοντι. The main point of debate surrounding this verse, of course, is whether τέλος here has a teleological or temporal sense—that is, whether Paul meant to say that the law culminates in some sense with Christ or that Christ abrogates and does away with the law. The evidence cannot be reviewed for each position here. It only needs to be mentioned that, however one views the matter, the point Paul is seen to be making is no different from others he has made already. Paul is saying either that (faith in) Christ fulfills the law (being the goal of the law), or that (faith in) Christ rules out ethnocentric covenantalism. Either way, no new light is shed on Paul's concerns.[3] Perhaps he intends the phrase to be ambiguous and to

1. Cf. Mundle, 1932: 100 n. 3; Howard, 1969: 336; Wright, 1978: 83; *idem*, 1980: 98, 175, 122; Sanders, 1983a: 38; Räisänen, 1983: 174-75; *idem*, 1986c: 74-75; Dunn, 1988a: 587; *idem*, 1985: 530; Gaston, 1987: 129; Watson, 1986: 165; Ziesler, 1989: 256-57. Contra e.g. Westerholm, 1988: 114-15; Johnson, 1989: 157; Käsemann, 1980: 281.

2. In support of this reading of ἰδίαν is Dunn's observation concerning the significance of ἵστημι (1987a: 222; *idem*, 1988a: 588). He notes that this verb appears on occasion in Jewish literature to indicate the preservation of Israel's exclusive relationship with God in covenant. See esp. Sir. 44.20; 1 Macc. 2.27; cf. Jer. 34.18 (LXX 41.18); 35.16 (LXX 42.16); Sir. 11.20; 44.20.

3. Räisänen's comment is, to a certain extent, quite appropriate: 'the never-ceasing controversy about the meaning of Rom. 10.4 seems immaterial' since both the teleological and temporal possibilities within this verse are contained elsewhere in Paul's writings (1986a: 10-11). Cf. Howard, 1969: 332.

include both meanings,[1] for he goes on in 10.5-13 to argue both points from Scripture. In fact, however, because of its immediate connection with Paul's case in 10.5 (cf. the explanatory γάρ of 10.5), the temporal sense seems to have been uppermost in his mind, as we will see.

In 10.6-10, Paul argues that righteousness which comes by faith in Christ has been foretold in the scriptures (Deut. 30.12-14),[2] thereby fulfilling scriptural prophecy: 'The word is very near to you, on your lips and in your heart'. Paul understands this to be the 'word of faith which we preach' (10.8). The confession of Jesus as Lord equals the word 'on the lips', and the belief in Jesus' resurrection equals the word 'in the heart' (10.9-10). Thus Paul reads Deut. 30.12-14 with Christ in view, and demonstrates from scripture that faith fulfils the law apart from ethnic qualifications.

To reinforce this point, in 10.11 and 10.13 Paul quotes two other passages of Scripture. In each, the key word is πᾶς, 'all', which is coupled in Isa. 28.16 with 'faith',[3] and in Joel 3.5 with calling upon God. Moreover, to bolster his point all the more Paul once again calls up the principle of divine impartiality, which he had already established in Romans 1–3: 'there is no difference between Jew and gentile, for the same one is Lord of all' (10.12; cf. 3.29-30).

In Paul's mind, all this evidence rules out the principle upon which 'righteousness from the law' (nomistic service) is founded—that 'the one who does them [the commandments] shall live by them' (10.5).[4] Paul quotes this scriptural passage (Lev. 18.5) and understands it as expressing a fundamental premise of ethnocentric covenantalism: 'do

---

1. Cf. e.g. Harrington, 1980: 62; Wedderburn, 1985: 615; Kuss, 1959: 3.752-53; Leenhardt, 1961: 266. Jewett insists that this option is the least defensible (cf. Räisänen, 1983: 53), considering it to be theologically motivated with little attention paid to the context in order to gain the advantages of both Lutheran and Calvinist exegesis (1985: 353). Jewett's polemic at this point is unwarranted.

2. Several scholars argue that Paul did not quote from Scripture in 10.6-8; cf. Sanday and Headlam, 1902: 289; Davies, 1980: 153-54; Barrett, 1957: 199. Conversely, see e.g. Badenas, 1985: 126.

3. πᾶς does not occur in the Greek or Hebrew of Isa. 28.16. Paul has inserted it himself.

4. We read Rom. 10.5 according to UBS 3 = Nestle-Aland 26 editions, considering internal evidence to render a mute judgement on the proper reading while external evidence favours the ὅτι being placed after νόμου, with the other textual discrepancies following accordingly. Cf. Seifrid, 1985: 12-13. Seifrid also defends the adversative sense of the grammatical construction γάρ. . . δέ in 10.5-6 (1985: 16-17).

and live'. That is, the one who obeys the commandments of the law (ὁ ποιήσας αὐτά) which God has given exclusively to Israel will retain his place within the ethnic community of the righteous people of God (ζήσεται). This is precisely how Paul's contemporaries seem to have understood the relationship between 'do' and 'live'. In *Pseudo-Philo*, for instance, God states concerning his people: 'I gave them my Law and enlightened them in order that by *doing these things they would live* and have many years and not die' (23.10; cf. *Pss. Sol.* 14.2-3). This appears in the heart of the covenant renewal ceremony between Israel's God and his exclusive people, Israel. Paul recognizes this popular understanding of 'do and live', with all its ethnocentric connotations, and, accordingly, cites Lev. 18.5 as characteristic of the attempt to hoard the covenant within Jewish boundaries by making it 'their own' (10.3; cf. 9.31), an attempt which is proven to be illegitimate the light of (1) other scriptural passages exegeted by Paul, and (2) the principle of divine impartiality referred to once again in 10.12.

It is interesting to note that, in its original context, Deut. 30.12-14 functioned in the same manner as Lev. 18.5. That is, it encouraged the maintenance of Israel's obedience to God by the doing of the law, a practice which distinguished them from the pagan nations. As such, this passage from Deuteronomy promoted the ethnocentric covenantalism which Paul attempts to discredit. It even has the same verb of Lev. 18.5 which, for Paul, characterized Jewish attempts to hoard righteousness for themselves—ποιεῖν, the doing of the commandments in order to distinguish the people as righteous in contrast with the other nations. In Paul's hands, however, Deut. 30.12-14 contests the attempt to restrict the covenant of God's righteousness to an ethnic group. For this reason, he neglects to include the mention of 'doing' (ποιεῖν) in Deut. 30.14[1] since it appears to him to connote the maintenance of ethnocentrism. We might find this peculiar, but from Paul's standpoint such a reading was the self-evident meaning of the passage. If Paul seeks to apply Scripture to his current situation, he also applies his situation to Scripture. It is little wonder then that he 'hears the motif "righteousness by faith" speaking out of the law'.[2]

---

1. Cf. Beker, 1980: 246.
2. Rhyne, 1985: 498. Dunn contends that Deut. 30.12-14 was already uprooted from its ethnocentric context, functioning instead in a more universal context (1987a).

It is also curious that Paul cites Lev. 18.5 in an effort to set it aside as invalid while admitting that it is an utterance of Moses himself. Although Paul elsewhere claims that his gospel has Mosaic authority (9.15; 10.19; 1 Cor. 9.9), here his case is more complex. Paul's words in 10.5 approximate to those of other passages in which Moses' significance is downplayed in the present age. In Rom. 5.14, for instance, Paul relegates Moses to the Adamic, pre-Christ age (cf. 1 Cor. 10.2; 2 Cor. 3.7-15). The same temporal delineation has evidently influenced Paul's portrayal of Moses in 10.5: what Moses wrote in Lev. 18.5 is not a valid expression of the covenant in the present age. (In this way, the temporal sense of τέλος in 10.4 should be highlighted: Christ puts to an end the law as a way of life; with the change of the ages, previous ways of life have become irrelevant, and only faith is salvifically sufficient.)

Paul's citation of Lev. 18.5 also needs to be understood within the context of his earlier discussion concerning the *knowledge* of God (cf. the fourfold γάρ construction throughout 10.2-5). He argues in 10.2-3 that Jewish ethnocentrism is rooted in ignorance of God's eschatological ways; in 10.5 he cites Lev. 18.5 as an example of that ignorant perspective, one which is no longer an appropriate guide of understanding and behaviour since it fails to be enlightened by the events of the present age. It is a relic of the past, but not one to be honoured, for, when practised, it impedes the righteousness of God in the present.[1]

A word of clarification must be registered here. I am not intimating that Paul saw the need to *overrule* Moses. Paul considered himself wholly in line with Mosaic tradition, and firmly believed that Scripture supports his position, as the many proof-texts within Romans illustrate. Nonetheless, as his proof-texting of Rom. 10.5-8 indicates, he seems to have considered that the temporal boundary which marks off the ages also runs throughout Scripture; in at least one passage (and a good number more![2]), what God has revealed to and through Moses does not apply as a description of his eschatological ways since

---

1. Accordingly, if he did not mean this in 10.4 anyway, Paul could have expanded his comments of 10.4 to say that Christ was the end of a former understanding of God's ways (cf. 2 Cor. 3.12-18). Cf. Dugandžic, 1977: 287. See Williams's discussion of 10.4 within the context of proper and improper knowledge (1980: 282-84).

2. The doing of God's law is equated with life in Deut. 4.1; 5.32-33; 6.24-25; 8.1; 30.15-20; Ezek. 18.9, 21; 20.11, 13, 21; 33.19; Neh. 9.29.

it is not in line with his self-revelation in Christ and the gospel of faith.[1] Paul's handling of Lev. 18.5 is due to his understanding of the process of salvation history; various passages of Scripture are pertinent to each stage of that process, so that the development within those stages provides for some temporal 'discrepancies' within scripture. In this way Paul can undermine the authority of other perspectives (even if they are contained within Scripture) in order to defend his own 'innovation'.[2] It is not wholly accurate, then, to say that, for Paul, 'Moses was incorrect'.[3] Nor do we think it accurate to say that Paul considered Lev. 18.5 to prescribe a *theoretical* way of salvation, but one which is impossible in practice.[4] Paul's handling of Lev. 18.5 is explained by the temporal aspect of his understanding of salvation history and, accordingly, of Scripture. Paul relegates Lev. 18.5 to a previous age, although precisely how it pertains to the old age is not altogether clear from Paul's brief case here.

In all this, then, an intriguing dynamic within Paul's argument and scriptural proof-texting has been noticed. On the one hand, Paul can claim that his understanding of God's eschatological acts has been testified to by the law (3.21), establishes the law (3.31) and was foretold by Moses himself (9.15; 10.19). His proof-texting in Romans indicates the extent to which he attempts to root his gospel in Scripture. On the other hand, Paul's handling of Scripture in 10.5 results from his schematization of salvation history; he does not attempt to align a passage like Lev. 18.5 with his own case but considers it to represent a perspective which, with the dawning of the new age, has been shown to be inappropriate within the eschatological age. The temporal boundary between the ages of salvation history is critical for Paul's hermeneutic; whatever scriptural evidence can be used against his case is considered to be the residue which is left over from a pre-

---

1. Cf. Dunn: 'Lev. 18.5 speaks for the old epoch before Christ, represented by Moses, while Deut. 30.12-14 speaks for the new age of God's wider grace introduced by Christ, characterized by "the righteousness from faith"' (1987a: 219).

2. Those scholars who argue that Paul could not have juxtaposed Lev. 18.5 and Deut. 30.12-14 do so on the basis that Paul 'would never make Scripture contradict itself' (Guthrie, 1969: 102). Cf. Bring, 1971: 47; Badenas, 1985: 121, 123; W.S. Campbell, 1980: 78. However, this is too simplistic a view. Paul's hermeneutic contains a temporal distinction which he perceived to be inherent within Scripture itself.

3. Sanders, 1983a: 41.

4. Lindars, 1961: 229. Cf. Westerholm, 1988: 145 n. 16; Gundry, 1985: 18-19. See too Ridderbos's strained case concerning Moses' real intention (1975: 156-57).

vious age. Such scriptural passages lead to a misunderstanding of God's self-revelation made manifest in Christ and are not to trespass the eschatological boundary into the eschatological 'now'. Paul hears, in a sense, 'two voices of the law',[1] which have their respective places on either side of the eschatological boundary. Moreover, all this corresponds with Paul's comments in 3.27 where he made a distinction between the 'law of (ethnocentric) works' (= Lev. 18.5) and the 'law of (christocentric) faith' (= Deut. 30.12-14).

Paul's mission was a controversial one, and his attempts to legitimate it are marked by a tension between received tradition and (revelatory) innovation, between established 'doctrine' and (eschatological) experience. In Rom. 10.5-10, this same tension is apparent in Paul's reading of Scripture. As R.B. Hays suggests, if 'Paul's temporal sensibilities are apocalyptic in character, the same must be said of his hermeneutics'.[2] So too J.L. Martyn observes that Paul's hermeneutic demonstrates 'an inextricable connection between eschatology and epistemology' which is due to 'the new means of perception' gained in the new age.[3] This new perception, which was foretold in the law (1.2; 3.21) and which has come to light with the change of the ages, necessitates the abandonment of previous perceptions of God's ways and the abandonment of previous practices of covenant fidelity, even if they be attributed to Moses himself, for those perceptions and practices have no place in the new age, as the scriptures themselves professed.

With these results from Rom. 3.21-31 and 9.30–10.13 as the backdrop, Rom. 7.7–8.4 will prove to be significant for Paul's presentation and its legitimation.

---

1. Johnson, 1989: 155.
2. Hays, 1989: 191. He continues: 'Scripture must be read with new eyes. The reader who stands at the turn of the ages can no longer believe that Scripture merely authorizes religion-as-usual for Israel; instead, it must promise the New Creation. Scripture must adumbrate, for those who have eyes to see, the coming of eschatological transformation.'
3. Martyn, 1967: 272. He writes later: Paul 'is saying that there are two ways of knowing and that what separates the two is the turn of the ages. . . There is a way of knowing which is characteristic of the old age. . . and by clear implication there is a way of knowing which is proper either to the new age or to that point at which the ages meet' (p. 274).

13.3. *Insider and Outsider Ethics: 7.7–8.4*

In Rom. 7.7-25 Paul describes in vivid detail an encounter between the 'I' (ἐγώ) and the law, wherein the 'I' explains his frustration at his inability to do the law on account of sin. Precisely who this 'I' represents is not altogether clear. As Westerholm says:

> No chapter in the Pauline corpus has aroused more controversy than Romans 7, and no question in that difficult chapter is more disputed than the identity of the 'I' who speaks there.[1]

On this matter, interpreters have generally tended to follow one of three basic approaches, thinking that Paul is speaking of either (1) his 'pre-conversion' experience, (2) his christian experience, or (3) the experience of unregenerate humanity from the perspective of christian faith. In the following section (§13.3.1), this issue will be addressed and a general approach to Rom. 7.7–8.4 will be set out which will be followed in the closer analyses of §13.3.2 to §13.3.4.

13.3.1. *Identifying the 'I' of Romans 7.7-25.* Those who advocate the 'pre-conversion' interpretation consider 7.7-25 to be Paul's confession of personal inadequacy before God prior to putting his faith in Christ. So J.S. Stewart writes:

> Romans 7 is Paul as he was right up to the eve of the Damascus journey— torn in spirit, disintegrated in personality, sunk into an abyss of self-loathing and despair.[2]

A modified version of this interpretation has recently been proposed by G. Theissen. Interesting himself in the 'psychological aspects' of Paul's thought, Theissen argues that Romans 7 portrays the inner frustration of Paul's 'pre-conversion' days, although Paul was unaware of this frustration until he encountered the risen Christ; only then did Paul come to realize what lay in his unconscious mind all along.[3]

Others maintain the 'christian experience' interpretation, finding in Rom. 7.14-25 Paul's portrait of the frustration felt by believers in their struggle against the power of sin, a struggle which continues as long as they remain 'in the flesh'. Paul's 'already'–'not yet' tension,

---

1. 1988: 52. Hübner gives a good survey of interpretation, 1987: 2668-76.
2. 1935: 108. Cf. Gundry, 1980; Sanday and Headlam, 1902: 186-87.
3. Theissen, 1987.

this interpretation contends, is not just a scheme of salvation history but realizes itself even within the life of the believer. The boundary between the two ages of history runs even through those who identify themselves with Christ; although they have died with Christ, they have yet to be resurrected with him, and although they live in newness of life, they have yet to experience the fulness of the resurrected life. Accordingly, while they are 'in the flesh', believers still stand with one foot in the Adamic age, which will not give way until death is finally overcome. As such, they are still prone to attack from the power of sin.[1]

A third approach, the 'anthropological' interpretation, reacts against the first two interpretations, both of which highlight the experiential, biographical aspect of Paul's account in 7.7-25: what Paul writes he himself feels or has felt. In contrast, the 'anthropological' interpretation, associated especially with W.G. Kümmel,[2] undermines the biographical aspect of 7.7-25 in Paul's own experience, finding in Paul's words an accurate description neither of life before Christ nor of life between the ages. Instead, it is a *christian reflection* upon what life is like apart from Christ (whether 'before' or 'without'). That is, Rom. 7.7-25 is simply a caricature of 'unregenerate man' apart from faith, as seen through the eyes of faith.

Not one of these approaches has proven itself beyond doubt, and even within the last decade or so each approach has had its vigorous supporters. It would take too much space to reiterate once again all the evidence for consideration when identifying the 'I' of Romans 7. However, one point is fundamental in this matter: in 7.7-25 Paul depicts the condition of impotent slavery to the all-encompassing power of sin (cf. 7.14). It seems unlikely that such a scenario could apply, first of all, to the believer in Paul's scheme. While he recognizes that the believer is *vulnerable to attack* from the forces of the old age while living in the flesh (cf. Rom. 6.12-13; Gal. 5.17), this is different from *living in the control of sin*, which Paul insists is inappropriate for the believer who has died with Christ (6.1-14; cf. Gal. 5.24), who is no longer a slave to sin but to righteousness (6.15-23), and who lives by the Spirit (8.1ff.). In 7.7-25, only one force is at

---

1. This position has become associated with such notable scholars as Nygren (1949), Barrett (1957), Cranfield (1975a: 341-42), and Dunn (1975; 1988a: 404-12). Cf. also Espy, 1985; D.H. Campbell, 1980; Wenham, 1980; Rowland, 1988b: 40.

2. Kümmel, 1929.

work: sin. The 'I' is sold to sin (7.14), a helpless wretch, who does not know from where his deliverance will come (7.24). It seems highly unlikely that Paul could have aided his case by portraying *the believer* in the terms of 7.14-25. It is precisely this situation of total failure which he thinks can be overcome when one participates in the christo-centric covenant, the covenant which is confirmed in the giving of the Spirit who brings the hope of victory both now and in the future when the process of salvation history comes to completion.[1] For Paul, then, the norm for the believer is not the frustration vividly expressed in 7.14-25 but the realization that he can now hope to overcome that frustration by living 'according to the Spirit' (8.4; cf. 7.6).[2]

The same point is problematic for the 'pre-conversion' view also. The description of slavery to sin which Paul gives in 7.7-25 does not fit well with what Paul tells us elsewhere about what he thought of his life 'under the law'. In Phil. 3.6, for instance, he quite proudly relates how he had been blameless in terms of righteousness under the law. Various considerations may lessen the apparent tension between the two portrayals, but 7.7-25 is, in the end, difficult to reconcile with the 'consciousness' of the pious Jew (replicated by Paul in Phil. 3.6) whose own sin in no way contributed to a sense of slavery to the power of sin in the absence of grace. (Theissen's reconstruction avoids this criticism but seems to owe as much to speculation as to evidence; despite the extent of his work, a psychological approach is limited in view of the nature of the sources.) It is unlikely, then, that the pre-christian Paul would have written Rom. 7.7-25, or that the christian Paul is providing a *factual* account of how it felt to be an unbelieving Jew.

The approach that seems to have the most in its favour is the third, outlined above, which finds Paul's reflections in 7.7-25 to be the prod-uct of a christian mind as it reflects upon the state of existence outside the christian community. In its traditional form, however, we do not find this interpretation to be wholly convincing. This approach has traditionally found Romans 7 to depict 'the basic nature of human

---

1. In 7.25a, Paul anticipates his description of christian existence of 8.1ff. with an interjection of confidence in God. This interjection should not be used as evidence of the identity of the 'I'; Paul is thanking God that he is not like the sinner he is describ-ing. Cf. Watson, 1986: 155; R.N. Longenecker, 1964: 113-14.

2. Cf. the criticisms by Kümmel, 1929: 104-10; Ridderbos, 1975: 127; Räisänen, 1983: 110; Martin, 1981; Theissen, 1987: 183; Gundry, 1980: 236-38.

existence in general',[1] 'the general human predicament in this world',[2] or '[e]ach of us. . . under the curse of Adam's fall'.[3] Paul's analysis of this desperate situation is carried out through the voice of 'the pious Jew',[4] the 'Jew under the law',[5] who, it is said, represents *homo religiosus*—a microcosm of humanity apart from Christ, the epitome of human striving for salvation.[6] But from what we have already seen of Paul's case, very little of this is evident in Romans 1–11; the fundamental problem with 'the pious Jew' for Paul is not so much his perversity in thinking he can earn salvation through his own striving apart from God's grace but his ethnocentrism, whereby he considers himself to be righteous by reason of God's grace upon the people Israel, symbolized by their possession of the law. If Paul intends the 'I' of Romans 7 to give voice to the frustration (from a christian perspective) of 'the pious Jew', his argument throughout the rest of Romans should provide the context for interpreting who it is that 'the Jew' represents. Paul characterizes 'the Jew' as one who, although he may boast in the law (2.17-20), fails to keep it (2.1-3, 21-27) and is condemned by the law (2.12b). The law, in fact, causes trespasses to increase (5.20) because 'the Jew' remains in the Adamic condition (1.18-3.20; cf. 5.12-21), under the power of sin (3.9). He has zeal for God but misses the mark (10.2); he pursues the law but fails to 'reach' it (9.31). This is precisely what is portrayed in Romans 7, wherein Paul addresses his Jewish 'brothers' ('those who know the law' and who had been 'bound to the law', 7.1-2). If Romans 7 is to be read with Paul's interests in Romans 1–11 in view, the 'I' is not 'the pious Jew' understood as the representative of all humanity in its sinfulness, but 'the pious Jew' understood as the representative of the non-believing Jewish community. Paul's critiques of 'the Jew' throughout Romans have all been motivated by his interest in undermining Jewish ethnocentrism. It may be suspected, then, that the description of the 'I' ('the Jew') in Romans 7 is not meant to be an all-encompassing portrait of the whole of unredeemed humanity, an 'Existentialanalyse des Menschen'.[7] Instead, Paul's sights are narrower, being focused

1. Bornkamm, 1969b: 94.
2. Dahl, 1977: 85.
3. Käsemann, 1980: 205-206. Cf. Barclay, 1988: 248; Dunn, 1988a: 404.
4. Käsemann, 1980: 195.
5. Stauffer, 1955: 93.
6. Cf. esp. Bultmann, 1952: 247.
7. Schlier, 1977: 228.

precisely upon the ethnocentric Jew. In the paragraphs to follow, fuller reason will be given why this view should be considered as a valid interpretative option which does justice to the broader interests of Paul's case.

The first thing to notice is the structural relationship between 7.1-6 and 7.7–8.11. As most commentators agree, 7.5-6 serves not only as a summary statement for 7.1-6, but also as the springboard into his discussion in 7.7–8.11.[1] What unites the whole of 7.1-6 is Paul's emphasis on being 'released from the law' (7.2, 3, 6) or 'dying to the law' (7.4) in the present time (νῦν) after a period of being subordinated to the law (7.1, 2, 5).[2] It is in 8.1ff. that Paul's description of the age of the Spirit in the 'now' begins (picking up his point of 7.6), while his description of the 'then' of subordination to the law is described in 7.7-25 (elaborating his point of 7.5). There is, then, a structural indicator within 7.5-6 to the developments within 7.7–8.11 (7.7-25 complements 7.5 while 8.1-11 complements 7.6). This is significant since several important themes operate in terms of this structural outline of 7.5-6 and give clues as to the character and meaning of Paul's case in 7.7–8.11, as we will see below.

Before proceeding along those lines, however, it is necessary to notice that, when speaking of being 'released from the law' in 7.1-6, Paul is not referring to the law in its function of declaring faith in Christ as the badge of the eschatological covenant. Instead, he has in mind the law in another sense—the law as a symbol of Jewish security and superiority, the law as a catalyst of a nomistic way of life. In the 'now', claims Paul, two things have become obvious: (1) the law is established by christian faith (3.31; cf. 3.21b, 27; 9.31-32), and (2) the connection between law and ethnocentric definitions of the covenant has been broken (e.g. 3.27; 9.30–10.13). The law appears in Paul's case either positively or negatively, depending upon the context of his thought at any given point. Many scholars dispute such a view, but it is firmly rooted in such passages as 3.27 and 9.31-32 wherein Paul distinguishes between two ways of attempting to 'reach' the law: faith and

---

1. Cf. Bornkamm, 1969b: 88; Luz, 1969: 166.

2. Paul's discussion in 7.1-6 is directly related to his comment in 6.14: 'Sin will have no dominion over you, since you are not under law but under grace'. In this verse, Paul introduces the law into his case of 6.1-13 that, having died with Christ and been made alive to God in Christ Jesus, the believer is freed from sin. However, Paul has nowhere demonstrated the fact that the believer is freed from the law, as he claims in 6.14, and so he addresses the issue finally in 7.1-6.

works. Although Paul makes no programmatic distinction in 7.1-6, he has only the 'negative' side of the dichotomy in view (the law in its connection with 'works'). Dunn writes of the law in this case:

> It is not the law per se from which Paul speaks of being liberated; it is the law as manipulated by sin and death (especially 7:9-13), the law operating within the context of the age of Adam (5:20-21), the law understood at the level of the flesh and outward definition (γράμμα).[1]

Throughout 7.1-6, what Paul envisages when he speaks of 'release from the law' is the believer's freedom from the law as a symbol of Jewish ethnocentrism (cf. χωρὶς νόμου, 3.21a)—that is, the law within the context of ethnocentric, rather than christocentric, covenantalism.

With this in mind, we turn to themes within 7.5-6 which, operating within the 'then'–'now' structure established there, indicate the context of Paul's thought. The first to be noticed is Paul's contrast between 'the Spirit' and 'the letter' in 7.6. Paul states that, because believers have been released from the law, they now serve by the newness of the Spirit, not by the oldness of the letter. Paul has employed the same 'Spirit'–'letter' contrast earlier in 2.29 (cf. 2.27) where he juxtaposed the one who thinks himself to be a Jew by reason of the external mark of circumcision with the one who is truly a Jew by reason of the inner circumcision of the heart, carried out 'by the Spirit, not the letter'. Before getting into his survey of 7.7–8.4, Paul makes precisely the same juxtaposition in 7.6 as in 2.29 (cf. 2 Cor. 3.6-12). Evidently, then, a connection can be traced between Paul's case in 2.29 and 7.6. Since, in the former, Paul contrasted (*in nuce*) ethnocentric and christocentric covenantalism, it would not be surprising to find the same juxtaposition being established in 7.6, the springboard to his case of 7.7–8.4. The point is that if 7.7-25 describes the 'then', the 'I' described therein is none other than the ethnocentric Jew who has yet to be freed from the law as a symbol of Jewish privilege and superiority (the law as 'letter') and who, in fact, transgresses the law, just as Paul stated in 2.27 that 'the Jew' whose life is defined by the letter of the law is a transgressor of the law.

Support for this comes from Paul's use of σάρξ in 7.5. This term is sometimes employed by Paul to characterize Jewish confidence in their ethnic status; they boast 'in the flesh' (Phil. 3.3-6 [twice]; Gal. 3.3;

1. 1988a: 419.

4.29; 6.13; cf. Col. 2.11, 13; Eph. 2.11; it refers to ethnic lineage in Rom. 1.3; 4.5; 9.3, 5-9; 11.14; 1 Cor. 10.18). In Rom. 2.28, before contrasting the Spirit and the letter in 2.29, Paul decried circumcision 'in the flesh' (ἐν σαρκί) as salvifically irrelevant, despite the expectation of 'the Jew'. The same overtones can be heard in 7.5: whereas we lived then 'in the flesh' (ἐν τῇ σαρκί), we now live by the Spirit. Paul then describes life 'in the flesh' in 7.7-25 and life in the Spirit in 8.1ff. This again suggests that the 'I' of 7.7-25 describes the inadequacy with regard to the law of the one who lives 'in the flesh' by nomistic practice.

Paul's characterization of the law in 7.5 suggests a similar point. There he describes the law (within the ethnocentric context) as the means through which the sinful desires were provoked 'in our body parts' (cf. 7.23), leading us unto death. This, of course, is what Paul depicts in 7.7-25; when one is 'in the flesh' the law is hijacked by sin, thereby producing every kind of sinful desire, preventing the doing of God's law, and resulting in death. The plural referent 'we' of 7.1-6 has changed to the 'I' of 7.7-25, but the pattern is precisely the same. Earlier in Romans Paul has spoken of the law in this same connection with sin and death. In 2.27, Paul states that those for whom the law operates within the realm of the 'letter' are transgressors of the law. This same charge is elaborated in striking terms in 5.20, wherein Paul claims that the law actually caused the trespass to increase and death to result. That situation arises whenever one is 'in Adam', apart from Christ. This characterization of the law with sin and death is carried out in the light of Paul's case in 1.18–3.20, wherein he denounces Jewish ethnocentrism. There Paul argued that the law should force 'the Jew' to recognize his Adamic condition (3.9-20). When the law is placed in that Adamic context, instead of symbolizing Jewish superiority and security, the law actually aids in the process of condemnation, sin and death (5.20; cf. 4.15). This is what Paul is describing in 7.7-25: the law encountered by the ethnocentric Jew.

If we skip over 7.7-25 momentarily, we can see from 8.1ff. that Paul's concern there is still to discredit the law as a regulator of nomistic practice. Although the point is controversial, we will defend below the view that Paul's words in 8.2 demonstrate again the two contexts in which Paul speaks of the law—the christocentric and the ethnocentric (as in 3.27 and 9.31-32). There Paul contrasts 'the law of the Spirit of life' with 'the law of sin and death'. It is the latter, says Paul, from which believers have been freed. No doubt this theme of

freedom from the law in 8.2 carries on the same theme of 7.1-6
wherein Paul denounced the salvific efficiency of nomistic living.
Accordingly, in the context immediately preceding and following 7.7-
25, Paul's concern is to discredit the salvific necessity of nomistic
practice, even portraying the law as the 'law of sin and death' when it
is used to promote ethnocentric practices. Since 7.7-25 is closely
bound to its surrounding context (cf. 7.5-6; 8.1), it too must be animated by Paul's same concern to undermine Jewish ethnocentrism.

Moreover, the (convoluted) analogy in 7.1-3 confirms this suggestion in yet another way. There Paul composes a characterization of a
married woman who is freed from her marital responsibilities upon
the death of her husband, thereby allowing her to marry another.
Scholars often make the case that the only point which Paul wants to
make in the analogy is simply that 'death dissolves obligations valid
throughout life'.[1] As Räisänen notes, however, this is incorrect; the
theme of death is not the *only* point of the analogy. In 7.4, where Paul
reflects upon the analogy of 7.1-3, his reflection is not simply upon the
theme of death and the removal of obligation but also includes reference to marrying another (εἰς τὸ γενέσθαι ὑμᾶς ἑτέρῳ), picking up
directly from his words in 7.3 where he contrasts marriage to one
man with marriage to another man (ἐὰν γένηται ἀνδρὶ ἑτέρῳ
... γενομένην ἀνδρὶ ἑτέρῳ).[2] From this, it would seem that we need
to reflect upon this theme of successive marriages to the two 'partners'
(as Paul does in 7.4) if we want to do full justice to Paul's analogy;
and to do so, the identity of the two husbands would seem to be where
the point of the 'marriage' theme lies. It seems best to understand the
first husband as representing not the law,[3] nor God,[4] but Adam;[5] the
second husband is, of course, Christ. Paul has juxtaposed these two
key figures already in 5.12-21, and here, evidently, his thoughts run
along the same lines. As such, Paul's analogy works in this way: the
death of the woman's first husband represents the death of the
believer's connection with Adam; the woman's marriage to the second
husband signifies the believer in connection with the second Adam,
Christ. In the process the believer has been released from obligation to
the law (the law in its connection with ethnocentrism). In this way

1. Käsemann, 1980: 187. Cf. Dunn, 1988a: 369.
2. Räisänen, 1983: 62 n. 93.
3. Contra Derrett, 1970: 466-71; Räisänen, 1983: 61; Schoeps, 1961: 192.
4. Contra Theissen, 1987: 247-48.
5. Cf. Wright, 1980: 148.

Paul maintains that nomistic practice actually binds one to the Adamic condition, as he has already suggested throughout (2.27; 3.20, 27; 5.20); only when one is 'in Christ' does that bond with the Adamic condition become severed, thereby nullifying one's duty to the law— that is, the law in its connection with Adam (5.20), the law as a way of life (3.21a, 27), the law as a symbol of Jewish security (2.17-20), the law of sin and death (8.2). The thrust of Paul's argument, of course, is that ethnocentric definitions of the covenant sink the covenant in the Adamic condition of sin which it was thought to correct. 7.7-25 goes on to describe precisely that fact.

From these considerations, it seem best to think that 7.7-25 furthers Paul's attempt to discredit ethnocentric definitions of the covenant. His strategy is to describe, from the perspective of christian faith, the anguish of the Jew who tries to accomplish the law while remaining outside of the community of faith. This is the Jew who understands the law to be a symbol of national security whereby he, as a member of the ethnic people of Israel, naturally participates in the community of grace.

Romans 7.7-25 places us, therefore, within the arena of ethical polemic, for the issue is the performance of the ethical requirements of the law—an indicator of one's standing *vis-à-vis* the covenant of grace. By definition, the one inside the community of grace fulfils the law while the one outside that community fails to keep the law. Thus, Paul talks about the righteous requirement of the law being fulfilled by the christian community (8.4), just as later he talks of love as the fulfilment of the law, by which he means love demonstrated within the christian community (13.8-10; cf. Gal. 5.14). Both claims stem from the underlying conviction that those within the community of grace fulfil what the law requires.[1] This explains why Paul's letters to his churches have such a heavy emphasis on ethical behaviour; if the communities which he has established among the gentiles cannot evidence within themselves ethical integrity, they have little claim to embody the community of grace. To make bold claims about one's community demands that those claims be demonstrated ethically.

---

1. Ziesler argues that since δικαίωμα is singular rather than plural, Paul does not mean in 8.4 that believers fulfil the *whole* law, but only the commandment against covetousness mentioned in 7.7-8 (1988: 50; *idem*, 1989: 206-207). Better, however, is T.R. Schreiner's explanation of the singular: 'the singular in 8.4 is used to show that the moral norms of the law could be fulfilled as a unity by the power of the Spirit' (1989: 61).

The whole of Rom. 1.18–3.20 is established on this conviction. There, Paul seeks to discredit 'the Jew's' ethnocentric definition of the covenant by means of ethical polemic. Whether or not 'the Jew' *was* morally deficient matters little for Paul's argument; the 'grammar' of covenantal definition allows for such a charge. Because 'the Jew' is not a participant in the community of God's grace, so Paul can charge him with failing to live up to the ethical demands of the law.

In essence, then, Paul's sights turn in 7.7-25 to 'the Jew' in order to fill out this ethical charge, for the 'I' of 7.7-25 is none other than the Adamic (= ethnocentric) Jew of 1.18–3.20, who now admits his own ethical failure. Paul here is a ventriloquist, projecting his voice into the mouth of his 'dummy', 'the Jew' of Romans 2–3. For Paul, since the christian community enjoys the grace of God, its members fulfil the requirements of the law (8.4). Accordingly, Paul hopes to show that the Jew who puts his hopes in his ethnic position and considers himself to have natural rights to God's grace finds his expectations dashed by the realization that he fails to fulfil the law's requirements, despite whatever desires he might have to do so. (No doubt, Paul's Jewish contemporaries would not have perceived their situation as Paul describes it here, as was the case also in Romans 2 ['You do the same!', 2.1]. These passages are polemical denunciation of a sort that does not rely upon empirical observation but which follows on from prior convictions concerning the boundaries of covenant grace.)[1] This realization is described for us by Paul, as if by 'the Jew' himself, in Rom. 7.7-25. The 'we' of 7.1-6 has become a single representative, just as 'the Jew' of Romans 2–3 represented the whole of the unbelieving Jewish community. Evidently, then, the dialogue partner of Romans 2–3 has here reappeared, having recognized that the problem of the anthropological condition of sin permeates even himself, an ethnic Jew, and that, just as Paul argued in Romans 2–3, sin operates within him to prevent him from doing the ethical requirements of the law.[2] Paul's diatribe partner now accuses himself of the same charge laid against him earlier by Paul. Thus, Paul's 'you' of Romans 2

1. Cf. Räisänen: Paul's 'thesis is clear in advance, and Paul snatches up more or less suitable arguments to support it wherever he meets them' (1983: 113).
2. Dunn argues that the pious Jew cannot be the subject of Rom. 7.7-25 since, as Phil. 3.4-6 illustrates, Paul had never known such despair before putting his faith in Christ (1988a: 394). It is illogical, says Dunn, to see both 7.7-25 and Phil. 3.4-6 as descriptions of the pious Jew. But Dunn seems to be working with a definition of logic which excludes polemic.

resurfaces here as 'the Jew's' 'I' (cf. 'the Jew's' κἀγώ of 3.7); the charge imposed earlier upon the ethnocentric Jew by Paul is here self-imposed.

We have attempted to show that structural and thematic considerations combine to indicate that the 'I' of 7.7-25 is not 'the hidden Jew in all of us',[1] but as Wright well states, 'the hidden Adam in Israel'.[2] Wright claims:

> Insofar as 7.7-25 'describes' anybody, it describes, with Christian hindsight, the Jew who (rightly) rejoices in the law, but whom the law binds to Adam so that he cannot but sin, that is, break the law.[3]

Romans 7.7-25 depicts 'the Jew' who, because he is not a member of the community of God's grace, is not able to perform the law. This depiction is arrived at by the rules of the logic of covenant self-definition; those outside the boundary of grace fail, by definition, to do the law. In 7.7-25, Paul lays out for his readers a description of the kind of frustration felt by this Adamic (= ethnocentric) Jew in order to solidify his own christocentric definition of the covenant. In 8.1ff., Paul begins the ethical legitimation of his own position. In 8.4, then, he states that those in Christ meet in full 'the righteous requirement of the law' by the Spirit. His main point in all this is that the law is in the 'possession' of the christian community; that community wears the badge of covenant membership spoken of in the law (faith), and their identity as the community of grace is verified in their ethical fulfilment of what the law requires. In 8.2, he even describes the law as 'the law (= Torah; see below) of the Spirit of life', a characterization possible when the law is rooted within a christocentric context. Those (Jews) who are outside the christian community of faith and who claim to be the possessors of the law are actually in bondage to 'the law of sin and death', for the law is impotent and cannot bring life when one remains in the weakness of the flesh (8.3). Thus, the law is a law of life only within the community of believers who have been set free from the law of sin and death.

Before analysing Rom. 7.7–8.4 in closer detail, two final points deserve mention. First, there is general agreement that in Romans 6 Paul is motivated to defend his case against the charge that freedom from the law promotes libertinism and immorality. We saw such a

1. Käsemann, 1969: 186.
2. Wright, 1980: 152; *idem*, 1982: 15.
3. 1980: 148.

charge in 3.7-8 where Paul brushed aside such objections to his case as nonsensical. In Romans 6, Paul constructs his defence against the charge. In 6.1 he frames the issue in the terms of his discussion in 5.12-21: 'Shall we go on sinning that grace may increase?' In 6.15 he asks the same thing, this time in terms which include the law: 'Shall we sin because we are not under law but under grace?' In each case Paul replies, 'By no means'. In 6.1-14 Paul's point is made by means of his emphasis on the death of believers with Christ, wherein they die to sin. In 6.15-23 the same point is made by a complementary analogy—that of having been released from slavery to sin and becoming slaves to righteousness. In Paul's definition, although believers are not 'under the law' (6.15), neither are they 'lawless' in an amoral sense. In fact, it is precisely because they are not 'under the law' as a way of life that they have escaped the dominion of sin.

Paul expands upon this defence in 7.7–8.4. There he first depicts the frustration of the Jew who, expecting his ethnic standing to assure him a position within the covenant of grace, finds that his behaviour does not match the demands of covenantal ethics, as laid out in the law. In this way, Paul hopes to demonstrate that such a Jew is sold under sin (7.14) despite his noble desire to fulfil the law; it is precisely his ethnocentrism which causes him to 'carry on in sin' (6.1; cf. 3.8). Conversely, it is the believer who escapes the condition of sin, having been set free (8.2) to meet in full the requirement of the law (8.4). Accordingly, in 7.7–8.4, Paul is motivated to defend his case against the charge that release from a nomistic lifestyle leads to ethical depravity; instead, says Paul, it is Jewish ethnocentrism which results in ethical impotency, as 7.7-25 depicts. Paul has fully answered his objectors who lie behind 3.8. There he could only rebuke them briskly; herein is his full defence and reversal of their charges against him. In the process, he has undermined their restrictive definition of the covenant.

Second, it should be noted that a close parallel to this description is found in Ezra's words in *4 Ezra* 3.20-36, wherein he too demonstrates the great anguish of the Jew who, despite his ethnic laurels, cannot find it within himself to do the law because of the sinful condition which he shares with Adam. In contrast to some Jewish writers, however, both Paul and the author of *4 Ezra* are sympathetic towards 'the Jew', for whom God's grace is not at present effective. As a result, they transform the expected grammar of ethical denunciation. That is, in each of their presentations, the Adamic (= ethnocentric) Jew is not depicted in the same light as the Jewish apostates of, for instance, the

Psalms of Solomon or the *Thanksgiving Hymns* of Qumran, wherein the Jewish 'outsiders' are said to have flagrantly disregarded the law in order that they might revel in perverse sin. Instead, both authors of this study portray the Adamic Jew as intent on doing the law but, ultimately, as unable to do so. As we will see, Paul's more sympathetic rendering of the Adamic Jew is explained by his concern for his people's salvation.[1] Despite his sympathies, however, Paul is convinced that the ethnocentric Jew now stands (by his lack of faith) outside of the boundaries of divine grace, in the anthropological condition of sin, and therefore is unable to do the law.

At this point, now that the 'I' has been identified on the basis of contextual matters, and now that Paul's basic motivation throughout this section has been noted, Rom. 7.7–8.4 can be analysed more closely.

13.3.2. *Romans 7.7-13*. Paul has been talking in 7.1-6 of release from the law in its connection with Adam (viz. the law in the context of ethnocentric covenantalism). In fact, throughout the whole of 6.1–7.6, whenever the law has appeared in Paul's case it has stood 'on the same side as "sin" and "death"',[2] just as in 5.12-21 (especially 5.20). In 7.7-13, Paul seeks to clarify his argument concerning the law. Although the law has received some 'bad press' from Paul, he nonetheless wants to vindicate the law to a certain extent, which he carries out in 7.7-25—Paul's 'apology for the law'.[3] Thus he asks initially whether the law itself is sin, and answers with an emphatic 'No' (7.7). In 7.10, in fact, he describes the law (now in terms of the 'commandment', the 'representative summation of the Mosaic law'[4]) as being 'unto life' (εἰς ζωήν), and in 7.12 it is said to be 'holy and righteous and good'.

This aspect of Paul's argument should not be overlooked. Paul affirms the inherent value of the law as something intrinsically life-giving in and of itself, and proceeds to show that the problem lies not with the law itself but with sin. As he says, sin worked its way 'through the commandment' (7.8, 11) so that what was good (the commandment/law) became an instrument of sin unto death (εἰς

---

1. Ezra's sympathy transpires from the fact that, instead of denouncing Jewish sinners, his project is to indict God.

2. Theissen, 1987: 181.

3. Cf. Beker, 1980: 105; Stendahl, 1976: 92; Bornkamm, 1969b: 88; Dunn, 1988a: 376-77.

4. Moo, 1986: 128.

θάνατον) (7.10-11). The culprit is not the law, but sin. So Paul emphatically denies that the law/commandment itself promotes death (7.13). Instead, sin works death through what is good (the law/commandment) in order that it (sin) might be recognized as sin (7.13). Had the commandment not been good in itself, sin would not have been shown to be its opposite. Paul always keeps sin as the middle term between the (good) law/comandment and death; without that middle term, the result would be life rather than death (7.10; 8.7).

It is important to notice that Paul presents the 'I' ('the Jew') in terms which call to mind Adam's fall into death by his transgression of God's order in the garden. As E. Käsemann has remarked: 'There is nothing in the passage which does not fit Adam, and everything fits Adam alone'.[1] That Paul's description is styled upon the story of Adam's fall is especially apparent in 7.9-11: Adam alone can be said to have existed in a time that had no law (χωρὶς νόμου), and Adam alone can talk of the coming of the commandment as the occasion when sin sprang to life.[2]

This, then, explains why Paul introduces this section with a reference to the law but then proceeds to talk about the commandment; the commandment is the command given by God to Adam in the garden. Paul here seems cognizant of the idea that the Mosaic law was contained within the single commandment given to Adam.[3] Paul sees in this identification of the Mosaic law and the Adamic commandment a corresponding identification of the ethnocentric Jew and Adam who sins unto death.[4] Throughout Romans, 'Paul's theologizing about Adam is aimed specifically at the Jewish nationalistic self-conscious-

---

1. Käsemann, 1980: 196. The sin of covetousness described in 7.7-8 fits this portrayal since covetousness was perceived by many Jews as the fundamental condition of sinfulness. See Theissen, 1987: 204-206; Wedderburn, 1980: 420-21. By 'covetousness' Paul is not thinking simply of sexual lust; contra Gundry, 1980; Watson, 1986: 151. He uses the term more broadly to include 'all kinds of covetousness' (πᾶσαν ἐπιθυμίαν), and is thinking more generally of 'the passion to assert oneself against God and neighbor' (Käsemann), of 'wanting what is not one's own, and especially wanting it at the expense of one's neighbour' (Ziesler, 1988: 47).

2. For other parallels, see Watson, 1986: 152; Theissen, 1987: 202-208. He concludes: 'Paul unmistakably has the model of Adam in view in Rom. 7:7ff.' (p. 208).

3. Cf. Philo, *Spec. Leg.* 4.84-94; *Decal.* 142, 150, 173; *Apoc. Mos.* 19.3; *Apoc. Abr.* 24.10; *4 Ezra* 7.20; *TgNeof* Exod. 20.17 and Deut. 5.18; *Mekilta* on Exod. 20.17. See Wedderburn, 1980: 420; Käsemann, 1980: 196; Dunn, 1988a: 379; contra Deidun, 1981: 197.

4. Cf. Moo, 1986: 128; Leenhardt, 1961: 186.

ness'.[1] Paul inserts the ethnocentric Jew into the story of Adam's fall, just as in 1.25 he recalled Israel's idolatry before the golden calf as demonstrative of the anthropological condition of sin, described in 1.18-32. The point, of course, is that the ethnocentric Jew, rather than having been rescued from the Adamic condition of sin, stands firmly in sin and remains outside the boundaries of the community of grace. Paul argued this point strongly already in 1.18–3.20. Now, instead of arguing his point, Paul paints a picture of 'the Jew' in his desperate situation, stuck in the anthropological condition of sin.

13.3.3. *Romans 7.14-25*. It is not wholly proper to separate this section from 7.7-13, as the γάρ of 7.14 well indicates.[2] Paul here continues along similar lines as he did in 7.7-13 to arrive at the same place: the vindication of the law. Nonetheless, in 7.14, Paul's argument begins to follow a somewhat different track to make this point.[3] Still at issue, then, is the negation of the idea that the law of God produces death (7.13); it simply cannot be the case that the law works evil since God would necessarily be indicted as the mastermind of the crime. Paul does not allow God to be culpable of this offence, asserting that the problem is not on account of the law of God. This was the point of 7.7-13 as well. What is new in 7.14-25 is his defence of the 'I' himself. Paul is intent on showing in 7.14-25 that, just as the problem does not lie with the law, so neither does it lie ultimately with the 'I'; although the 'I' is fleshly, his earnest desire is to do the good. The culprit, then, is neither the law (7.7-13, 14-25), nor the 'I' (7.14-25), but sin (7.7-13, 14-25). What Paul highlights in 7.14-25 is the unwillingness of the 'I' to cooperate with sin, although he is inevitably enslaved to its overbearing power (7.14). As K. Stendahl says: 'The argument is one of acquittal of the ego, not one of utter contrition'.[4] If, as we suspect, the 'I' is Paul's own caricature of 'the Jew', 7.14-25 expands

---

1. Garlington, 1990: 148.

2. Bornkamm: 'The connection between the two sections (7-13 and 14-25) cannot be overemphasized' (1969b: 95). Some scholars make a separation between 7.12 and 7.13. Cf. Wilckens, 1978: 2.74-75; Wright, 1980: 151-54. We follow the structural outline set out by, for instance, Theissen, 1987: 184.

3. We do not overemphasize the shift to present tense verbs within this section. This shift only serves to contemporize the Adamic past of 7.7-13 which is now no longer in Paul's view; Paul 'has moved from story to analysis' (Ziesler, 1989: 193). Cf. Watson, 1986: 155; Martin, 1981: 43.

4. 1976: 93.

Paul's case to include an 'apology for the ethnocentric Jew' who is zealous for God but who 'misses the mark' nonetheless (10.2-3).

Paul introduces this section in 7.14 by juxtaposing the *spiritual* quality of the law with the *fleshly* quality of the 'I' (7.14). Here, Paul sets up two 'planes' of existence—the spiritual and the fleshly, as in 7.5-6 and 2.28-29. The law belongs to the spiritual plane, the 'I' to the plane of the flesh which is susceptible to attack from the power of sin. The despair of the 'I' arises because, although he desires the good, he does not stand on the same plane as the law. Instead, he is enslaved to sin because he is in the flesh, 'the workshop of sin'.[1] Of course, Paul works his case to show that this desperate situation is overcome when one 'participates' in the spiritual plane (the natural habitat of the law, 7.14), a situation which Paul describes in 8.1-4 wherein the law is said to be fulfilled by the believer who walks 'according to the Spirit' (8.4). Much is to transpire in Paul's argument before reaching that solution.

Although Paul begins in 7.14 speaking of the law in singular fashion as the spiritual law (the Torah), his argument proceeds in 7.22–8.2 seemingly to force a division within the law itself so that it (the Torah) is split into two, each 'law' being polarized. In the latter verses of Romans 7, Paul makes mention on two occasions of 'the law of God' (ὁ νόμος τοῦ θεοῦ, 7.22, 25). This should be understood as referring to the Torah, which is spiritual (7.14), and holy (7.12), just as in 8.7 the same expression is used in reference to the Torah.[2] The 'I' rejoices in this law in his inner self (7.22), describing it in fact as 'the law of my mind' (ὁ νόμος τοῦ νοός μου, 7.23).

Paul also mentions, however, 'another law' (ἕτερον νόμον, 7.23) which is at work 'in my members' (ἐν τοῖς μέλεσίν μου, 7.23) and which the 'I' serves 'with (my) flesh' (τῇ σαρκί, 7.25). This is 'the law of sin' (νόμος τῆς ἁμαρτίας, 7.23, 25) whose results end in death (7.24). The question, then, is whether this νόμος also refers to the Torah or, as many think, to a 'principle' of sin. In our estimation, the former has more in its favour. We have seen how 7.7-25 expands upon Paul's words in 7.5, where νόμος clearly refers to the Torah,

---

1. Käsemann, 1980: 205.

2. Attempts to see the νόμος τοῦ θεοῦ as 'the will of God' are unconvincing, and inevitably must qualify this to mean, as Ziesler does, the will of God 'as expressed in the Torah' (1989: 198). Three sentences later Ziesler drops all talk of 'God's will' and reverts wholly to talk of 'the Law of God'; 'the power of sin . . . perverts *the Law of God*'.

albeit the Torah in the 'context' of ethnocentric covenantalism. A constellation of ideas which relate to the νόμος of sin in 7.23-25 has already appeared in relation to the νόμος (= Torah) in 7.5: when one is in the flesh (ἐν τῇ σαρκί), the law (= Torah) is the instrument (διὰ τοῦ νόμου) through which sinfulness arises in the members of the body (ἐν τοῖς μέλεσιν) unto death (τῷ θανάτῳ). The parallels in thought and expression signify that the equation νόμος = Torah in 7.5 is to be continued in 7.23-25 when Paul speaks of the νόμος of sin. Within these verses, then, Paul presents the Torah in a double function as the Torah of God and (provocatively) the Torah of sin (cf. the Torah of faith and the Torah of works in 3.27).

A similar situation arises in 8.2, where Paul juxtaposes the νόμος of the Spirit of life and the νόμος of sin and death. Whereas the law of sin and death must be the law (= Torah) of sin mentioned in 7.22-25 (cf. freedom from the νόμος [= Torah] in 7.1-6 and freedom from the νόμος [= Torah] of sin and death in 8.2), so the law of the Spirit of life (the spiritual law [7.14] empowered by the Spirit) must be equivalent to the law (= Torah) of God mentioned in 7.22-25. Here too Paul seems to be making a distinction with regard to the law, the νόμος in each case referring to the Torah. This is supported from Paul's case in 8.3ff., which elaborates 8.2 (cf. the connective γάρ) and wherein νόμος appears three times, each referring to the Torah (8.3, 4, 7).

Throughout 7.22–8.7, then, we find νόμος to refer consistently to the Torah.[1] What is at variance is not the referent of νόμος but the context to which it is applied; the Torah itself is not a primary character in the drama of Romans 7 except when acted upon by various powers. Just as in 3.27 (cf. 9.31-32), so here too the genitive modifiers of νόμος are the determining factors of Paul's various statements concerning the law in 7.14–8.2, or, as Snodgrass argues:

---

1. Cf. Lohse, 1982; Hahn, 1976: 48-49, 60; Moule, 1974: 181-87 (but see his concession, 1987: 48); Hübner, 1984a: 144-48; Meyer, 1980: 73; Dunn, 1988a: 416-17; Theissen, 1987: 256-57; Stuhlmacher, 1985: 99; Wilckens, 1978: 2.90, 122-24; Osten-Sacken, 1975: 226-34; *idem*, 1989: 13-23; Snodgrass, 1988; Reike, 1985: 243-44; Wright, 1980: 153. Contra e.g. Ziesler, 1989: 202; Luz, 1968: 153 n. 173; Räisänen, 1986d; *idem*, 1986e: 113-14. See Hübner's review of the secondary literature, 1987: 2682-91.

The determinant for the law is the sphere in which it is placed. . . [I]n Paul the law does not stand for itself; it occurs in a context and in connection with something else. It refers to the law as used in various specific ways.[1]

In the spiritual sphere or plane (cf. 7.14), the law operates as the 'law of God'; in that context it is holy, just and good, and something in which to rejoice. But the law within the plane of 'the flesh' operates so differently as to be a different law, a 'law of sin'. In this situation, the law is nothing other than 'the Torah in the possession of a man unable to keep it: it is a treasure, but when set in an unworthy context (cf. v. 14) it becomes a liability, a dispensation of death at work "in the members"'.[2] Accordingly, the simple portrayal of the law as operating on the spiritual plane in 7.14 becomes fragmented in 7.22–8.2 by the recognition that it can also work on the fleshly plane, hijacked by the power of sin.

After setting up the alternative 'planes' in 7.14, the 'I' exclaims: 'I do not know what I am doing' (7.15a). This is explained more fully on three occasions (7.15b-16a; 7.18-19; and 7.21), each of which highlights the fact that the 'I' wants to do the good but simply cannot accomplish it; instead he ends up doing the evil that he does not want to do. This dilemma, stated thrice, is the basis for three conclusions in 7.16b-17, 20 and 22-23. In 7.16b-17, because the 'I' is unhappy with his inability to do the good, the fault of doing evil lies not with him so much as with the power of sin: 'But now it is no longer I working this but sin which dwells in me' (7.17). Although sin dwells in the body of the 'I', it is not a welcome guest there. It has hijacked the body parts and controls them, without the cooperation of the 'I', who is unable to dislodge the power of sin. Herein, then, Paul has furthered his accusations against 'sin' to include an explicit defence of the 'I'. The same point is made in exactly the same terms in 7.20. Thus 7.18-20 makes no progress on 7.15b-17,[3] but simply reiterates the point that the 'I' himself is not wholly to blame for his condition under sin.

Evidently, then, Paul wants to emphasize this point. He takes great care not to depict the 'I' in terms in which the speaker of the Qumran

---

1. 1988: 99, emphasis his.

2. Wright, 1980: 153. Cf. especially Dunn, 1988a: 416-17. Contra e.g. Keck, who understands 'the law of sin' as a simple reference to the ability of sin to enslave one in its web, as if 'the law of sin' could be translated as 'the *power* of sin' without reference to the Torah (1980: 49). As Snodgrass states, 'If that is true, Paul has stretched the word [νόμος] almost beyond recognition' (1988: 106).

3. Cf. Kuss, 1957: 2.454-55.

Thanksgiving Hymns (for instance) describes Jewish apostates who are included under the designation 'Sons of Darkness' (cf. Rev. 2.9: 'the synagogues of Satan'). For that author, the Jews who fall outside the covenant loathe the law and take no delight in the commands of God (1QH 15.18). Paul, however, is not prepared to portray 'the Jew' who falls outside the boundaries of the community of faith in such an extreme fashion. The 'I', representing unbelieving Israel, is not in an irretrievable position, for he is desirous of the good, although he cannot accomplish it because he is 'in the flesh'. At present 'the Jew' remains within the domain of sin, but Paul does not depict his condition as unsalvable. Is there a possibility for correction? Paul's characterization in 8.1-4 would suggest that there is, and his hope for his gentile mission and for the future conversion of unbelieving Israel, expressed in Romans 11, would support this contention. This point will be further discussed below.

The final mention of the dilemma (that good desire does not translate into doing the good) appears in 7.21. The problem has been cited twice since 7.14: it is sin (7.17, 20). In 7.22-23, Paul applies this dilemma to the issue of the law,[1] and it is here that the separation within the law (= Torah) first appears. First, Paul states that the 'I' rejoices in the 'law of God' (7.22; cf. 8.7),[2] but then introduces into his discussion what he first calls a 'different law' (7.23: ἕτερον νόμον). This different law works 'in my body parts' (ἐν τοῖς μέλεσίν μου) and must equal what Paul calls in 7.23 'the law of sin', for Paul says of both that they operate 'in my body parts' (cf. 7.5). This 'different law' ('the law of sin') wages war on 'the law of God', the law which the 'I' wants to uphold ('the law of my mind'). In 8.2 Paul resolves the tension between these two 'laws', saying that those in Christ are freed from 'the law of sin and death' by 'the law of the Spirit of life'.[3] As we have seen, Paul does not have two laws (or

---

1. As he indicates in 7.21 where the νόμος again refers to the Torah: 'So I find with regard to the Torah that, while I wish to do the good, evil is right there with me'. Properly translated, εὑρίσκω has two direct objects: νόμος and the ὅτι clause. (My thanks are due to Dr A.J.M. Wedderburn for solidifying my thoughts on this matter.) Cf. Snodgrass, 1988: 105; Gaston, 1987: 176; Dunn, 1988a: 393.

2. I take the 'inner man' (τὸν ἔσω ἄνθρωπον) here to be simply the 'I' in his desire to do the law.

3. Räisänen (1986d: 115-16) notes that if νόμος is to mean Torah in 8.2, then Paul is saying that believers' freedom is acquired by means of the Torah itself. This is a strange position for the Torah to be in. Accordingly, Räisänen suggests that, in fact, νόμος in 8.2 does not mean Torah. But if νόμος is not the Torah, another

'principles') in mind here so much as the one law (= the Torah) as it operates within two different situations. In 8.2-4, Paul makes the same point as in 7.5-6, affirming that believers have been freed from the law of sin and death by the Spirit (8.2), adding here that in this way the righteous requirement of the law is fulfilled in them (8.4); for believers the law is 'the law of the Spirit of life'. The problem, as Paul states in 8.3, is that the law is impotent when in the context of the flesh, so that only those who walk by the Spirit, not by the flesh, fulfil the law (8.3)—the law which is spiritual by nature (7.14). In fact, however, the passive sense of the verb should be highlighted, for the fulfilment of the law is not achieved by means of an active campaign on the part of believers but by the Spirit working in and through them.[1]

From Paul's comments in 7.22–8.4 it has again become apparent how tenuous it is to speak without qualifications of Paul's view of the law, for the law (= Torah) stands on both sides of the eschatological boundary and is qualified by the context in which it appears: in the context of the flesh, the law is the law of sin, whereas in the context of the Spirit it is the 'law of God', the 'law of the Spirit of life'. What determines one's position *vis-à-vis* the law of God or of sin is where one stands in relation to the eschatological boundary. The ethnocentric Jew who has no recourse to the Spirit remains trapped within the old age of the flesh; in that situation, the law is nothing more than a 'law of sin', a law which perpetuates the Adamic condition by causing the trespass to increase (5.20). The full force of this realization allows the 'I' to cry out: 'I am a wretched man. Who will deliver me from this body of death?' (7.24).

Immediately, Paul supplies the answer, in anticipation of Romans 8: 'Thanks be to God through Jesus Christ our Lord' (7.25a).[2] Rescue is

---

irregularity arises between 8.2 and 8.3 where νόμος appears again, and clearly in reference to the Torah. Räisänen argues that νόμος in 8.4 must refer to the Torah, since it does so in 8.3 and since 'Paul cannot have intended *nomos* to change its meaning abruptly' (1983: 67). Unfortunately, Räisänen does not apply the same logic to the νόμος of 8.2 and 8.3.

1. Cf. Ziesler, 1989: 208. Unlike Ziesler (p. 207), I find no 'contradiction' between 7.1-6 (wherein believers are said to be free from the law) and 8.4 (where believers are said to be passive fulfillers of the law); the different contexts of flesh and Spirit allows for the different evaluations of the law.

2. Cf. Watson: 7.25 'is merely an interjection anticipating the description of liberation from the law of sin in 8:1ff' (1986: 155). Cf. R.N. Longenecker, 1964: 113-14.

possible only in the community of the Spirit. Paul does not wait until the 'I' has stated his conclusion (in 7.25b) to introduce the eschatological solution (in 8.1-4) but speaks with his own voice in 7.25a to interject the obvious answer to the desperate outcry of 7.24. Finally, the 'delayed conclusion'[1] to the whole of 7.14-25 is stated in the voice of the 'I': although I (the ethnocentric Jew) want to serve the law of God,[2] I end up serving only the law of sin by means of my flesh.

13.3.4. Romans 8.1-4. In the preceding discussion the main function of this section has been noted: Paul's primary concern herein is to juxtapose the position of the 'I' as a slave to sin, for whom the law is a law of sin and death, with the position of those in Christ Jesus, for whom there is no condemnation since, by the Spirit, the righteous requirement of the law is fulfilled in them (8.4). It is only when the spiritual nature of the law (7.14) is matched by the possession of the Spirit by those in Christ that the ethical requirement of the law is fulfilled; it is only then that the condemnation spoken of in 2.1-29 is avoided, for the ethical failings of 'the Jew' are corrected only by the Spirit in the christian community. In 8.5-11 Paul develops further the juxtaposition of walking by the Spirit and by the flesh. In 8.12-17, he characterizes the believer's existence as one of sonship to God, thereby transposing to a higher key his tone of 6.15-23, wherein the believer is depicted as a slave, albeit to righteousness; in fact, says Paul, the believer's credentials are even more impressive, for the slave of righteousness is a son of God—a co-heir with Christ in his glory, although at present the co-heir shares also in Christ's sufferings. These, however, are not worth comparing to the greater glory of those who await their (full) adoption as sons (8.18-27), leading Paul to a confident celebration of God's ways (8.28-30) on behalf of those whom Paul has described throughout as the (sole) beneficiaries of divine grace: those who are 'in Christ Jesus' who have been freed from the law of sin and death.

Throughout the present chapter two aspects of Paul's understanding of the law have been noted—one concerning the identity markers pre-

---

1. Dahl, 1977: 85, rather than a scribal gloss (most recently, Ziesler, 1989: 199, 209).
2. Literally, 'I serve with my mind the law of God'—that is, 'with my volition', indicating again the great desire of the 'I' to do the law.

scribed by the law for the eschatological age (3.21-31; 9.30–10.13), the other concerning the ethical dimension of the law (7.7–8.4). In this regard, some have suggested from time to time that Paul's perception of the law is explained by a distinction between (1) the cultic and ritual aspects of the law and (2) the moral aspects of the law. For Paul, the suggestion goes, the latter continues to be in force while the former has been abrogated.[1] This interpretative option has generally fallen out of favour, primarily because no such distinction functioned within Early Judaism; the law was recognized to be a unity. Several comments need to be made in this regard.

It is not enough to say that, since the law was perceived as a unity in Early Judaism, Paul could not have made a distinction between the ethical law and the ritual law. As we have seen, much of Paul's case depends upon just such a distinction, just as his case often fails to coincide with traditional Jewish perceptions. In Romans 2, for instance, Paul argues in such a manner as to remove circumcision from the arena of 'doing the law'. His (polemical) argument there proceeds from the basis that to do the law is to live ethically. In this regard he both argues that gentiles can keep the law (2.14, 26-27) and denies that Jewish rituals have anything to do with keeping the law (2.25-29). Similarly, in Romans 14 Paul seems to be arguing that *ethnic* dietary practices are salvifically irrelevant. In both cases, Paul's is a most provocative case because it introduces a distinction in the law where none seems to have existed for most of his contemporaries. By discarding circumcision (Rom. 2.25-29) and dietary observances (Rom. 14) from the necessary prescriptions of the law, Paul is attacking what was an accepted 'given' for his Jewish contemporaries—the unity of the law.[2] In some sense, then, it is true to Paul's message to speak of the negation of the ritual law and the fulfilment of the ethical law by believers. What was a 'given' in Early Judaism (the unity of the law) both confronted, and was challenged by, Paul; in his capacity

---

1. Cf. most recently, T.R. Schreiner, 1989: 59-65.

2. Although indifference towards Jewish identity markers would have forced Paul to the periphery of Early Judaism, such a move was not unprecedented. Something of the sort seems to have motivated the messages of John the Baptist and Jesus (although perhaps in a less pronounced manner and in a more restrictive context). Moreover, we know from Philo of some Alexandrian Jews who denied that such practices as circumcision were meant to be observed literally, thinking them to be ethical symbols of inner transformation (cf. *Migr. Abr.* 89-94). Paul's case in Romans 2 is hardly different.

as the apostle to the gentiles, he forced, in effect, a distinction within the law, distinguishing the law as a moral code from the law as prescriptive of ethnically restrictive practices.

Several qualifications need to be registered here, however. First, although Paul wants to affirm the fulfilment of the law as a moral code by the christian community in 8.4 and 13.8-10 (cf. Gal. 5.14), he does not seem concerned, at least thoughout most of his (extant) letters, to work out his prescriptions for community ethics on the basis of Torah commands. In general, rules of conduct are not founded upon scriptural prescriptions for moral behaviour.[1] When he states that believers fulfill the law by love he 'is describing, not prescribing, Christian behavior'.[2] He is 'not commanding their observance, but arguing that Christian love inevitably meets the standard set by the law'.[3]

Second, Paul does not set out *programmatically* to negate the 'ritual law' and uphold the 'ethical law'. A dichotomy of this sort does not *explain* Paul's understanding of the law, but it is a *result* of his arguments at various places.[4] Räisänen may be right to say that such a distinction was unrecognized by Paul himself and was made possible by the fact that the term 'law' lacks consistent definition in Paul's letters.[5]

Third, in partial explanation of the second point above, the distinction between moral and ritual is itself not framed in terms appropriate to Paul's case; what seems more fundamental to it is the temporal distinction of the ages—a distinction which falls even within the law, or so Paul seems to have thought. We have suggested, on the basis of Rom. 10.5-8, that for Paul the eschatological divide corresponded to a divide permeating Scripture itself. Scriptural prescriptions which promote ethnocentrism belong to the past age and are not appropriate in the present age (10.4-5), for the law prescribed that the sole identity marker valid for the eschatological 'now' is faith. By prescribing what for Paul were both ethnocentric (Lev. 18.5) and universalistic

---

1. Cf. Lindemann: 'Ethik ist für Paulus also keinesfalls die Praktizierung der Tora. . . Christen führen ihr Leben "in Christus". . . Dies ist für Paulus der Ursprung der ἀγάπη, an der als höchstem Wert sich das Handeln auszurichten hat' (1986: 265). Cf. Räisänen, 1983: 48-50, 200; Westerholm, 1984. But see T.R. Schreiner, 1989: 59-65; Deidun, 1981: 188-93.

2. Westerholm, 1988: 201.

3. Westerholm, 1988: 202.

4. Cf. Segal, 1986b: 373; Sanders, 1983a: 105.

5. 1983: 25, 28, 199, 201.

(Deut. 30.12-14) identity markers, the law itself includes a temporal distinction which encompasses both sides of the eschatological boundary. If Paul is granted this temporal argument, the unity of the law in some sense remains intact. That is, Paul makes no distinction between the law's prescription for the *eschatological* membership (faith) and for ethical behaviour fulfilled by love; both are maintained in the christian community. For Paul, the law's ethical prescriptions and its prescriptions concerning the badge of covenant membership in the eschatological age are both fulfilled only by the 'in Christ' community; that community alone fulfils the law *as a unity in the 'now'*, or *as it was meant to be a unity in the eschatological age*. Conversely, unbelieving Jews demonstrate their failure to fulfil both aspects of the one law; they do not exhibit the proper mark of covenant membership in the eschatological 'now' and their position outside of the covenant of grace is evidenced (in Paul's polemic) by their failure to keep the ethical prescriptions of the law. The only thing untypical in this is Paul's perception of the prescribed marker for membership in the eschatological covenant, but once that is granted to him the unity of the law is maintained. Ironically, the only way Paul's case can have the effect of keeping the law as a unified entity in the eschatological age, while at the same time making the claim that the law is fulfilled by the christian community of faith, is by undermining the validity of the law for the present wherever it seems to prescribe ethnocentric practices as badges of covenant membership (such as Lev. 18.5).

In this way, the temporal disjunction between the two ages provides the scaffolding for two seemingly contradictory phenomena in Paul's case: (1) the resulting dichotomy between the law's requirements concerning (a) moral behaviour and (b) the ethnocentric distinguishing marks of the Jewish people; and (2) the claim to uphold the whole law appropriately in the eschatological present by faith (3.31).

One final issue remains to be noted before concluding this chapter— what might be called 'affective' influences on Paul's depiction of 'the Jew' throughout 7.7-25. It will be argued here that Paul's presentation of 'the Jew' in this section has itself been determined to a significant extent by an underlying motivation which does not arise out of the inner workings of Paul's gospel but which springs ultimately from his great concern for his fellow Jews. We learn of his great affection for his people in 10.1: 'My heart's desire and prayer is that they might be saved' (cf. 9.1-3; 11.14). It is precisely because of this affection on

Paul's part that his portrayal of 'the Jew' is not wholly dismissive.[1] Although 'the Jew' fails at present to belong to the community of faith, Paul guards his disparaging depiction of him, taking care not to portray him in terms of the deliberate and flagrant sinner who has no chance of ever participating in the 'in Christ' community.[2] 'The Jew' is not in a position beyond hope; although he currently does not know from where his salvation will come, his earnest desire is for salvation, just as Paul's desire for him is the same. In the case of the Jewish people, Paul considers the soil to be fallow; all that is needed is proper seeding and harvesting. So, as we have seen, he recognizes them to be zealous for God although their zeal is not properly targeted. Accordingly, Paul's comments in 7.14-25 are rightly understood not only as a vindication of the law but also as a curious apology for unbelieving Israel.[3]

Moreover, similar lines of thought seem to underlie Paul's convictions and hopes in both 7.7–8.4 and 11.11-14. In Romans 11, Paul expresses his hope that the Jews will become jealous of the fact that salvation is bypassing them and going to the gentiles; spurred on by their jealousy, they too might enter the covenant community. Like the mule who follows the carrot wherever it goes, so too will the Jews follow salvation; when they recognize that they cannot contain it within an ethnocentric community, they will join the community wherein grace is at work (or so Paul hopes). This involves a process of disorientation (they have been bypassed) and reorientation (they enter the covenant community). And it is this process which Paul describes in Romans 7–8: the 'I' of Romans 7 is the disoriented Jew who recognizes that he cannot keep the law; in Romans 8, Paul shows how 'the Jew's' dilemma can be resolved when he (re)orients himself within the 'in Christ' people, the community which encompasses even the gentiles by their faith (Rom. 3.21–4.25) and whose constituents are slaves to righteousness, having been freed from enslavement to sin (6.1-23).

---

1. Räisänen notes the perplexity of many scholars at Paul's 'too favourable picture of the unredeemed man's will and "mind" in this passage' (1983: 110). When the interpretation suggested herein is accepted, such perplexity falls away.

2. Contrast 9.22, where unbelieving Israel are described as objects of God's wrath 'prepared for destruction', an estimation which he 'corrects' in 11.11-32 (esp. 11.26).

3. This is not to deny that Paul's case here is intended as a chastisement of 'the Jew', but simply to point out why the chastisement is not wholly incriminating.

It would seem, therefore, that alongside Rom. 10.1, 9.1-3, and 11.11-32, Rom. 7.7–8.4 provides us with insight into the character of Paul's affection for his people. So great was that affection that it influenced the manner in which he portrayed the problem of the unbelieving Jew. Paul does not portray him as a flagrant sinner for whom there is no hope of salvation whatsoever. Instead, such a Jew is depicted by Paul as the unwilling victim of sin who simply needs correction for his sinfulness to be put aside. It is this same concern which shapes his expectations of the manner in which salvation history will unfold to include those of Israel who are presently excluded from the covenant people, an issue with which the next chapter of this book deals.

Chapter 14

THE ETHNIC COMPONENT OF
CHRISTOCENTRIC COVENANTALISM

In Romans 9–11, Paul reargues his case concerning christocentric
covenantalism, but this time he does so with one issue specifically in
mind: God's relationship to Israel. Underlying this whole section is the
question of God's faithfulness to Israel. Paul's gospel is open to the
charge that God is favouring the gentiles at the expense of the Jews. If,
as Paul has argued, God's covenant grace is operative within the
christocentric community, and if most Jews are 'outsiders' to that
community, then God's promise to Israel has come to nought and he
has been unfaithful in his constancy towards them. This 'Jewish problem' impinges on the persuasiveness of Paul's own gospel, for if it can
be concluded that God is unfaithful in his relationship to Israel, there
is little reason to think that he should be otherwise in his relationship
with the christian community.

It might appear strange for Paul to concern himself with the question of God's faithfulness to Israel, for Paul has been arguing
throughout Romans 1–8 that those in relationship with God are members of the christian community, without regard for race. Has Paul set
aside his arguments in Romans 1–8? Such might be a proper conclusion were it not for several indications found within his earlier case
that there does exist a bond between God and Israel which the principle of divine impartiality does not negate. Paul recognized in Romans
2–3 that Jewish possession of the law gives evidence of a relationship
between God and Israel (2.17; 3.1-2). Although he rejects Jewish
claims to superiority, Paul does not reject the basis for that claim:
God's relationship with Israel, symbolized by Israel's possession of the
law. As we saw in Chapter 12, the discussion throughout 3.1-8 was
facilitated by Paul's two convictions (1) that God is impartial, and (2)
that a relationship of some sort exists between God and Israel. In

Romans 9–11, Paul analyses the latter with regard to his case for christocentric covenantalism.

Throughout this chapter, the primary goal will be to evaluate Paul's claim in 11.26 that 'all Israel will be saved' in the light of his fuller case in Romans 9–11, especially 11.11-32. Section 14.1 provides a brief overview of Romans 9–11 so that Paul's strange, but fascinating, argument in Romans 11 (examined in §14.2) might be located within its larger context.

14.1. *An Overview of Romans 9–11*

Paul sets his new agenda around the issue of Israel in Rom. 9.1-5. After stating in explicit terms his concern for his fellow Jews, Paul recognizes that to them belong special privileges: the adoption, the glory, the covenants, the giving of the law, the temple worship, and the promises. Moreover, from them have come the patriarchs (οἱ πατέρες) and, even more, the Messiah (ὁ Χριστός; cf. 1.3).[1] Here Paul is continuing the list of Jewish advantages referred to in 3.1 (Jewish advantage is 'much in every way'), after having cited only one example in 3.2. As he begins this section of this epistle, Paul does not skirt the issue of God's relationship with Israel but establishes it in bold relief at the outset, as if to suggest that what follows concerns this very fact.

In 9.1-5, Paul looks back on Israel's history from the beginning (the patriarchs) to the recent culmination of that history (the Messiah), and claims that God is the one who has directed the whole process of that history ('God is over all').[2] But if salvation history, directed by God and culminating in the Messiah, progresses in such a way as to exclude unbelieving Jews from participating in salvation, if the relationship between God and Israel has had no beneficial result for Jews who do not believe, the implication is that God himself is culpable. But Paul curtails such a conclusion, arguing in fact that 'God's word has not failed' (9.6). He explains this in 9.6-13, stating that Israel's advantages were never intended to be enjoyed by the whole of Israel inclusively,

---

1. More than anywhere else in the Pauline corpus, the titular sense of Χριστός is evident in 9.5.

2. This phrase in 9.5, ὁ ὢν ἐπὶ πάντων θεός, is not a christological but a theological description, and refers most probably to God's role in the process of the unfolding drama of salvation history. Cf. Barrett, 1957: 175; Luz, 1968: 27; Käsemann, 1980: 260; Lübking, 1986: 56.

but have always been restricted to one part of that group. Here Paul no longer speaks of Israel collectively, as he did in 9.4-5, but draws out two strands within the one people; not all of Israel are Israel in the true sense of the word (9.6),[1] not all of Abraham's offspring are his children (9.7). Paul demonstrates this from Israel's history, as told in Scripture: God chose Isaac not Ishmael, Jacob not Esau (9.7-13).

Since God has always been one to choose a part from within the whole to be the beneficiaries of his grace, so he cannot be said to be unjust if the same is currently happening. As his dealings in history well show, God has always been characterized by his acts of hardening as much as by his mercy (9.15-18). The same applies to his dealings with Israel. God's calling of Israel entails that both his mercy and his hardening fall on respective parts of that one people; some within Israel enjoy his mercy while others experience his hardening. The point is made further by the analogy of the potter and his clay: from the one lump of clay can come two separate objects, some of the clay being used for honourable objects and some for dishonourable objects (9.21). Both parts of the one lump are useful to the potter; as Paul explains in 9.22-23, God is being patient with the 'objects of his wrath' (unbelieving Israel) in order that the riches of his glory might be enjoyed by 'the objects of his mercy'.[2] Those objects of divine mercy are called from the ranks of both Jews (the remnant) *and* gentiles (9.24, where Paul makes his 'first distinctively Christian claim of the argument'),[3] and again Paul supports this from Scripture (9.25-29). The obvious results of Paul's argument are (1) ethnic heritage in itself is no assurance of God's grace, and (2) God's ways in the present are as they have been from the start; his word has not failed.

Moreover, it is important to note that, while distinguishing between those Jews who are rightly Abraham's children and those who are not (9.6-13), Paul maintains that the latter are useful to God and perform

---

1. οὐ γὰρ πάντες οἱ ἐξ Ἰσραὴλ οὗτοι Ἰσραήλ. Some scholars contend that Paul here identifies true Israel with the christian community, as he does in Gal. 6.16. Cf. Ellis, 1957: 137-39; Williams, 1980: 281; Aageson, 1987: 55. But those whom Paul has in mind here are almost certainly those of ethnic Israel who have faith in Christ, the *true* members of Israel, in contrast to the rest of ethnic Israel. Cf. Mussner, 1984: 29; Hübner, 1984a: 58; Beker, 1980: 316; W.S. Campbell, 1981b: 32; B.W. Longenecker, 1989: 96-97.

2. That the hardening of some leads to the salvation of others is also inherent in Paul's reference to God's hardening of Pharaoh in 9.17.

3. Johnson, 1989: 148.

a function for which they were chosen within the process of salvation history (9.19-23). God is being patient with them now, thereby putting off the final day and allowing the riches of his glory (which belong to Israel; cf. 9.4) to go to the full number of God's eschatological people. This point will be fundamental to Paul's case in 11.11-32: God is working his design even through the disobedient members of Israel.

Romans 9.30–10.13 has already been examined in some detail. Israel has stumbled by their lack of faith (as Isaiah prophesied), for they considered the covenant to be restricted to the community of the Jews, whereas Scripture foretold that no such restrictions would apply in the eschatological age. It is not that Israel has not heard (10.14-18). They simply remain disobedient (10.21) while gentiles enter into covenant with God (10.20), thus provoking Israel to jealousy (10.19). Paul leaves this latter point undeveloped until 11.11-32.

Paul then makes the claim that God has not rejected his people (11.1), as demonstrated by the existence of the remnant who live by grace (11.2-6). The remnant ('the elect') now obtain what the rest of Israel so zealously pursued (11.7; cf. 9.31; 10.2-3), and in fact, says Paul, God is the one who has caused the rest to stumble (11.7b-10). Here Paul is building on his case of 9.6-29 that God's ways include the choosing of some and the hardening of others, and just as he argued in 9.22-23 that the hardening of one part of Israel works for the benefit of others, so in 11.11-16 he makes the same point: unbelieving Israel has stumbled and by their stumbling salvation has gone to the gentiles. God's hardening of them has a purpose within the larger scope of his design in salvation history.

In 11.11-16, however, a new development appears in Paul's case. He argues that, despite their stumbling, unbelieving Israel has not fallen; instead, provoked by jealousy at the sight of the gentiles being saved, the 'fulness' of unbelieving Israel will copy their remnant counterpart and enjoy God's salvation (11.11-12, 15). Paul expresses his hope that his gentile mission will aid in the process, so that some Jews may be saved (through jealousy) as a result of it (11.14). Within this section, then, Paul entertains a note of optimism concerning the future of unbelieving Israel which is unprecedented thus far in Romans 9–11. No longer are they depicted as 'objects of wrath, prepared for destruction' (9.22). Paul has stepped back to bring into view a broader scope of salvation history and perceives a favourable scenario for the 'fulness' of Israel alongside the remnant.

In 11.17-24, Paul presents his extended olive tree analogy which expands upon 11.11-16. Two aspects of Paul's case in 11.11-16 facilitate the analogy: (1) the conviction that unbelieving Israel is playing a role in the process of salvation history, and (2) the hope that, as the process of salvation unfolds, it will come to include those of unbelieving Israel who at present have been cut off. Paul elaborates on these points, arguing that although gentiles have been grafted in, they are not natural participants, whereas unbelieving Israelites are natural members; although unbelieving Israelites have been lopped off at present, their regrafting is likely. Despite the disparate courses of believing and unbelieving Israel, Paul highlights their common heritage and entertains the hope of their common destiny.

Paul takes this one step further in 11.25-32 where, as in 9.1-5, both parts of Israel are again spoken of as a single entity, here under the designation 'all Israel'. Paul repeats the point of 11.11-16 once again (the hardening of a part of Israel has facilitated the salvation of the fulness of the gentiles, 11.25) and again he is optimistic for the future salvation of unbelieving Israel. Whereas this optimism had been expressed in 11.17-24 as a hope for the ingathering of unbelieving Israel, here it is stated as a certainty, a mysterious certainty which includes *all* of Israel—that is, both parts: 'all Israel will be saved' (11.26).[1] Paul explains the certainty of Israel's salvation on the basis of their election: 'they are loved on account of the patriarchs (διὰ τοὺς πατέρας; cf. 9.5), for God's gift and his call are irrevocable' (11.28b-29). Finally, Paul states once again that their election has involved their hardening by God in order that God might be merciful to others (11.31), and, in the end, might be merciful to all (nations) (11.32). In a concluding doxology (11.33-36), Paul salutes God's sovereign ways in history—ways which transcend all human expectations.

14.2. *Paul's Understanding of Salvation History in Romans 9–11*

With this overview in mind, it is obvious that Paul's case in 11.11-36, which facilitates his claim that 'all Israel will be saved' (11.26), is not necessary to his case throughout 9.6–11.10 where he insisted that

---

1. There is no reason to believe that Paul means in 11.26 to identify the christian community as 'all Israel'. Contra Whiteley, 1964: 97; Wright, 1980: 193-210; Güttgemanns, 1971: 47-49; Aageson, 1986: 284-85; Jeremias, 1977: 193-205. See B.W. Longenecker, 1989: 96-97 for further elaboration.

God's faithfulness is not compromised if some of Israel remain outside the boundaries of his grace.[1] Romans 11 could well have concluded at 11.10 with no loose ends remaining. Nonetheless, Paul continues along a somewhat different path to argue a somewhat different point in 11.11-36. I want to show, however, that the two sections (9.6–11.10; 11.11-36) are not necessarily incompatible theologically. The worst that Paul can be accused of is having a large agenda on the subject of ethnic Israel. In this regard, his claim that 'all Israel will be saved' cannot be fully understood without a proper understanding of his view of salvation history. Two aspects are of special importance: (1) the *temporal* aspect of Paul's view of salvation history, wherein the 'already' awaits the 'not yet', and (2) the *ethnic* (as opposed to *'ethnocentric'*) aspect of Paul's understanding of salvation history, wherein salvation is going out to all humanity by God through the instrument of his chosen people, Israel. These two aspects will be examined in §§14.2.1 and 14.2.2 below. In §14.2.3, both will be compared with popular eschatological expectations in Early Judaism.

14.2.1. *Israel and the temporal distinction in Paul's view of salvation history.* If we are right to recognize in Paul a hope for the salvation of all Israel, that hope will need to be placed within the larger context of his presentation in Romans.

Throughout Romans 1–8, Paul concerns himself with the requirements for being a member of the people of God in the present age. Paul's case is that, in the present age, the identity marker of the people of God is not an ethnic peculiarity but faith and living by the Spirit. In that way, one has membership with the eschatological people of God. Nonetheless, although Paul thought the previous age to have given way with the death and resurrection of Christ, he still awaited the consummation of the present age. Those 'in Christ' have life now, but with the culmination of the age they will have resurrection (6.5) and glory (5.2; 8.17-18). They have the Spirit now (5.5), but only the firstfruits of the Spirit (8.23); the full harvest is yet to come. They are sons of God (8.14-16) and heirs with Christ (8.17), but they have yet to receive their full adoption as sons (8.23). Just as all creation groans in anxiety while awaiting the final day (8.19-22), so believers too groan inwardly and await the redemption of their bodies (8.23-25). In

---

1. Cf. Noack: 'the paragraphs from ix.1 to xi.10 do not contain the slightest hint at the final solution' of 11.11-36 (1965: 166).

this way, Paul's vision of the present age is proleptic, always marked by anticipation; the penultimate of salvation history is already present, but the ultimate is yet to come.

It is this same plan of the temporal stages within salvation history (the 'already' and the 'not yet'), established in Romans 1–8, which facilitates Paul's two estimates of ethnic Israel in Romans 9–11 (namely 9.6–11.10 and 11.11-36): in the present age, ethnic lineage has no part in determining the membership of the community of grace; with the culmination of this age, however, all Israel will be turned to faith in Christ—that is, their godlessness (unbelief) will disappear.[1] This temporal distinction is one of the determining factors underlying Paul's various estimates of Israel. It is best seen in Paul's use of the stumbling motif. In 9.32, for instance, with his eyes on the present time, Paul states that Israel has stumbled (προσκόπτειν). The implication is that they are down, and therefore out. They have lost the race (cf. 9.30-31). In 11.11, however, when he turns his sight to the future, Paul distinguishes between stumbling (πταίειν) and falling (πίπτειν). Israel has stumbled, but they have not fallen. In fact, Paul looks forward to the time when they will recover from their stumble and, in their fulness, come into membership with God's people of faith.

In this way Paul's view of Israel is determined by a temporal factor. With his sights focused on the present stage of salvation history, Paul excludes all considerations of race. Those of Israel who do not believe are excluded from membership in the community of God's grace. Although their disobedience has been used by God to bring others into the people of God, they themselves fall outside of this community. *In the present age,* therefore, Israel is said to be an 'enemy' on account of the people of God (11.28). *In the culmination of this age,* however, Israel will be shown to be 'loved on account of the patriarchs, for God's gifts and his call are irrevocable' (11.28-29). Because they are elect, a deliverer (probably Christ himself)[2] will come to Israel and

---

1. Some have argued that Paul expected unbelieving Israel to be saved apart from faith in Christ. Cf. Mussner, 1976; Gaston, 1987: 92-99; Stendahl, 1976: 4, 40; Williamson and Allen, 1989: 34-39, 82-84; Lapide, 1984: 51; Gager, 1985: 261-64; Klappert, 1981: 58-137. Räisänen calls this interpretation 'simply insupportable' (1988: 189). See arguments against it in B.W. Longenecker, 1989: 98-101; Räisänen, 1988: 189-92; *idem,* 1987a: 2917-18; and esp. Johnson, 1989: 176-205.

2. For discussions of this issue, see B.W. Longenecker, 1989: 98; Stuhlmacher, 1971: 561; Hübner, 1984b: 114.

their sinful condition (unbelief) will be turned away. They are a part
of the chosen people and will not be forsaken, in spite of their present
hardening. Ultimately, God will prove his faithfulness to Israel once
and for all; in the end, even those whom he has hardened will be
turned to faith in the Messiah of God, *precisely because of their membership in the ethnic race of the Jews.* As J.C. Beker writes: 'At the
end, Israel's beginning, that is, its election by God, will be
confirmed'.[1]

In this temporal scheme of the stages within salvation history, the
tension between (1) Paul's case for salvation by faith, where ethnic
boundaries are disqualified, and (2) his certainty concerning the ultimate salvation of Israel, can be accounted for somewhat; both aspects
of his case pertain to different stages in the unfolding drama of salvation. Nonetheless, one significant question remains: what is the basis
for Paul's optimism concerning Israel's future incoming into the community of faith? The answer to that lies in the recognition of the ethnic character of Paul's understanding of salvation history, a vital
aspect of Paul's case which will be examined in §14.2.2.

14.2.2. *The ethnic character of Paul's view of salvation history.* Just as
his sketch of salvation history within Romans 1–8 includes the whole
picture, from beginning to end, from Adam to the resurrection, so
also he answers the Israel question within this broader frame of reference (but, as we have seen, with different verdicts at different points
of the drama). In Rom. 11.11ff., Paul pulls back from his case concerning the present stage of salvation history and broadens his sights
to include the events of the future and Israel's place in them; all Israel
will be saved by the deliverer who will turn away their godlessness
(11.26). Paul repeatedly explains that the inclusion of the gentiles is
itself a way to bring unbelieving Israel to salvation; salvation is
presently going to the gentiles in order to provoke Israel to jealousy
and to lead them to salvation. Although his ministry might appear to
some to concern itself solely with bringing salvation to the gentiles,
Paul wants his readers to understand that there is a deeper motivation
behind his mission—that is, the salvation of Israel, for whom he has
already expressed his great concern (9.1-3). Although he is the apostle
to the gentiles, he does not presume that his ministry entails God's
abandonment of Israel. In a roundabout way, in fact, Paul understands

---

1. Beker, 1980: 87. Cf. *idem*, 1986: 14; Käsemann, 1980: 305.

his gentile mission as a rescue operation for Israel's sake. Although Paul is working for the salvation of the gentiles, that does not mean that the gentiles have taken centre stage in God's plan. God has not transferred his favour to the gentiles at the expense of the Jews. He still has Israel in view and in fact, as we have seen, the process of salvation culminates with them. He argues, then, that even his gentile ministry is a catalyst for the eventual salvation of Israel.[1]

As soon as Paul has established this point in 11.11-16, he proceeds immediately to warn the gentiles against boasting (11.17-24), just as he had earlier condemned *Jewish* boasting (2.17-24; 3.27). Paul seems aware at this point that his characterization of his gentile ministry could be misperceived as indicating that Israel is indebted to the gentiles for their ultimate salvation, that Israel has no existence apart from the christian community, that it is the gentiles who are in a position to save Israel, rather than vice versa. Furthermore, Paul's own gospel of salvation apart from ethnic boundaries may well have motivated an anti-Jewish sentiment within some gentile circles of the christian community, just as it did less than a century later in the theology of Marcion (85–160 CE).[2] Paul recognized this danger and took immediate steps to steer clear of it by clarifying, specifically for his gentile readers, what he was *not* saying. Although gentile believers are 'inside' and unbelieving Israel are 'outside' of the community, gentile believers have no grounds to boast in themselves at the expense of the Jews. Paul hopes to undermine their pride, and his olive tree analogy serves this purpose well.[3] With this analogy, Paul portrays the com-

---

1. Kim has suggested that *from the very beginning* Paul conceived of the gentile ministry as ultimately bringing about the salvation of all Israel (1981: 82-96). Better, however, is Räisänen's argument that Paul's views developed in the light of his later experiences in ministry (1986c) and represents an attempt at theological legitimation (1988: 187-88, 195-96). Cf. Dunn, 1987b.

2. Many think that Paul was aware of anti-Jewish tendencies within the Roman churches. See, for instance, W.S. Campbell, 1981a: 36; *idem*, 1981b: 37; Minear, 1971: 79; Mussner, 1984: 35-36; Davies, 1984c: 144. On the other hand, Käsemann writes: 'The admonitions of vv. 16-24 arise naturally *out of the problem of the chapter* and give evidence of Paul's foresight, but tell us little about the situation in Rome' (1980, 305; emphasis added). Cf. Schlier, 1977: 333; Dunn, 1988a: 673.

3. I was evidently wrong to state in 1989 that Paul's olive tree analogy is horticulturally problematic (1989: 119 n. 40; cf. Shaw: 'horticultural nonsense' [1983: 171]); Baxter and Ziesler have re-argued that the process of ingrafting wild olive branches was a common practice in Paul's day which allowed a diseased olive tree to be reinvigorated (1985). I remain somewhat sceptical, however, of their conclusion that 'the main point. . . [is] the rejuvenation of the tree' (1985: 29). Although this

plexities of his view of salvation history. He perceives it to involve a process whereby God's promises to Abraham unfold (= the root[1])—a process which works through an ethnic people (= the natural branches), some of whom have turned to faith in the Messiah of their God while others are expected to believe only during the final stage of the process. But since faith is the means of admission into this stage of salvation history, the process is no longer exclusive to that ethnic group; gentiles (= the unnatural branches) are admitted on the same basis. They must, however, be aware of their place, for they are like wild branches grafted into a tree who, in fact, function merely as parasites which become productive only when they are nourished by the nutrients of the root. The process itself does not end with them. It culminates, as it began, with Israel, for if the wild olive branches were grafted into a cultivated olive tree, how much more readily will the natural branches be grafted back into their own tree.

Here Paul has stepped back and surveyed the whole of salvation history in order to place the present situation into its fuller context. That is, when the whole picture of salvation history is in view, those of the present age who are admitted as members of the people of God apart from Jewish heritage must recognize that what they are participating in is fundamentally an *ethnic* process whereby the salvation of all humanity is effected. Gentiles are welcome to take part and, at this stage of the process, can enter fully into it. However, what gentile believers have associated themselves with is the salvation which God has effected through the vehicle of the Jewish people.[2] God began the process of salvation with an ethnic people (9.4-5). Ethnic Jews keep up with the process when they believe in their Messiah. Only then can they claim to be the true Israel (9.6). As the programme of salvation history unfolds, some of the ethnic people with whom it began have 'evolved' with it by their faith in Christ. Others, however, have lagged behind by their lack of faith. Nonetheless, Paul retains a central role in the process of salvation history for those of Israel who do not believe; by their disbelief they have made room for others to join the

would fit well with Paul's general concerns, Paul works his analogy to show the indebtedness of the gentiles to Israel, rather than the opposite.

1. What is meant here is that the unfolding of God's promises to Abraham constitutes the root, rather than a more precise identification of the root as a specific person or group (Abraham, the patriarchs, Israel, the remnant or Jesus Christ).

2. Cf. D.W.B. Robinson: 'the very pattern of salvation remains part of the heritage of Israel, and can only be learned by the Gentiles from Israel' (1974: 235).

ranks of God's people. Even their disobedience is a medium whereby salvation goes to those who will believe.[1] God is working the salvation of others through those of Israel who have stumbled. They have a vital role in the process in which God is now recognized to be the God not only of the Jews, but of the gentiles as well (3.29). When the process, of which they are a part, is completed, they themselves will be turned to faith in the Messiah. Thus, things at present are not as they will be finally. Paul awaits the culmination of the age when God's ethnic agents, through whom he brings salvation to all, will be saved.

Since Paul perceives every stage of salvation history as operating through the agency of the ethnic race of the Jews, Paul draws out significant implications of this for his gentile-christian audience, whose apostle he is. He advises them that the benefits which they have received must always be kept in their proper perspective, for he views them as the *proleptic deposit of what God will bestow upon Israel at the culmination of salvation history*. This is the whole point, for instance, of Paul's jealousy motif: When Israel realizes that the gentiles are taking part in the salvation which was promised to them (Israel), they will be provoked to jealousy and be saved by faith themselves. In this respect, it is interesting to examine what Paul says about adoption. On one hand, he states that believers are presently awaiting their full adoption as sons (8.23). On the other hand, he says that adoption as sons belongs to Israel (9.4). The relationship between these two statements is explained later in 15.27 where Paul speaks of the gentiles as *sharing in the spiritual blessings of the Jews*. In the present stage of history, those who believe in the Jewish Messiah are (proleptically) participating in the eschatological salvation of all Israel. At present, only the firstfruits of those blessings are evident. Paul looks forward to the time when all Israel (that is, both 'parts') will be saved by faith in Christ, for only then will the whole of salvation history be complete and the full blessings of Israel fall upon the community of believers. This community does not displace Israel. Instead, it is 'an extension of the promises of God to Israel. . . the proleptic dawning of the future destiny of Israel'.[2]

---

1. Contra e.g. Segal: 'Paul. . . seems unwilling to allow the Jews any significant part in the salvation of mankind until the fulfillment of history' (1986a: 172).

2. Beker, 1980: 332, 316. He continues: Paul 'intends to show that the true *ekklesia* is a future eschatological reality that will only be realized when it comprises the whole people of Israel'.

At this point, Paul's presentation of the course of salvation history, and the place of Israel and the gentiles respectively within that process, needs to be compared with other eschatological expectations in the Judaism of his day in order to highlight points of continuity and innovation in his understanding of salvation history.

14.2.3. *Paul's ethnic view of salvation history in comparison with popular expectations in Early Judaism.* As on most issues, no uniformity existed in Early Judaism concerning Israel and the gentiles at the final day. Despite the diversity of Jewish opinion, one conviction was presupposed by them all: 'that Judaism as the one true religion was destined to become the universal religion'.[1] As Zechariah proclaimed: 'The Lord will be king over the whole earth. On that day there will be one Lord, and his name the only name' (14.9). This prophetic announcement captures a fundamental assurance of Judaism: 'The golden age in the future, the goal toward which all history moved, was, above everything else, the fulfillment of Israel's destiny'.[2] The literature of Early Judaism demonstrates repeatedly the common belief that, in the end, the religion of the true God will be established at the expense of all others (cf. e.g. *Pss. Sol.* 17).

If this can be said to be a given of Jewish eschatological expectations, the specifics which describe how that supremacy is awarded to the Jewish religion vary. In general, however, they can all be contained within one of three categories: the nations will be (1) subjugated, (2) destroyed, or (3) converted.[3] For our purposes, it is, of course, the conversion of the nations which is of particular concern.

Within the book of Isaiah, especially, God commissions his people to be a means towards the establishment of his rule for all humanity: 'I will make you a light to the gentiles, that you may bring my salvation to the ends of the earth' (Isa. 49.6; cf. 51.4). Similarly, in the last days, it is said that Mt Zion will be established above all others,

> and all the nations will stream to it. Many peoples will come and say, 'Come, let us go up to the mountain of the Lord, to the house of the God of Jacob. He will teach us his ways so that we may walk in his paths.' The law will go out from Zion, the word of the Lord from Jerusalem (2.2-3 = Mic. 4.1-2).

1. Moore, 1927: 1.323.
2. Moore, 1927: 1.225-26.
3. Russell, 1964: 297-303; Moore, 1927: 2.371. Sanders finds six basic prophetic predictions concerning the gentiles in the end-times (1985b: 214), but all his categories are included in these three more general classifications.

Elsewhere, it is said that those of other nations who bind themselves to
the Lord, and who serve, love and worship him will be brought to
Zion and into the house of prayer, for God's house 'will be called a
house of prayer for all nations' (56.6-7). In this way, God will gather
to himself both Israel and other nations with them (56.8). Zechariah
also proclaimed that, in the end, members of all nations will grab hold
of the skirts of the Jews in order to enter Jerusalem with them and
worship their Lord (Zech. 8.20-23). On that final day when God will
live in Zion with his people, many nations will be joined with the
Lord and will become his people (2.11). In these passages, salvation is
not granted without conversion to the Jewish religion. That is, salvation comes to the gentiles only as they learn the ways of God and walk
in his paths by aligning themselves with the law and its practices, and
this itself comes about through the instrumentality of the people of
Israel.

This same expectation is evident in much of the literature of Early
Judaism,[1] so much so, in fact, that Sanders estimates that most Jews of
Paul's time who gave the issue any consideration would have expected
the gentiles to be converted to the true (Jewish) religion at the end of
the age.[2] Whether or not it is true that *most* Jews believed this, the
conviction was certainly in the air in Paul's day and had strong roots
in the prophetic tradition. In the end, Israel will be vindicated and the
true religion will emerge uncontested as all the world turns to worship
the God of Israel. Contending religions would be wiped out by the
emptying of their membership ranks by means of conversion to the
true religion, thereby ensuring the final triumph of God over all creation. Salvation lay with Israel's God, and the way to him was through
his people. So J. Jocz writes:

> Between the God of Israel and the Gentile world stands the Jewish people.
> To come to God meant primarily to come to the Jews. Without first coming to
> Israel, the way to God remained barred.[3]

1. *1 En.* 10.21; 50.2-5; *Sib. Or.* 3.115-31, 195; *T. Dan* 9.2; 10.5, 9-11; *T. Levi*
14.4; *Pss. Sol.* 17.34-35; Tob. 14.6-7.
2. Sanders, 1985b: 216-18. Davies is more cautious, finding this expectation to be
'well marked' in Early Judaism (1984a: 126). Cf. Levenson, 1985: 126; Beker,
1980: 248.
3. 1979: 306.

In this way, the universalism of Judaism's outlook is 'nothing more than an extension of particularism, implying the absorption of the Gentile world by the chosen people'.[1]

Paul evidences the same ethnic view of salvation history and the ingathering of the gentiles. The process began with an ethnic entity, continues as some of that ethnic entity places their faith in their Messiah, and will be completed when all of that ethnic people have turned to faith, after first allowing others to enter the covenant by the absence of some of its own members. All this follows from Paul's christocentric definition of the covenant. Because Judaism proper has outgrown its previous garb and is now marked out by faith, so even the gentiles can participate in this eschatological form of Jewish religion and share proleptically in the blessings which are Israel's. All of salvation history is rooted in the history of Israel and will be completed with Israel. In the process, God will have mercy on all humanity, and Israel will have been the instrument of his grace. In essence, the gentiles are coming to salvation on the skirts of the Jews—the whole point of Paul's olive tree analogy. For Paul, gentile faith in the Jewish Messiah is the actualization of the Jewish hope for the eschatological ingathering of the nations. Paul must have considered his gentile mission as fulfilling the 'eschatological expectation of the Old Testament that in the latter days the nations will come to worship the God of Israel'.[2] Of course, by insisting that nomistic practice has no salvific significance, Paul has changed the guise of Jewish religion,[3] but he maintains a fundamental Jewish conviction that in the end 'Judaism as the one true religion was destined to become the universal religion'. Paul's point is not simply that gentile believers *cannot exist without* Israel but, even more, when the whole scope of salvation history is in view, gentile believers *cannot exist except within* Israel.[4] In this way, God's salvation is going to the ends of the earth by way of Israel, just as God foretold (Isa. 49.6).[5]

1. Guignebert, 1939: 157.
2. Hultgren, 1985: 136.
3. Cf. Byrne: 'Paul represents a Judaism *one stage ahead* of Palestinian Judaism in the apocalyptic programme' (1979: 232).
4. Cf. Getty, 1988: 459; W.S. Campbell, 1988: 10.
5. This is an essential aspect of Paul's presentation in Rom. 1–11. It is not, then, simply an expediential move on Paul's part to pacify christian Jews (Watson, 1986: 171-73), nor is it a later interpolation into the text (Plag, 1969: 41-45).

In the light of these considerations, it is not right to say, as does J. Klausner, that Paul 'took from the Jewish Messianic idea its universalistic side, and ignored. . . its politico-national side'.[1] Such a distinction did not exist in Paul's mind and does not do justice to his case in Romans 9–11. Instead, his universalism is an extension of his peculiar view of the unfolding drama of Israel's history, through which God works the salvation of the world. In an elaborate argument, Paul asserts two fundamental convictions: (1) one does not need to adopt the *ethnic symbols of the people of Israel* in order to experience God's grace; and (2) God works the salvation of the world *through an ethnic people, Israel.* Both aspects of his case are maintained in complementarity by a dynamic awareness of the process whereby God works in history with a particular people for the salvation of humanity. The fact that Paul allows for no ethnocentricity in the present age does not deny the ethnic character of his understanding of salvation history; he simply gives different answers to different issues. Within Paul's christocentric covenantalism there is an ethnic component which roots his innovative understanding of God's eschatological ways firmly in the soil of the history of the Jewish people.

---

1. Klausner, 1943: 446. Correctly, Munck, 1959: 258-59; Richardson, 1969: 133; Hahn, 1982: 223-24.

Part IV

Conclusions

Chapter 15

COMPARISON OF 4 EZRA AND ROMANS 1–11

15.1. *Comparison of 4 Ezra and Romans 1–11*

This study has analysed two texts of Early Judaism whose authors
were each confronted by a 'crisis event' which proved to be a serious
challenge to prevalent Jewish perceptions and expectations, at least for
them. For the author of *4 Ezra*, that event appears right at the outset
of his work, as if to frame the whole of what transpires: the destruction of Jerusalem. Throughout the rest of *4 Ezra*, the implications of
that event are worked out, and Ezra (the author's 'alter ego' in the
process of transformation) arrives at a new perspective which is presented as 'the source of understanding, wisdom and knowledge'
(14.47). This perspective is proven to be valid by its experiential 'cash
value': that is, it alone restores comfort and confidence in God. For
Paul, the critical event is not mentioned explicitly in Romans
(although it lies behind the whole of his presentation there), but it is
referred to elsewhere in his letters: the revelation of Jesus Christ (Gal.
1.12) who appeared to him (1 Cor. 15.8; cf. 1 Cor. 9.1; Acts 9.17;
26.16) in exalted form (cf. Rom. 1.4; 2 Cor. 4.6; Acts 9.3; 22.6;
26.13) and who commissioned him to be the apostle to the gentiles
(Rom. 1.1-5; Gal. 1.16). As a consequence of this event, Paul declares
his perspective to have been dramatically altered (2 Cor. 5.16); what
he clung to previously he has relinquished for something far greater
(Phil. 3.7-9; 2 Cor. 3.7-11). This event, then, 'is clearly the watershed
that is responsible for the work and thought of the Apostle'.[1]

As a consequence of these events and the theological reflection
which they necessitated, each author considered himself to be the
beneficiary of the true understanding of God's ways, in contrast with
the majority of the Jewish constituency. The author of *4 Ezra* recog-

1. Hagner, 1980: 157.

nized his perception to be shared by, and valid for, only a few; the rest of Israel ('all the people. . . from the least to the greatest' [13.40]) are ignorant of it. Paul too held convictions which, despite his claim to the authentic form of Judaism (cf. 9.6), were perceived by most of his contemporaries as idiosyncratic innovations, if not 'heresies'. Paul, however, believed that any perspective which went contrary to his own was 'not according to knowledge' (10.2).

For both authors, the claim to proper knowledge was substantiated by the fact that their perceptions were informed by, and corresponded with, God's eschatological ways. Such claims to exclusive truth were, of course, in no way novel. Nor is the manner whereby those claims were substantiated; the claim to have true insight concerning God's eschatological ways is fundamental to the majority of apocalyptic texts. What is seemingly novel, however, is the general thrust of their respective perceptions; that is, for each author, proper knowledge involves the rejection of what we have called 'ethnocentric covenantalism'. Although various Jewish groups seem to have defined the covenant in various ways (envisaging differently what loyalty to the covenant entailed), few seem to have undermined the basic ethnocentric character of the covenant. They simply (re)defined that ethnocentric element according to their respective social situations. So, the Qumran sectarians considered themselves to be the true Israel—the remnant who alone embodied what Israel as a whole was meant to be. Similarly, those who produced and circulated *Jubilees* considered that, by their observance of the solar calendar in distinction from the majority of their contemporaries, they alone upheld the covenant between God and Israel. The examples are numerous. Each one includes an ethnocentric slant, although each one interprets it along different lines.

This is not the case, however, for either Paul or the author of *4 Ezra* (although this will have to be nuanced somewhat with regard to both). The revelation of God's eschatological ways has forced them to reject the ethnocentric slant of traditional Jewish covenantalism. Quite simply, in both *4 Ezra* and Romans 1–11, eschatology does not complement but, in fact, disqualifies ethnocentrism. In *4 Ezra*, Uriel's constant pointing to the eschaton (wherein only the few will be saved by their perfect works) forced Ezra to abandon (eventually) his historical perspective which focused with singular interest upon the merciful character of God in relation to his people and his creation. Similarly, Paul's christological solution, which is set within an eschatological context throughout (cf. 1.16-17; 3.21a, 26; 5.12-21; 7.1-6; 8.1-17; 10.4-8), contravenes any ethnocentric interest. For both authors, then, knowing how God operates in the eschatological age erases any prior convictions concerning Jewish ethnocentrism in relation to the covenant.

Moreover, the manner by which both authors facilitate the breakdown of ethnocentrism is precisely the same; that is, they both dwell on the Jewish commonplace that all are guilty of sin, manipulating it to such an extent as to discredit an ethnic sense of security in God's favour. In the light of the desperate condition of sin which pervades the whole of humanity, the very justice of God would be compromised if his mercy were ethnically conditioned (cf. Rom. 2.1-11; 3.5-8; *4 Ezra* 7.17-25). Each author maintains the spotlight on the anthropological condition of sin at the expense of traditional ethnocentric explanations of the covenant as the corrective to that condition.

While the problem to be solved is the same in each work (human sinfulness), the corrective to that condition is, of course, quite different in the respective works. For the author of *4 Ezra*, human sin must be countered by human effort in accordance with the standard of the law; in the eschatological age, God will (in his 'mercy') save the few who have proven themselves to be worthy of salvation by their works. For Paul, the decisive initiative has already been taken by God and the responsibility rests with his creatures to respond properly (i.e. without ethnic restraints) to that divine initiative. Since God's grace is restricted to the boundaries of the christian community of faith, Paul seems to *accuse* ethnocentric Jews of a type of legalism (trying to earn salvation by their ethnocentric works in a context apart from God's grace; cf. 4.4-5). Conversely, the author of *4 Ezra prescribes* a type of legalism in which salvation is attained to by works of merit, thereby earning the right of God's 'grace' in the eschaton. Accordingly, whereas Paul substitutes one community self-identity for another, the author of *4 Ezra* seems to abandon a community identity in favour of individual piety and perfection (although what this entails in practice is never stated).

The fundamental differences between these two solutions are these. First, for Paul, God's grace is a *present reality*, whereas such is not the case for the author of *4 Ezra*. Second, for Paul, the eschatological age has *already* begun, whereas for the author of *4 Ezra* that age is *not yet*. These two aspects are explained by the nature of their respective crisis events. Paul's crisis event was a *positive* one which revealed something definitive about the way God is working now in the new age. The eschatological life has already been inaugurated (but not fully 'realized') for those 'in Christ'—those who uphold the law (3.31) and fulfil what it requires (8.4; 13.8-10). The crisis event for the author of *4 Ezra*, conversely, was a *negative* one which demonstrated for him God's absence in history. Although God has left his standard of judgment behind, he himself takes no part in the course of events; his mercy is restricted to the bounds of the future eschatological age and is available only to those who merit his favour by their works in accordance with the law (that is, grace is available to those who have no need of it!).

But while the *nature* of their crisis experiences explains something of the differences between these two authors, it does not ultimately explain the radical cases set forward by them in contrast with their respective contemporaries. That is, the fact that Paul's experience was positive does little to explain his case in distinction from other believing Jews who rejoiced in God's salvific dealings in Christ. Similarly, the destruction of Jerusalem was most likely a negative experience for the majority of Jews of the late first century CE, but there is little evidence that they considered this event to indicate the absence of God's grace in the present apart from ethnic consideration. In this regard, it is not simply the *nature* of their respective crisis events but the *profundity* of these events which leads to each author's innovative case. This is not to suggest that they were in any sense more perceptive than others to the 'real meaning' of those events. Our point is only a psychological one, suggesting that each author took to heart his crisis event in a manner quite distinct from the majority of his contemporaries. In this regard, each author shows his dissatisfaction with traditional explanations of God's ways; he grappled to understand the significance of his crisis event, even if that process involved discarding some long-treasured tenets of belief or practice. For each, Jewish ethnocentrism was considered 'loss', resulting in the radical alteration of his perceptions, beliefs and expectations.

What is intriguing about their respective cases is the manner in which each author handles the concepts of 'law' and 'Israel'. When challenging ethnocentric definitions of the covenant, each one encounters similar difficulties. One issue to be answered is: what then of the law? In answer to this pressing issue, these authors demonstrate similar techniques of self-definition and legitimation. First, each one stakes his claim to scriptural authentication on his eschatological perspective (cf. *4 Ezra* 7.129-30; Rom 1.2; 3.21b, 31; etc.), as most pious Jews would have done.

Second, each one makes *a distinction* with regard to the law. Since the Jewish scriptures cannot be convincingly drained of *all* their particularistic quality, and since each author needs to substantiate his challenge of ethnocentrism in the light of those same scriptures, so the necessary distinctions with regard to the scriptures appear as a consequence. For Paul, that distinction is between what is and is not a valid prescription for the eschatological age; if the whole of Scripture serves a function, only some of it (those passages which Paul can cite in support of his case for faith and equality of membership) functions within the boundaries of the eschatological 'now'. If other passages can be cited which challenge or repudiate his case, they are illegitimate within the eschatological age. The law is properly the 'law of faith' (3.27), a law which is 'pursued' properly by faith rather than by ethnocentric works (9.31-33). If others consider the covenant to be an ethnocentric phenomenon and stake their own claim to the law, what they have in their possession is not the law which is 'unto life' (7.10), the 'law of God' (7.22, 25; 8.7), the 'law of the Spirit of life' (8.2); instead they possess the law as a 'law of works' (3.27) which leads them to attempt to earn salvation outside the boundaries of God's grace (4.4-5) and which keeps them enslaved to sin (7.14), thereby becoming for them 'the law of sin and death' (8.2; 7.23, 25). In this way, Paul legitimates his own case in terms of the law while discrediting the claims of others who cite Scripture in support of their counter-cases.

The author of *4 Ezra* proceeds with precisely these two concerns in mind: (1) to legitimate his case, and (2) to discredit any attempts to negate his case on scriptural grounds. Although the author makes his claim (via Uriel) to Mosaic authority on one occasion (7.129-30), this is a unique reference; proof-texting does not have any further part in his case. At places, it might appear that the author wants to *redefine* the nature of the law, or to infuse the concept 'law' with a meaning which is in line with his eschatological perspective (13.54; 14.20-22). Ultimately, however, his real technique of legitimation lies in his public–private distinction; that is, claiming continuity with Moses, the author distinguishes between what Moses *publicly revealed to the people* and what he *secretly withheld from them* (14.5-6). These have been called 'the public law' and 'the private law' respectively. The problem with the public law is that it is incomplete and, as such, pro-

motes a perspective (ethnocentrism) which is inadequate for understanding the ways of God. The people have in their possession this
public law. Just as Ezra drew on these twenty-four books for his
expectations of God in Episodes I–III (especially in his initial speeches
of each, thereby contributing to his lack of understanding), so 'all the
people' are guided by the same public law and, accordingly, misjudge
their position before God. In this way, any challenge to the author's
case is, naturally, in error, even if it has scriptural support, since such
a challenge arises from an inadequate understanding of Scripture
itself. The twenty-four books are revealed to both 'the worthy and the
unworthy' (14.45), which is to say that the public law *alone* has no
definitive quality. Only the seventy books (a numeric metaphor) provide wisdom and understanding (14.47), and then only to the few who
are wise. The author does not suggest, however, that the private law
renders the public law superfluous. He seems to maintain that the public and private belong together, almost as text and interpretation; the
true meaning of the public law comes to light only when it has the
benefit of its proper interpretative key—that is, the private law, which
brings understanding.[1] Accordingly, without the eschatological wisdom of the private law to enlighten the true meaning of the public
law, the public law itself (the Jewish scriptures) promotes a *mis*understanding (ethnocentrism!) of God's ways.

In this fashion, both authors can be seen to treat the law in similar
ways. Not only do they each claim to have true insight into the law, as
may be expected, but each substantiates that claim by making a distinction within the concept of 'law' itself; for the author of *4 Ezra*, the
distinction is between the public law and the private law, while for
Paul the distinction is between the law of works and the law of faith.
In each case, the former is rejected—that is, the law as a symbol for,
and promoter of, Jewish ethnocentrism. In this way, each author hears
two voices within the law: one voice promotes ethnocentrism, while
another disqualifies ethnocentrism in view of the revelation of God's
eschatological ways. Paul has the luxury of restricting the former to a
previous age, since the new age has already dawned. The author of *4
Ezra* does not share this option, since, for him, the new age is still to
come; accordingly, he attributes an ethnocentric reading of the law to

---

1. It is little wonder, then, that biblical proof-texting plays such a minor role in
Uriel's case!

an inadequate understanding, an understanding shared by nearly all except the few who are wise.

It needs to be noted, however, that such distinctions are not programmatically set out by either author; they are employed to legitimate their 'innovations' *vis-à-vis* claims of legitimacy by others. Distinctions of the sort illustrated above allow for a degree of one-upmanship; what is possessed by the particular author is the law in its fullest character, in contradistinction to others who claim to uphold the law. Paul's distinction is most clearly seen in 3.27 (cf. 9.31-32; 7.22–8.2), and, although he does not maintain the distinction *in explicit terms* (cf. the undifferentiated 'law' of 3.31), it nonetheless explains his various references to the law, both positive and negative. For example, when he speaks of the law positively (e.g. 3.31), it is because his gospel is wholly in line with the law in its proper character as the spokesman of faith; when he speaks of it negatively (e.g. 7.1-6) it is because the law has been hijacked by others to promote ethnocentrism in the eschatological age.

For the author of *4 Ezra*, the distinction within the law is made explicit only at the end of his piece in order to legitimate his preceding case. Apart from that, the law appears without distinction and always as a guide to proper living, the divine blueprint for salvation. Nonetheless, although the distinction between public and private is not explicit until Episode VII, it is necessary for the author's case throughout. As soon as the law is removed from the context of God's abiding covenant mercy on behalf of his people and is put into a context of (what Sanders calls) 'legalistic perfectionism', it takes on a new nature; although it remains *the standard* of divine judgment, *the system* in which it operates forces an implicit distinction within the law itself. This is evident in the case of the law's provisions for repentance of, and atonement for, transgression—an aspect which cannot be included in the law which the author wants to uphold, since, for him, transgressions themselves rule out the possibility of salvation altogether. Repentance and atonement have salvific import only if God's grace is presupposed, but such is not the case for the author. The consequence of this for his view of the law is readily obvious: although he speaks of the law without distinction throughout Episodes I–VI, an implicit distinction within the law is necessary to his case, a distinction made explicitly in VII.

The second major issue for each author is 'the Jewish problem': what, then, of ethnic Israel? In their respective cases, each author initially narrows the concept of Israel to a small number—a remnant. Several things must be noted in this regard. First, for Paul, the Jewish remnant (11.1-7; cf. 9.6) includes those who embody what Israel is meant to be, because of their participation in the christian community undergirded by God's grace. The remnant concept evident in *4 Ezra*, however, is quite different. There the remnant (the few, those who remain) are not portrayed as a community *per se*, and especially not a community undergirded by God's grace.[1] Instead, 'the remnant' is the collective term applied to those few individuals who merit eschatological salvation by their own stringent efforts in obedience to the law. In both Romans 1–11 and *4 Ezra*, the concept of (true) 'Israel' is (initially) reduced to a remnant, but the character of that remnant is at variance in each presentation.

Second, after narrowing the concept of (true) Israel to a remnant, both authors broaden the concept of Israel to include a much larger group once again. Paul argues a case throughout Rom. 1.16–11.10 that God's righteousness is not negated by the fact that only some of Israel (the remnant) have believed in the Messiah. Nonetheless, Paul puts a different perspective on things in 11.11-32, demonstrating a dimension of salvation history which his earlier case did not touch on (except in 3.1-8, where he left it inchoate). In 11.11-32, Paul shows how unbelieving Israel perform a function within the process of salvation history—a function in line with their election by God whereby he (the potter) uses them (a part of the clay) for his purposes to bestow his mercy on all humanity. Their temporary displacement does not entail their ultimate rejection; instead, it is an outworking of their calling (cf. 9.22-24)—a calling which is incontrovertible (11.28-29) and which assures their ultimate salvation (11.26). His argument in 11.11-32 is not necessary to the case which precedes it in 1.16–11.10, but it demonstrates Paul's dissatisfaction at the prospect of leaving 'Israel' (in the sense of *true* Israel) as only a small remnant; in the end, 'Israel' will embrace both the remnant and those Jews outside the remnant.

The author of *4 Ezra* maintains that only a few out of all the people are righteous. Like Paul, he too argues that this does not negate God's righteousness; the fault lies not with God but with the people them-

---

1. If *4 Ezra* was intended as a piece of community 'evangelization', such a community is barely evident throughout the pages, and its inner cohesion would result from phenomena other than the notion of divine grace.

selves (cf. Uriel in 7.19-25, and the transformed Ezra in 9.30-37 and 14.28-31). Nonetheless, the author expects salvation to be enjoyed by an innumerable group consisting not only of the few but also of the ten tribes who were preserved in another land (13.39-47). The final constituency of eschatological Israel, then, is not just the 'remnant' from within the two tribes but a magnificent twelve-tribe conglomerate. One suspects, however, that the author is simply posturing on this score in order to root his innovation more firmly in traditional expectations, or, restated, to protect the righteousness of God in a way which the rest of his case could not. The salvation of a twelve-tribe entity offers no reprieve to 'all the people', who remain in their ignorance, destined for destruction. In this regard, the author's description of the twelve-tribe entity of eschatological salvation is somewhat feeble, transparent and unconvincing, at least from our 'detached' point of view. Paul too may be guilty of posturing somewhat in Rom. 11.11-32, but he does seem to have integrated his argument there more successfully into his larger case than does the author of *4 Ezra* at 13.39-47.

A word must be included about naming the 'patterns of religion' observed herein. It has been argued that both authors are discontent with traditional ethnocentric definitions of the covenant. Paul's gospel has the effect of removing the adjective 'ethnocentric' while keeping a type of covenant structure;[1] God's initiating grace offsets the anthropological condition of sin for those who bear the mark of covenant membership, faith. Although Paul does not make much use of the term 'covenant' in Romans 1–11,[2] a covenant perspective gives his case coherence at every point. What he ends up with we call *christocentric* covenantalism—'christocentric' in that faith in Christ excludes the salvific import of ethnic practices. Nonetheless, even this christocentric covenantalism contains within it an ethnic (as opposed to 'ethnocentric') clause: all Israel plays a part in salvation history and will be saved as the final stage of the process. Moreover, even in this christocentric covenantalism, Paul cannot bring himself to renounce the law; legitimating his definition of the community of christian believers is what Paul calls the 'law of faith', the 'law of the Spirit of

1. Cf. Wright: 'Paul, in rejecting the *nationalist* view of the covenant, does not reject covenant theology itself' (1982: 14).
2. διαθήκη is found only in 9.4 (plural) and 11.27 (quoting Scripture), and both times it has reference to ethnic Israel.

life'—that is, something like 'the law given by God to promote faith in Christ apart from ethnocentric works within the boundaries of the eschatological age'. Thus, when writing to the Roman christian communities, Paul takes great pains to ensure that his case does not repudiate the covenant of Israel's history. Contrary to Sanders's insistence, Paul did *not deny* the 'two pillars common to all forms of Judaism: the election of Israel and faithfulness to the Mosaic law'.[1] Granted, Paul has profoundly *revalued* the significance of these 'pillars'; nonetheless, they remain significant aspects of his case. Paul's redefinition of them only testifies to the diversity within Early Judaism (cf. §1.3). I cannot speak, then, as Sanders does in the conclusions to his study, of 'Paul and the Break with Judaism',[2] nor, as V.P. Furnish does, of 'Paul's conversion to Christianity...*from* Judaism'.[3] If the term 'conversion' is used with reference to Paul, it must be done with historically sensitive care in order to do full justice to the way Paul himself viewed his own efforts. Paul, it seems, wanted to insist that the communities which he was founding were the embodiment of what God, who long ago revealed himself on Mt Sinai to the Jewish people, intended the covenant community to be in the eschatological age; those communities, then, represent for Paul the 'full flowering' of Judaism. His argument in Romans 1–11 is carried out with this demonstration in view, as he revalued the covenant in the light of the eschatological Christ-event.

In the case of *4 Ezra*, a definitional label is harder to obtain. What transpires looks more like an individualistic legalism than anything else—'individualistic' in that a community dynamic is (almost?) absent from the text,[4] and 'legalism' in that, for all intents and purposes, God's grace is removed from the scene altogether, the onus being placed on individuals to forge their own salvation by works apart from a community identity. Nonetheless, the author dresses up his innovation with the garb of covenantalism, perhaps even an ethnocentric covenantalism; that is, he would argue that his case upholds the

---

1. 1983a: 208.
2. 1983a: 207-10.
3. 1989: 338, emphasis his.
4. The individual is not urged to remain with or join the remnant community wherein is salvation, for there is no obvious community referred to in the text. As Meeks says, *4 Ezra* comes close to 'personal salvation' (1986: 95). Cf. Kolenkow: 'What one sees in *4 Ezra*. . . may be called salvation in the private sphere. . . *4 Ezra* emphasizes the possibility of ascetics saving themselves' (1982: 249).

grace of God (but only as an eschatological reflex to human merit), the law as the divine standard of judgment (apart from divine grace), and the salvation of a twelve-tribe Israel (although that translates into very little salvific hope for 'all the people'). But the system into which the author drops these characteristics is about as foreign to their traditional context as can be imagined; divine grace and the salvation of a twelve-tribe Israel are better understood as legitimating posturings rather than the core of his perspective.

Finally, four implications of this study may be in order concerning the character of Early Judaism and the relation of these authors to it. First, it needs to be said that if Paul's letters and *4 Ezra* represent exceptions to a generally predominant 'pattern of religion', they are exceptions which help to prove the rule. That is, these works give indication that ethnocentric covenantalism (cf. Sanders's 'covenantal nomism') *was* prevalent in Early Judaism; in fact, the author of *4 Ezra* characterizes it as being shared by 'all the people'. Whereas other Jewish works indicate the various ways in which ethnocentric covenantalism took form in various situations, *4 Ezra* and Paul's letters (especially Romans and Galatians) are exceptional in their attempts to undermine such a system (ethnocentrism) altogether.

Second, it is telling to notice the techniques whereby ethnocentric covenantalism is discredited in Romans 1–11 and *4 Ezra*. Paul's extended 'attack' upon ethnocentrism is found in Romans 2. Therein, his technique is to extrapolate principles which were common in Early Judaism and to apply them in a new manner (e.g. the impartiality, kindness and judgment of God, salvation by works). This is fair enough; Paul has every right to perceive principles in a new fashion (appealing to divine revelation as the basis for his new perception, 1.17-18; 3.21a). However, the point is that in his attempt to discredit the ethnocentrism of 'the Jew', Paul does not do full justice to the prevalent convictions of his Jewish contemporaries. 'The Jew' who appears in that context is a sort of 'man of straw' who is never quite allowed to speak for himself, and so his position is naturally shown to be indefensible. Paul is not to be faulted for this; such is the nature of polemic. (The same thing is noticeable, for instance, in the letter of James, where a 'Pauline' position seems to be set up in order to be knocked down [Jas 2.14-26].[1]) The point to notice is that, for whatever

---

1. Cf. Hengel, 1987.

reason, Paul never really comes to grips with the ethnocentric covenantalism against which he launches so many arguments.

In *4 Ezra*, conversely, ethnocentric covenantalism *is* given a fairly honest voice in Ezra's initial speeches of Episodes I–III. But as a result, the author (speaking through Uriel) has no rational arsenal against it; it is simply wrong. He has one reason why it is wrong (it does not explain God's ways) but that reason is mediated by means of eschatological description and apocalyptic revelation rather than logical deduction. This partially explains the great length of the dialogues and their open-ended closure; Ezra was looking for rational solutions to explain his dilemma, but none was satisfactory, and he remained unconvinced by rational persuasion (cf. 9.14). His 'conversion', then, takes place outside the context of argumentative debate. In fact, it is not even recorded for the reader; Ezra simply appears in Episode IV a transformed character. It might be supposed that the author knew of no way to transcend the traditional mindset by means of rational deductions. He simply knew that such had to be done.

Taken together, then, these two texts give evidence of the cohesion and compellingness of the system of *ethnocentric* covenantalism. One author (Paul) mounts argument after argument against it but, from my perspective, fails to orchestrate an ultimately convincing rebuttal of it *for its own sake*.[1] The other (the author of *4 Ezra*) portrays it in its own terms, but then has no real arguments to level against it. It is little wonder, then, that Paul's career seems to have been plagued by the constant blockages erected by unconvinced Jewish believers and their gentile sympathizers; and it is little wonder that the author of *2 Baruch* (writing after *4 Ezra*, we think) found the need to offset the idiosyncracies of *4 Ezra*, placing the events of 70 CE once again within the context of a confident ethnocentric covenantalism.[2] Neither Paul nor the author of *4 Ezra* did much to *prove* that ethnocentric covenantalism was wrong; they simply believed that such had to be the case in the light of their respective crisis events.

Third, if it can be said that the notion of divine grace is the foundation for Jewish practice and theological reflection in Early Judaism and in emerging rabbinic Judaism (as Sanders and Segal argue[3]), this notion is shared wholly by Paul, but not by the author of *4 Ezra*

---

1. The italicized words make up an important qualification.
2. Cf. Sayler, 1984; Murphy, 1985; Willett, 1989: 77-125.
3. Sanders, 1977: 33-288; *idem*, 1980; Segal, 1985. Cf. Rowland, 1985: 25.

(except as an eschatological concept which has been redefined to the point of losing all salvific substance). On this score, then, Paul is a better representative of the prevailing ethos within Judaism, despite his untypical definition of the covenant. On the other hand, if it can be said that 'Judaism was. . . much less concerned about "right *belief*" than about "accepted *practice*"',[1] then, on this score, Paul is representative of very little within Early Judaism. Conversely, despite the idiosyncratic perspective of the author of *4 Ezra*, one can expect that his practice remained within the bounds of acceptable praxis in Early Judaism and nascent Rabbinic Judaism; there is little indication to the contrary. All in all, then, the theological innovations of these two first-century Jews help to contribute to our understanding of the diversity of Early Judaism.

In this way, the two authors, writing twenty-five to thirty years or so after their respective crisis events, demonstrate something of the direction of the Judaisms which they represent—on the one hand, the need of the christian movement to work out its self-identity in the light of its ever-increasing gentile constituency, and, on the other hand, the post-destruction rabbinic concern to regulate more specifically what faithfulness to the law entailed without recourse to the temple. For its part, the christian movement would develop along the 'universal' side of Paul's case while all too often neglecting the 'ethnic' component of his case. For its part, the rabbinic movement shared the concern of the author of *4 Ezra* for exactitude in practice, although, if Sanders and Segal are correct, that movement tended not to share a legalistic motivation with the author of *4 Ezra*.

Fourth, one final observation should be registered. Mention has already been made of the manner in which both authors allow the anthropological condition of sin to overrun ethnocentric covenantalism; the encyclopaedic problem means that the people of Israel cannot rest on their ethnic laurels for salvation. Paul does not introduce a new anthropological understanding on this point; he leaves intact the notion of universal sinfulness and replaces an ethnocentric solution with a christocentric solution. We may ask of him, then, why one solution is structurally any better than the other? Could not ethnocentric Jews have argued that if the human condition of sin is used to undermine their perspective, it can be used just as well to undermine Paul's case? Unless Paul is willing to insist that sin is altogether for-

---

1. Russell, 1967: 155. Cf. Urbach, 1981: 289, 292-93.

eign to christian existence (which he is not willing to do; cf. Gal. 5.17; 6.1), may not Paul's criticisms of 'the Jew' in Romans 2 be returned to him with the same amount of polemical 'spin' to discredit his own solution? The fact that Paul thinks of sin as *a power* from which believers are to be released (despite the inevitable transgression) does not dispel this possibility, since Paul's argument in 2.1–3.20 operates on the presupposition that transgression is itself evidence of the fact that 'the Jew' is 'under (the power of) sin' (3.9). No doubt, Paul would not allow the same presupposition to be used against his own case.[1] Judging from his comments in 3.5-8, 6.1 and 6.15, however, something of the sort seems to have happened in response to his case by other believers who accused him of promoting ethical libertinism and antinomianism. Evidently, then, in the process of christian self-definition, polemical arguments were being thrown back and forth which followed similar lines, despite their different points of origin within the christian movement. This phenomenon seems to have been facilitated by the fact that the Jewish commonplace of human sinfulness remained a commonplace within christian redefinitions of God's covenant mercy.

The author of *4 Ezra*, however, sidesteps this arena of debate, but only by allowing an exception clause to modify the human dilemma: a few manage to escape the anthropological condition of sin. Since divine grace is excluded from the scene, salvation must be by human effort with the hope of transcending the otherwise all-encompassing condition. Here is a radical anthropology which is able to transcend the kind of polemic evident between Paul and his 'opponents', but its radicalness is achieved at the expense of the notion of divine mercy.

The point, then, is this. In the christian movement, because traditional views on anthropology were retained (at least on the point under discussion here), so too was the traditional solution retained: divine grace. How that grace is mediated was not so obvious within the movement, facilitating the inevitable disputes concerning the identity markers and social make-up of the new movement. In *4 Ezra*, however, a new view on anthropology is arrived at which allows for an obvious solution (perfection by works), but only by negating, for all intents and purposes, the notion of divine grace (and community self-definition).

---

1. Cf. Räisänen: 'Paul has double standards when evaluating Jewish and Christian transgressions respectively' (1983: 100; cf. 117, 148-49).

15.2. *Summary*

This project has traced the cases of two pious Jews in provocative re-evaluation of the covenant *vis-à-vis* the eschatological insight afforded them. For each, their respective experiences of crisis so profoundly shaped their outlook that they discarded prevalent traditions, which they previously had embraced, and adopted new understandings of salvation which they thought to be properly aligned with the eschatological ways of God. Neither author considered his case to entail a rejection of YHWH; neither abandoned the conviction that the God who revealed himself on Mt Sinai was altogether righteous. If traditional Jewish covenantalism did not explain the ways of God adequately, another perspective was necessary, for the righteousness of God could not be doubted. If God's actions did not match the traditional understanding of his ways, the former was not to be questioned, but the latter.

What animates Romans 1–11 and *4 Ezra* is primarily the repudiation of Jewish ethnocentrism and, consequently, the revaluation of the law and the people of God. We do well to recall S. Sandmel's appropriate characterization of common Jewish conviction: 'Israel and the Torah constituted a blended entity; without Israel the Torah had no significance, and without the Torah Israel had no uniqueness'.[1] It is this conviction with which both Paul and the author of *4 Ezra* grapple as they attempt to reconcile their own 'crisis' experiences with the conviction that YHWH is a righteous God. It is this inseparable bond between the ethnic people and the law which they are forced to break, or at least redefine, thereby rendering God's ways free from ethnocentrism. Their writings illustrate the extremes to which each had to go in order to accomplish this task in the light of contemporary understandings of the law and the people of God.

---

1. 1978: 182.

BIBLIOGRAPHY

1. *Texts and Translations*

The Armenian Version of IV Ezra (trans. M. Stone; UPATS, 1; Missoula, MT: Scholars Press, 1979).

Biblica Hebraica Stuttgartensia (ed. K. Elliger and W. Rudolph; Stuttgart: Deutsche Bibelgesellschaft, 1967–77, 1983).

The Dead Sea Scrolls in English (trans. G. Vermes; 2nd edn; Harmondsworth: Penguin Books, 1975).

'4 Esdras' in *The Old Testament in Syriac according to the Peshitta Version, Part 4: Apocalypse of Baruch, 4 Esdras* (ed. R.J. Bidawid; Leiden: Brill, 1973).

The Greek New Testament (ed. K. Aland, M. Black, C.M. Martini, B.M. Metzger, and A. Wikgren; 3rd edn; New York: United Bible Society, 1975).

Josephus (ed. H.St.J. Thackeray, R. Marcus *et al.;* Loeb Classical Library; 9 vols.; London: Heinemann, 1926–65).

Der lateinische Text der Apokalypse des Esra (ed. A.F.J. Klijn; Berlin: Akademie Verlag, 1983).

The Old Testament Pseudepigrapha (ed. J.H. Charlesworth; 2 vols.; Garden City: Doubleday, 1983, 1985).

Philo (ed. F.H. Colson, G.H. Whitaker *et al.*; Loeb Classical Library; 12 vols.; London: Heinemann, 1929–53).

Psalms of Solomon (ed. H.E. Ryle and M.R. James; Cambridge: Cambridge University Press, 1891).

Septuaginta (ed. A. Rahlfs; 2 vols.; Stuttgart: Württembergische Bibelanstalt, 1962).

Die Texte aus Qumran: Hebräisch und Deutsch (ed. E. Lohse; Munich: Kösel, 1971).

The Mishnah: Translated from the Hebrew with Introduction and Brief Explanatory Notes, by H. Danby (London: Oxford University Press, 1933).

2. *Secondary Literature*

Aageson, J.W.
  1986   'Scripture and Structure in the Development of the Argument in Romans 9–11', *CBQ* 48, pp. 265-89.
  1987   'Typology, Correspondence and the Application of Scripture in Romans 9–11', *JSNT* 31, pp. 51-72.
Alexander, P.S.
  1988   'Retelling the Old Testament', in *It is Written: Scripture Citing Scripture. Essays in Honour of Barnabas Lindars, SSF* (ed. D.A. Carson and H.G.M. Williamson; Cambridge: Cambridge University Press), pp. 99-121.

Badenas, R.
   1985   *Christ the End of the Law: Romans 10.4 in Pauline Perspective* (JSNTS, 10; Sheffield: JSOT Press).
Barclay, J.
   1988   *Obeying the Truth: A Study of Paul's Ethics in Galatians* (Edinburgh: T. & T. Clark).
Barth, M.
   1974   *Ephesians* (2 vols.; Garden City: Doubleday).
Barrett, C.K.
   1957   *A Commentary on the Epistle to the Romans* (London: A. & C. Black).
   1977   'Rom 9:30–10:21: Fall and Responsibility in Israel', in *Die Israelfrage nach Rom 9–11* (ed. L. de Lorenzi; Rome: St Paul Abbey), pp. 99-121.
Bassler, J.M.
   1982   *Divine Impartiality: Paul and a Theological Axiom* (SBLDS, 59; Chico, CA: Scholars Press).
   1984   'Divine Impartiality in Paul's Letter to the Romans', *NovT* 26, pp. 43-58.
Baxter, A.G., and J.A. Ziesler
   1985   'Paul and Aboriculture: Romans 11.17-24', *JSNT* 24, pp. 25-32.
Beale, G.K.
   1984   *The Use of Daniel in Jewish Apocalyptic Literature and in the Revelation of St. John* (London: University Press of America).
Beker, J.C.
   1980   *Paul the Apostle: The Triumph of God in Life and Thought* (Edinburgh: T. & T. Clark).
   1986   'The Faithfulness of God and the Priority of Israel in Paul's Letter to the Romans', in *Christians among Jews and Gentiles* (ed. G.W.E. Nickelsburg and G.W. MacRae; Philadelphia: Fortress Press), pp. 10-16.
Berlin, A.
   1983   *Poetics and Interpretation of Biblical Narrative* (BLS, 9; Sheffield: Almond Press).
Bickermann, E.
   1979   *The God of the Maccabees: Studies on the Meaning and Origin of the Maccabean Revolt* (trans. H.R. Moehring; Leiden: Brill).
Bidawid, R.J.
   1973   '4 Esdras', in *The Old Testament in Syriac according to the Peshitta Version, Part 4: Apocalypse of Baruch, 4 Esdras* (Leiden: Brill).
Black, M.
   1973   *Romans* (NCB; London: Oliphants).
Blenkinsopp, J.
   1981   'Interpretation and the Tendency to Sectarianism: An Aspect of Second Temple History', in *Jewish and Christian Self-Definition*, vol. II: *Aspects of Judaism in the Greco-Roman Period* (ed. E.P. Sanders, with A.I. Baumgarten and A. Mendelson; Philadelphia: Fortress Press), pp. 1-26.
Boers, H.W.
   1988   'The Foundation of Paul's Thought: A Methodological Investigation—The Problem of the Coherent Center of Paul's Thought', *ST* 42, pp. 55-68.
Borgen, P.
   1983   'Paul Preaches Circumcision and Pleases Men', in *idem, Paul Preaches Circumcision and Pleases Men* (Trondheim: Tapir), pp. 33-43.
Bornkamm, G.
   1963   'Gesetz und Natur (Röm 2,14-16)', in *Studien zu Antike und Urchristentum: Gesammelte Aufsätze II* (BEvTh, 28; Munich: Chr. Kaiser Verlag), pp. 93-118.

1969   'Sin, Law and Death: An Exegetical Study of Romans 7', in *Early Christian Experience* (trans. P.L. Hammer; London: Harper & Row), pp. 87-104.
1971   *Paul* (trans. D.M.G. Stalker; London: Hodder & Stoughton).
1977   'The Letter to the Romans as Paul's Last Will and Testament', in *The Romans Debate* (ed. K.P. Donfried; Minneapolis: Augsburg), pp. 17-31.

Bousset, W.
1926   *Die Religion des Judentums im späthellenistischen Zeitalter* (3rd edn; ed. H. Gressmann; Tübingen: J.C.B. Mohr).

Boyarin, D.
1972   'Penitential Liturgy in 4 Ezra', *JSJ* 3, pp. 30-34.

Box, G.H.
1912   *The Ezra-Apocalypse* (London: Pitman & Sons).

Brandenburger, E.
1962   *Adam und Christ: exegetisch-religionsgeschichtliche Untersuchungen zu Rom 5,12-21 (1 Kor 15)* (WMANT, 7; Neukirchen-Vluyn: Neukirchener Verlag).
1981   *Die Verborgenheit Gottes im Weltgeschehen: Das literarische und theologische Problem des 4. Esra Buches* (Zürich: Theologischer Verlag).

Breech, E.
1973   'These Fragments I have Shored against my Ruins: The Form and Function of 4 Ezra', *JBL* 92, pp. 267-74.

Bring, R.
1971   'Paul and the Old Testament: A Study of the Ideas of Election, Faith, and Law in Paul, with Special Reference to Rom. 9.30–10.13', *ST* 25, pp. 21-60.

Brockington, L.H.
1961   *A Critical Introduction to the Apocrypha* (London: Duckworth).

Broyles, C.C.
1989   *The Conflict of Faith and Experience in the Psalms: A Form-Critical and Theological Study* (JSOTS, 52; Sheffield: JSOT Press).

Buchanan, G.W.
1970   *The Consequences of the Covenant* (NovTSup, 20; Leiden: Brill).

Bultmann, R.
1910   *Der Stil der paulinischen Predigt und die kynisch-stoische Diatribe* (FRLANT, 13; Göttingen: Vandenhoeck & Ruprecht).
1952   *Theology of the New Testament* (trans. K. Grobel; 2 vols.; London: SCM Press).
1955   'Christ the End of the Law', in *Essays Philosophical and Theological* (trans. J.C.G. Grieg; London: SCM Press), pp. 36-66.
1956   *Primitive Christianity in its Contemporary Setting* (trans. R.H. Fuller; Philadelphia: Fortress Press).
1967   'Glossen im Römerbrief', in *Exegetica: Aufsätze zur Erforschung des Neuen Testaments* (ed. E. Dinkler; Tübingen: J.C.B. Mohr [Paul Siebeck]), pp. 278-84.

Burkitt, F.C.
1914   *Jewish and Christian Apocalypses* (London).

Byrne, B.
1979   *'Sons of God—Seed of Abraham': A Study of the Idea of the Sonship of God of All Christians in Paul against the Jewish Background* (Analecta Biblica, 83; Rome: Biblical Institute Press).

Campbell, D.H.
1980   'The Identity of ἐγώ in Romans 7:7-25', in *Studia Biblica 1978: III. Papers on Paul and Other New Testament Authors. Sixth International Congress on Bibli-*

cal Studies. Oxford, April 1978 (ed. E.A. Livingstone; JSNTS, 3; Sheffield: JSOT Press), pp. 51-64.

Campbell, W.S.
1980 'Christ the End of the Law: Romans 10:4', in *Studia Biblica 1978: III. Papers on Paul and Other New Testament Authors. Sixth International Congress on Biblical Studies. Oxford, April 1978* (ed. E.A. Livingstone; JSNTS, 3; Sheffield: JSOT Press), pp. 73-81.
1981a 'Romans III as a Key to the Structure and Thought of the Letter', *NovT* 23, pp. 22-40.
1981b 'The Freedom and Faithfulness of God in Relation to Israel', *JSNT* 13, pp. 27-45.
1988 'Did Paul Advocate Separation from the Synagogue?', cited from proofs.

Charles, R.H.
1896 *The Apocalypse of Baruch* (London: SPCK).

Charlesworth, J.H.
1979a 'A History of Pseudepigraphic Research: The Re-Emerging Importance of the Pseudepigrapha', *Aufstieg und Niedergang der römischen Welt*, II.19.1 (ed. W. Haase; Berlin & New York: de Gruyter), pp. 54-88.
1979b Review of A.L. Thompson, *Responsibility for Evil in the Theodicy of IV Ezra*, *JBL* 98, pp. 465-67.
1985a 'Prayer of Manasseh', in *Old Testament Pseudepigrapha*, vol. II (ed. J.H. Charlesworth; London: Darton, Longman & Todd), pp. 625-37.
1985b 'The Triumphant Majority as Seen by a Dwindled Minority: The Outsider according to the Insider of the Jewish Apocalypses', in *'To See Ourselves as Others See Us': Christians, Jews, 'Others' in Late Antiquity* (ed. J. Neusner and E.S. Frerichs; Chico, CA: Scholars Press), pp. 285-316.
1987 'From Jewish Messianology to Christian Christology: Some Caveats and Perspectives', in *Judaisms and their Messiahs* (ed. J. Neusner, W.S. Green and E. Frerichs; Cambridge: Cambridge University Press), pp. 225-64.
1988 *Jesus within Judaism: New Light from Exciting Archaeological Discoveries* (New York: Doubleday).

Cohen, S.J.D.
1987 *From the Maccabees to the Mishnah* (LEC; Philadelphia: Westminster Press).

Collins, J.J.
1974 'The Symbolism of Transcendence in Jewish Apocalyptic,' *BR* 19, pp. 5-22.
1984a *The Apocalyptic Imagination: An Introduction to the Jewish Matrix of Christianity* (New York: Crossroad).
1984b *Daniel, with an Introduction to Apocalyptic Literature* (FOTL, 20; Grand Rapids: Eerdmans).
1985 'A Symbol of Otherness: Circumcision and Salvation in the First Century', in *'To See Ourselves as Others See Us': Christians, Jews, 'Others' in Late Antiquity* (ed. J. Neusner and E.S. Frerichs; Chico, CA: Scholars Press), pp. 163-86.

Cook, J.E.
1988 'Ezra's Confession: Appeal to a Merciful God', *JSP* 3, pp. 89-100.

Cranfield, C.E.B.
1975a *The Epistle to the Romans* (2 vols.; ICC; Edinburgh: T. & T. Clark).
1975b 'Some Notes on Romans 9:30-33', in *Jesus und Paulus: Festschrift W.G. Kümmel* (ed. E.E. Ellis and E. Grässer; Göttingen: Vandenhoeck & Ruprecht), pp. 35-43.

Dahl, N.
 1977   *Studies in Paul: Theology for the Early Christian Mission* (Minneapolis: Augsburg).
Davies, W.D.
 1980   *Paul and Rabbinic Judaism: Some Rabbinic Elements in Pauline Theology* (Philadelphia: Fortress Press; orig. pub. 1948).
 1984a   'Law in First-Century Judaism', in *Jewish and Pauline Studies* (Philadelphia: Fortress Press), pp. 3-26.
 1984b   'Paul and the Law: Reflections on Pitfalls in Interpretation', in *Jewish and Pauline Studies*, pp. 91-122.
 1984c   'Paul and the People of Israel', in *Jewish and Pauline Studies*, pp. 123-53.
Deidun, T.J.
 1981   *New Covenant Morality in Paul* (AnalBibl, 89; Rome: Biblical Institute Press).
Derrett, J.D.M.
 1970   *Law in the New Testament* (London: Darton, Longman & Todd).
Dodd, C.H.
 1932   *The Epistle of Paul to the Romans* (London: Hodder & Stoughton).
Doeve, J.W.
 1953   'Some Notes with Reference to TA ΛΟΓΙΑ ΤΟΥ ΘΕΟΥ in Romans 3:2', in *Studia Paulina in honorem J. de Zwaan* (ed. J.N. Sevenster and W.C. van Unnik; Haarlem: Bohn), pp. 111-23.
Donaldson, T.L.
 1989   'Zealot and Convert: The Origin of Paul's Christ–Torah Antithesis', *CBQ* 51, pp. 655-82.
Drane, J.W.
 1975   *Paul: Libertine or Legalist? A Study in the Major Pauline Epistles* (London: SPCK).
Dugandžic, I.
 1977   *Das 'Ja' Gottes in Christus: Eine Studie zur Bedeutung des Alten Testament für das Christusverständnis des Paulus* (Würzburg).
Dunn, J.D.G.
 1975   'Romans 7:14-25 in the Theology of Paul', *TZ* 31, pp. 257-73.
 1977   *Unity and Diversity in the New Testament: An Inquiry into the Character of Earliest Christianity* (Philadelphia: Westminster; London: SCM Press).
 1980   *Christology in the Making: An Inquiry into the Origins of the Doctrine of the Incarnation* (London: SCM Press).
 1983   'The New Perspective on Paul', *BJRL* 65 (1983), pp. 95-122.
 1985   'Works of the Law and the Curse of the Law (Galatians 3.10-14)', *NTS* 31, pp. 523-42.
 1987a   ' "Righteousness from the Law" and "Righteousness from Faith": Paul's Interpretation of Scripture in Romans 10:1-10', in *Tradition and Interpretation in the New Testament* (ed. G.F. Hawthorne with O. Betz; Grand Rapids: Eerdmans), pp. 216-28.
 1987b   ' "A Light to the Gentiles": The Significance of the Damascus Road Christophany for Paul', in *The Glory of Christ in the New Testament: Studies in Memory of G.B. Caird* (ed. L.D. Hurst and N.T. Wright; Oxford: Clarendon Press), pp. 251-66.
 1988a   *Romans* (WBC, 38; Dallas: Word Books).
 1988b   'Pharisees, Sinners, and Jesus', in *The Social World of Formative Christianity and Judaism* (ed. P. Borgen, J. Neusner et al.; Philadelphia: Fortress Press), pp. 264-89.

Ellis, E.E.
    1957   *Paul's Use of the Old Testament* (Grand Rapids: Eerdmans).
Espy, J.M.
    1985   'Paul's "Robust Conscience" Re-Examined', *NTS* 31, pp. 161-88.
Evans, C.A.
    1984   'Paul and the Hermeneutics of "True Prophecy": A Study of Romans 9–11', *Bib* 65, pp. 560-70.
Evans, C.R.
    1989   *To See and Not Perceive: Isaiah 6.9-10 in Early Jewish and Christian Interpretation* (JSOTS, 64; Sheffield: JSOT Press).
Ferch, A.J.
    1977   'The Two Aeons and the Messiah in Pseudo-Philo, 4 Ezra and 2 Baruch', *AUSS* 15, pp. 135-51.
Franklyn, P.N.
    1987   'The Cultic and Pious Climax of Eschatology in the Psalms of Solomon', *JSJ* 18, pp. 1-17.
Friedrich, G.
    1954   'Das Gesetz des Glaubens, Röm 3,27', *TZ* 10, 401-17.
Furnish, V.P.
    1989   'Pauline Studies', in *The New Testament and its Modern Interpreters* (ed. E.J. Epp and G.W. MacRae; Philadelphia: Fortress; Atlanta: Scholars Press), pp. 321-50.
Gager, J.G.
    1981   'Some Notes on Paul's Conversion', *NTS* 27, pp. 697-704.
    1985   *The Origins of Anti-Semitism: Attitudes toward Judaism in Pagan and Christian Antiquity* (Oxford: Oxford University Press).
Garlington, D.
    1990a   *The Obedience of Faith: A Pauline Phrase in Historical Context* (WMANT, 2.38; Tübingen: J.C.B. Mohr [Paul Siebeck]).
    1990b   'ΙΕΡΟΣΥΛΕΙΝ and the Idolatry of Israel (Romans 2.22)', *NTS* 36, pp. 142-51.
Gaston, L.
    1987   *Paul and the Torah* (Vancouver: University of British Columbia Press).
Getty, M.A.
    1988   'Paul and the Salvation of Israel: A Perspective on Romans 9–11', *CBQ* 50, pp. 456-69.
Grabbe, L.L.
    1989   'The Social Setting of Early Jewish Apocalypticism', *JSP* 4, pp. 27-47.
Gray, M.L.
    1976   'Towards the Reconstruction of 4 Esdras and the Establishment of its Contemporary Setting' (Oxford University: unpublished B.Litt. thesis).
Green, W.S.
    1985   'Otherness Within: Towards a Theory of Difference in Rabbinic Judaism', in *'To See Ourselves as Others See Us': Christians, Jews, 'Others' in Late Antiquity* (ed. J. Neusner and E.S. Frerichs; Chico, CA: Scholars Press), pp. 49-69.
Gruenwald, I.
    1973   'Knowledge and Vision: Towards a Clarification of Two "Gnostic" Concepts in the Light of their Alleged Origins', *IOS* 3, pp. 63-107.
    1979   'Jewish Apocalyptic Literature', in *Aufstieg und Niedergang der römischen Welt*, II.19.1 (ed. W. Haase; Berlin & New York: de Gruyter), pp. 89-118.
    1980   *Apocalyptic and Merkavah Mysticism* (Leiden: Brill).

Grundmann, W., with G. Quell, G. Bertram and G. Stählin
  1964 'ἁμαρτάνω, ἁμάρτημα, ἁμαρτία', in *Theological Dictionary of the New Testament* (ed. G. Kittel, trans. G.W. Bromiley; Grand Rapids: Eerdmans), pp. 267-316.

Guignebert, C.
  1939 *The Jewish World in the Time of Jesus* (trans. S.H. Hooke; London: Kegan Paul, Trench, Trubner & Co.).

Gundry, R.
  1980 'The Moral Frustration of Paul before his Conversion: Sexual Lust in Romans 7:7-25', in *Pauline Studies: Essays Presented to Professor F.F. Bruce on his 70th Birthday* (ed. D.A. Hagner and M.J. Harris; Grand Rapids: Eerdmans; Exeter: Paternoster Press), pp. 228-45.
  1985 'Grace, Works and Staying Saved in Paul', *Bib* 66, pp. 1-38.

Gunkel, H.
  1900 'Das vierte Buch Esra', in *Die Apokryphen und Pseudepigraphen des Alten Testaments*, vol. II (ed. E. Kautzsch; Tübingen: J.C.B. Mohr), pp. 331-401.

Guthrie, D.
  1969 *Galatians* (NCB; London: Thomas Nelson & Sons).

Güttgemanns, E.
  1971 'Heilsgeschichte bei Paulus oder Dynamik des Evangeliums; zur strukturellen Relevanz von Röm 9–11 für die Theologie des Römerbriefes', in *Studia linguistica neotestamentica* (Munich: Chr. Kaiser Verlag), pp. 34-58.

Hagner, D.A.
  1980 'Paul in Modern Jewish Thought', in *Pauline Studies: Essays Presented to F.F. Bruce* (ed. D.A. Hagner and M.J. Harris; Exeter: Paternoster Press; Grand Rapids: Eerdmans), pp. 143-65.

Hahn, F.
  1976 'Das Gesetzesverständnis im Römer- und Galaterbrief', *ZNW* 67, pp. 29-63.
  1982 'Zum Verständnis von Römer 11.26a: ". . . und so wird ganz Israel gerettet werden"', in *Paul and Paulinism: Essays in Honour of C.K. Barrett* (ed. M.D. Hooker and S.G. Wilson; London: SPCK), pp. 221-34.

Hall, D.R.
  1983 'Romans 3.1-8 Reconsidered', *NTS* 29, pp. 183-97.

Hann, R.R.
  1988 'The Community of the Pious: The Social Setting of the Psalms of Solomon', *SR* 17, pp. 169-89.

Harnisch, W.
  1969 *Verhängnis und Verheissung der Geschichte* (FRLANT, 97; Göttingen: Vandenhoeck & Ruprecht).
  1981 'Die Ironie der Offenbarung: Exegetische Erwägungen zur Zionvision im 4. Buch Esra', in *SBL 1981 Seminar Papers* (ed. K.H. Richards; Chico, CA: Scholars Press), pp. 79-104.
  1983 'Der Prophet als Widerpart und Zeuge der Offenbarung: Erwägungen zur Interdependenz von Form und Sache im IV. Buch Esra', in *Apocalypticism in the Mediterranean World and the Near East: Proceedings of the International Colloquium on Apocalypticism. Uppsala, August 12-17, 1979* (ed. D. Hellholm; Tübingen: J.C.B. Mohr [Paul Siebeck]), pp. 461-93.

Harrelson, W.
  1980 'Ezra among the Wicked in 2 Esdras 3–10', in *The Divine Helmsman: Studies on God's Control of Human Events, Presented to Lou H. Silberman* (ed. J.L. Crenshaw and S. Sandmel; New York: Ktav), pp. 21-40.

Harrington, D.
1980   *God's People in Christ* (Philadelphia: Fortress Press).

Hayman, A.P.
1975   'The Problem of Pseudonymity in the Ezra Apocalypse', *JSJ* 6, pp. 47-56.

Hayward, R.
1990   'The Vine and its Products as Theological Symbols in First Century Palestinian Judaism', *DUJ* 82, pp. 9-18; cited from the author's manuscript.

Hays, R.B.
1983   *The Faith of Jesus Christ: An Investigation of the Narrative Substructure of Galatians 3:1–4:11* (SBLDS, 56; Chico, CA: Scholars Press).
1989   '"The Righteous One" as Eschatological Deliverer: A Case Study in Paul's Apocalyptic Hermeneutic', in *Apocalyptic and the New Testament* (ed. J. Marcus and M.L. Soards; Sheffield: JSOT Press), pp. 191-215.

Hengel, M.
1974   *Judaism and Hellenism: Studies in their Encounter in Palestine during the Early Hellenistic Period* (trans. J. Bowden; 2 vols.; Philadelphia: Fortress Press).
1987   'Der Jacobsbrief als antipaulinische Polemik', in *Tradition and Interpretation in the New Testament: Essays in Honor of E. Earle Ellis* (ed. G.F. Hawthorne and O. Betz; Grand Rapids: Eerdmans; Tübingen: J.C.B. Mohr [Paul Siebeck]), pp. 248-78.

Herford, R.T.
1933   *Talmud and Apocrypha: A Comparative Study of the Jewish Ethical Teaching in the Rabbinical and Non-Rabbinical Sources in the Early Centuries* (London: Soncino).

Hooker, M.D.
1989   'πίστις Χριστοῦ', *NTS* 35, pp. 321-42.

Howard, G.E.
1969   'Christ the End of the Law: The Meaning of Romans 10:4ff', *JBL* 88, pp. 331-37.
1970   'Romans 3:21-31 and the Inclusion of the Gentiles', *HTR* 63, pp. 223-33.

Hübner, H.
1984a   *Law in Paul's Thought* (trans. J.C.G. Greig; Edinburgh: T. & T. Clark).
1984b   *Gottes Ich und Israel: Zum Schriftgebrauch des Paulus in Römer 9–11* (Göttingen: Vandenhoeck & Ruprecht).
1987   'Paulusforschung seit 1945: Ein kritischer Literaturbericht', in *Aufstieg und Niedergang der römischen Welt* II.25.4 (ed. W. Haase and H. Temporini; Berlin & New York: de Gruyter), pp. 2649-2840.

Hughes, H.M.
n.d.   *The Ethics of Jewish Apocryphal Literature* (London: Charles H. Kelly).

Hultgren, A.J.
1985   *Paul's Gospel and Mission* (Philadelphia: Fortress Press).

James, M.R.
1917   'Ego Salathiel qui et Ezras', *JTS* 18, pp. 167-69.

Jaubert, A.
1963   *La notion d'alliance dans le judaïsme aux abords de l' ère chrétienne* (Paris: Editions du Seuil).

Jeremias, J.
1977   'Einige vorwiegend sprachliche Beobachtungen zu Römer 11,25-36', in *Die Israelfrage nach Röm 9–11* (ed. L. de Lorenzi; Rome: St Paul Abbey), pp. 193-205.

Jervell, J.
1960   *Imago Dei: Gen 1,26f. im Spätjudentum, in der Gnosis und in den paulinischen Briefen* (Göttingen: Vandenhoeck & Ruprecht).
1977   'The Letter to the Romans as Paul's Last Will and Testament', in *The Romans Debate* (ed. K.P. Donfried; Minneapolis: Augsburg), pp. 61-74.

Jewett, R.
1985   'The Law and the Coexistence of Jews and Gentiles in Romans', *Int* 39, pp. 341-56.

Jocz, J.
1979   *The Jewish People and Jesus Christ: The Relationship between Church and Synagogue* (3rd edn; Grand Rapids: Baker Book House).

Johnson, E.E.
1989   *The Function of Apocalyptic and Wisdom Traditions in Romans 9–11* (SBLDS, 109; Atlanta: Scholars Press).

Kabisch, R.
1889   *Das vierte Buch Esra auf seine Quellen untersucht* (Göttingen: Vandenhoeck & Ruprecht).

Käsemann, E.
1969   *New Testament Questions of Today* (trans. W.J. Montague; London: SCM Press).
1980   *Commentary on Romans* (trans. and ed. G.W. Bromiley; Grand Rapids: Eerdmans; London: SCM Press).

Keck, L.E.
1980   'The Law and "The Law of Sin and Death" (Rom 8:1-4): Reflections on the Spirit and Ethics in Paul', in *The Divine Helmsman: Studies on God's Control of Human Events, Presented to Lou H. Silberman* (ed. J.L. Crenshaw and S. Sandmel; New York: Ktav), pp. 41-57.
1989   ' "Jesus" in Romans', *JBL* 108, pp. 443-60.

Kee, H.C.
1981   ' "The Man" in Fourth Ezra: Growth of a Tradition', in *SBL 1981 Seminar Papers* (ed. K.H. Richards; Chico, CA: Scholars Press), pp. 199-208.

Kim, S.
1981   *The Origin of Paul's Gospel* (WUNT, 2.4; Tübingen: J.C.B. Mohr [Paul Siebeck]; Grand Rapids: Eerdmans, reprinted 1982).

Kirschner, R.
1985   'Apocalyptic and Rabbinic Responses to the Destruction of 70', *HTR* 78, pp. 27-46.

Klappert, B.
1981   'Traktat für Israel (Römer 9–11): Die paulinische Verhältnisbestimmung von Israel und Kirche als Kriterium neutestamentlicher Sachaussagen über die Juden', in *Jüdische Existenz und die Erneuerung der christlichen Theologie* (ed. M. Stöhr; Munich: Chr. Kaiser Verlag), pp. 58-137.

Klausner, J.
1943   *From Jesus to Paul* (trans. W.F. Stinespring; London: Allen & Unwin).
1956   *The Messianic Idea in Israel* (trans W.F. Stinespring; London: Allen & Unwin).

Klein, C.
1978   *Anti-Judaism in Christian Theology* (trans. E. Quinn; London: SPCK).

Klijn, A.F.J.
1981   'Textual Criticism of IV Ezra: State of Affairs and Possibilities', in *SBL 1981 Seminar Papers* (ed. K.H. Richards; Chico, CA: Scholars Press), pp. 217-27.
1983   *Der lateinische Text der Apokalypse des Esra* (TUGAL, 131; Berlin: Akademie Verlag).

Klinzing, G.
1971   *Die Umdeutung des Kultus in der Qumrangemeinde und im Neuen Testament* (SUNT, 7; Göttingen: Vandenhoeck & Ruprecht).
Knibb, M.A.
1979   'The Second Book of Esdras', in *The First and Second Books of Esdras* (CBC; Cambridge: Cambridge University Press), pp. 76-307.
1982   'Apocalyptic and Wisdom in 4 Ezra', *JSJ* 13, pp. 56-74.
Knowles, M.
1989   'Moses, the Law, and the Unity of 4 Ezra', *NovT* 31, pp. 257-74.
Köberle, J.
1905   *Sünde und Gnade im religiösen Leben des Volkes Israel bis auf Christum: Eine Geschichte des vorchristlichen Heilsbewusstseins* (Munich).
Koch, K.
1978   'Esras erste Vision: Weltzeiten und Weg des Höchsten', *BZ* 22, pp. 46-75.
Kolenkow, A.B.
1982   'The Fall of the Temple and the Coming of the End: The Spectrum and Process of Apocalyptic Argument in 2 Baruch and Other Authors', in *SBL 1982 Seminar Papers* (ed. K.H. Richards; Chico, CA: Scholars Press), pp. 243-50.
Kümmel, W.G.
1929   *Römer 7 und die Bekehrung des Paulus* (Leipzig: Hinrichs); reprinted in 1974: *Römer 7 und das Bild des Menschen im Neuen Testament: Zwei Studien* (Munich: Chr. Kaiser Verlag), pp. ix, 160.
Kuss, O.
1957   *Der Römerbrief* (3 vols.; Regensburg: F. Pustet; vol. 1, 1957; vol. 2, 1959; vol. 3, 1978).
Lacocque, A.
1981   'The Vision of the Eagle in 4 Esdras: A Rereading of Daniel 7 in the First Century C.E.', in *SBL 1981 Seminar Papers* (ed. K.H. Richards; Chico, CA: Scholars Press), pp. 237-58.
Lafargue, M.
1985   'Orphica', in *Old Testament Pseudepigrapha*, vol. 2 (ed. J.H. Charlesworth; London: Darton, Longman & Todd), pp. 795-801.
Lapide, P.
1984   *Paul: Rabbi and Apostle* (co-authored with P. Stuhlmacher; trans. L.W. Denef; Minneapolis: Augsburg).
le Roux, J.H.
1981   'The "Last Days" in Apocalyptic Perspective', *Neot* 12, pp. 41-74.
Lebram, J.C.H.
1983   'The Piety of Jewish Apocalypticists', in *Apocalypticism in the Mediterranean World and the Near East: Proceedings of the International Colloquium on Apocalypticism. Uppsala, August 12-17, 1979* (ed. D. Hellholm; Tübingen: J.C.B. Mohr [Paul Siebeck]), pp. 171-210.
Leenhardt, F.J.
1961   *The Epistle to the Romans* (trans. H. Knight; London: Lutterworth).
Levenson, J.D.
1985   *Sinai and Zion: An Entry into the Jewish Bible* (Minneapolis: Winston).
Levison, J.R.
1988   *Portraits of Adam in Early Judaism: From Sirach to 2 Baruch* (JSPS, 1; Sheffield: JSOT Press).
Limbeck, M.
1971   *Die Ordnung des Heils: Untersuchungen zum Gesetzverständnis des Frühjüdentums* (Düsseldorf: Patmos).

Lindars, B.
1961   *New Testament Apologetic: The Doctrinal Significance of the Old Testament Quotations* (London: SCM; Philadelphia: Westminster Press).

Lindemann, A.
1986   'Die biblischen Toragebote und die paulinische Ethik', in *Studien zum Text und zur Ethik des Neuen Testaments: Festschrift zum 80. Geburtstag von Heinrich Greeven* (ed. W. Schrage; Berlin: de Gruyter), pp. 242-65.

Lohse, E.
1982   'ὁ νόμος τοῦ πνεύματος τῆς ζωῆς: Exegetische Anmerkungen zu Röm 8,2', in his *Die Vielfalt des Neuen Testaments* (Göttingen: Vandenhoeck & Ruprecht), pp. 128-36.

Lombard, H.A.
1981   'The Character, Epoch (Period), Origins (Motives) and Methods of Jewish Apocalyptic', *Neot* 12, pp. 20-40.

Longenecker, B.W.
1989   'Different Answers to Different Issues: Israel, the Gentiles and Salvation History in Romans 9–11', *JSNT* 36, pp. 95-123.

Longenecker, R.N.
1964   *Paul, Apostle of Liberty* (New York: Harper & Row).
1977   ' "The Faith of Abraham" Theme in Paul, James and Hebrews: A Study in the Circumstantial Nature of New Testament Teaching', *JETS* 20, pp. 203-12.

Lübking, H.-M.
1986   *Paulus und Israel im Römerbrief: Eine Untersuchung zu Römer 9–11* (Frankfurt: Peter Lang).

Luz, U.
1968   *Das Geschichtsverständnis des Paulus* (BEvTh, 49; Munich: Chr. Kaiser Verlag).
1969   'Zum Aufbau von Röm. 1–8', *TZ* 25, pp. 161-81.

Martin, B.L.
1981   'Some Reflections on the Identity of ἐγώ in Rom. 7:14-25', *SJT* 34, pp. 39-47.

Martyn, J.L.
1967   'Epistemology at the Turn of the Ages: 2 Corinthians 5.16', in *Christian History and Interpretation: Studies Presented to John Knox* (ed. C.F.D. Moule and R.R. Niebuhr; Cambridge: Cambridge University Press), pp. 269-87.

McCullough, W.S.
1975   *The History and Literature of the Palestinian Jews from Cyrus to Herod: 550 B.C. to 4 B.C.* (Toronto & Buffalo: University of Toronto Press).

Mead, G.R.S.
1929   'Chairman's Introductory Remarks', in C.G. Montefiore, *IV Ezra: A Study in the Development of Universalism* (London: Allen & Unwin), pp. 7-10.

Meade, D.C.
1986   *Pseudonymity and Canon: An Investigation into the Relation of Authorship and Authority in Jewish and Earliest Christian Tradition* (WUNT, 39; Tübingen: J.C.B. Mohr [Paul Siebeck]).

Meeks, W.
1986   *The Moral World of the First Christians* (London: SPCK).

Metzger, B.M.
1983   'The Fourth Book of Ezra', in *Old Testament Pseudepigrapha*, vol. 1 (ed. J.H. Charlesworth; London: Darton, Longman & Todd), pp. 517-60.

Meyer, P.
1980   'Romans 10:4 and the End of the Law', in *The Divine Helmsman: Studies on God's Control of Human Events, Presented to Lou H. Silberman* (ed. J.L. Crenshaw and S. Sandmel; New York: Ktav), pp. 59-78.
Minear, P.
1971   *The Obedience of Faith: The Purposes of Paul in the Epistle to the Romans* (SBT 2.19; London: SCM Press).
Montefiore, C.G.
1914   *Judaism and St. Paul: Two Essays* (London: Max Goschen).
Moo, D.J.
1983   ' "Law", "Works of the Law", and Legalism in Paul', *WTJ* 45, pp. 73-100.
1986   'Israel and Paul in Romans 7.7-12', *NTS* 32, pp. 122-35.
1987   'Paul and the Law in the Last Ten Years', *SJT* 40, pp. 287-307.
Moore, G.F.
1921   'Christian Writers on Judaism', *HTR* 14, pp. 197-254.
1927   *Judaism in the First Centuries of the Christian Era: The Age of the Tannaim* (3 vols.; Cambridge, MA: Harvard University Press; vol. 1, 1927; vol. 2, 1927; vol. 3, 1930).
Morris, L.L.
1972   *Apocalyptic* (Grand Rapids: Eerdmans).
Moule, C.F.D.
1974   ' "Justification" in its Relation to the Condition (Rom. 8:1-11)', in *Battesimo e giustizia in Rom 6 e 8* (ed. L. de Lorenzi; Rome: St Paul Abbey), pp. 177-87.
1987   'Jesus, Judaism and Paul', in *Tradition and Interpretation in the New Testament: Essays in Honor of E. Earle Ellis* (ed. G.F. Hawthorne and O. Betz; Grand Rapids: Eerdmans; Tübingen: J.C.B. Mohr [Paul Siebeck]), pp. 43-52.
Moxnes, H.
1988   'Honour and Righteousness in Romans', *JSNT* 32, pp. 61-77.
Mueller, J.R.
1981   'A Prolegomenon to the Study of the Social Function of 4 Ezra', in *SBL 1981 Seminar Papers* (ed. K.H. Richards; Chico, CA: Scholars Press), pp. 259-68.
Münchow, C.
1981   *Ethik und Eschatologie: Ein Beitrag zum Verständnis der frühjüdischen Apokalyptik mit einem Ausblick auf das Neue Testament* (Göttingen: Vandenhoeck & Ruprecht).
Munck, J.
1959   *Paul and the Salvation of Mankind* (trans. F. Clarke; London: SCM Press).
Mundle, W.
1929   'Das religiöse Problem des IV. Esrabuches', *ZAW* 47, pp. 222-49.
1932   *Der Glaubensbegriff des Paulus* (Leipzig: Heinsius).
Murdoch, W.
1967   'History and Revelation in Jewish Apocalypticism', *Int* 21, pp. 167-87.
Murphy, F.J.
1985   *The Structure and Meaning of Second Baruch* (SBLDS, 78; Atlanta: Scholars Press).
1988   'Retelling the Bible: Idolatry in Pseudo-Philo', *JBL* 107, pp. 275-87.
Mussner, F.
1976   ' "Ganz Israel wird gerettet werden" (Röm 11,26): Versuch einer Auslegung', *Kairos* 18, pp. 241-55.
1984   *Tractate on the Jews* (trans. L. Swidler; Philadelphia: Fortress Press).
Myers, J.M.
1974   *1 and 2 Esdras* (Garden City: Doubleday).

Neusner, J.
1973   *From Politics to Piety: The Emergence of Pharisaic Judaism* (Englewood Cliffs: Prentice-Hall).
1981   ' "Judaism" after Moore: A Programmatic Statement', in *Method and Meaning in Ancient Judaism II* (BJS, 15; Chico, CA: Scholars Press), pp. 19-33.
1987   *Judaisms and their Messiahs at the Turn of the Christian Era* (ed. J. Neusner, W.S. Green and E. Frerichs; Cambridge: Cambridge University Press).

Newton, M.
1985   *The Concept of Purity at Qumran and in the Letters of Paul* (SNTSMS, 53; Cambridge: Cambridge University Press).

Nickelsburg, G.W.E.
1981   *Jewish Literature between the Bible and the Mishnah* (Philadelphia: Fortress Press).
1983   'Social Aspects of Palestinian Jewish Apocalypticism', in *Apocalypticism in the Mediterranean World and the Near East: Proceeding of the International Colloquium on Apocalypticism. Uppsala, August 12-17, 1979* (ed. D. Hellholm; Tübingen: J.C.B. Mohr [Paul Siebeck]), pp. 641-54.
1985   'Revealed Wisdom as a Criterion for Inclusion and Exclusion: From Jewish Sectarianism to Early Christianity', in *'To See Ourselves as Others See Us': Christians, Jews, 'Others' in Late Antiquity* (ed. J. Neusner and E.S. Frerichs; Chico, CA: Scholars Press), pp. 73-92.

Nickelsburg, G.W.E., and M.E. Stone
1983   *Faith and Piety in Early Judaism* (Philadelphia: Fortress Press).

Noack, B.
1965   'Current and Backwater in the Epistle to the Romans', *ST* 19, pp. 155-66.
1970   'Celui qui court: Rom. ix, 16', *ST* 24, pp. 113-16.

Nolland, J.
1981   'Uncircumcised Proselytes?', *JSJ* 12, pp. 173-94.

Nygren, A.
1949   *Commentary on Romans* (Philadelphia: Fortress Press).

Oesterley, W.O.E.
1933   *II Esdras* (London: Methuen).
1935   *An Introduction to the Books of the Apocrypha* (London: SPCK).

Osten-Sacken, P. von der
1975   *Römer 8 als Beispiel paulinischer Soteriologie* (FRLANT, 112; Göttingen: Vandenhoeck & Ruprecht).
1989   *Die Heiligkeit der Tora: Studien zum Gesetz bei Paulus* (Munich: Chr. Kaiser Verlag).

Perrot, J., D.J. Harrington, J. Cazeaux and P.-M. Bogaert
1976   *Pseudo-Philon. Les Antiquités Bibliques* (SC, 229-30; Paris: Cerf).

Pfeiffer, R.H.
1949   *History of New Testament Times: With an Introduction to the Apocrypha* (New York: Harper and Brothers).

Plag, C.
1969   *Israels Wege zum Heil: Eine Untersuchung zu Römer 9 bis 11* (AT, 40; Stuttgart: Calwer Verlag).

Ponthot, J.
1985   'The Jewish Apocalyptic Tradition: Features and Purposes of the Literary Genre', *LumVit* 40, pp. 153-66.

Porton, G.C.
1976   'The Grape-Cluster in Jewish Literature and Art of Late Antiquity', *JJS* 27, pp. 159-76.

Räisänen, H.
1983   *Paul and the Law* (WUNT, 29; Tübingen: J.C.B. Mohr [Paul Siebeck]).
1986a   'Paul's Theological Difficulties with the Law', in *The Torah and Christ: Essays in German and English on the Problem of the Law in Early Christianity* (PFES, 45; Helsinki: PFES), pp. 3-24.
1986b   'Legalism and Salvation by the Law: Paul's Portrayal of the Jewish Religion as a Historical and Theological Problem', in *The Torah and Christ*, 25-54.
1986c   'Paul's Call Experience and his Later View of the Law', in *The Torah and Christ*, pp. 55-92.
1986d   'Das "Gesetz" des Glaubens und des Geistes', in *The Torah and Christ*, pp. 95-118.
1986e   'Sprachliches zum Spiel des Paulus mit NOMOS', in *The Torah and Christ*, pp. 119-47.
1986f   'Zum Verständnis von Röm 3.1-8', in *The Torah and Christ*, pp. 185-205.
1987a   'Römer 9–11: Analyse eines geistigen Ringens', in *Aufstieg und Niedergang der römischen Welt*, II.25.4 (ed. W. Haase and H. Temporini; Berlin & New York: de Gruyter), pp. 2891-2939.
1987b   'Paul's Conversion and the Development of his View of the Law', *NTS* 33, 404-19.
1988   'Paul, God and Israel: Romans 9–11 in Recent Research', in *The Social World of Formative Christianity and Judaism* (ed. P. Borgen, J. Neusner *et al.*; Philadelphia: Fortress Press), pp. 178-206.
Refoulé, F.
1985   'Note sur Romains IX, 30-33', *RB* 92, pp. 161-86.
Reicke, B.
1985   'Paulus über das Gesetz', *TZ* 41, pp. 237-57.
Rhyne, C.T.
1981   *Faith Establishes the Law* (Chico, CA: Scholars Press).
1985   'Nomos Dikaiosynês and the Meaning of Romans 10:4', *CBQ* 47, pp. 486-99.
Richardson, P.
1969   *Israel in the Apostolic Church* (SNTSMS, 10; Cambridge: Cambridge University Press).
Ridderbos, H.
1975   *Paul: An Outline of his Theology* (trans. J.R. de Witt; Grand Rapids: Eerdmans).
Robinson, D.W.B.
1974   'The Priesthood of Paul in the Gospel of Hope', in *Reconciliation and Hope: New Testament Essays on Atonement and Eschatology presented to L.L. Morris on his 60th Birthday* (ed. R.J. Banks; Exeter: Paternoster Press), pp. 231-45.
Rowland, C.
1982   *The Open Heaven: A Study of Apocalyptic in Judaism and Christianity* (New York: Crossroad; London: SPCK).
1985   *Christian Origins: An Account of the Setting and Character of the Most Important Messianic Sect of Judaism* (London: SPCK).
1988a   'Apocalyptic Literature', in *It Is Written: Scripture Citing Scripture. Essays in Honour of Barnabas Lindars, SSF* (ed. D.A. Carson and H.G.M. Williamson; Cambridge: Cambridge University Press), pp. 170-89.
1988b   *Radical Christianity: A Reading of Recovery* (Cambridge: Polity Press).
Russell, D.S.
1964   *The Method and Message of Jewish Apocalyptic* (Philadelphia: Westminster Press).
1967   *The Jews from Alexander to Herod* (London: Oxford University Press).

1987   *The Old Testament Pseudepigrapha: Patriarchs and Prophets in Early Judaism* (London: SCM Press).

Sanday, W., and A.C. Headlam

1902   *The Epistle to the Romans* (ICC; Edinburgh: T. & T. Clark).

Sanders, E.P.

1976   'The Covenant as a Soteriological Category and the Nature of Salvation in Palestinian and Hellenistic Judaism', in *Jews, Greeks and Christians: Studies in Honour of W.D. Davies* (ed. R. Hamerton-Kelly and R. Scroggs; Leiden: Brill), pp. 11-44.

1977   *Paul and Palestinian Judaism* (Philadelphia: Fortress Press).

1980   'Puzzling out Rabbinic Judaism', in *Approaches to Ancient Judaism II* (BJS, 9; ed. W.S. Green; Chico, CA: Scholars Press), pp. 65-79.

1982   'Jesus, Paul and Judaism', in *Aufstieg und Niedergang der römischen Welt*, II.25.1 (ed. W. Haase; Berlin, New York: de Gruyter), pp. 390-450.

1983a   *Paul, the Law and the Jewish People* (Philadelphia: Fortress Press).

1983b   'Testament of Abraham', in *Old Testament Pseudepigrapha*, vol. 1 (ed. J.H. Charlesworth; London: Darton, Longman & Todd), pp. 871-902.

1983c   'The Genre of Palestinian Jewish Apocalypses', *Apocalypticism in the Mediterranean World and the Near East: Proceedings of the International Colloquium on Apocalypticism. Uppsala, August 12-17, 1979* (ed. D. Hellholm; Tübingen: J.C.B. Mohr [Paul Siebeck]), pp. 447-59.

1985a   'Judaism and the Grand "Christian" Abstractions: Love, Mercy and Grace', *Int* 39, pp. 357-72.

1985b   *Jesus and Judaism* (London: SCM Press).

Sandmel, S.

1978   *Judaism and Christian Beginnings* (New York: Oxford University Press).

Sayler, G.B.

1984   *Have the Promises Failed? A Literary Analysis of 2 Baruch* (SBLDS, 72; Chico, CA: Scholars Press).

Schechter, S.

1909   *Some Aspects of Rabbinic Theology* (London: A. & C. Black).

Schlier, H.

1977   *Der Römerbrief* (Freiburg: Herder).

Schmeller, T.

1987   *Paulus und die 'Diatribe': Eine vergleichende Stilinterpretation* (NA, 19; Münster: Aschendorff).

Schmithals, W.

1975a   *The Apocalyptic Movement: Introduction and Interpretation* (trans. J.E. Steely; Nashville: Abingdon Press).

1975b   *Der Römerbrief als historisches Problem* (StNT, 9; Gütersloh: Gütersloher Verlagshaus [G. Mohn]).

Schoeps, H.J.

1950   *Aus frühchristlicher Zeit: Religionsgeschichtliche Untersuchungen* (Tübingen: J.C.B. Mohr [Paul Siebeck]).

1961   *Paul: The Theology of the Apostle in the Light of Jewish Religious History* (trans. H. Knight; Philadelphia: Westminster Press).

Schreiner, J.

1981   'Das 4. Buch Esra', *JSZ* 5.4, pp. 291-412.

Schreiner, T.R.

1984   'Is Perfect Obedience to the Law Possible? A Re-Examination of Galatians 3.10', *JETS* 27, pp. 151-60.

1985 'Paul and Perfect Obedience to the Law: An Evaluation of the View of E.P. Sanders', *WTJ* 47, pp. 245-78.

1989 'The Abolition and Fulfillment of the Law in Paul', *JSNT* 35, pp. 47-74.

Schürer, E.

1973 *The History of the Jewish People in the Age of Jesus Christ (175 B.C.–A.D. 135)* (3 vols.; rev. and ed. G. Vermes and F. Millar; Edinburgh: T. & T. Clark: vol. 1, 1973; vol. 2 [rev. and ed. with M. Black], 1979; vol. 3 [rev. and ed. with M. Goodman], 1986–87).

Scroggs, R.

1976 'Paul as Rhetorician: Two Homilies in Romans i–xi', in *Jews, Greeks and Christians: Studies in Honour of W.D. Davies* (ed. R. Hamerton-Kelly and R. Scroggs; Leiden: Brill), pp. 271-98.

Segal, A.F.

1985 'Covenant in Rabbinic Writings', *SR* 14, pp. 53-62.

1986a *Rebecca's Children* (Cambridge, MA: Harvard University Press).

1986b 'Romans 7 and Jewish Dietary Law', *SR* 15, pp. 361-74.

Seifrid, M.A.

1985 'Paul's Approach to the Old Testament in Romans 10.6-8', *TrinJ* 6, pp. 3-37.

Shaw, G.

1983 *The Cost of Authority: Manipulation and Freedom in the New Testament* (London: SCM Press).

Sigal, P.

1988 *Judaism: The Evolution of a Faith* (Grand Rapids: Eerdmans).

Silberman, L.

1974 'The Human Deed in a Time of Despair: The Ethics of Apocalyptic', in *Essays in Old Testament Ethics* (ed. J.L. Crenshaw and J.T. Willis; New York: Ktav).

Simon, M.

1967 *Jewish Sects of the Time of Jesus* (trans. J.H. Farley; Philadelphia: Fortress Press).

Simonsen, D.

1911 'Ein Midrasch im IV. Buch Esra', in *Festschrift zu Israel Lewy's 70. Geburtstag* (ed. M. Brann and J. Elbogen; Breslav), pp. 270-78.

Snodgrass, K.

1986 'Justification by Grace—to the Doers: An Analysis of the Place of Romans 2 in the Theology of Paul', *NTS* 32, pp. 72-93.

1988 'Spheres of Influence: A Possible Solution to the Problem of Paul and the Law', *JSNT* 32, pp. 93-113.

Stauffer, E.

1955 *New Testament Theology* (trans. J. Marsh; London: SCM Press).

Steck, O.H.

1977 'Die Aufnahme von Genesis 1 im Jubiläen 2 und 4 Esra 6', *JSJ* 8, pp. 154-82.

Stendahl, K.

1976 *Paul among Jews and Gentiles* (Philadelphia: Fortress Press).

Stern, M.

1974 *Greek and Latin Authors on Jews and Judaism* (3 vols.; Jerusalem: Israel Academy of Sciences and Humanities; vol. 1, 1974; vol. 2, 1980; vol. 3, 1984).

Stewart, J.S.

1935 *A Man in Christ: The Vital Elements of St. Paul's Religion* (London: Hodder & Stoughton).

Stone, M.E.
1968   'The Concept of the Messiah in 4 Ezra', in *Religions in Antiquity: Essays in Memory of Erwin Ramsdell Goodenough* (ed. J. Neusner; Leiden: Brill), pp. 285-312.
1973   'Judaism at the Time of Jesus Christ', *Scientific American* (January), pp. 80-87.
1979   *The Armenian Version of IV Ezra* (UPATS, 1; Missoula, MT: Scholars Press).
1981   'Reactions to the Destruction of the Second Temple: Theology, Perception and Conversion', *JSJ* 12, pp. 195-204.
1983   'Coherence and Inconsistency in the Apocalypses: The Case of "the End" in 4 Ezra', *JBL* 102, pp. 229-43.
1984   'Apocalyptic Literature', in *Jewish Writings of the Second Temple Period* (ed. M. Stone; CRINT, 2; Philadelphia: Fortress Press), pp. 383-441.
1987   'The Question of the Messiah in 4 Ezra', in *Judaisms and their Messiahs at the Turn of the Christian Era* (ed. J. Neusner, W.S. Green and E. Frerichs; Cambridge: Cambridge University Press), pp. 209-24.
1989   *Features of the Eschatology of IV Ezra* (HSS, 35; Atlanta: Scholars Press).
Stowers, S.K.
1981   *The Diatribe and Paul's Letter to the Romans* (SBLDS, 57; Chico, CA: Scholars Press).
1984   'Paul's Diatribe with a Fellow Jew in Romans 3.1-9', *CBQ* 46, pp. 707-22.
1988   *'The Diatribe' in Greco-Roman Literature and the New Testament: Selected Forms and Genres* (ed. D.E. Aune; SBLSBS, 21; Atlanta: Scholars Press), pp. 71-83.
1989   ''Εκ πίστεως and διὰ τῆς πίστεως in Romans 3:30', *JBL* 108, pp. 665-74.
Stuhlmacher, P.
1971   'Zur Interpretation von Röm 11,25-32', in *Probleme biblischer Theologie: G. von Rad zum 70. Geburtstag* (ed. H.W. Wolff; Munich: Chr. Kaiser Verlag), pp. 555-70.
1985   'Paul's Understanding of the Law in the Letter to the Romans', *SEA* 50, pp. 87-104.
1989   *Der Brief an die Römer* (NTD, 6; Göttingen: Vandenhoeck & Ruprecht).
Syreeni, K.
1987   *The Making of the Sermon on the Mount: A Procedural Analysis of Matthew's Redactional Activity* (AASFDHL, 14; Helsinki: Academia Scientiarum Fennica).
Theissen, G.
1987   *Psychological Aspects of Pauline Theology* (trans. J.P. Galvin; Philadelphia: Fortress Press; Edinburgh: T. & T. Clark).
Thompson, A.L.
1977   *Responsibility for Evil in the Theodicy of IV Ezra: A Study Illustrating the Significance of Form and Structure for the Meaning of the Book* (SBLDS, 29; Missoula, MT: Scholars Press).
Torrey, C.C.
1945   *The Apocryphal Literature: A Brief Introduction* (New Haven: Yale University Press).
Trocmé, E.
1985   'The Jews as Seen by Paul and Luke', in *'To See Ourselves as Others See Us': Christians, Jews, 'Others' in Late Antiquity* (ed. J. Neusner and E.S. Frerichs; Chico, CA: Scholars Press), pp. 145-61.
Tyson, J.B.
1973   ' "Works of Law" in Galatians', *JBL* 92, pp. 423-31.

300 *Eschatology and the Covenant*

Urbach, E.E.
1981   'Self-Isolation or Self-Affirmation in Judaism in the First Three Centuries: Theory and Practice', in *Jewish and Christian Self-Definition*, vol. 2: *Aspects of Judaism in the Greco-Roman Period* (ed. E.P. Sanders, with A.I. Baumgarten and A. Mendelson; Philadelphia: Fortress Press), pp. 269-98.

Vermes, G.
1981   *The Dead Sea Scrolls: Qumran in Perspective* (2nd edn; Philadelphia: Fortress Press).

de Villiers, P.G.R.
1981   'Understanding the Way of God: Form, Function and Message of the Historical Review in 4 Ezra 3:4-27', in *SBL 1981 Seminar Papers* (ed. K.H. Richards; Chico, CA: Scholars Press), pp. 357-78.

Watson, F.
1985   'The Social Function of Mark's Secrecy Theme', *JSNT* 24, pp. 49-69.
1986   *Paul, Judaism and the Gentiles* (SNTSMS, 56; Cambridge: Cambridge University Press).

Wedderburn, A.J.M.
1980   'Adam in Paul's Letter to the Romans', in *Studia Biblica 1978: III. Papers on Paul and Other New Testament Authors. Sixth International Congress on Biblical Studies. Oxford, April 1978* (ed. E.A. Livingstone; JSNTS, 3; Sheffield: JSOT Press), pp. 413-30.
1985   'Paul and the Law', *SJT* 38, pp. 613-22.
1988   *The Reasons for Romans* (Edinburgh: T. & T. Clark).

Wenham, D.
1980   'The Christian Life: A Life of Tension? A Consideration of the Nature of Christian Experience in Paul', in *Pauline Studies: Essays Presented to Professor F.F. Bruce on his 70th Birthday* (ed. D.A. Hagner and M.J. Harris; Grand Rapids: Eerdmans; Exeter: Paternoster Press), pp. 80-94.

Westerholm, S.
1984   'Letter and Spirit: The Foundation of Pauline Ethics', *NTS* 30, pp. 229-48.
1988   *Israel's Law and the Church's Faith* (Grand Rapids: Eerdmans).

Whiteley, D.E.H.
1964   *The Theology of St. Paul* (Oxford: Basil Blackwell).

Wiefel, W.
1977   'The Jewish Community in Ancient Rome and the Origins of Roman Christianity', in *The Romans Debate* (ed. K.P. Donfried; Minneapolis: Augsburg), pp. 100-19.

Wilckens, U.
1974   'Die Bekehrung des Paulus als religionsgeschichtliches Problem', in *Rechtfertigung als Freiheit: Paulusstudien* (Neukirchen-Vluyn: Neukirchener Verlag), 11-32.
1978   *Der Brief an die Römer* (3 vols.; EKK 6.1-3; Neukirchen-Vluyn: Neukirchener Verlag; vol. 1, 1978; vol. 2, 1980; vol. 3, 1982).
1982   'Zur Entwicklung des paulinischen Gesetzesverständnis', *NTS* 28, pp. 154-90.

Willett, T.W.
1989   *Eschatology in the Theodicies of 2 Baruch and 4 Ezra* (JSPS, 4; Sheffield: JSOT Press).

Williams, S.K.
1980   'The "Righteousness of God" in Romans', *JBL* 99, pp. 241-90.
1987   'Again *Pistis Christou*', *CBQ* 49, pp. 431-47.

Williamson, C.M. and J. Allen
    1989   *Interpreting Difficult Texts: Anti-Judaism and Christian Preaching* (London: SCM Press).

Wright, N.T.
    1978   'The Paul of History and the Apostle of Faith', *TynBul* 29, pp. 61-88.
    1980   'The Messiah and the People of God' (Oxford University: unpublished D.Phil. thesis).
    1982   'A New Tübingen School? E. Käsemann and his Commentary on Romans', *Themelios* 7.3, pp. 6-16.
    1988   'History and Theology', in *The Interpretation of the New Testament 1861–1986*, by S. Neill and T. Wright (Oxford: Oxford University Press), pp. 360-449.

Ziesler, J.A.
    1988   'The Role of the Tenth Commandment in Romans 7', *JSNT* 33, pp. 41-56.
    1989   *Paul's Letter to the Romans* (TPINTC; London: SCM Press).

INDEXES

INDEX OF BIBLICAL REFERENCES

OLD TESTAMENT

NEW TESTAMENT

QUMRAN LITERATURE

JOSEPHUS

PHILO